HOLLYWOOD
GODFATHER

HOLLYWOOD GODFATHER

THE LIFE AND CRIMES OF

BILLY WILKERSON

W. R. WILKERSON III

CHICAGO REVIEW PRESS

An A Cappella Book

Published by Chicago Review Press Incorporated
814 North Franklin Street
Chicago, Illinois 60610
ISBN 978-1-61373-660-9

Portions of this book have previously appeared, in substantially different form, in the *Los Angeles Times*, the *Hollywood Reporter*, and the author's previous book *The Man Who Invented Las Vegas* (Beverly Hills, CA: Ciro's Books, 2000).

Library of Congress Cataloging-in-Publication Data
Names: Wilkerson, W. R., 1951– author.
Title: Hollywood godfather : the life and crimes of Billy Wilkerson /
  W. R. Wilkerson III.
Description: Chicago, Illinois : Chicago Review Press Incorporated, [2018] |
  Includes bibliographical references and index.
Identifiers: LCCN 2018021889 (print) | LCCN 2018028459 (ebook) | ISBN
  9781613736616 (PDF edition) | ISBN 9781613736630 (EPUB edition) | ISBN
  9781613736623 (Kindle edition) | ISBN 9781613736609 | ISBN
  9781613736609 (cloth edition)
Subjects: LCSH: Wilkerson, Billy, 1890–1962. | Businessmen—United
  States—Biography. | Publishers and publishing—United States—Biography.
Classification: LCC HC102.5.W544 (ebook) | LCC HC102.5.W544 A3 2018
  (print) | DDC 647.95793/135092 [B] —dc23
LC record available at https://lccn.loc.gov/2018021889

All images are property of Wilkerson Archives
Typesetter: Nord Compo

Printed in the United States of America
5 4 3 2 1

This one's for you, Pop . . .

Never forget a friend. Never forgive an enemy.

—Billy Wilkerson

CONTENTS

PREFACE
DISCOVERING
MY FATHER

I NEVER KNEW MY father the way most sons know their dads—the way I wish I had. I was robbed of that opportunity one September morning in 1962, when I was ten years old and my father slipped out of my life forever. He didn't live long enough for the dust from his wings to fall on me, and his death left a void that was never filled and cast a pall over our house that never lifted.

At first, like most kids, I wasn't curious about what his life had been like. I was already carrying so many painful memories of the years with him; for almost my whole life I'd watched him suffer from emphysema and dementia. His health battles had seemed titanic and endless. And my preteen mind was preoccupied with other things—not the least of which was the appearance less than two years after my father died of the Beatles on *The Ed Sullivan Show*. The moment I saw that broadcast, I knew what my calling was.

But in 1972, after the dust of rock 'n' roll settled, I began to think more about my dad. I was a freshman at the University of Southern California, and I began to write to the man who many had told me knew Billy Wilkerson better than anyone: George Kennedy, his secretary of thirty years. George had been at my father's side (or just steps outside his open office door) since 1933, from his early years at the helm of the *Hollywood Reporter*, as he opened many of Hollywood's most renowned cafés, restaurants, and clubs, and through the whole rest of his life. George had a front row seat to both my father's business dealings and his chaotic personal life.

It was George himself who had opened the door to our correspondence, sending me a first-edition James Joyce volume signed by his Paris publisher,

Sylvia Beach, for my eighteenth birthday. And our relationship was made easier by the fact that George was also my baptismal godfather. When the time came for that Catholic sacrament—and my father was always a devout Catholic—Billy Wilkerson could have chosen from any number of his famous and powerful friends. He chose his faithful secretary.

George had been living in happy retirement in Ramona, California, following my father's death. I had not seen him in all those years, but we began to exchange letters, and as we did, my curiosity about my father deepened. When my film history professor at USC gave us an assignment to write a twelve-page typewritten paper on a well-known figure in the entertainment industry, it was a no-brainer. My father had been among the most well-known men in the entertainment industry in his day, and the more I learned about him, the more I wanted to learn. I wrote to George to ask for his help with my research into Billy Wilkerson's life. I had no idea, of course, that that paper would ultimately take me on a forty-year odyssey.

From that point on, every Friday after class I climbed into my orange MG roadster and made the two-hour drive from the house just above the Hollywood Bowl that I shared with my girlfriend at the time to George's home in Ramona, near San Diego. George lived in a modest house filled with an eclectic mix of antiques and signed paintings and photographs, many by the famous photographer Carl Van Vechten. He also lived in what felt to me like a library: every room in his house was filled floor to ceiling with books. At the time of his death decades later, he had more than seventy-five hundred volumes.

For the next several months I spent my weekends drinking in every story George told about my father. We spent early evenings on his veranda, gin and tonics in hand, watching the sunset as George told tales. He was usually uninhibited in his storytelling, despite the fact that he had kept my father's secrets for thirty years. He was sixty-four that year, and he asked me to please not use a tape recorder; he had a terrible stammer that was exacerbated when he was nervous, and some of the memories were unnerving. I understood, and I got good at listening closely, followed by hours spent writing notes.

Some days when I prodded for information, George was struck mute by the power of his own memories. He would sink into his armchair and dissolve in tears, and for a while he stopped telling stories. There could be no disputing the raw truth he offered me; if for a moment I'd imagined he was inventing, when I heard him at night screaming in his sleep, reliving some of the darkness he had witnessed and overheard, I knew he was telling me the unvarnished truth about my father.

One stifling summer night George's screaming woke both of us. I wandered out to the kitchen in my underwear and T-shirt and found him there. We opened all the windows in the house to let in what little breeze there was, and we made hot chocolate and continued the conversation we had left earlier. Neither of us seemed capable of sleep, so we parked ourselves in the living room. Mindful of the air force of moths and mosquitoes just outside the windows screens, we lit just one light to keep them from invading. We sipped our chocolates and shared a whole pack of Winston filter cigarettes.

That night George was talking about my father's many wives, the sixth and last of whom was my mother, Tichi. For the first time, he dug out the breakup letter Dad had received from Edith Gwynn, his second wife. She was the partner who had been with him when he first catapulted to success, and she was the one who had stayed on at the *Reporter* for the next several decades, becoming one of the trade paper's best-known writers. George handed me her twelve-page typewritten missive. He wanted me to read it to myself, but I insisted he read it aloud. And so, by the light of that single lamp, he slowly read Edith's letter, which sounded like a cry from the soul.

I've always believed writing to be a great emotional exorcist. Why there is magic made when we siphon painful memories from our hearts and minds and commit them to the page remains a mystery, but magic I know it to be. And because I knew George carried many demons from those years—as did so many of those who crossed my father's path—I encouraged him on many of our late afternoon walks to take up the pen of exorcism. He shied away from the task, but to this day I believe if he had, it would have saved his life. What I know for certain is this: if anyone was qualified to write a book about my father, it was George Kennedy. He was a remarkably gifted writer—he loved words—and he knew my father inside and out.

After I had written my USC film paper, I began to hector George to write a biography about my dad. I was even prepared to pay him a king's ransom of a salary: a dollar a page, which was an enormous sum for a college student at that time. I had inherited a little money from my father, which made this proposal possible—and I couldn't imagine a better way to spend it. But the closest I got were George's replies to my questions via mail. Over time I realized that in these short snippets, answers to questions I posed, George had created a comfort zone that allowed him to write about my father in the only way he could.

George had also pointed me in the direction of the other individuals who knew my father best. I got in touch with Tom Seward, my father's former business partner; his longtime attorney, Greg Bautzer; and his barber, Harry Drucker, who had been a kind of consigliere. I prodded all three just as I prodded George. But as I listened to the stories they told, I came to believe they were feeding me a whitewashed version of the man. Their tales only echoed the glowing obituaries and articles I had collected. Each one seemed to parrot the others, offering a résumé of a man who sounded far too good to be true, and a man whose image didn't square with Edith Gwynn's characterization.

I realize all these years later that the principals were hesitant to share the dark side of the story. After all, I was the man's son, and I suppose they were trying to protect me from hard-to-swallow truths. Others who had known my father intimately—people like Lana Turner and my father's faithful lieutenant Joe Rivkin—would not talk about his dark side, either; they seemed too devoted to him to do so. And my mother, who'd had a difficult relationship with my father, would speak only about incidents that did not involve their painful marriage. But I kept probing and digging, because the man who people told me had had the Midas touch, the man who had created so many palaces of splendor—from Hollywood's Café Trocadero and Ciro's to the infamous Flamingo Hotel in Las Vegas—this man of extraordinary vision who also had a shadowy past, now seemed to have enormous holes in his life story, and pieces were not adding up.

After a while, stories about Dad's politics, his feud with the Hollywood studio chiefs, and the card games he hosted with stunning dexterity began to contrast with earlier stories I'd heard. I'd envisioned him as a kind of Catholic saint, but as I learned more and more about his closest allies and fiercest enemies—men like the mobster Johnny Rosselli, who adored him, and Bugsy Siegel and Willie Bioff, who wanted him either dead or financially fleeced—I was certain some of their dirt had worn off on him.

It took a long time, but finally a breakthrough in understanding my father's life came in a conversation with Tommy Seward, my father's business partner and once-upon-a-time brother-in-law. When I contacted him initially, he was not happy about being asked about my father. The two men had been locked in bitter litigation in the early 1950s, and that had led to an irrevocable split.

But why? For more than fifteen years, these two men had been inseparable. Indeed, my father considered Tommy the brother he never had. The lawsuit cited corporate malfeasance on my dad's part—absconding with corporate money for personal use. This also seemed unbelievable. My father was very comfortable financially. So why would he need to siphon off corporate profits? None of it made sense.

After the sixth phone interview, Tommy finally cracked. I pushed Tom to explain discrepancies in the stories I was hearing, and finally he confessed with restrained emotion that my father had suffered from a chronic gambling addiction.

When Tom offered this revelation, I was sitting in my home office in Hollywood on a sweltering summer day. I had no air-conditioning and I was mopping my brow. His words became my Rosetta stone. Until I learned about the gambling addiction, my father's involvement with organized crime and his never-ending vendetta against the movie studio owners never made sense. And although the news made me unhappy, it also provided the outline of an explanation—for his Mafia friends, for the regular card games. But it also raised more questions. For instance, if my father had been as inveterate a gambler as Tom described, how had he acquired the funds to build his palaces of splendor? So, armed with this new information, I returned to the principals to confront them with further inquiries.

When I called Greg Bautzer and told him what I had learned from Tom Seward, he didn't deny it. He did, however, discourage me from writing about it; neither Greg nor Tom nor Harry Drucker wanted my father's glittering image tarnished. I struggled with the meaning of the stories the three men began to confess. My father's criminal activities were becoming clearer to me, but no matter how hard I tried, I couldn't verify events.

I consoled myself with the fact that at least I had George Kennedy's letters, the notes I had made after our many conversations, and those tape-recorded interviews I had done with the others George told me to speak to. But in December 1976 disaster struck: my mother informed me that our family home in Bel-Air had been burglarized. It was the home my father had built in 1935, and it was where the family kept all our treasures. It's where I had stored my notes and recordings neatly in a briefcase, as I was moving into new digs in a month's time. I'd placed the briefcase in the garage with some of my other belongings, and when it went missing, my mother told me it had been stolen in a burglary. I couldn't help but believe that, in truth, she did not want me to write about my father; I'm sure she didn't want me stirring up unwanted skeletons that had been so deeply buried in the family closet.

When I learned the material was gone, I was devastated. I abandoned the idea I'd had about writing about my father and decided to wait for George's book. I convinced myself that one day he would write it. But it turned out George was enjoying retirement too much to be bothered with what he thought of as simply more clerical work. He lived for gardening, donning his straw hat and gloves and spending his days trawling in the earth under a blistering sun. The thought of punching typewriter keys reminded him too much of those thirty years he'd toiled as a secretary. I once asked him why he never worked for anyone else after my father's death, and he looked at me, smiled, and said simply, "Your father was my job for thirty years." That said it all.

Having given up on the book project, I devoted myself to finding work in the entertainment industry as a songwriter. But my father's hidden dark side followed me wherever I went. Whenever I tried to gain a foothold in the music industry, I found gates closed to me. Some people took meetings with me out of courtesy to my family's business, but in the end they always disappeared quietly into the night. By the time I was twenty-five, I wondered whether my failure to crack the music world was the result of a lack of talent or if it was simply bad luck.

I began to see a pattern. Time and again, as I neared the finish line—a song I'd written under serious consideration, a contract being dangled—the offer either never came to fruition or was suddenly dropped with no explanation. My disappointments usually coincided with a negative review in the *Hollywood Reporter* or a *Reporter* gossip column's unfavorable swipe at the company or person with whom I was hoping to do business. Results were most often predictable and catastrophic. When your family has long been in the business of critiquing, maligning, and even destroying others' careers, you're likely to be on the top-ten enemies list. Sometimes when I was trying to place a song with someone, I'd suddenly recognize the signs—I'd see my interviewer barely able to contain himself, and often in the middle of our interview he'd blurt out, "Your father was a sonofabitch . . ." It didn't matter that this was the 1970s and my father's misdeeds had occurred decades earlier; there seemed to be no recovering from the sins of the father.

In early 1978 I married and moved to England to try to reinvent myself. Two weeks after my arrival in London, Steve Rowland, a transplant from Los Angeles who was running Hansa Records, a successful independent record label, asked to meet with me through my manager at the time, Sue Francis. His request had a sense of urgency. I knew Steve's uncle was Louis B. Mayer, the studio tyrant who had run MGM studios during the era when my father was running his empire. Steve knew a thing or two about being the victim of a Hollywood witch hunt. And when I sat down in his plush London office, he confessed that he too had had a difficult time making it in L.A. He wasted no time imparting his message: "They resent you there [in Hollywood]," he said. "You did good coming here." I never placed any songs with Steve, but his advice and insight were pure gold.

But even in the UK, I could not escape my family's history. I changed my name to Kurt Langdon, and despite that, at almost every turn I came across someone who had tangled with my family's newspaper and knew who I was. In one instance, an A&R man told me how the *Reporter* had given the band he was managing a negative review, and because of that the label that had been about to sign the band dropped them. The band broke up, the manager lost his income, and his wife divorced him because he had no money. With no one else to blame, I became the convenient whipping boy.

I returned to Los Angeles in 1983 and continued to try to make it in the music industry. After years of dog-paddling, I called it quits in 1989 and became a writer. But Billy Wilkerson's story was not among the projects I pursued.

Then, twenty years after George Kennedy and I began our conversations about my father, when George was eighty-four, the memories that had so plagued him caught up with him. On November 14, 1991, he removed the signed studio portrait of Billy Wilkerson that had hung on his wall for decades. He placed it on his bed, lay down beside it, pressed a revolver to his skull, and pulled the trigger.

When my mother's secretary called to tell me the news, I was crushed, but I understood that in the end George had been unable to let go of the ghost of my father, unable to shake the anguished love he'd felt for so long.

The next day I drove to his house and watched the relatives he had despised dismantling that home—moving photographs and paintings, furniture and clothing, all the treasures of my beloved friend's life. When I could not take the sight any longer, I walked out into his garden, the sight of so many memorable afternoons, and let the hot breeze dry my tears. It was there I said farewell to the first man I had ever loved. That was the last time I set foot in George's house. It was also the beginning of my journey as my father's biographer.

For years I blamed myself for George's death. I saw myself as a pushy, arrogant young man and was certain that my unchecked aggression and endless probing all those years earlier had opened a door George was never able to close. I believed that ever since then he'd been flooded with memories and haunted by the darkness so many of them evoked. If I hadn't pushed, I might still have had him to talk to and walk with, to listen to and commiserate with over the legacy my father had left. Perhaps, I thought, those memories were better left forgotten. After all, I had collected memories at the expense of the life of someone I loved.

As time passed, though, I began to realize that if I did not tell my father's story, George's tragic suicide would be in vain. So I spent the next two years picking up the pieces of those stories I had begun to gather, pulling together the threads of stories I hadn't yet heard. I returned to a cardboard box of things I had culled from George, things that had not been stolen back in 1976. I had a trickle of articles about my father, a handful of yellowed newspaper pieces, and several obituaries extolling Billy Wilkerson as a visionary and a genius— the man who had created Hollywood glamour. I read and reread everything, but I learned nothing new. So many of the threads were broken that the story would not come together.

I began to slowly read through the daily editorials my father had penned for more than thirty years. Billy Wilkerson had not just run a publishing and nightclub empire in Hollywood from 1930 to 1962; he had also written a front-page editorial for the *Hollywood Reporter* five days a week for all those years. There were approximately 8,320 editorials to read, and as I did so, I came to understand that in those thirty-two years all the threads of Hollywood's history, golden and sordid and everything in between, had intersected at my father's desk.

I tracked down and read all the editorials I could find, and in them I learned that the story of Billy Wilkerson is the story of Hollywood, and that the story of Hollywood is not about movies or glamour but about power. Movies and glamour were mere by-products of Hollywood's unending power struggles, and throughout those decades Billy Wilkerson was at the epicenter of those struggles. I kept reading, and soon realized I couldn't accommodate the rich and vast history of my father's life in a single volume. I had to make some tough choices about what would stay and what must go.

Much of what remained would have to include conversations reconstructed from memory, from the notes and recordings that had been stolen decades earlier. I found few other records, though over time, as I learned more, I was certain that my father had colluded with his friend Joe Schenck at 20th Century Fox and mobster Johnny Rosselli in a misguided scheme to extort millions from the studios. Everything Seward, Bautzer, and Drucker had told me showed that this was true, but nothing in the public record corroborated their stories. That made sense, of course: George had told me that in 1952 he and my father incinerated all the paperwork housed at the *Reporter* from its founding in 1930 to that date.

I decided to stick to the evidence. But that smacked me hard against a barrier concerning my father's biography, so I put the project on hold. I hadn't had a father when I was growing up, so I decided to devote my time to raising my own son. I wanted to give him what I had never had, a father's presence, since while my father was alive his was so often interrupted.

Then one night, eighteen months after I gave up, I was having dinner with my good friend David Neely, a Tennessean just like my dad. For the first time I confided some of the unsavory stories. I told him about my father's underworld associates, about the fact that he had been involved with J. Edgar Hoover. I confessed that I didn't know what to do with these stories. David smiled, leaned across the table, and reminded me of something that changed my life: "The very nature of organized crime is secrecy."

I couldn't shake that statement, and, as strange as it seems, that was the night I finally understood that the stories surrounding my father's life—the man I so often thought of not as Dad but by any of his many monikers, "Billy Wilkerson" or "the Hollywood Godfather" or "the Man with the Midas Touch"—were shrouded in mystery precisely because they were illegal. Of course no one had recorded those stories; of course those who knew them, including many of the people I interviewed, had taken the details to their graves. They were incriminating, and not only of my father. I decided that these were exactly the stories that needed to be included in any biography of my father if it wasn't going to be just one more whitewash. Even if these stories' secret nature made them impossible to verify, even if they challenged the well-known accounts already on the public record, they needed to be told before they disappeared forever.

I thanked David and dived back into the project with renewed vigor, though my father's associates continued to discourage me from going near one particular aspect of my father's life. That was his involvement in the late 1940s with the anti-Communist movement in Hollywood. He had written scathing editorials, often harping for months at a time on the same subject. In them, he condemned "card-carrying Communists" in the movie industry—men and women, he claimed, who had openly pledged their allegiance to the Communist Party and thus were supporters of Joseph Stalin, the brutal Soviet dictator whose regime would ultimately claim the lives of tens of millions of innocent people. In some cases this was indeed true. But others were targeted for old and fleeting political connections or even the connections of their friends and family. Ultimately, my father's editorials became the seeds of the now-infamous blacklist, which ushered in one of the darkest eras of American history. Senator Joseph McCarthy coopted what had begun as my father's campaign and turned it into a nationwide witch hunt. Maybe it was not my father's intention to destroy lives, but it's clear that by naming names, some of them innocent, Billy Wilkerson and the *Hollywood Reporter* had helped to do just that.

My father's primary goal with these editorials was something different but still ugly: he wanted revenge on the Hollywood studio chiefs who he believed had blocked his dreams years before, as part of their illegal monopoly over the film industry. If anything about Billy Wilkerson's life is clear it is that he lived by a code of fairness; he loathed monopolies because he believed they were patently unfair. Still, I understood that if I wrote about what he had done in those dark years in the late 1940s, I was likely to stir up the same sort of resentments that had impeded my career in the music industry.

Finally, in 1999, I took my first steps toward bringing my father's true legacy into the light of day. Taking back my name and once again becoming a Wilkerson, I published *The Man Who Invented Las Vegas*, the story of my father's involvement with the Flamingo Hotel. With only the blessing of a handful of good friends, I published the book against my family's wishes. I was stunned by the universal praise the book received, and buoyed by that support. At last I had accomplished something without running into a roadblock.

Another decade passed. I authored several books not related to my father or my family. And then, in 2010, I woke up one morning and realized I'd had a change of heart. It might have been wishful thinking, I knew, but I believed I was finally free of the tractor beam of my father's legacy; I felt that the blacklisting that had plagued me for decades had ended. I was certain that, after eighty years, the rumblings of events surrounding my father's life and the volcanic eruptions he had caused had subsided. I partnered with a distant cousin and respected TV writer, Ron Wilkerson, on a TV project about my dad. Together with the talented Canadian showrunner Robert Cooper, we decided to dramatize Billy Wilkerson's life. We created a series concept for American TV titled *Dreamland*, working on the project for six years. Often our project would be moving along just fine when suddenly, at the last minute and always without explanation, it would be dropped. I hadn't warned my two partners about the difficulties I'd endured because of my dad's misdeeds; I had stayed quiet because I thought that curse had passed. Still, with each rejection, I became more and more aware of the fact that the story of Billy Wilkerson, even all these years later, was too controversial for Hollywood. After a litany of legal wranglings and numerous options that went nowhere, we had to throw in the towel.

It was discouraging, of course, but I was convinced then and am convinced still that we cannot know the greatness of a person's life if we do not know his flaws. Omitting those flaws from the story of Billy Wilkerson's life might have landed us a TV deal, but it would have been at a great cost to the truth, to history, and to all those whose lives were so strongly affected by my father's deeds and misdeeds.

I do not believe my father's accomplishments are diminished by his many wrongdoings both great and small, and because I know his story is worth telling, I decided I must do so without pulling punches. When Billy Wilkerson died in 1962, everyone in the film world knew who he was. A mere decade after his death, the New York nobody who rose to become the most powerful man in the entertainment industry had faded into obscurity. That amazed me, frustrated me, haunted me, dogged me, and pushed me to resurrect the man, in all his glory and infamy.

1 | THE CORPSE

GEORGE KENNEDY, dressed in his best blue pinstriped suit, stepped over the body of the man who had been his employer for the last thirty years. Billy Wilkerson, my father, lay facedown on the linoleum floor of the master bathroom, naked and emaciated, a plastic tube with a metal clamp protruding from his abdomen. A few feet away, a cigarette had burned itself out, charring the white floor in a brown, wormlike trail. It was a little after 6:30 AM on Sunday, September 2, 1962.

It was the first time Kennedy had seen his employer naked. He was shocked at how undignified he looked. "Death swept away all his greatness," he would later recall. He bent down and placed two fingers on Wilkerson's neck to check for a pulse. Tichi, my mother, was waiting, standing there. He told her that her husband was gone. Then he broke down, sobbing uncontrollably, dropping to his knees. When he had sufficiently recovered, he nervously began reciting the Lord's Prayer over the dead body. "It was a futile gesture," he admitted decades later, "but I was at a loss for what to do at that moment."

Wilkerson's small beige poodle Pierre came in. It licked its owner's cold face and immediately launched into a fit of howling so haunting it raised the hair on the back of Kennedy's neck. Tichi, unnerved, interrupted Kennedy's prayer abruptly and asked him to remove the dog. Kennedy muffled his sobs with his handkerchief, picked up the dog, took it downstairs, and locked it in the kitchen.

Billy Wilkerson had apparently risen from his bed at approximately 3:30 AM and, in the dark, made his way unsteadily, limping, to the bathroom.

13

His widow remembered the sounds of her husband feeling his way along the walls in the darkness. In the pitch blackness of the bathroom, he sat down on the toilet and, out of sheer habit, lit a cigarette. Judging by what was left of it, he had inhaled only a few times before a heart attack overcame him. The cigarette fell onto the floor. Wilkerson's own fall was precipitously halted when his open mouth caught the small reading table in front of him. The coroner later determined that he was dead before his face made contact with the table.

Tichi told Kennedy that her husband had risen twice during the night to go to the bathroom. At approximately 4:30, when he did not return to bed the second time, she went to investigate. She switched on the bathroom light and found him on the toilet, his upper jaw clinging precariously to the reading table. With great effort, she unhooked his head from the table and shifted his body to the floor. Not knowing what to do after that, she immediately summoned Kennedy, who made the long drive from his Pasadena home to his employer's Bel-Air residence to find my mother still dressed in a white silk bathrobe and utterly bewildered.

A few evenings before, Wilkerson had slipped and fallen on that same linoleum floor in his bathroom. His dog had tipped over its water bowl. My father's screams, which echoed throughout the house, were so agonizing that I had plugged my ears with my fingers. I was only ten years old.

But on that Sunday morning, my sister, Cindy, and I were still asleep. After my mother called the coroner's office, she locked the master bedroom door to prevent us from inadvertently entering.

The coroner arrived just before 7:00 AM and officially pronounced Billy Wilkerson, age seventy-one, dead. The death certificate later listed the cause of death as heart failure. At 7:30 AM, Cunningham & O'Connor Mortuary collected the body.

It was close to eight o'clock when I came downstairs and found my mother and George Kennedy seated in silence in the dark, wood-paneled den where my father had spent so much of his leisure time.

When my mother spotted me in the doorway, she quickly escorted me upstairs and sat Cindy, who had just risen, with me on my bed. She put her arms around us and told us that our father had passed away during the night. Cindy cried. I didn't.

"It's a relief," said our mother. "It's over." We knew what she meant. For years our father had been struggling with poor health. His suffering had come to seem unendurable.

At that moment we heard howling coming from the kitchen. It was the same beige poodle. We couldn't stand it. My mother told Kennedy to take the animal away.

Billy Wilkerson perished one day before the thirty-second anniversary of the *Hollywood Reporter*. The trade paper he created had come to dominate the entertainment industry, and by the end of the following day, all three of Los Angeles's major newspapers carried a prominent notice of Wilkerson's passing.

To moviegoers, Billy Wilkerson was not a household name like Frank Sinatra or Lana Turner. He never made studio policy, nor did he run a motion picture company. His name appeared on the movie screen only a few dozen times, and that was in the 1920s. Yet the publisher was universally eulogized in print. Newspapers and magazines hailed Wilkerson as one of Hollywood's pioneers, one of its founding fathers and architects, the "Mentor of the Sunset Strip."

Hundreds of cables and phone calls poured into our residence and to the *Reporter* offices by the hour. Tributes mounted. Film producer and director Joe Pasternak, who made his first movie, *Help Yourself*, with Billy Wilkerson, wrote, "There comes a time in our lives when we cannot find adequate words to express our great sorrow." (Pasternak would later recall that the day my father died "it seemed like the whole world stopped.")

Those same sentiments were echoed in a cable from radio columnist Walter Winchell: "There are no words."

"As a matter of fact," wrote Thomas M. Pryor, the editor of *Daily Variety*, "a memory I cherish, Billy was the first to call and congratulate me and wish me good luck when I became editor of this paper. Our friendly relations remained unchanged when we became, in a sense, competitors in the same field."

"It is always a matter of deep sorrow to see fine, vibrant leaders taken away from our industry, and particularly so in the case of your late husband," wrote Barney Balaban, president of Paramount Pictures. "For his was a voice of great significance to the entire film business, and his powerful vision was dedicated in every way to the furtherance of the motion picture both as an art and a worldwide entertainment."

Spyros P. Skouras, chairman of 20th Century Fox, who knew Wilkerson during his salad days when he worked in Kansas City under Carl Laemmle, head of Universal Pictures, wrote, "He was a wonderful human being and will be greatly missed by all who knew him."

"He was a part of Hollywood and his departure leaves a void no one else can fill," wrote Harry Brand, Fox's head of publicity.

"I am one among thousands," wrote actress Joan Crawford, "who considered Billy a dear and wonderful friend." Actor Kirk Douglas wrote, "He was a marvelous man and a dynamic leader in our industry. He will be sorely missed."

Billy Wilkerson should have lived longer than seventy-one years. But his self-destructive lifestyle made that impossible. Amid the tributes, newspapers were quick to note his five failed marriages and his long battle with ill health.

What they neglected to mention were his ties with organized crime; or how he had been instrumental in the rise of Las Vegas; or how he had helped orchestrate the Hollywood blacklist; or his role in the assassination of Bugsy Siegel; or his involvement in *United States v. Paramount Pictures*, the case that broke Hollywood's distribution monopoly. Nobody mentioned that Billy Wilkerson had once been the most powerful man in the entertainment industry. Nobody mentioned it because almost nobody knew.

But condolences arrived, too, from those who knew some of his secrets, including his gangster friend Johnny Rosselli. "I did not see Bill too often in late years," he wrote. "I always considered him my very good friend." Considering the criminal favors they had done for each other, that tribute might have been the most understated we received.

Blessed Sacrament Catholic Church, a large beige building in the style of the Italian Renaissance, dominates a block not far from the corner of Sunset Boulevard and Highland Avenue in Hollywood and can accommodate approximately fourteen hundred people. But on Wednesday, September 5, 1962, at 10:00 AM its capacity was tested. The numbers swelled to more than double that as relatives, friends, acquaintances, coworkers, and industry figures crowded the large church to pay their final respects to Billy Wilkerson. Rows of nuns lined the back pews, their faces pressed in handkerchiefs, quietly whimpering. The overflow of mourners from the standing-room-only crowd spilled out of the church onto the pavement.

"We come into this world with nothing," said Rev. Harold Ring, SJ, in his eulogy, "and it is for certain we take nothing out. But Billy Wilkerson has left us a very rich legacy which will stand for all time."

A simple spray of white roses adorned the bronze casket. The pallbearers were all men who had worked under Wilkerson for decades, like his secretary, George Kennedy, who visibly struggled with his grief.

The day before, a fight had broken out between Kennedy and my mother. She had insisted on a closed casket, but Kennedy protested. "The closed casket infuriated mourners wishing to pay their final respects," Kennedy later recalled. But Tichi Wilkerson was adamant. "I wanted them"—meaning us, the children—"to remember him as he was when he was alive."

There were detractors, opponents, and enemies by the score who avoided Wilkerson's funeral. Tom Seward, my father's right-hand man for close to a decade and a half, was noticeably absent. "A lot of people hated Billy's guts," Seward remembered, "myself included. It made no sense to attend."

Still, a three-hundred-car cortege wound its way to the interment. On that balmy, overcast afternoon near a large poplar tree that still shadows his grave, void of fanfares or salutes, Billy Wilkerson was laid to rest at Holy Cross Cemetery in Culver City, California, where his mother, Mary, had been buried two years earlier.

The man people in Hollywood considered their godfather, whom they came to rely upon as their guiding spirit, had finally expired. The question on everyone's lips now was how the industry would survive without Billy Wilkerson.

2 | ROSEBUD

WHEN BILLY WILKERSON DIED, his longtime secretary, George Kennedy, at the instruction of his widow, cleaned out the desk at his Hollywood office. In the top left drawer he found a small cardboard box containing a wooden printing block, a copperplate of Billy Wilkerson's first infant picture. For a moment Kennedy mused over it before adding it to the box containing everything else. He knew that some of his employer's happiest memories were of his childhood and speculated that he had kept the printing block as a reminder.

"We all have our Rosebuds," said Kennedy, referring to the Orson Welles epic *Citizen Kane*.

The story goes that on the night Wilkerson was born, his father sat at a poker game in a Nashville saloon, inebriated. After losing a considerable sum, he passed out in a corner booth. The next morning when he came to, it was pouring rain. Hungover, he walked the short distance to the hospital, where he learned that his wife had given birth to a boy. Cleaned out at the card table, he couldn't afford the hospital bill. But Wilkerson Sr. was one of the most recognized figures in Nashville, and the hospital knew he was good for the money.

All his life, William Richard Wilkerson Sr. had been a professional gambler whose fate and fortunes were dictated by the turn of a card. Indeed, in the 1900 US Census, "Big Dick," as he was affectionately known, would list his occupation as "gambler." The game of choice for the portly man with the flamboyant waxed handlebar mustache was poker, and people speculated that his nickname derived from the size of his sexual organ. No one who was in a position to know ever verified this, and it seems more likely the name derived from his girth.

What we do know is that Big Dick loved to drink, so much so that his imbibing often deteriorated into barroom brawling. For certain, it interfered with his gambling. "He always lost when he was drunk," said Wilkerson Jr.'s business partner Tom Seward.

When Big Dick was sober and coherent, he managed to amass fortunes at the card tables. By all accounts, he was erudite and eloquent, an engaging storyteller, an orator par excellence who left audiences spellbound. Drunk or sober, Big Dick was something of a gambling legend in the Old South. He would make gambling history one night in 1902 when he won the Coca-Cola concession and bottling rights for thirteen southern states in a poker game. Such a boon could have made him a legendary financial titan, the Warren Buffet or Bill Gates of his day, but Big Dick was a professional gambler, not an investor. Thinking the franchise was worthless, he traded the rights for a movie theater, which he sold two weeks later for $4,000. After another night of heavy drinking and card playing, the cash evaporated too.

Just the opposite of the alcoholic gambler was Big Dick's wife, Mary, whom everyone affectionately called "Mamie." The petite, frail Mary Maher from County Cork, Ireland, gave the outward appearance of being almost saintly. Governed by common sense, patience, and steely determination, traits sadly lacking in her husband, Mary became the pillar Dick leaned on. Although they were an unlikely pair, everyone noted she was devoted to her husband.

"She quickly learned how to roll with the punches," said Kennedy.

Indeed, Big Dick's gambling led to a turbulent domestic life. At times, the couple knew untold riches; then, just as easily, Dick's losses tumbled the family into debt. They could go from owning plantations with cotton fields as far as the eye could see and employing hundreds of African American workers, to picking cotton in the very fields they'd once owned.

Mary, especially, had ugly memories of the bailiffs arriving at their door, coming to confiscate all their possessions. Dick ordered his wife into the next room while he fought off the bailiffs, but they returned hours later with police reinforcements, who restrained Big Dick while they removed the family's belongings.

It was into this domestic turmoil that Billy Jr. was born in Nashville on September 29, 1890. He was to be Big Dick and Mary's only child and would inherit all his father's obsessive and dangerous passions—despite his mother's best efforts. By the time of Billy Jr.'s birth, Mary had had enough of her husband's drinking and gambling and decided the remedy was relocation to a new life in the country, where they could offer a safe and decent upbringing for their son. They would take up farming. It would be hard work but a welcome distraction from the Nashville saloons and gambling parlors.

Mary always had the final word, so the Wilkersons purchased a hundred-acre farm in Springfield, Tennessee, thirty miles south of the Kentucky line. The seat of Robertson County, Springfield boasted rolling hills and woods traversed by rivers and creeks. Cash crops during the 1890s included tobacco, corn, and soybeans. The Wilkersons grew tobacco.

But Big Dick could always find action; as Kennedy put it, "He had an uncanny gift for smelling out a poker game." The next decade would regularly find him straying from the farm in search of his next big score, occupying pieds-à-terre in Knoxville, Birmingham, even back in Nashville. Though records sometimes indicated that his wife and son were with him, according to Kennedy they rarely visited him at these "gambling addresses." Instead, Billy Jr. spent his formative years in Springfield, just as his mother had planned. In a life saturated with intrigue, controversy, and tragedy, the Hollywood Godfather would count those years on the farm among the happiest of his life.

———

At the close of the nineteenth century, styles were changing: the ragged look that had defined the Tennessee frontiersman was being replaced by the Parisian look, favoring a cleanly cropped head of hair. At age five, Billy Jr. sported golden curls that cascaded down his shoulders, so Big Dick transported his son to a local barber, where Billy Jr. sat patiently while the barber did his work. When he was done, he handed young Wilkerson a mirror.

"I turned the mirror from side to side," said Wilkerson, "and felt my head to see if it matched the image in the mirror."

Wilkerson Jr. burst into tears, threw himself onto the floor, and vainly tried to reattach his curls. Back home, he locked himself in his room and did not reappear until the following morning.

This was my father's earliest childhood memory, and a story he recounted at dinner tables for the rest of his life. There is no obvious reason why this event would tug at him perpetually, but it apparently did. Perhaps he saw it as the moment that inaugurated a long train of abuse at his father's hands.

My father also recalled reaching school age and tying his belt around his books, slinging them over his shoulder, and following the sun to school. He described the single-room red schoolhouse, remembering its dilapidation in detail, down to the ceilings that leaked during thunderstorms. "It was just a single room crammed with twenty students and there was a stove in the middle for heat."

My father's failing grades were evidence of his attitude toward school. As he put it, "Books were boring. And anything that was boring was just a plain waste of time." This attitude earned him a regular place in the corner of the schoolhouse, sitting on a stool and wearing a dunce cap. He donned it so many times that eventually his name came to be inscribed on it. As he put it, "I spent more time wearing that stupid cap than learning anything useful." It comes as no surprise, then, that he was often in trouble for truancy as well. "Billy got lickings from his dad for missing school," said Tom Seward. His lack of scholastic enthusiasm endured for the rest of his life; no one ever saw Billy Wilkerson reading a book.

So it's perhaps ironic that a big part of my father's boyhood came straight out of Mark Twain. He clocked hours lazing by the creek. He would park himself on the bank, his back leaning against the bend of a tree trunk. From a pocket he pulled a fishing kit—string wrapped around a sturdy twig. He had a makeshift metal hook created from something out of his mother's sewing kit, with freshly killed bugs in a tin box for bait. Barefoot, a straw hat pulled sleepily over his face, he daydreamed until he felt the tug of the twig between his fingers.

Later in life at the family dinner table, he often waxed lyrical about his ramblings through the woods surrounding the family farm. He told of catching live snakes, pinning them at the base of the neck with a pronged twig, but his mother's mortal fear of snakes prevented him from bringing them home. In the Tennessee wilderness Billy Wilkerson found his rapture, and throughout his life, during moments of turmoil and grief, whenever he reflected on this period, he immediately was restored to tranquility, able to carry on.

But catching snakes and fishing were not just idle fun; they ultimately became necessary for self-preservation from a deadly foe. His relationship with his father was seismic. Big Dick was abusive, frequently stumbling home in a drunken stupor from a poker game and exorcizing his demons on his son. Mary did not intervene, but during one early beating, according to George Kennedy, one of the farm's canines came to my father's rescue. From this indelible experience sprang his lifelong love of dogs.

After a decade, Mary's dreams of a decent country life for her son also fell apart. The restless Wilkerson Sr. had little luck with his tobacco crop, and in 1900 the family sold the farm and followed Big Dick to his latest gambling address: Hot Springs, Arkansas. His physical abuse of his son worsened, and by the time Billy was twelve, Mary feared for his safety. She spirited him away to Cullman, Alabama, to a school run by Benedictine monks. Billy Wilkerson would always be grateful to his mother for finally intervening, and despite the austere conditions at the school, there, at last protected, he flourished.

His attraction to the religion of his new protectors was immediate and adhesive. In Catholicism he found sanctuary, the kind he knew in few other realms. It became his safe haven from the troubled waters of the world. For the rest of his life, Billy Wilkerson's loyalty to the Church would never falter. He attended Mass every Sunday, irrespective of where he was or the state of his health. He carried pictures of the Savior and the Blessed Virgin Mary in his wallet and later would insist that my sister and I attend parochial schools.

While young Billy Jr. was grateful and happy to be safe from his father, his hatred of education traveled with him, and again his grades reflected his disposition. His academic underachievement raised a thorny issue for the boy after he transferred to Mount St. Mary's Prep School in Maryland, a boarding school run by Jesuits, in 1904. During his second year at the new school, a priest propositioned him, promising to improve his grades in return. Wilkerson wasn't the least bit surprised by the sexual solicitation. According to my mother, although this was the only proposition he ever received from a priest, he understood that such advances were, unfortunately, a pervasive part of Church culture. Nonetheless, he declined the priest's offer.

"The boy's grades next to me dramatically improved," he noted.

Without illicit aid, Wilkerson was forced to repeat his second and third years at St. Mary's. Nevertheless, he was a hard worker—according to his second wife, Edith Gwynn, he labored like a demon to erase his broad south-ern drawl—and he possessed a boyish charm that never abandoned him. The 1906 Mount St. Mary's portrait of Billy Wilkerson shows a confident teenage boy with rugged features and a dark complexion. At sixteen, he looked set to become a snappy dresser, another of his lifelong trademarks.

Billy Wilkerson Sr., meanwhile, cognizant of his own charisma, launched a bid to represent Arkansas in the US Senate in 1904. He went to the trouble of having a campaign photo taken and made into a button—one of the mementos my father held on to that somehow survived the passage of time. There's no evidence that Big Dick ever filed papers, however, and his political aspira-tions remain largely unknown. Some theorize that his reputation as a gambler became enough of a liability that he was drummed out of the race.

His ambitions having been shattered, Big Dick was unsympathetic a few years later when his son announced his career aspirations. In his final year at Mount St. Mary's, Billy Jr. went home for Christmas and declared that he was studying for the priesthood. It's difficult to know where Big Dick's religious sympathies lay, but unlike his wife, he was likely an atheist who conveniently prayed for divine intervention at the card tables. In any event, when Billy shared his intentions, Big Dick raged. Mary calmed her husband and encouraged him to make amends, but when he went to the boy's room to apologize and talk some sense into him, he found Billy on his knees praying by candlelight.

That was it. According to Billy, Big Dick demolished the room, breaking every candle in half and throwing them and every ecclesiastical book out the window into the pouring rain. In fury, he delivered his dictate: Billy Jr. would be going to medical school. Two months later, he was on a train to Philadelphia to attend Jefferson Medical College, where his father expected him to learn to be a good doctor.

Wilkerson later admitted that his heart was never in medicine. The time spent in and out of labs, in classrooms and lecture halls, yielded few posi-tive results. Instead of focusing on his studies, he tried his hand at amateur theatrics and took up the mandolin. He serenaded the nursing students from under their balconied windows. And as his academic failures mounted and his interest failed to spark, he retreated into playing the track and betting on the World Series, with catastrophic consequences.

He also added drinking and frequent visits to the local bordellos to his list of pastimes. "He spent more time in the cathouses than he did in any school classroom or lab," Kennedy noted. Even when Billy was passed out drunk, his private horse and carriage conducted themselves through the streets to his college digs or to a bordello. They knew the way from memory.

During his second year, in addition to contracting bad grades, Billy contracted gonorrhea. When he realized his condition, he took matters into his own hands, sneaking late into the lab while everyone else was sleeping. He looked up the antidote and learned that one of the treatments was a dose of arsenic. "He reasoned," said Kennedy, "that if he gave himself double the dose, he could really knock it for a loop."

After that night, Billy was sick for at least two weeks, but he had achieved his purpose: the double dose eradicated his venereal disease. It had another apparent consequence: the treatment, he believed for much of his life, had left him sterile.

Billy's second-year report card, dated May 23, 1912, revealed that out of seven courses, he'd passed only four: organic chemistry, urinalysis, hygiene, and physical diagnosis and symptomatology. If Billy decided to return for a third year of medical school, he would have to repeat the courses he had flunked—but fate had already made that decision for him.

The previous year, Billy's parents had moved from Hot Springs to Birmingham, Alabama, as Big Dick continued to chase new opportunities for enrichment. The earth in Alabama is mostly red clay, ideal for farming cotton, which at the time was the state's cash crop. And those who found farming too challenging could find work in Birmingham's burgeoning steel mills. The Wilkersons had no need to resort to working in the mills; when they planted cotton, their fortunes changed.

But their good luck didn't last. Big Dick Wilkerson died on February 5, 1912, while Billy was in his second year of medical school. He passed away at a local Birmingham infirmary after an operation for appendicitis.

Billy did not attend his father's funeral. Some say his absence was out of spite for the man he grew up hating. But others say the young medical student was on a bender for an entire week, and it was only when he surfaced that he learned his mother had just buried his father.

What is unquestionably true is that Big Dick died penniless. Soon after his death, creditors took possession of everything the family owned and were soon demanding payment for the balance. As my father put it, "The only thing I knew I would inherit from my father were his debts."

With his father gone, Wilkerson Jr. opted not to stay on the path Big Dick had laid out for him; he dropped out of medical school after his second year. He also made two lifetime vows. The first was that he would never let poverty touch him. The second was that he would always take care of his mother. "They struck a bargain," Kennedy remembered. "They would always look out after each other."

After Big Dick's death, Mary surrounded herself with dogs and was passionate about gardening. From picking cotton in fields to pruning her own flowers and trees, Mary had an almost supernatural gift when it came to horticulture. With touching fidelity, she never remarried, living the rest of her life entirely for her son, cooking his meals and doing his laundry. Wherever she lived, she always had a room ready for him. And everywhere he lived, he made sure that his mother resided no more than thirty minutes away.

When a friend once asked Wilkerson who the most important person in his life had been, he said without hesitation, "My mother." Mary would be, forever, the one constant in his life. "I believe she was the only woman he truly loved," my own mother told me.

3 | LUBINVILLE

AFTER DROPPING OUT OF MEDICAL SCHOOL, my father had to figure out how to make a living. His job search took him to the Lubin Manufacturing Company, a film company that produced low-budget one-reelers out of its Philadelphia studio. Known locally as "Lubinville," the studio boasted a soundstage, editing rooms, and a film lab. Lubin produced many comedic shorts, introducing such stars as Pearl White and Oliver Hardy.

Billy Wilkerson knew nothing about the motion picture business, but even in those days he had an aversion to starting at the bottom of any ladder. According to his lifelong friend producer Joe Pasternak, Billy talked his way into Lubin. "Billy wasn't a gofer. That wasn't his style. He was too much of a wheeler-dealer. . . . He was a great con artist when he wanted to be. He probably said he had all this experience and they believed him."

Before the days of online background checks or electronic résumés, a little fibbing could mean the difference between food on the table and starving. So it's likely Billy Wilkerson fibbed, since in 1912 Lubin signed him on as a film producer and distributor. At first the film novice merely viewed this as an employment opportunity, but it was at Lubin that his love affair with the silver screen began.

———————

Another love affair began that same year. In mid-1912 Wilkerson began courting Helen Durkin, a twenty-year-old redhead. One story has it that the two met while he was still a medical student and she was one of the subjects of his mandolin serenades. Others disagree. Whatever the start, their relationship blossomed, and they married in Wilmington, Delaware, on September 14, 1912. Little record of their relationship survives beyond a few photos of the couple taken while on their honeymoon at Lake Saranac, New York, with friends.

Even less of a record remains of his work for Lubin, where he produced, directed, or wrote dozens of shorts during his tenure. Sadly, all his credits have been lost due to the volatility of the film stock used in early cinema. At the time, film was made from nitrocellulose, a highly flammable compound that needs no outside air to keep burning once ignited, as the reaction itself produces oxygen. This made nitrate film fires particularly difficult to extinguish; they could continue fulminating even after being doused with water. (Contact with water produced another deadly side effect: increased toxic smoke.) Nitrate film warehouse fires not only claimed all of Wilkerson's Lubin work but also destroyed the related logs and catalogs, which means that even the movie's titles and who starred in them are unknown.

At the time, such warehouse fires were commonplace, and finding stable environments to house developed film was a nightmare, since nitrocellulose gradually decomposes and releases nitric acid, which hastens the film's destruction; eventually it is reduced to a flammable powdery dust. The devastation left in the wake of this unstable technology is difficult to fathom; 70 percent of all silent films have been lost either by fire or through decomposition.

And destructive fires were not always accidental. According to Kevin Brownlow, an expert on Hollywood's silent era, arsonists reduced film studios to ashes with "startling regularity." It was the work, Brownlow elegantly argues, of rival film corporations that would stop at nothing to rid themselves of their competition. Wilkerson would never forget the devastating fire that destroyed Thanhouser Studios in New Rochelle, New York, in 1913, while he was employed at Lubin. Many, like Wilkerson, believed it was arson.

Fire wasn't the studios' only way of maintaining dominance. It was commonplace for revolver-wielding thugs to muscle their way onto active film sets; they could knock out production for a period of time with a few well-placed gunshots—usually one to the camera magazine and one to the camera mechanism itself. Wilkerson recalled that his own studio employed guards who patrolled the grounds twenty-four hours a day, on the lookout for rival studios' saboteurs.

But guards hadn't protected the studio from another weapon in its rivals' arsenals: lawsuits. In the previous decade, the ever-litigious Thomas Edison had sued Lubin, charging that the company's Cineograph projector infringed on Edison's patent. By the time of Wilkerson's employment, Lubin had surrendered, paying royalties to Edison and becoming a partner in his Motion Picture Patents Company, also known as the Edison Trust. The trust strengthened Edison's hold over the nascent film industry—but with greater control came creative stagnation and the threat of government antitrust action. The partners, including Lubin, began to flounder, and just four years after Billy was hired, on September 1, 1916, the studio was forced to close its doors.

Billy Wilkerson was out of a job. He, wife Helen, and mother Mary were packing up their belongings and planning a move back to Birmingham when Wilkerson bumped into an old medical school buddy who announced that he had won a bet on the World Series. The bet was worth $90,000 but had been paid off in real estate: he was now the owner of a nickelodeon.

"What the hell am I going to do with a nickelodeon?" his friend complained, to which my father, thinking on his feet, quickly replied, "I'll manage it and we'll split the profits."

"I call it Wilkerson luck," Kennedy noted. "All his life, Mr. Wilkerson always pulled a rabbit out of his hat at the last minute."

———

Nickelodeons, the precursors to modern movie theaters, became the historical starting line for the rise of cinema. In the beginning, these establishments primarily showcased live vaudeville acts, which would perform on a front stage while movies were shown on screens on the back wall. Most nickelodeon films were "one-reelers," comedies lasting less than fifteen minutes. Joe Pasternak explained they were known as "chasers," since they were used to sweep the audience out for the next live show.

These venues were anything but glamorous. Converted storefronts festooned with ornamented facades and gaudy posters to attract patrons, they were havens for pickpockets and prostitutes. Inside were hard wooden chairs (often mere benches), bare floors, and walls that dripped with condensation from body heat and poor ventilation. Few had ceiling fans. Spittoons were strategically placed at the end of each aisle, and the overpowering smell of body odor was disguised by a thick fog of tobacco smoke. "Now that I think about it, they were really unsanitary," recalled Pasternak. But those who patronized the cramped movie houses were tolerant of the filthy accommodations.

Between 1907 and 1908, the number of nickelodeons in the United States doubled to around eight thousand. By 1910, twenty-six million Americans were visiting these theaters every week. Attendance grew so rapidly that by 1913 they became victims of their own success: longer films doubled ticket prices from five to ten cents and larger audiences necessitated bigger auditoriums. The early nickelodeons typically seated fewer than two hundred people, but as audiences began to demand more film content and the length of the movies increased, the live acts were silenced and larger nickelodeons sprouted that accommodated well over a thousand moviegoers.

The placement of these theaters was based on demographics: they were located in areas with high residential volume. Originally relegated to slum neighborhoods where pedestrian traffic was highest, as the art form evolved the theaters began to creep into middle-class neighborhoods. Once seen as proletariat amusements, disdained by the well-to-do, after World War I the middle class would begin flocking in droves to the venues. In their heyday, nickelodeons dominated city life just as saloons once had and speakeasies would during Prohibition.

Billy Wilkerson took note of another sea change in the evolution of the nickelodeon: interest in shorts was dwindling with the emergence of feature films, which at the time lasted close to an hour. But it was director D. W. Griffith who raised the feature to a new art form with the release of his film *Birth of a Nation*, a staggering twelve reels and three hours long, presented in two parts separated by an intermission. When *Birth of a Nation* was released on February 8, 1915, to both fanfare and controversy, Wilkerson saw that there was money to be made screening longer films.

So in 1916, he, Helen, and Mary moved to Fort Lee, New Jersey, the site of the nickelodeon his friend had won. The name of the place is lost to us, but we know it was well situated. New Jersey, particularly Fort Lee, was the cradle of the motion picture industry in those days, and Wilkerson installed himself and Helen in an apartment above the theater. He moved Mary into an apartment down the street.

He quickly saw he had inherited a sad excuse of a place. Grimy and run down, with bare wooden floors and benches, the venue reeked. To separate himself from the competition, he envisioned upgrades with the goal of attracting the well-to-do. His theater would be plush and serve refreshments, and for this increased quality he would charge fifteen cents, an exorbitant figure at the time and by far the highest ticket price in the area. Instinctively he knew his target clientele could easily support such luxuries. This emphasis on quality first became Billy Wilkerson's signature, one that he would inscribe on all his future projects.

Wilkerson imparted his vision to his friend and new business partner, and put the arm on him to finance the renovations. The partner agreed, and work began with the stripping of the benches and the resanding of every wooden surface. Next they laid carpeting and installed rows of fixed seating padded in velvet. Billy was clear that he wanted no live acts; his nickelodeon would show only films.

Even without live performers to worry about, managing and running a movie theater was not without idiosyncratic headaches. The biggest peril to cinema owners during the early decades of the twentieth century was the same one that plagued film warehouses of the time: fire sparked by volatile nitrate film. It was a worry that incessantly gnawed at Wilkerson.

The exact number of theater fires due to nitrate films is unknown, as record-keeping was poor and small theaters and nickelodeons that were victims of nitrate fires with no loss of life did not make headlines. Several fatal incidents did garner attention, including the 1926 Dromcollogher cinema fire in County Limerick, Ireland, which claimed forty-eight lives, and the 1929 Glen Cinema disaster in Paisley, Scotland, which killed seventy-one children. "Every time there was one of these awful tragedies," said Joe Pasternak, "there was talk of banning films altogether, because they were considered too dangerous, if you can believe that now. But back then, after a theater fire leaving many dead, people had second thoughts about going for a long time."

In his nickelodeon, Wilkerson, a lifelong smoker, instituted a no-smoking policy in his projection room. He also installed bottled fire extinguishers, which ringed the projection booth, and a metal fire door on the booth to prevent any potential fire from spreading to the auditorium.

The Wilkersons worked long hours to make their place a stunning show-piece and hired a small staff to help run it. Helen was the ticket taker. The establishment flourished, and within six months of operation, Billy was doing so well he was able to purchase his first car, a Ford Model T.

This new form of transportation presented its own problems, of course. Like so many others, Wilkerson struggled to navigate the unpaved dirt roads of America, which quickly turned into muddy troughs after downpours. Even just setting out for a drive could prove hazardous. "Cars then were hand cranked," noted George Kennedy. "Mr. Wilkerson twice broke his arm when the engine kicked while he was trying to start the car." But in most ways, life for Billy Wilkerson was good.

The annals of film history are littered with tales of ordinary people who walked into a movie theater only to see their lives transformed by the time they walked out. Many of these individuals became industry pioneers and figureheads, and Billy Wilkerson was one. What began in 1912 with the Lubin Manufacturing Company was cemented by 1916 in his nickelodeon. In that darkened room, the images on his screen cast a spell over him in a way no other art form ever would.

On April 6, 1917, the US entered World War I on the side of its French and English allies. President Woodrow Wilson presided over the start of the first military draft since the Civil War, and on August 5 of that year Billy Wilkerson was drafted into the US Army.

How long and in what capacity he served is impossible to determine. In 1973, a fire at the National Personnel Records Center in St. Louis destroyed tens of millions of military personnel files. Wilkerson's file was apparently one of them. One of the few records that survived was his draft card; the signature is unmistakably his, but the card includes a few odd discrepancies: he misstates his birth year as 1891 and his birthplace as Birmingham, and claims to be a "traveling salesman" for Fox Film Corp. rather than an independent theater owner. Whether any of this was part of some scheme to evade military service is unknown, though he did also claim "dependents" (his wife and mother) as a reason to exempt him from the draft.

He was still shipped out, though, most likely to Fort McClellan outside Anniston, Alabama, where units from New York and New Jersey were assigned for basic training. The Department of War had formally established Fort McClellan only a month earlier, believing that the Choccolocco Mountains were ideal for artillery training. In late August the first troops arrived. A photo of Billy Wilkerson in his WWI doughboy's uniform was most likely taken at McClellan. It shows him seated next to three of his buddies, one of them unabashedly grasping a bottle of hooch.

After training at Fort McClellan, soldiers would be on their way to France—but Billy Wilkerson could not picture himself huddled in a French foxhole. Without his military record, we can't know how he avoided seeing combat, though no one close to Wilkerson made any mention of him serving overseas. Perhaps the genius conniver talked his way into a cushy support role stateside, maybe in the arena of entertainment, to keep himself out of harm's way.

Wilkerson's own story of how he avoided combat is more romantic. In later years, he'd talk of how, during a medical exam, the medical officer was called out of the examination room to take an urgent phone call. Alone, Wilkerson pondered his open file, and in a flash of inspiration surmised that with no military record to prove his existence, he could safely disappear. He dressed quickly and stuffed the file down his shirt, buttoned it, threw on his coat, and hastily exited the building. He wasted no time incinerating the file.

Whether he served his time quietly or contrived some untraceable act of desertion, by the following year he was back in Fort Lee running his nickelodeon. Though he'd been spared the death and suffering of world war, another international calamity soon found its way to his back door: the influenza pandemic of 1918, which ultimately claimed the lives of an estimated 675,000 Americans. By mid-September, attendance at Wilkerson's nickelodeon began to dwindle. Later that month, a mortuary down the block from the theater began stacking coffins on the sidewalk, and a furious Wilkerson confronted the mortician, charging him with chasing away his customers with this display of empty coffins. The mortician countered that the coffins weren't empty. He led Wilkerson into the funeral parlor, where every hallway and room save the mortician's bedroom, kitchen, and bathroom were lined with full caskets. Kennedy recalled my father talking about the terrible stench.

On his way back to the theater, Wilkerson noticed smoke rising from surrounding backyards and quickly realized these fires weren't caused by people burning garbage; people were being forced to burn the bodies of the dead. Even the gravediggers and morticians were dying. Horrified by what he saw, Wilkerson demanded that Mary stay in her apartment that day. The very next day she learned that two of her bridge partners had passed away. A few days later, Wilkerson learned that his projectionist had died.

To restrain the spread of the disease, public health departments issued strict ordinances to curb person-to-person contact. They distributed gauze masks and issued orders for people to wear them in public; hefty fines were imposed for those who did not. Funerals were restricted to fifteen minutes in length; stores were not permitted to hold sales. They shut down churches, schools, and anywhere else that more than fifteen people gathered.

Theaters were of course included. A few days after his projectionist passed away, Wilkerson found a public health closure notice tacked to the front door of the nickelodeon. By November 11, 1918, when it was safe and legal to remove his mask, a despondent Wilkerson informed his partner that he would no longer be managing the theater. He wanted nothing more to do with Fort Lee. This was the kind of impulsive decision he would continue to make throughout his life.

Later that same month the Wilkerson family moved out of New Jersey and relocated to an apartment in Upper Manhattan, at 559 West 190th Street. Once settled there, Wilkerson talked his way into a job in film distribution at Universal Studios, under owner Carl Laemmle. The job consisted of hopping on and off trains with canisters of film under each arm, delivering finished movies to theaters up and down the East Coast.

Wilkerson vividly recalled the hotels he stayed in during this time, particularly those in the South. Many southern hotels, he said, kept a boa constrictor in each room to curb the rodent problems that plagued the hot and humid cities and towns. Wilkerson recalled waking up many a time to find the snake coiled up on his chest. Later, at the family dinner table, he remembered the creatures fondly: "Snakes love warmth. They'll go anywhere to find it."

A year after he started his new job, Universal promoted Wilkerson to district manager of film distribution in Kansas City. Mary and Helen stayed in Manhattan while he divided his time between Kansas City and New York. According to sources who knew Wilkerson well, he excelled at his new job—

but "it became too easy for him," remembered Joe Pasternak. With his success came the characteristic boredom that would infect my father for the rest of his life. The adrenaline junkie who was always scouting for a new adventure began to feel a growing disinterest in his occupation.

In addition, Wilkerson hated Kansas City, in part because it wasn't New York, in part because he resented spending time away from his wife. Helen, too, must have felt stir crazy in the days alone. On his next return to New York in December 1920, he found one less person waiting for him. Mary broke the news: his wife had run away to the Bahamas with another man.

By all accounts, Wilkerson had been deeply in love with Helen, and her departure was cataclysmic—eight happy years of marriage had ended. According to Edith Gwynn, Wilkerson's second wife, one of the problems between Billy and Helen was her desire for a family. She understood that her husband was sterile, but she believed she could endure it. They had even talked of adoption, but Wilkerson would consider only biological offspring. So he leaned on his Catholicism, counting on God to produce a miracle child.

For the rest of his life, rather than speak of the failure of his first marriage, my father told people that Helen had perished in the 1918 flu pandemic and that he had buried her in the back garden of the nickelodeon. This seemed to be his way of disposing of some of his hurt and anger.

Wilkerson's more immediate plan to deal with the loss of Helen was to announce to his mother that he needed to get away for a while, speculating he would be gone for one month. He and Helen had been saving to buy a home; that money, he told Mary, would fund his "Lost Weekend" of 1921. Frugal Mary had also set aside savings, so she told her son not to worry about her.

In early 1921 Wilkerson quit his job at Universal and left New York by steamer, headed for Europe. The complete itinerary of this journey, his first abroad, is unknown. No one knows, either, where his first port of call was, but Kennedy thought it was likely England, where he would not face the barriers of a foreign language. The original projected month turned into four, then six. Postcards he mailed to Mary reveal that he visited London, Rome, Prague, St. Petersburg, and Madrid, though there is no record of the how long he stayed in each city. "He couldn't remain in one place for too long," said Joe Pasternak. "It was an emotional safari."

If his Rome visit is any indication, he did little sightseeing. Decades later he told George Kennedy that in that iconic Italian city he drank himself into a stupor every day. He barely recalled eating, much less how he made it back to his hotel room each night.

His visit to St. Petersburg was more memorable. In Russia just years after the Bolshevik Revolution, he witnessed Communism in practice. He saw a pitiless system devoid of cherished rights such as free speech, thriving on oppressive control over a vast, impoverished wasteland. That trip solidified Wilkerson's devotion to capitalism. Forever after he loathed anything that hampered the free market. To Wilkerson, Communism was synonymous with suppression.

But as his journey abroad continued, less philosophical concerns about money arose. After six months, Mary's finances ran out, and she asked her son's permission to draw from the savings account. He also cabled her for money. By October 1921, Wilkerson acknowledged to friends that the exercise of pulling himself out of his grief was failing.

One day in Madrid, after Mass had ended, he sat alone in the empty church, tears streaking his cheeks. The exiting priest spotted him and sat down next to him. It was lucky for Wilkerson that the priest had a grasp of English. As the story goes, the priest, hearing his story, put an arm around Wilkerson and said, "In our hour of need God always brings us a sign, an answer. What that is, is always a mystery. But God brings everyone miracles and he will bring you one, too. But you must have faith." Dissatisfied with that promise, Wilkerson thanked the priest and headed for the nearest bar.

The next morning he boarded a train for Paris, and years later he recounted the story of the moment he stepped off that train. The torment that had shuttered him so completely for a year suddenly and mysteriously vanished. He was swept up into the magical, uplifting vortex of the famed City of Light—the passion of the Parisians, the benediction of the food, the romantic mélange of sidewalk cafés, music wafting through the air, each cobblestone street steeped in culture and history. All these distilled into a medicinal tonic that calmed his turbulent spirit. The Spanish priest was right: Billy Wilkerson had gotten his miracle.

"Paris was it," said Tom Seward. "He didn't have to visit another city."

Wilkerson spent a week in Paris, but instead of booze he drank in the sights and the sounds, and he became convinced that this was where he wanted to spend the rest of his life. When he told Mary, she said she would have nothing to do with relocating to a foreign country where they spoke a language she did not understand. And with that, his pipe dream evaporated. He knew he had to return to the States.

But his Parisian epiphany did leave him with a burning ambition. If he could not live in France, he would transport the culinary and cultural splendor of that city to America. Wilkerson would spend the rest of his life doing again and again what no other nightclub or café owner in America had done: successfully replicating the charm of the French capital on his own country's soil, transplanting the delights of Paris to Hollywood, creating a glamorous empire that swept people off their feet.

Wilkerson boarded a train for Le Havre and the ocean liner back to the States, back to his mother, back home. "I believe that receiving the Spanish priest's comforting words and seeing Paris was the Catholic miracle that allowed him to move on," Kennedy said.

"It was certainly Billy's year of wandering," said Greg Bautzer. "I think that's where he found himself—his life's purpose, if you will."

———

By early 1922 Wilkerson was again finding success as a film salesman in New York City, in the distribution department of the Famous Players–Lasky Corporation. Lasky was one of the biggest film companies of the silent film era; over the next five years, it would morph into Paramount Pictures.

It was at Lasky's Long Island studios that Wilkerson met Joe Pasternak, a young Hungarian immigrant laboring as a busboy in the studio commissary. The salesman made an indelible impression on Pasternak the first time he saw him. "I would come out from the kitchen," Pasternak remembered, "and see a man sitting at a table with the most beautiful girls I had ever seen. I wanted to meet the man who was with all these beautiful women all the time. I managed to get around, clean up his table, get some more coffee and all that stuff, and finally I met him."

During this period Wilkerson was seldom without a beautiful woman on each arm. He was, after all, doing well financially, and that combined with his good looks, charm, and snazzy dress attracted women. He was surrounded by starlets at the studio and engaged in a multitude of mindless encounters that served to fill the void left by Helen.

During his first year with Famous Players–Lasky, Wilkerson went on a sales trip to Hollywood, where he witnessed the progress of the film industry's migration toward this lazy hacienda thick with orange groves. Prior to 1915, the movie industry was based firmly in New York City and its environs, but the area's unstable weather made it hard to schedule film shoots. Southern California, on the other hand, was an ideal spot for location filmmaking, one that offered both cooperative weather and a wide range of topographies. What's more, California courts refused to enforce the patents of the Edison Trust, so independent studios could do business without fear of legal action. By the time of Wilkerson's visit, directors were fleeing their dark New York sets for sunny Hollywood.

Over the course of 1922, Wilkerson also took breaks from film sales to make two more trips abroad, both times by ship. His sojourn the year before had instilled him with a love of travel he would never lose, and on nearly every trip his first port of call would be Paris. He referred to these voyages as his "thinking trips." "It was a way of letting his mind uncoil," observed Pasternak.

By the end of 1923, Wilkerson was once again itching to explore horizons beyond his current job. He left Famous Players–Lasky and explored a number of different career opportunities in New York City. He spent the first six months in 1924 as the assistant manager of the Academy of Music theater on Fourteenth Street in Manhattan, between Third Avenue and Irving Place. The latter part of that same year, from July to November, he worked as manager of the Jewel Exchange, a film distribution network. Then in 1925 he got a job selling advertising and writing ad copy, articles, and movie reviews for Wid Gunning's *Film Daily*, the primary motion picture trade paper during this era. (*Variety* had been around since 1905, but at the time it was a weekly publication, and associated more with vaudeville than with film.)

As he bounced from one position to another, Wilkerson never found the satisfaction he'd enjoyed in the early days running his nickelodeon in Fort Lee. He was forced to acknowledge an unwavering truth about himself: he was an entrepreneur at heart. Working for others would never bring him contentment—nor the financial rewards he desired.

For now, though, Wilkerson was still working for Wid Gunning, whose whip-cracking tyranny was legendary. The trade paper publisher was a perfectionist with no social graces, prone to screaming rants that often lasted the better part of a day. Wilkerson later commented that it was impossible in Gunning's office to get any work done. "We were like a Roman slave ship," he recalled. "Every day we were in the galley being lashed by Gunning."

By 1926 Wilkerson had had enough, and he quit *Film Daily*. By that time, he was fully steeped in the movie industry. He hadn't been an actor, but he had done just about everything there was to do in back of the camera. He had produced, directed, and written movies. He had run a movie theater. He had been a salesman, a marketer and promoter of films. He'd been a trade paper columnist and film critic. But he continued to search for the holy grail, that position that would enable him to be his own boss and keep his profits. No matter how many times he thought it through, his thinking led him back to the same idea: he needed to establish his own film studio.

"All you needed to do was to look at [MGM's] Louis B. Mayer or [Columbia Pictures'] Harry Cohn," said Harry Drucker, "and you could see where the big money was."

At this point, the money was also in California. In the decade since the release of *Birth of a Nation*, fewer and fewer films had been made in New York. Within the next year, with the introduction of the "talkies," the writing would be on the wall: the film capital had permanently shifted to Hollywood. Still, "the industry bigwigs at the time," said Joe Pasternak, "didn't take California seriously." After all, George Kennedy recalled, "in the teens Hollywood was hardly what anyone would care to call 'glamorous.'"

But Wilkerson was not so complacent. According to Joe Pasternak, he'd been toying with the idea of moving to California for years. He was motivated in part, Pasternak said, by his hatred of shoveling snow in New York winters, but the first train trip he made to Hollywood in 1922 had cemented his desire. So in May 1926 he hopped a westbound train to lay the foundation for his dream of owning a film studio in Hollywood. To make that dream a reality, he knew he needed a convincing package that included a big-name actor and director, and once again serendipity showed him a path.

The same month Wilkerson moved to Los Angeles, Joe Pasternak became a citizen of the United States. The busboy had dreamed of being an American film director ever since departing from Hungary. Against the advice of others, Pasternak quit his job at the Famous Players–Lasky commissary, and immediately after obtaining citizenship he too boarded a Hollywood-bound train.

Pasternak arrived in a city quickly transforming to accommodate its growing film industry presence. Many of the streets of Hollywood were still unpaved in 1926, but that was about to change. Despite the pleas from the Save-Our-Trees Committee and silent film superstar Mary Pickford, the pepper and eucalyptus trees and orange groves lining the boulevards would soon be removed to make room for paved roadways.

Pasternak made the rounds among his transplanted New York friends in the industry, asking for a job. When the last one, Eddie Sutherland at Paramount Pictures, turned him down, he drifted across the street to a little restaurant to grab a cup of coffee. According to his 1956 autobiography, *Easy the Hard Way*, it was there that he ran into Billy Wilkerson, seated at the counter "with a Coca-Cola in one hand and a Piedmont cigarette curling smoke in the other." Pasternak recalled Wilkerson as being immaculately tailored with a waxed mustache.

The old acquaintances greeted each other, and Wilkerson asked Pasternak what he was doing there. After pressing, the young Hungarian confessed that he was trying to make a Hollywood connection to fulfill his lifelong ambition of becoming a film director. Wilkerson took a sip from his Coke. "Let's you and me move in together. We'll do something. Something big. I've got an idea. How much money you got?"

Pasternak had all of thirty dollars, and Wilkerson asked him if he could get more. When Pasternak told him that Eddie Sutherland was always offering him money, Wilkerson instructed him to go see Eddie again. Fifteen minutes later, Pasternak returned with a check for $100.

Pasternak told Wilkerson he had taken a room on Marathon Street, right next to Paramount's studio lot, but Wilkerson called it a fleabag. Almost before Pasternak knew what was happening, Wilkerson had found them a handsome apartment to share. As he recalled, "Billy was a very resourceful man, but even I was amazed at what he could do."

The day after they moved in, Pasternak overheard Wilkerson on the phone calling about a classified ad. "He was looking for a butler with flawless qualifications," Pasternak wrote, "a boy thoroughly experienced in serving two demanding gentlemen." Wilkerson also wanted someone reliable who could furnish a bond of $250 to guarantee his reliability.

Pasternak was mortified when he overheard the conversation, and after Wilkerson hung up, he demanded his new partner explain. Wilkerson waved away his concerns about money, and the next day three Filipino boys arrived at the apartment. "We chose one," Pasternak wrote, "who not only filled the bill perfectly but asked Billy if he could just deposit with him the sum of two hundred and fifty dollars in cash as a token of his honesty."

Wilkerson surprised Pasternak again when later that day he drove up to the apartment in a brand-new Packard automobile. Again, Pasternak was aghast, but Wilkerson placated him, saying, "You're a big director, understand? You've directed pictures," and instructed him to grab his hat and get in the car.

The two men drove to Paramount Studios, where Wilkerson parked just outside the main gate. He told Pasternak to wait and went inside. Moments later he returned with actor/comedian El Brendel, one of America's top box office draws. Wilkerson introduced Pasternak to Brendel as "the great European director Josef von Pasternak."

"In those days," Pasternak told me, "European directors were all the rage. Billy knew that if you had the right last name, it was a cinch to get work."

Sitting in the car, the three men talked business. "Brendel was still looking at the new car," wrote Pasternak in his memoir. "There was a little vase—automobile designers thought of everything in those days—and Billy, or our boy, had put a little rose in it." Wilkerson seemed to know Brendel had been in a fight with Paramount. Wilkerson told Brendel that Pasternak might be willing to direct him in a two-reeler and assured the actor that they had a story already prepared. The actor agreed to star—much to the astonishment of "Josef von Pasternak."

"We did not have enough money for next month's rent," Pasternak wrote, "not to mention the car payment, nor the butler's salary. To talk about making a motion picture was fantastic. . . . I was worried about my limited experience, about our lack of money, and not least of all about what El Brendel would do when he found out what we had done to him."

Back at their apartment, Pasternak raged, convinced that they would be discovered and arrested. On the verge of packing his bags and heading back to New York, the emotional Hungarian let Wilkerson have it, but Wilkerson somehow calmed his friend down and told him not to worry, that he had it all figured out.

"I don't know why I calmed down," Pasternak told me. "I think I had every right to be concerned. What Billy was doing was sheer lunacy, if not illegal. But he had a way of explaining things that somehow always made sense, don't ask me why."

Their film would have to be self-financed. Pasternak himself borrowed to the limit on his insurance policy and wired relatives in Hungary for anything that they could spare, while Wilkerson raised what he could. The two men dreamed up a story about a well-meaning but clumsy busboy who, in the process of trying to be helpful, only succeeds in making a mess. "It was more than faintly autobiographical," wrote Pasternak. They called it *Help Yourself.*

Billy Wilkerson put the deal together for the cast and crew, with everyone working for a share of the profits. Rather than pay the fifty-dollar-a-day rental for space at the old Christie Studio, Wilkerson made an arrangement with a friend who worked there: on a day when the studio was dark, the friend sneaked the Wilkerson-Pasternak production inside via the back entrance of the Lasky Ranch (now Warner Bros. Studios). The expenditures for *Help Yourself* came to just under $600, most of which was spent on raw film stock and extras.

But once the film was finished, Pasternak wrote, "we were in terrible trouble." The production was a disaster from a technical perspective, with massive continuity errors and other problems caused by his inexperience as a director. But Wilkerson once again had a plan. He brought in the veteran silent film director Wesley Ruggles. "He was one of the finest makers of comedy in our country," Pasternak wrote. Ruggles reviewed the film and made a few suggestions, enough that the filmmakers could at least get the picture into marketable shape.

Then Ruggles paid Pasternak a compliment: despite his technical shortcomings, he had managed to make the busboy character sympathetic, real, and likable. Such personal details were a rare gift, Ruggles said. "Most directors forget about them." The veteran director invited Pasternak to come work for him as his assistant.

From there on, Pasternak's film career would progress steadily. By 1936 he had produced *Three Smart Girls* for Universal Pictures; it reportedly saved the studio from bankruptcy. He moved on to Metro-Goldwyn-Mayer, where he was one of the three most important people in the company. His film career as a producer ultimately spanned forty years and earned him two Oscars and three Golden Globe nominations. He produced more than ninety feature-length films, directing and producing a number of classics, including 1945's *Anchors Aweigh* and *Please Don't Eat the Daisies* in 1960.

But in 1956, with the release of Pasternak's memoir *Easy the Hard Way*, the two men would have a falling out over the chapter Pasternak devoted to the serendipitous meeting with Billy Wilkerson that had spawned *Help Yourself* and kick-started his film career. "Believe it or not," Pasternak said, "that chapter happened just like that. Unfortunately, Billy didn't think what I said was about him was true—even though it was."

Pasternak had also written the following:

> [Billy] has always been a perfectionist, in life as well as in love. Having achieved perfection, he loses interest. Though I lived with him, he was a mystery to me, as he has remained a mystery to me ever since. I once told him he was the most kind-hearted cruel man I ever met. If Billy wants something, nothing had better stand in his way. And yet he is a man capable of the warmest gestures, a man whose only fault (if it is a fault) is that he is always shooting for the moon, and nothing less than perfection will suffice for him. . . . I liked him when I first met him and I've never ceased loving him.

That night in 1926 Pasternak and Wilkerson celebrated Pasternak's new appointment with champagne that Wilkerson had somehow finagled. "We were both broke," Pasternak told me. "Every penny we had had been spent on the film. To this day I don't know where Billy got the money to buy the champagne."

Two months later, Wilkerson was back in New York, shopping *Help Yourself* to the movie studios. If he was going to form his own motion picture company, which he planned to call Wilkerson Studios, he needed their support.

At that time, although the Edison Trust had long since been dismantled, almost the entire movie industry was controlled by a new monopoly owned by a handful of autocratic studio moguls. Among the toughest roughneck industrialists in America, they rivaled the robber barons, the Carnegies and Mellons. Where Edison had relied on his patents to maintain control of the industry, the current studio heads simply *owned* everything, from the raw talent to the production and distribution machinery to the theater chains that screened the finished films. Even equipment was difficult to procure without their say-so.

And they might still, as in Wilkerson's days with the Lubin Manufacturing Company, resort to arson or other sinister methods to intimidate an upstart rival. Without an invitation from the cartel, he had no chance of getting his studio off the ground.

But courting the studios would take time, and meanwhile, Wilkerson had to eat. So by October 1926 he was chasing profits in a completely different market.

In the early part of the twentieth century, powerful temperance movements, largely spearheaded by women, sprouted in America. They popularized the belief that alcohol was the nectar of Satan, responsible for most of the personal and social problems plaguing the nation. Most of these groups, the largest of which was the Christian Temperance Union, were composed of working-class women fed up with the domestic violence and loss of household income they associated with alcohol. Their message was so deafening that local bans began to spread across the country, and on January 16, 1919, the US Congress ratified the Eighteenth Amendment, prohibiting the production, distribution, and sale of alcoholic beverages anywhere in the United States, which went into effect one year later.

Prohibition became America's first large-scale experiment in legislating morality and was the template for the so-called "moral wars" to follow—those fighting drugs, prostitution, and gambling. Its supporters believed that it would serve as a cure-all for the nation's violence, crime, and poverty. Several communities were so convinced of the amendment's power to reform society that they even sold their jails.

But the experiment ultimately had the opposite effect. Most Americans ignored the ban, and promptly went on a drinking binge. Prohibition quickly became synonymous with decadence as illegal saloons, or speakeasies, sprung up across the country. In Manhattan alone there were twenty-two thousand speakeasies, far more than there had ever been legitimate bars. By the mid-1920s these establishments had only grown more popular, and so lucrative that they continued to flourish despite routine raids carried out by zealous Prohibition agents. Even the sight of speakeasy operators and patrons being hauled away in handcuffs did little to frighten away customers.

Seeking a profitable business venture as he pursued his film studio dream, Billy Wilkerson smelled opportunity in the speakeasy market. Surveying the current players, which included opium dens and bordellos, he instantly saw the same gap he had filled with his Fort Lee nickelodeon. To distinguish himself from the competition, he'd need a spectacular venue, where he could charge the highest prices and thus attract the most exclusive clientele.

In November 1926 Wilkerson took over a luxury Manhattan townhouse owned by auto magnate Horace Dodge, on Fifth Avenue near Saint Patrick's Cathedral. There he opened his first speakeasy.

"The townhouse was the first really glorified 'speak' in town," wrote George Murphy. In 1926 the future US senator was a struggling actor and a friend of Wilkerson's. When Murphy had no place to stay, Wilkerson let him live in an empty top-floor room over his "speak." From the outset, Wilkerson displayed an instinct for running high-class operations. "He was a natural," said Joe Pasternak, another friend who saw Wilkerson's Manhattan club operations firsthand.

With the success of his first speakeasy, Wilkerson quickly opened another: an exclusive club on the corner of Fifty-Second Street and Park Avenue. (Unfortunately, the names of all of Wilkerson's "speaks" are lost to us.) Opened in February 1927, it required members to pay an initiation fee of $1,500 per person—in today's dollars, about $20,000.

The speakeasy owner justified such prices by bringing an elegance to his venues that had been lacking in Prohibition-era New York. He offered the finest menus and wine list in the city, and he put on stunning floor shows, with live bands featuring the best entertainment he could hire. He also hired the best help to ensure top-notch service. In addition, it was said that Wilkerson was the first to institute a strict dress code for his customers. In his speakeasies, formal attire was mandatory. He himself was always dressed in a tuxedo and spats, complemented by a fresh carnation in his lapel and his waxed mustache, which curled up like the horns of a bull. And he was not beyond encouraging additional vices to improve his bottom line: he ensured that the back rooms had ongoing card games and parked beautiful women at the bar (and received a cut of the monies they received for their "services").

But while his new venture found him encouraging others' vices, it also motivated him to curb one of his own. Until Prohibition, Wilkerson had been, like his father, a heavy drinker, but this changed suddenly one night at one of his clubs. He and two of his bouncers were ejecting an unruly drunk when the man vomited all over Wilkerson's tuxedo. "From that moment on," remembered Tom Seward, "he hated drunks."

"A boozer is a loser," Wilkerson was often heard to say. He eventually came to have three deep-seated hatreds: drunks, Communists, and people who stole from him.

He replaced his weakness for alcohol with a passion for a softer drink. "The only drink Billy would allow to touch his lips was Coca-Cola," Joe Pasternak recalled. "He literally chain-smoked Coca-Colas. He never drank alcohol, not to my knowledge. But Coke is worse than drinking—cocaine, acid soda." Once, on a 1927 trip to Berlin to visit Pasternak, Wilkerson was desperately looking for a Coke. Pasternak told him they could find one about six blocks away. Pasternak recalled, "We took a taxi to get a Coca-Cola. Nine dollars was the cab fare! It was the most expensive Coke he ever drank!" I don't know if my father was aware, but the irony has not escaped my notice—the franchise my grandfather, Big Dick, owned for a brief moment ultimately became his son's favorite beverage.

In order to run a successful speakeasy, Wilkerson had to walk both sides of the street. To ensure that the doors to his illegal establishments stayed open, he quickly learned the wisdom of making payoffs to police captains and beat cops, to judges and district attorneys. "If you wanted to stay in business," said Seward, "you had to make your payoffs." (Years later my father would muse that repealing Prohibition was one mistake politicians would never repeat, for overnight they lost a hefty cash cow.)

Benefits of the "insurance" money paid to the appropriate authorities included early warnings of impending raids. According to George Kennedy, when Wilkerson got word that Prohibition agents were incoming, he relied on an elaborate system by which he'd temporarily transport his liquor inventory to a warehouse. He purchased a fleet of trucks to effect the transfer, but once those trucks reached their destination, they remained parked and loaded inside the warehouse until the raid or threat of a raid had passed. Once the booze was returned to his clubs, the trucks went back to the warehouse, where they were stored inside until they were next needed. On the day of a raid, Wilkerson would close the club and schedule himself to be elsewhere. Seward explained that these painstaking precautions were the reason Wilkerson never went to prison.

But Wilkerson also possessed a secret weapon: a lawyer named Isaac Goldenhorn, well known for routinely fixing cases for organized crime and speakeasy owners. When Wilkerson actually was raided, which was rare, he went to "Judge Goldenhorn," as he was known, who got him off in exchange for a hefty fee. When Wilkerson himself was victim of a police bust—an equally rare occurrence—Goldenhorn was his protection against prosecution.

One of Judge Goldenhorn's daughters, Edith, worked for her father, and one day Wilkerson was in the lawyer's office when Edith walked in. He was instantly smitten with the petite, dark-haired girl with flashing green eyes. Decades later Edith observed, "Of course every woman believed that their dreamboat had come in when they met Billy."

Before long Edith discovered one of Wilkerson's fetishes: he liked to have sex in phone booths. "Billy would wrap his trench coat around me in a phone booth and we would do it," she confessed to George Kennedy in 1934. She went on to disclose that her boyfriend had an interesting anatomical anomaly: a hooked penis, which amplified her pleasure when they made love.

Wilkerson didn't just make friends with lawyers and law enforcement. He also had to forge connections with the Mafia, who were just as essential to keeping one's establishments in business. The mob was the only source of high-quality alcohol. "Only the finest booze came from gangsters," said Seward. But other gangsters periodically showed up in Wilkerson's speakeasies demanding a piece of his operation. Some threatened to interrupt his alcohol supply if he failed to comply with their demands. Others simply exerted force.

"It was broken-nose politics," said Seward. "You either cut people in or you kill them. It was that simple." And so Wilkerson paid protection money to associates in organized crime, and for this service they "took care" of others attempting to infringe on his territory, and made sure he was never without quality booze.

Wilkerson also took delivery of weapons stored in his mob cohorts' alcohol shipments—though they weren't for his own use, he certainly knew they were part of the deal. "It only happened a few times," said Seward. "But it was just like the movies. Booze and tommy guns packed in the same wooden crates filled with straw." He stored the weapons in his cloakrooms, covering them with overcoats and jackets and scarves until the men working for one of his suppliers showed up to claim them.

Some argue that organized crime as we now know it was born during Prohibition. Certainly in this period the criminal demimonde acquired a quasi-legitimacy, even an aura of glamour. So it was with one such individual Wilkerson worked with during this period: Joe Kennedy, father of future president John F. Kennedy. Kennedy was one of his faithful suppliers of fine liquors, which he usually smuggled in through Canada. The two men may have met during Wilkerson's stint in Hollywood, as Kennedy was also a film producer and financier, who later produced movies for Gloria Swanson and cofounded RKO Pictures. Kennedy was also a fellow Catholic, which cemented their connection, but Wilkerson never let morals or religion stand in the way of profit. Although his other liquor suppliers remain unknown, they likely included a Who's Who of gangsters, including men like Meyer Lansky and Bugsy Siegel.

With allies on both sides of the law, Wilkerson had the opportunity to compare their effectiveness. He came to believe that politicians were inept, and he surmised they never would be key to his success. They drowned business owners in red tape and frequently broke promises—even after he paid them off. Not only did he not trust them, he believed they did not truly hold the reins of power. And they never matched the efficiency of his associates in organized crime, who for a fee always produced tangible results. "He always got what he paid for and was seldom disappointed," George Kennedy explained. Throughout his life, he would rely on gangsters when all other avenues failed him.

———————

The 1920s in New York City were prosperous in large measure because of the speakeasies, and the prosperity continued under the mayoralty of James

J. Walker, or Jimmy Walker, who was elected in 1926. The flamboyant young mayor was colorful, to say the least, known for his affairs with chorus girls and his tolerance for girlie magazines, casinos, and speakeasies. In addition, despite a threatened transit union strike in 1926, he kept city residents happy by maintaining the five-cent subway fare.

One night Mayor Walker visited Wilkerson's Park Avenue speakeasy and was so impressed that on the spot he asked Wilkerson to run his venues as well—for the mayor was in the speakeasy business himself. Walker knew that any successful operation potentially involved organized crime, and getting killed by rival gang members or going to prison was a significant downside. By turning over his clubs to Wilkerson, the dashing young mayor believed he would be safe; if Wilkerson were busted, he would take the fall. "Walker was a smart politician," Seward said. "He knew he couldn't afford to get his hands dirty." And naturally Wilkerson's services did not come cheap; he insisted on a 45 percent take of all proceeds.

By all accounts, the two men got along famously and their partnership was a resounding success. Walker wisely stayed out of Wilkerson's way and let the money pour in. With six profitable speaks, Wilkerson was raking in a fortune, close to $1 million a year—more than $13 million in today's dollars.

Unfortunately, the vast majority of Wilkerson's take evaporated each night, as he haphazardly tossed the fruits of his labor back onto the card tables. While the origins of Wilkerson's gambling addiction can be traced to his medical school days, speakeasy cash accelerated his disease. Work and religion remained lifelong sources of refuge, but it was gambling that offered him an escape. "When he gambled," observed Kennedy, "it was as though he was purging himself of success."

No one was more horrified by his growing addiction than Mary Wilkerson. Mary was Billy's rock, always there for her only son; whenever he lost every penny at the card tables, she gave him what little she had. But she never made any secret of her disappointment that he had inherited his father's fatal flaw. Mary saw her son as another gambling, cavorting rogue who took chances with life at every turn, while she was just the opposite: a steadfast saver who believed not in entrepreneurial endeavors but in the virtue of working steady jobs for other people. This stunning difference in their characters would cause friction throughout the rest of their lives.

A fervent Catholic like her son, she had prayed that Billy would not follow in his father's footsteps. When she saw history repeating itself, she lit a fire in her fireplace and, in a rage, yanked the crucifix from her wall and tossed it in. She then consigned her Bible and three sets of rosary beads to the flames. After the mid-1920s, she never again attended church or uttered a Catholic prayer.

4 | THE CRASH

IN MID-JUNE 1927, Wilkerson decided he needed a vacation from the speakeasy world, so he and Edith Goldenhorn hopped aboard a train bound for Hollywood. The couple spent ten days looking around. Wilkerson's dream of founding a Hollywood film studio hadn't faded; one evening over dinner he said, "One day, this will be our home." Then, without missing a beat, he popped the question. Edith accepted.

On June 22, 1927, they were married in Los Angeles by a justice of the peace. Billy was thirty-seven; Edith, twenty-five. We don't know if they had Judge Goldenhorn's approval, though in the dozens of interviews I conducted over the years I found no indication of his dissent. The couple honeymooned in Niagara Falls, New York, for another two weeks before returning to New York City.

Shortly after their return, Prohibition agents came through the skylight of Wilkerson's Park Avenue club and raided it. It was only a fluke that on this night Wilkerson was in Long Island on other business, but the fact is, he hadn't seen this one coming. "The raid really shook Billy up," said Joe Pasternak. "He should have been tipped off."

Within a week, Wilkerson's speakeasy in the Dodge townhouse was also unexpectedly raided and shut down. He surmised that either new agents were on the job and wanted to make a name for themselves, or someone who wanted a cut of his business had not yet been paid off. "It didn't matter who he paid off, there was always someone new who came in from the wings that made things difficult," Pasternak said.

"Billy never found out who the rat was," said Tom Seward. "There were so many people to deal with and pay off that you couldn't blame anyone for getting confused."

Wilkerson could have continued running Jimmy Walker's operations, but with two raids in close succession, he knew he was now on law enforcement's radar. What's more, he was now a married man, and his new wife was not shy about expressing concern over the dangers associated with his work. This made it a good time to leave the business. So in August 1927 he decided enough was enough and tendered his resignation to Mayor Walker.

With his speakeasies shuttered, his quest to get Wilkerson Studios off the ground took on greater urgency. But this venture, too, was meeting with harsh resistance from the powerful men he'd counted on to support him.

By 1928 Wilkerson had screened *Help Yourself* for every major studio, banking on the notion that a major star (El Brendel) and a "European" film director (Joe Pasternak) would be enough to land him a distribution deal. "Billy really hungered to start his own studio," remembered Pasternak. "He talked about it all the time. With Brendel as part of the package, it should have been a shoo-in." But *Help Yourself* was a dud and Wilkerson knew it. While the studio heads were keenly aware of his acumen as a salesman and distributor and as a producer of one-reelers ("He had done a lot for the studios," Tom Seward said), they turned up their noses.

Wilkerson believed that religion played a part in the moguls' rejection. Most of these men were nonobservant Jews living in a Christian-dominated nation, immigrants who had fled persecution in their countries of origin and still faced heavy discrimination in their new home. Barred from virtually all respectable business, they found refuge in an industry that dignified gentile society initially looked down upon. In fact, some historians believe they created the studio system in part as a fortress to protect themselves from the Christian elite. All the principals interviewed for this book claimed that the moguls were slow to trust those in the business world who did not share their religious background. Others, such as George Kennedy, went so far as to speculate that the all-Jewish film enclave couldn't allow a non-Jew to compete with them—something Wilkerson himself suspected. But considering the number of gentiles who rose to the top of the industry, from Frank Capra to Cecil B. DeMille, such charges smack of sour grapes. In any event, Wilkerson eventually had to accept that his dream of owning his own movie studio was over before it began.

As for *Help Yourself,* Wilkerson kept the only print in his possession, and what happened to it remains a mystery. What is no mystery is what happened to the negative. Wilkerson neglected to pay the lab bill, so the lab destroyed it. As Pasternak explained, "Labs incinerating prints and negatives for nonpayment was a common practice in those days."

To say that my father was heartbroken by his failure is an understatement. His second wife, Edith, said, "It was a bitter pill to swallow."

This was, it appears, the seminal moment in Billy Wilkerson's life. While most take rejection on the chin and move on, he took it personally and decided no one who had stood in the way of his dreams would get off lightly. "They refused to let him into their club," said Greg Bautzer. "That was a huge mistake."

Filmmaking dreams were replaced by a deep desire for revenge, and Wilkerson made it his life's mission to crush the studio monopoly and along with it the movie brass. As Pasternak reiterated, "Anyone who got in his way he annihilated." From that point on, my father would no longer wait for an invitation from Hollywood. Instead he decided to become its self-anointed czar. One morning he stepped out of the shower and announced to his wife that he had a new idea for a business that would both be lucrative and support his desire to move to California. "From there," Edith remembered, "it took off like a forest fire."

The idea he was formulating was to start the first daily trade paper for the motion picture industry in Hollywood. With the industry now firmly ensconced in Southern California, Wilkerson knew the demand for such a publication would be high. But he'd also learned during his time with *Film Daily* in New York that a trade paper's words could have a powerful effect on the industry; a single bad review could flatten a film. He surmised that a similar publication in Hollywood would give him a club with which to pummel the men who had shut him out of "their" business.

Of course, he needed capital to make this venture feasible. His classic resourcefulness led him in February 1929 to acquire a half interest in a faltering

Manhattan film trade paper, the name of which is lost to history. He pumped life back into the paper and sold it seven months later for $20,000. This sum was more than adequate for his needs, but he wanted more cash before taking off for California. In October, just after he turned thirty-nine, Wilkerson bumped into a Wall Street chum, who advised him to play the market. Naturally, he jumped; in those days it seemed everyone was making money hand over fist with stock trades.

On a dangerous whim that echoed his gambling, he borrowed an additional $25,000 from a loan shark he knew, agreeing to repay it in full within a few months. The short turnaround time might have worried another man, but not Wilkerson. Tom Seward explained that his game plan was to double his money playing the market and then head to the West Coast. Wilkerson walked into the New York Stock Exchange at ten in the morning and dumped all $45,000 in cash on a single stock his friend had recommended. Forty-five minutes later, he stood dazed on the paper-strewn floor of the exchange; the date was October 29, 1929—Black Tuesday, the day the market crashed. Along with thousands of others, Wilkerson watched as his entire investment was wiped out.

The results of the Wall Street crash rippled across the nation. Consumer confidence plummeted and business and industry hit the skids. Before long, nervous depositors would be lining up at banks, desperate to withdraw their money for fear that the institutions were about to fail. The nation entered the Great Depression, and countless Americans lost everything they had—including Mary Wilkerson. It wasn't the first time Mary had lost all her money in a financial crash. Thirty-five years earlier, in May 1893, she'd suffered the same fate when the Dime Savings Bank of Chicago closed its doors. When history repeated itself, Mary changed her ways. This is when she began to keep her money in used coffee cans, which she stored in her kitchen cupboard.

Her son, meanwhile, would never again trust the stock market or any other form of investment, including real estate. Billy Wilkerson adopted the philosophy that the only investment worth making was in himself. He never hesitated to take risks to further his own career. "They were hard times," remembered Seward. "You had to use your wits and your fists to get by."

But Wilkerson's more immediate problem was his now-unpayable debt to the loan shark. When Edith learned of it, she was incensed. She knew the consequences of reneging on such commitments; she'd witnessed the results firsthand in her father's legal practice. "It was a cardinal rule," Seward explained, "that you never borrowed money from the mob. Never."

And Wilkerson understood his wife's ire; he knew it was only a matter of time before the loan shark came calling. He had no option but to act quickly. Fortunately, Edith knew her husband's weakness for gambling and had squirreled money away. "It was their escape money," said Kennedy. Wilkerson borrowed a few hundred dollars from another friend, and one morning in mid-December he woke up and packed Edith, Mary, and their dog, Fritz, into a dilapidated flivver, as small cars in those days were known. They made the arduous cross-country journey to Hollywood.

When Kennedy relayed this story my father had told him, he chuckled at the memory. "They nearly didn't make it. Their car broke down half a dozen times." And on top of the difficulties of the journey itself, neither Edith nor Mary let up on him about his stupidity in the stock market debacle. "They must have harangued Billy nonstop from one coast to another," Pasternak said.

They left behind a Manhattan apartment in a building known as the Windsor, at 100 West Fifty-Eighth Street. Their monthly rent was $141.67 (about $2,000 in today's dollars). Edith urged her husband to hold on to the place, so if things didn't work out in California, they could settle matters with the loan shark and return. "Edith particularly was suffering from a terrible case of cold feet," said Kennedy. "She was a real New Yorker. She hated the idea of leaving."

But Wilkerson would not return to the Windsor. He would never again live in New York City.

5 | LIFE IN THE WEST

THE MOST SUCCESSFUL FIGURES in the entertainment industry—people like film producers Mike Todd, Sam Spiegel, and David O. Selznick, and movie tycoons like Joe Schenck—shared a sense of determination, an ability to weather massive misfortune. Like these men, my father could not be crushed. After a bruising defeat (often at the card tables), Wilkerson typically shrugged it off with "Tomorrow's another day." When he lost everything in the crash of 1929, he stuck with this rallying cry. It was not the first time he had fallen on hard times, and it would certainly not be his last, but like other industry pioneers of his era, he did not let failure stop him.

"Billy had an uncanny ability not to personalize his losses," remembered Greg Bautzer. He possessed unshakable self-belief, self-confidence that bordered on arrogance, in his knowledge that he would succeed. "When he made up his mind to do something," said Joe Pasternak, "that was it. He wasn't afraid of anybody."

Having been shunned by the studios only fed his sense of self. "Nobody else would take him seriously," said Harry Drucker, Wilkerson's barber and friend. "He had to believe in himself. That's how he became successful." And so, when Billy and Edith arrived in California in 1930, they immediately went to work on the idea of starting a daily film trade paper.

It would not, however, be the *first* daily trade paper in Hollywood. They'd been beaten to the punch the previous year by a publication called *Hollywood Daily Screen World*, the motto of which was "Today's Motion Picture News Today." Wilkerson's first instinct, apparently, was to join forces; on July 31,

55

1930, *Hollywood Daily Screen World*'s publisher, Louis Jacobino, wrote a letter to Billy Wilkerson in which he welcomed the idea of him coming on board as a partner. He sent this letter to the Wilkersons' New York address, and it was forwarded to their Los Angeles address: 1737 Whitley Avenue in Hollywood.

What exactly my father proposed to Jacobino is not known, but by the time the publisher's letter was drafted, Wilkerson had already decided to start a competing daily instead. On July 26, 1930, Wilkerson formed the Wilkerson Daily Printers Corporation, in partnership with Manhattan broker Herbert Sonn. Wilkerson had approached Sonn to borrow $5,000, with an option to borrow twice that. Sonn, whom Wilkerson knew through Edith's sister, Helen, instantly agreed, and with that agreement in place, Wilkerson rented offices at 1606 North Highland Avenue in Hollywood from which to produce the *Hollywood Reporter*.

The next order of business was to assemble a team. Wilkerson installed Frank T. Pope as news editor. He hired an adman, Vic Enyart, who would remain at the *Reporter* until Wilkerson's death. Frank Whitbeck, publicity and advertising head of Fox West Coast Theaters, was solicited to draw up a distinctive format for the *Reporter*, and John Wentworth designed the elegant art deco logo, which survived for five decades. The *Reporter*'s editorial pages would be printed in two colors: red and black.

Wilkerson never let scruples stand in the way of stealing a good idea, and he certainly was not above pilfering *Hollywood Daily Screen World*'s slogan, altering it slightly. It ran on the masthead as "Today's Film News Today." The paper's premise from the start was simple:

> The primary function of the *Hollywood Reporter* is reporting today's film news today. To evaluate the *Hollywood Reporter*'s need by the Motion Picture industry throughout this great nation, one must closely observe its outstanding editorial policy, fine reporting, meticulous printing and excellent format. The combination of these factors makes the *Hollywood Reporter* the leading motion picture trade paper on the West Coast of these United States of America.

On September 3, 1930, the first issue of the *Hollywood Reporter* rolled off the presses and hit the streets. At first, "the *Hollywood Reporter* was literally a handout," said George Kennedy. "It was just a bundle of papers thrown over the studio walls." In other words, it was not the *Washington Post*. It was not the *New York Times*. But in its pages my father developed a unique editorial jargon that was to become the industry standard, casting aside good English prose in favor of a staccato telex style. "Penned," for instance, meant authored, "inked" meant signed a contract, and "lensed" indicated principal photography—words that entered the Hollywood lexicon through the *Reporter*'s pages and have never left.

The new daily was twelve pages long, and at fifty dollars a page, the printing costs were hefty. "It was pretty grim," remembered Kennedy. "At times they were so hard pressed there was hardly enough petty cash in the till for postage." As Tom Seward put it, "It was a hand-to-mouth deal from the beginning. Literally a starvation deal."

After a while, to save money, Wilkerson closed out all the local free subscriptions, though he continued to send complimentary copies to eight thousand exhibitors. Even then, with subscriptions of ten dollars per year coming in, the overhead was unsustainable. The Oxford Press, located on Sunset Boulevard, was the paper's printer. A little over a month after the *Reporter*'s launch, in an attempt to mitigate some of its production costs, the paper purchased it. We don't know the circumstances of the purchase or how much Wilkerson paid, but we do know that as of that purchase, the *Reporter* had its own printing plant.

Calling on all the resourcefulness he could muster, Wilkerson at times could be found operating the Linotype machine and other printing equipment himself. He even occasionally pitched in to deliver the paper. Edith vividly remembered her husband returning home at night, his hands blackened by newsprint from delivery runs.

Edith handled the accounts and payroll, and her job also entailed fending off creditors, at which she was particularly adept. She also wrote the majority of the editorial copy for the paper, at first writing without a byline. As she sat at her desk banging out a story on her typewriter, a cigarette precariously dangling from the corner of her mouth, she always managed to look good. According to Kennedy, who would join the organization a few years later, Edith was a fashion plate who "looked like she just stepped out of the pages of a magazine. She was always immaculately put together." Those who worked with her recalled her hair as always perfectly coiffed and her trademark red lipstick and matching nail polish looked like they had been applied by a studio makeup artist. "She was continually taking out her compact and touching herself up," Kennedy remembered.

Despite Edith's care in presenting herself, she and Billy were hardly living like royalty. They woke to the same breakfast every morning: black coffee, fried eggs, and toast. They ate chicken sandwiches for lunch and consumed soup and saltine crackers for dinner. Few people knew of their hard times. "They never showed how badly off they were," said Joe Pasternak. "Billy had a philosophy of keeping up appearances."

While Wilkerson had never before shown a proclivity for politics, from the moment he launched the *Reporter* he displayed an eagerness to champion causes, whether out of principle or to boost sales of his paper. His most potent weapon was his daily front-page editorial, entitled Tradeviews. The column was a chatty opinion piece in which my father played the dual roles of gossip and self-appointed seer. The *Reporter* would have survived, even thrived, without Tradeviews, but there's no question that my father's politically charged writings put the paper on the map. Billy Wilkerson did not become famous because he started a newspaper. He made himself famous by writing Tradeviews.

Wilkerson's primary target, of course, was the studio system that had rejected him. "When Mr. Wilkerson began the paper in 1930, he was an unknown outsider," said Kennedy. "When they told him to go to hell, really his only option was to muscle in on their turf." Tradeviews put the studio heads in the crosshairs for the first time.

We don't know the definitive list of movie bosses Wilkerson had in his sights when he launched the *Reporter*. He may have focused on the specific executives who had rejected *Help Yourself* and foiled his studio plans, but it's likely that his broader target was the studio monopoly itself, which offended him both as a perceived victim of its exclusivity and as a firm believer in fairness. Certainly, two of his ongoing nemeses were MGM's Louis B. Mayer and Columbia Pictures' Harry Cohn.

The various studio heads generally hated one another, but they banded together whenever their mutual interests were threatened. And Billy Wilkerson was a threat, because he was keenly aware of their Achilles heel: their predominantly Jewish heritage made them targets in a time of persecution and discrimination. Despite their wealth and power, the chiefs frequently found themselves social exiles in Los Angeles, self-conscious about their religious background and desperately wanting to blend in. They were banned from such civic organizations as the Rotary and Lions Clubs and were categorically denied membership at exclusive country clubs. "They didn't have a seat at the Hearst dinner table," said Greg Bautzer. "They were never the invited guests of other prominent gentiles in town."

"They were Jews who didn't want to be Jews," remembered MGM publicity head Howard Strickling. "They did everything they could to fit in." Wilkerson took advantage of the precarious social position of the group of men he dubbed "the Synagogue," subtly and skillfully playing the bigotry card to attract allies to his side.

But my father's opposition to the studio bosses wasn't just about revenge or religious discrimination. He also hated the way the studios routinely bullied their employees, to keep their pay low and punish those who did not fall in lockstep with their bosses' line. The mechanics of the studio system gave the moguls particular power over their actors; talent contracts were so one sided and open ended that the studios essentially owned the actors they employed. When actors became stars, few saw salary increases until their contract was up for renewal—meaning that the studios, and not the performers themselves, reaped the benefits of their hard-earned celebrity. The harsh contracts also allowed the studios' publicity arms to rigidly regulate not just their careers but also their private lives. "We controlled every syllable they uttered," Howard Strickling confessed.

Such exploitive deeds fueled Wilkerson's desire to break the studio system. Joe Pasternak described him as "a real-life Citizen Kane. He wasn't afraid of anybody. If he didn't like the policies of a Harry Cohn or a Jack Warner, he would come right out and say so in print. Billy was an honest guy, and when you're an honest guy, you can't be a nice guy." "A paper man," said Harry Drucker, "if he says something good, they like him. If he tells the truth about somebody, they dislike him."

At first, the moguls saw Wilkerson as a mere upstart, a version of the movie sheriff who breezes into town with highfalutin notions of reforming an industry. They smugly assured themselves that the buffoon and his words soon would evaporate. But "overnight the paper's readership went off the chart," said Seward. And as the *Reporter*'s criticism spread, the studio bosses' comfort level diminished. "They were all allergic to criticism," said Pasternak.

By early 1931 the studio heads had called an emergency meeting to discuss what to do about Wilkerson. There was no question in their minds that Adam needed to be expelled from the Garden of Eden. Each man had been thinking of ways to eliminate him. Harry Cohn suggested blackmail, an old but effective method. Ultimately, the men agreed that Louis B. Mayer, as the head of the Producers Association, should handle the task of dealing directly with Wilkerson.

The pudgy, bespectacled Mayer, who resembled a bank manager more than the head of an artistic organization, summoned Wilkerson to his office. One of the highest-paid executives in the United States and never one to waste time on pleasantries, Mayer told Wilkerson that as long as he printed what the studios wanted him to print, he could stay in business. "Those were the days when the studios could literally tell a newspaper what to print," said Kennedy. And they wanted puff pieces, not criticism.

But Wilkerson was not prepared to just roll over. "He told Mayer to go fuck himself," said Tom Seward. "That's right, right to his face!"

When news of the meeting got out, friends called Wilkerson and pleaded with him to reconcile with Mayer. Pasternak begged his friend to stop fighting with the studio titan, telling him it would cost him a fortune in ads. "Fuck 'em," Wilkerson said. "I'll do whatever I want."

"From that moment on," remembered Bautzer, "it was all-out war."

In an effort to drive Wilkerson out of business, Mayer convinced the studio chiefs to issue a complete ban on the *Reporter*, withdrawing all advertising support. Studio gates were closed to Wilkerson's reporters, and special details were ordered to stand guard to ensure no journalist from the paper trespassed. Studio employees were forbidden to return calls to the paper.

Winfield "Winnie" Sheehan, Fox's production head, issued instructions to the studio mailroom to gather up all copies of the *Reporter* first thing every morning when they came over the studio walls. He ordered them to be torched outside his office. Reportedly, he relished gazing out the window at the "wisps of smoke rising." And that launched a ritual. Attendants at all the other studios were directed to immediately douse their issues of the *Reporter* with gasoline and light them on fire. Seward also remembered studios dispatching their thugs to Southland newsstands to pressure newsstand owners not to sell the paper. In one incident studio strongmen took copies of the *Reporter* right off the newsstand, piled them in a heap on the sidewalk, doused them with gas, and burned them right there on the spot.

"When the studios put the ban on [Wilkerson]," recalled Seward, "he was just about ready to fold. But the minute they started letting him get to them, Billy became the bigger man."

Wilkerson understood something the studio heads didn't about the power of bad publicity. Because the studios owned their own theater chains, they could compel exhibitors to show their movies despite poor notices—but they didn't count on other newspapers across the country picking up the *Reporter*'s unflattering editorials and negative reviews, and delivering them directly to the moviegoing public. The studios could guarantee that their films would be screened, but before long Wilkerson had the power to dissuade audiences from seeing them.

He also had another ace up his sleeve: sources within the studio system who were ready to help him fight back.

One of Wilkerson's sources was film director Raoul Walsh, who would ultimately become the publisher's intelligence officer. Discovered in the early 1920s by D. W. Griffith, Walsh honed his image as a tough-guy director with a pencil-thin mustache. He had lost his right eye in an accident but refused to wear a prosthetic. Instead, he insisted on wearing an eye patch. He was one of the first directors who viewed action movies as an art form. "To Raoul Walsh," said Warner Bros. chief Jack Warner, "a tender love scene is burning down a whorehouse." Walsh was also one of the first directors not under exclusive contract to any studio, and he was known for discovering new talent. He plucked a young stagehand named Marion Morrison from the crew to star in his 1930 movie *The Big Trail*, and turned that young man into John Wayne.

He also possessed a peculiar sense of humor. When John Barrymore died in 1942, Errol Flynn (a longtime Barrymore fan) was apparently so bereft that Walsh paid the funeral home to dress the dead actor in a business suit. Walsh then transported the corpse in his car to Flynn's home, propped him up in a chaise, and placed a lit cigarette in his hand and a Martini glass in front of him. Flynn, Walsh joked, could thus share one last drink with his idol.

The eccentric director had a contentious relationship with the studio chiefs; few knew that he had long been collecting information on them. When Wilkerson began excoriating the moguls in the *Reporter*, Walsh recognized a kindred spirit. He secretly contacted Wilkerson to offer his services. The two men began to meet clandestinely each month.

"He had access to information impossible for Billy or any of his reporters at the time to get," said Don Carle Gillette, Wilkerson's last editor. "Walsh became Mr. Wilkerson's Deep Throat," said Kennedy.

Besides their shared desire to bring down the studio chiefs, the two men discovered their mutual love of card playing. Walsh frequently passed information during card games. In a 1972 interview, Walsh called his friend "a terrible card player and a sore loser." The two men did, however, create a formidable team that made the studio chiefs easy and frequent targets.

Another of Wilkerson's early sources was even more highly placed. Joseph Schenck had been a mega film producer responsible for discovering a roster of screen legends, including Buster Keaton. He was one of the few businessmen in the industry who was well regarded by Hollywood's creative talent—so much so that when Charlie Chaplin, Douglas Fairbanks, D. W. Griffith, and Mary Pickford formed their own studio, United Artists, to escape the movie moguls' reach, they hired Schenck to run it.

Though trusted by the talent, Schenck was no outsider. His brother, Nicholas, ran Loews Inc., which owned a lucrative theater chain and was the parent company of MGM. Between them, the Schencks controlled a sizable chunk of the entertainment industry. But in many respects, Joe was different from his fellow film moguls. While the other studio chiefs maintained a carefully crafted decorum, Schenck was an unapologetic carouser, and his behavior rankled the other tycoons, especially Louis Mayer, who oversaw his brother's studio.

While he differed from Mayer and his ilk, like Raoul Walsh he shared Billy Wilkerson's great passion. Despite Schenck's seemingly bottomless wealth, he used it to subsidize an equally bottomless gambling addiction. He managed his addictions with the same dexterity he used to manage his professional life. In 1928 he and other investors had constructed a sprawling gambling resort on the Mexican border called Agua Caliente; it featured a full casino, a golf course, a racetrack, plenty of available women, and boatloads of non-Prohibition booze. Apart from quenching its owner's gambling thirst, Agua Caliente was a popular weekend destination for the movie colony's power elite.

Schenck was, in the words of Charles Rappleye and Ed Becker, authors of *All American Mafioso*, "a large man of imperious bearing with a broad nose and sleepy eyes," and the gregarious film titan's likability earned him the nickname "Good Time Joe." But his affability masked a cutthroat business instinct and a willingness to play fast and loose with ethics. More than any other studio boss, Schenck would stop at nothing to snag any opportunity that presented itself. "If he had the chance to snatch the rug from underneath you, he would," noted Tom Seward, who knew the tycoon well. According to Paul Ivano, film cameraman and friend of United Artists superstar Rudolph Valentino, when Schenck learned that Valentino was suffering from a serious medical condition in 1926, he took out two $1 million life insurance policies on his life. When the idol perished, Valentino had one of the biggest funerals in recorded memory, but when it came to the interment, Schenck didn't lift so much as a finger to cover a final resting place befitting the movie star who had apparently made him millions. Valentino was tucked away in a nondescript crypt in Los Angeles.

As soon as my father began publishing Tradeviews, Schenck recognized that here was a dangerous potential adversary—and a powerful potential ally. He wasted no time telephoning Wilkerson to offer any assistance he could. The two men had actually first met sometime in the mid-1920s; Schenck may have been one of the studio heads who crushed Wilkerson's dream of starting a motion picture company. But my father saw the value of embracing their similarities. Their initial phone conversation resulted in a lifelong bond, and a powerful alliance.

6 | THE BET

BILLY WILKERSON'S ALLIANCE with Raoul Walsh and Joe Schenck gave him the inside track on his enemies within the studios, but he would not be able to stand up to them if he didn't also have muscle on his side. He'd learned in his New York speakeasy days how efficient the Mafia could be in that respect. So he was grateful when Schenck introduced him to local gangster Johnny Rosselli.

Rosselli had been part of the Chicago Outfit, but in the mid-1920s his bosses dispatched him to Los Angeles, where he set to work bringing gambling and prostitution to Hollywood. Traditional accounts name Jack Dragna as the head of the Mafia's operations in Los Angeles, but he did not control the entire city. According to both George Kennedy and Tom Seward, it was clear that Hollywood was Johnny Rosselli's domain—and he set his sights on making inroads into the film world.

Rosselli, whose nickname was "Handsome Johnny," possessed leading-man looks and frequently dated movie stars. He was vain, slim, tanned, and, like Wilkerson, a natty dresser. He possessed the charm and good manners of nobility. "He could charm the socks off you," George Kennedy remembered. "It was hard not to like him." Apart from his pronounced hawk nose, the gangster's most memorable feature was his steel-blue eyes. Accompanied by a "mirthful, infectious smile," as authors Charles Rappleye and Ed Becker called it, Rosselli's eyes either swept you off your feet or shot daggers at you. His eyes "laughed when they looked at you," remembered Tom Seward, who had much traffic with the gangster over several years. "I liked him."

According to Seward, who knew Rosselli well, the gangster yearned to be a successful film producer, which he saw as his ticket to legitimacy. But as a high-profile underworld figure, he would have a hard time making that sort of transition. So for the time being he would have to make do with his connections to Hollywood bigwigs like Joe Schenck and Columbia Pictures' Harry Cohn. Billy Wilkerson offered him another conduit into the business—and a way to gain some leverage over an industry he could not enter by legitimate means.

So began a long personal and business partnership between Rosselli and Wilkerson. Over the years, Wilkerson would make many social loans to the gangster, loans Rosselli always paid back in cash. Rosselli, in turn, would handle Wilkerson's insurance needs through the insurance company run by his associate Herman Spitzel. As Seward recalled, "Rosselli worshipped Billy. Whenever Billy needed anything or was in any sort of trouble, Rosselli took care of it."

Handsome Johnny also assisted Wilkerson in his early efforts to break the studio moguls' ban. Wilkerson had decided that a way to both build his reputation in the industry and keep the pressure on his enemies in the studios was to air their dirty laundry in the pages of the *Reporter*. He instructed his reporters to eavesdrop on studio conversations wherever they found them and to befriend studio secretaries, even bedding them in order to obtain information. He even ordered his reporters to climb studio walls and scale fences at night in search of embarrassing documents to publish, a venture for which Rosselli provided essential support.

In the early 1930s American companies did not have access either to paper shredders or to regular garbage collection, so they tended to incinerate their garbage. From his days working at *Film Daily*, Wilkerson had learned that studios did so every three or four days, assigning a studio attendant to the task, which generally took place at night. Thus, he knew that accessing their sensitive documents was simply a matter of timing. According to Tom Seward, Rosselli worked his industry connections, making sure he knew the garbage attendant at each studio, what his hours were, and when he burned the refuse. On nights when no burning was scheduled and the garbage lay unsupervised, Wilkerson's reporters would sneak in and sift through the refuse, retrieving the information before it met the flames. Rosselli would also post his boys to stand lookout as reporters broke into executive offices and rifled through file cabinets in search of documents to steal.

According to Vic Enyart, Wilkerson's top adman, the information culled from these nightly hauls was not anything today's readers would consider salacious. Instead, the *Reporter* found memos on salaries, who was getting hired and fired and why—the sort of details of studio politics infamously revealed in the 2014 Sony Pictures hacking scandal. Wilkerson never hesitated to publish such information on the front pages of his paper. "The *Reporter* was a scandal sheet," said Las Vegas promoter Herb McDonald, most famous for bringing the Beatles to Vegas in 1964. And Wilkerson's column, in particular, had a remarkable ability to scandalize.

Through his scoops, Wilkerson didn't just embarrass the studio heads; he also championed the cause of the blue-collar workers, studio technicians, writers, and directors, who hated the brass as much as he did. They, in turn, became his loyal fan base, and soon they were helping to supply the *Reporter* with more inside dirt. Over time, approximately 250 *Reporter* loyalists inside the studios began to send Wilkerson clandestine news reports, which they either mailed or personally delivered; Kennedy explained that it was too risky for them to telephone. In addition, readers faithful to the paper began to take out ads in a gesture of support. During its first year in print, the majority of the paper's ads came from writers, directors, producers, agents, and local businesses—not from the big studios. Although short lived, the *Reporter*'s fledgling period was its democratic era.

A loyal following could only get the publisher so far, though, and he schooled his sales staff to do whatever it took to secure more ads. Austrian director Berthold Viertel came to Hollywood around the same time as Wilkerson, to work for Fox Film Corp. and later Paramount, and he experienced the hard sell that was common at the *Reporter*. According to Berthold's son, writer Peter Viertel, Wilkerson's admen, known as "holdup men," would continuously visit the offices of directors, producers, and actors to put the arm on them for ads. This unabashed New York–style aggression repelled many Hollywood clients, but that didn't stop my father. "There's no question that Wilkerson was a genius at sucking ads out of people," noted Viertel.

By mid-1931 the *Reporter* was flush with advertising, and the studios realized their ban had backfired. "We were selling more space than ever before," remembered Enyart. The *Reporter* had already moved its offices from North Highland Avenue to 5746 Sunset Boulevard, today the site of the Hollywood Freeway, but now it had outgrown even this space. So the paper moved again, this time to a building at 6715 Sunset, formerly the address of its competitor *Hollywood Daily Screen World*. Around this time Wilkerson also purchased his mother a ranch at 17426 Sherman Way in in Van Nuys, twelve miles from Hollywood.

The other movie tyrants put pressure on Louis Mayer to make a deal with Wilkerson. Mayer summoned Wilkerson to his office and admitted that "they" had handled things badly. The studio titan told Wilkerson he could ask the other heads to end the advertising ban, but he could not guarantee that they would advertise extensively, because the *Reporter*'s circulation was too small. But Wilkerson knew that the *Reporter*'s influence depended on newspapers around the country frequently running its stories and reviews without credit. He bet Mayer that he could prove at least five hundred papers from all over the United States were doing just that. If he won, all the studios would take out yearly advertising contracts; if he lost, he would fold his operation and never again have anything to do with the entertainment industry. The men shook on the deal.

To test his claim, Wilkerson suggested that they concoct an absurdly phony story, one only the two of them would know about. The *Reporter* would run that story, and if other papers started to report it, they would know Wilkerson's paper was the source. But what should the story be? Mayer mentioned an MGM newcomer whom he felt wasn't terribly promising. He pushed the actor's glossy headshot across the desk toward Wilkerson. As Wilkerson studied the photo, Mayer told him to make some outrageous claim that he would become a star. And so, on July 13, 1931, the *Reporter* ran the following Tradeviews:

MR. EXHIBITOR: Watch out for Clark Gable!!

A new star is in the making. Has been made. A star that, to our reckoning, will outdraw every other star the pictures has ever developed. This Gable fellow is a sensation out here on the Coast and if he is not enjoying the same success in your town it is for the reason that your patrons, men and women, young and old, have not seen the new pictures he has been spotted in.

This reviewer has been looking at pictures for almost twenty years, has studied audience reactions to pictures and players, feels he knows a bit about both. Never have we seen audiences work themselves into such enthusiasm as when Clark Gable walks on the screen.

Maybe you don't know Gable. If you played "Dance, Fools, Dance" you may have caught him in the mob. If you saw "Secret Six" you will remember he played a flip reporter. He was a Salvation Army Captain in "Laughing Sinners" and did a refined brute in "A Free Soul." His unreleased pictures are Warner's "Night Nurse" and Metro-Goldwyn-Mayer's "Sporting Blood" and the lead opposite Garbo in "Susan Lennox."

All of this is not a build-up for Gable. He does not need it, but it is a tip for you, Mr. Showman. Grab everything you can get with Gable in it and watch your box-office thermometer rise, for not since the first days of Valentino has a player shot into the movie heavens with such rapidity. And he is going to stick at the top, for he has everything. The women will go into backflips at the mere mention of his name; critics will give him a big hand because he is an artist; men will flock to the theatre displaying his name because he is a man's man.

Gable is not limited to type, can play any part, is likable, has forceful personality, and, above all, has SEX written all over him in big letters.

Metro-Goldwyn-Mayer did not expect this avalanche of enthusiasm. They have only had him for six months, felt they had a bet, but nothing so sensational. Now they are scouring the world for stories to star him in.

Put this on your cuff and credit it to this column—after you have played "Susan Lennox" the name Clark Gable will be synonymous with top business. Yes, it's going to be a Gable year, Mr. Exhibitor—don't be caught napping.

For the next sixty days after this Tradeviews column ran, Wilkerson kept in close touch with his clipping service, directing them to forward any news article that picked up his invented story. When the results were in, he hurried over to MGM and showered Mayer's desk in a blizzard of five thousand press clippings. At first Mayer thought it was a prank, something Wilkerson had his men in the art department cook up. But after his publicity head, Howard Strickling, authenticated the clippings, Mayer grew pale.

Enyart said, "When Mayer realized he lost the bet, that was a big blow to somebody like him who always got his way."

The editorial had another unexpected result. Prior to the piece in the *Reporter*, Clark Gable had become discouraged with Hollywood. He was packing his bags, preparing to head back to his little stock company in Texas. But Gable knew the value of favorable press coverage, and after he read Wilkerson's glowing editorial, instead of heading back to Texas, the handsome young actor bought himself a brand-new white Cadillac convertible.

"From that single piece," said Joe Pasternak, "exhibitors really began taking notice of Gable and his career took off. I would go so far as to say that it was Billy's piece that made him a star."

Clark Gable would not become just any movie star. He became "the King."

As for Billy Wilkerson, with formidable allies like Joe Schenck and Raoul Walsh in his pocket, the working people of Hollywood on his side, and the studios committed to supporting his paper with advertising, he was well on his way to become Hollywood royalty of a different sort. Despite his success, however, the respect of the studio heads still eluded him. Whenever Wilkerson telephoned Louis Mayer or Harry Cohn, their secretaries, under instruction from their bosses, would tell the publisher they would take a message. But others in the studio system were coming around; at Christmas 1931 Carl Laemmle's son "Junior" Laemmle, who worked with his father at Universal, gave Wilkerson a gold-and-black enameled cigarette case as a peace offering. He joined Schenck and Walsh in befriending Wilkerson.

On the eve of the paper's second anniversary in 1932, Wilkerson reflected on how far he'd come in so short a time, and took a victory lap:

Two Years Ago
Two people, a dog and a few thousand dollars arrived in Hollywood with an idea to publish a daily motion picture paper for the dissemination of news of productions in particular and the entire motion picture industry in general.

We were told here, as we were told in New York—"Save your money, the picture business has too many papers now and a Hollywood paper WILL NEVER PAY." Being dumb and stubborn and still having a few thousand dollars, we paid no attention to this advice.

On August 1, 1930, we rented a $50 office, put in some second hand furniture, borrowed a couple of typewriters and started to work on that publishing idea. On September 3, 1930, the first edition of THE HOLLYWOOD REPORTER was printed and issued.

During the past twenty-four months this publication has grown from little more than a rumor and a few thousand dollars to the MOST IMPORTANT film publication printed. Our efforts have been rewarded by one of the largest paid circulations in the film industry and our advertising columns have carried more PAID advertising than all the Hollywood papers put together for the entire period of their existence.

WE ARE THANKFUL

During the next twelve months, we hope to serve you with a better paper, more news, more coverage and give you better values for your subscriptions and advertising.

W.R. Wilkerson
Publisher

7 | VENDÔME

IN THE FIRST FEW YEARS of the *Reporter*, both Billy and Edith Wilkerson had made extraordinary sacrifices to keep their paper alive, but now that business was humming, they vowed to reclaim their former life. "They made promises to each other," said Joe Pasternak. "It was very touching." Though expanded office space and the ranch for Billy's mother had taken priority, by late 1932 they were in a position to start investing in themselves as well. They purchased a modest house in the flats of Beverly Hills. A cream-colored Mexican adobe home with two bedrooms and two bathrooms, it would become Edith's lifelong residence.

The Wilkersons were most eager to resume their visits to restaurants, clubs, and other such locales that had characterized their lavish life in New York. In the New York days, according to Tom Seward, the couple rarely ate at home; in Hollywood, they'd rarely eaten out. Remembered Seward, "Billy told me that at night he and Edith would go to bed talking about the restaurants and nightclubs they missed in New York." Joe Pasternak agreed that this was a significant issue for the couple: "They were eating atrocious food. Sandwiches, soup and crackers. That wasn't Billy."

But it was more than poverty that kept the Wilkersons from dining out. Hollywood in the early 1930s could not compare to the Big Apple, where opportunities for extraordinary dining existed on practically every city block. In Hollywood, Wilkerson found few noteworthy eateries, especially within walking distance of the *Reporter* offices, and he began to muse to Edith that if they wanted a steady supply of excellent food, they might need to open a deli or grill of their own.

He also pointed out that opening a restaurant would give him an ideal place to meet with clients. By 1933 most of Wilkerson's day was eaten up by driving from one meeting to another, generally at the studios or agents' offices located miles away from the *Reporter*. "Mr. Wilkerson got tired of chasing people down all over town," said George Kennedy. Wilkerson ruminated on the idea of creating a venue that could function as a central meeting place, similar to the famed sidewalk cafés of Paris, where the literary giants of the 1920s had gathered.

In March 1933 Wilkerson rented a space at 6666 Sunset Boulevard, one block east of the *Reporter* offices. Associates were tight lipped about how the publisher funded ventures such as this; he likely relied on investors, but we don't know exactly who they were or what share of the business their investment brought them. A few sources hinted that, given my father's chronic gambling addiction, he may have accepted some funding from his organized crime connections. In any event, in the first week of May, he opened a delicatessen called Vendôme.

Initially Wilkerson had envisioned providing dinner at Vendôme in conjunction with the deli, but he was unable to get the necessary permit to conduct business at night. Instead he set his sights on the lunch market, installing a corner counter providing gourmet sandwiches. He had his own table built so that he could dine there as well. In order to ensure that the deli's produce, dairy products, and poultry came from a reliable source, he shipped them in from his mother's ranch in Van Nuys, which he renamed Vendôme Ranch. Within weeks of opening, the sandwich bar was so popular he couldn't resist the idea of serving luncheon and enlarged the building. Every day before the doors even opened at noon (Vendôme served hot meals between 12:00 and 2:00), a line of eager customers snaked halfway down the block.

In June a Hollywood friend returned from England with a gift basket from Fortnum & Mason, a famed London department store dating back to the 1700s. Wilkerson was so taken with the delicacies within that he made a special trip to London to explore the store for himself. He found it stocked with treats of every kind from all around the world, and realized that it offered a convenient way to supply his deli with exotic fare without having to scour the globe himself. He acquired exclusive licensing rights, becoming Fortnum & Mason's sole distributor in the United States.

As a result of this arrangement, Vendôme became a paradise for Hollywood's "royalty of the screen," as Wilkerson called the customers who eagerly devoured the procession of treats that arrived at his delicatessen by plane, train, and ship. And Wilkerson shamelessly trumpeted the parade of Fortnum & Mason products in daily full-page ads in the *Reporter*. Among other delicacies, the deli sold large gray-egged Russian caviar from pedigreed sturgeon, canned goose livers, smoky teas, Yarmouth bloaters, and Westphalian ham. English delicacies were particularly popular with such British expatriates as Charles Laughton and Charlie Chaplin who yearned for a bit of home. Thus, Wilkerson became not just a powerful publisher but also Hollywood's gourmet czar.

In truth, however, the deli's success was not just thanks to the extravagant food selection. In the waning days of Prohibition, it also filled another luxury consumer need. Unable to shake his speakeasy past, Wilkerson imported high-quality European booze via Canada and sold it under the counter to his highbrow European customers. "That alone immediately put the business on the map and in the black," said George Kennedy, who had finally arrived on the scene. Kennedy was a shy, handsome, dark-haired twenty-five-year-old when he was hired as my father's private secretary in the spring of 1933.

Kennedy was also gay, something Wilkerson didn't approve of, but the publisher preferred him to hiring a female assistant. Years later he explained to his fifth wife, Vivian DuBois, that female secretaries were likely to get pregnant and leave, and too prone to disclosing the boss's business in idle gossip with friends over drinks. Whether or not this was true, Kennedy proved himself both loyal and discreet; for decades, he'd be privy to juicy gossip for which the tabloids would have paid a tidy sum, but he was never tempted to betray his boss's confidence.

Wilkerson followed the same policy for the new hires at Vendôme: his servers would all be men. "Billy felt that female servers were too chatty and distracting to the customers," said Greg Bautzer.

My father's eye for luxury extended to the look of the restaurant itself. "The Vendôme in those days wasn't cheap," said Seward, and it had the distinctive Wilkerson style. The dark, wood-paneled walls bolstered the illusion of being an elegant European club. He hired a designer to create a crest for the deli, and included it in his advertising campaign. The pomposity of the crest said it all: a strip of film celluloid bearing the deli's name stretched diagonally across the banner, a chain-mailed hand held a silver goblet, a band of three stars sat regally at the top, and a lone mounted knight wheeled on a charger.

But celebrities and studio moguls flocked to the Vendôme for more than the food, drink, and ambience. They also came because they could be assured that their names would appear in the pages of the *Reporter* the day after they lunched. Wilkerson never hesitated to provide his readers with a roll call of names who had recently graced his establishment. Regulars over the years would include gossip columnist Louella Parsons, actor Clark Gable, actresses Marlene Dietrich, Mae West, and Joan Crawford, and super-agent Myron Selznick, brother of producer David O. Selznick.

And true to Wilkerson's original plan, the powerful of Hollywood would come to Vendôme to meet with the *Reporter*'s publisher. Instead of losing the entire day chasing people down at the studios, Wilkerson talked to an estimated one hundred people every day during lunch at his deli. "Instead of traveling to their studio offices in the San Fernando Valley," said Bautzer, "Billy made the studios meet him at Vendôme. He invented the power lunch." Recalled Kennedy, "Mr. Wilkerson had me make all his appointments to meet his clients at the Vendôme. Then he would just table-hop from appointment to appointment."

Vendôme quickly became the most widely celebrated haunt in town. Raoul Walsh remembered, "Billy stole all the clientele from the Brown Derby, and we guarded the door every day at Vendôme. It was a great meeting place for all the columnists and all the actors and actresses, and Billy enjoyed himself there. So did everybody that went there."

8 | THE CUT

EVEN AS BILLY WILKERSON prepared to launch his first swanky eating establishment for the Hollywood elite, back at the *Reporter* he was still championing the industry's put-upon working class, whose livelihoods were under threat as the Great Depression continued to roil the nation's economy.

On Monday, March 6, 1933, in an effort to stabilize the banking industry, newly elected president Franklin Delano Roosevelt declared a five-day nation-wide bank holiday. Five thousand banks were temporarily closed, forestalling bank runs by customers fearful of losing their savings. "I was in Palm Springs," said Wilkerson in a rare 1960 interview with *Hollywood Close-Up* magazine, "when I heard Roosevelt over the radio announcing the holiday lockup, and I put in a call to Louie." The publisher asked Louis Mayer what MGM was going to do if troubles with the banks persisted. Mayer told him he wasn't sure; the studio could go along for four weeks without access to banking services, but that was it.

The bank holiday and subsequent federal legislation ultimately succeeded in calming the financial system, and most of the banks quickly reopened. But shortly after his phone conversation with Wilkerson, using the bank holiday as an excuse, Mayer demanded that all MGM employees take a 50 percent pay cut for eight weeks. Vic Enyart remembered it as "take a cut in pay voluntarily or get fired." The other studios followed suit.

Wilkerson's inside man Raoul Walsh was tipped off that the studios intended to make the reductions permanent, and he passed along his finding to the publisher. Wilkerson phoned Mayer and confronted him with the information. As *Close-Up* magazine reported, Wilkerson said, "I advise you to see to it that the *Reporter* is reliably informed by somebody just what transpires at every meeting."

Mayer responded, "The paper can go to hell."

In light of the mogul's intransigence, Wilkerson felt the only way the industry's working people would have a happy ending was if they presented a united front. And, of course, he knew that their success would mean an embarrassing and costly failure for the hated studio heads. But at the time, only craftspeople such as electricians and set painters had unions to organize their resistance against the studios; writers and directors did not.

So Wilkerson contacted Hollywood scribe Howard J. Green and told him the writers should form a union. Green suggested reviving the old Screen Writers Guild, begun in 1921 largely as a social club. Wilkerson advised Green to sign up as many members as possible. Within the month he had mustered ten writers, including Lester Cole, John Howard Lawson, and John Bright; they met at the Hollywood Knickerbocker Hotel, where they reconstituted the guild as a trade union and elected Lawson as their president. With Wilkerson's backing, the Screen Writers Guild went into battle. "The writers organized," Wilkerson told *Close-Up* magazine, "and the studios had a fight on their hands."

Wilkerson wondered why the directors did not follow suit. "I got hold of a director named Bill Howard," Wilkerson said in his 1960 interview, "and asked why he didn't call a meeting that night of all the directors at the Roosevelt [Hotel]." Howard did just that, but few directors showed up. "Maybe the rest were scared," Wilkerson mused.

Nevertheless, under pressure from the Screen Writers Guild, and with the *Reporter* continuing to publicize the moguls' damaging secrets, the studios were forced to rescind their salary cuts. Mayer again summoned Wilkerson to his office. *Close-Up* reported that at that meeting Mayer ranted, "You've got these guys [the other studio owners] crazy. They want to arrange a sell-out. Why don't you sell the paper?"

"Well," said Wilkerson, "there's always a price for everything."

Mayer asked what he had in mind, to which Wilkerson responded, "I don't have anything in mind. What do you have in mind?"

Mayer went into his outer office and came back moments later with a personal check for $300,000. He placed it in front of Wilkerson. "You're telling me something I never knew before," said Wilkerson. "That I have a piece of valuable property." Indeed, that $300,000 would be worth nearly $6 million today—more than enough money for the Wilkersons to retire on. A prudent man would have taken a few days to ponder the offer. But in the sort of impetuous and reckless move that would come to define him, Wilkerson flicked the check off the desk with his finger, then got up to leave.

Mayer strongly suggested he take the money and run. Wilkerson never did. This was the last time he graced the studio titan's office with his presence. Later, Mayer would frame an unflattering Tradeviews column and place it on the wall immediately behind his desk, scrawling over the editorial in thick red grease pencil, "Never trust a man."

––––––––––––

From 1930 to 1933 the *Reporter* had supported the causes of the Hollywood everyman, who had returned the favor by loyally supporting him. "We went to war for the studio workers," said George Kennedy, "and they adored us for it." But in July 1933 an unwelcome development hastened the end of the *Reporter*'s democratic period. It was then that *Variety* first came to town.

Until mid-1933, *Variety* was still a weekly trade publication based in New York City. But its founder and publisher, Sime Silverman, eyed the *Reporter*'s success on the West Coast and decided he didn't want to miss this gold rush. In July he set up shop in Hollywood. On September 6, just weeks before Silverman passed away at the age of sixty, the first issue of *Daily Variety* saw print.

News of the competitor's arrival sent shockwaves throughout the *Reporter*'s newsroom. Everyone in the entertainment industry knew *Variety* was a well-established publisher with the power to blowtorch the *Reporter* into extinction, poaching both its scoops and its advertisers. Edith Wilkerson in particular went into a tailspin at the news; after struggling for three years to help their paper succeed, she and her husband might lose it all.

But Billy Wilkerson was undeterred. He'd launched his paper at the dawn of the Great Depression and built it into a thriving enterprise. Rather than derail him, hardships actually seemed to fuel my father. "All his life Billy was in love with the impossible," noted Joe Pasternak. He had a brand of luck all his own—"Wilkerson luck," George Kennedy called it—and it always allowed him to avert disaster, no matter how inevitable it seemed. "Billy believed the angels smiled on him," Pasternak recalled.

So when *Variety* threatened everything he'd accomplished, Wilkerson wasted no time in setting up a dirty tricks department at the *Reporter* to counteract its influence. Led by news editor Frank Pope and adman Vic Enyart, the task force had a simple strategy: thwart the new arrival at every turn. A top priority was holding on to their hard-won ad buys from the studios. Pope and Enyart built on their reporters' network of studio informants, instructing *Reporter* salesmen and other personnel to ingratiate themselves not only with all studio secretaries but with any studio staffers they could. They brought gifts and plied them with elaborate lunches, and in return these loyal informants would inform the *Reporter* in advance of appointments made by *Variety*'s admen. Thus Wilkerson's salespeople always arrived first.

Enyart also had the ad staff call *Variety* posing as ad buyers, tying up their phone lines with false leads. This left Arthur Ungar, *Daily Variety*'s editor, scratching his head, until one day it clicked: Billy Wilkerson was playing dirty. From then on, Ungar's hatred never abated. "Ungar hated Billy just because he was Billy Wilkerson," said Tom Seward. "Billy was smarter than him."

"Influence is a nice euphemism for power," commented Joe Pasternak, "and Billy had a lot of influence in Hollywood. If you wanted power, or at least a cut, you had to be just as ruthless as [the studios and other trade papers] were, otherwise you wouldn't survive. It was like gang warfare. You risked being squashed like a cockroach by the studios. I think that's the reason why so few people tried. The risk was too great. Billy was one of the few."

Wilkerson also benefited from having tied the studio to yearly advertising contracts, which he forced them to pay in advance. "Even in the '30s and '40s," noted Seward, "those amounts were enormous." If a studio decided to shut off advertising to the *Reporter*, the publisher held their money hostage.

But Wilkerson's hardball tactics didn't stop the studios from periodically withdrawing their ad support in response to an unfavorable review or another perceived provocation, sometimes for months at a time. "The studios were prone to shutting off advertising as if it were a biological function," Greg Bautzer said.

At times, George Kennedy recalled, his boss would grow terrified of losing vital revenue, especially if he'd recently suffered heavy gambling losses. Despite his power and his contempt for the studio chiefs, he would sometimes decide that an unfavorable review was not worth the risk. If a particular editorial slant was necessary to carry the paper through a rough financial patch, Wilkerson himself would edit the review or article to his satisfaction, or sometimes even write it himself under a reporter or reviewer's name. "Our reviews weren't always absolutely one hundred percent the reviewers' opinion," Kennedy said. "If Mr. Wilkerson was interested in somebody's writing, he'd see the review through and rewrite it—not often, but it could occur." Kennedy even intimated that when Wilkerson was gambling heavily, favorable reviews could be purchased with advertising.

Wilkerson's reliance on this kind of double dealing rubbed some observers the wrong way. "Billy started off as an idealist," said Vegas promoter Herb McDonald, "but became a fat cat just like the rest of the studio bosses." And according to author and screenwriter Peter Viertel, "The *Hollywood Reporter* as a trade paper published in a company town served the interests of the shakers and movers in the industry, such as L. B. Mayer and the Warner brothers. . . . Wilkerson became their mouthpiece in this regard." But his friends defended such compromises as an unfortunate necessity. "He was human," Joe Pasternak mused. "He wasn't pure as the driven snow. He was a businessman. He had to make hard choices sometimes, like we all do. He knew where his bread was buttered."

But whenever things were at their worst and the paper was on the verge of folding, an unexpected source always came along to bail Wilkerson out. "Luck always found Mr. Wilkerson at the last minute," Kennedy recalled. For instance, during one uncertain period, Wilkerson got a call from Max Albert Schlesinger, whose family owned nearly all the movie theaters in South Africa. Schlesinger had come to Hollywood to meet with the studio heads, in an effort to prove that they were infringing on his patents for sound films. Wilkerson told Schlesinger it was good he had gotten hold of him when he did, because the next day the paper was going out of business. Schlesinger was horrified. "But why are you closing?" he said. "I've been reading your paper. It's a good paper." Wilkerson confessed that the loss of ad revenue was killing him. When Schlesinger asked about the weekly budget and Wilkerson told him it was between $800 and $900, Schlesinger arranged for a loan until the first of the year. "That one pulled us out," remembered Kennedy. "That was two months, and it got us over the hump."

In such a high-pressure environment, Wilkerson expected a lot from his employees, including both complete loyalty and an unflagging work ethic. A reporter might find on his desk a typed memo with familiar initials at the bottom: "WRW." One sample memo read, "You should take the same time as you do in writing your column to go out and get scoop news. You won't get it sitting at your desk or phone all day. You have to get out and dig, dig, dig."

And when his staff really let him down, he was prone to outbursts of temper. These tongue-lashings, thought to have been inherited from his old boss Wid Gunning, were legendary. At times, said Kennedy, Wilkerson showered people with a stream of obscenities so acidic the recipient was reduced to "a quivering mass of jelly." Afterward he usually retained no recollection of the episode, but the unfortunate target was left with a reminder of the consequences of disappointing the boss.

News editor Frank Pope, however, was not so easily cowed. According to his colleagues, he was an editor of genius, the most gifted in Wilkerson's employ, but also quite the prima donna, in an office that only had room for one temperamental authority figure. Kennedy remembered the interactions between Pope and Wilkerson as a "battle of two titanic egos." They frequently locked horns, and their screaming matches often dissolved into physical confrontations. "Once they threw newspapers at each other," Kennedy said.

In spite of Wilkerson's temper and the periodic editorial meddling, his employees liked and respected him. He roared, but he could also be quite the charmer, and he was wonderfully supportive of their work. "If people were throwing rocks at them," Kennedy recalled, "he'd back them 100 percent." For the most part, publisher and staff worked together in harmony. "We were a close-knit bunch," recalled Vic Enyart. "Everyone knew what they were supposed to do."

In the midst of their early scrambling over *Daily Variety* came an impressive stamp of legitimacy. In the summer of 1933 Wilkerson received a handwritten letter from President Roosevelt requesting a subscription to the *Hollywood Reporter*. From then on, the president received a copy every day, airmailed special delivery to his desk at the White House. It was sweet vindication for the publisher whose paper was routinely slighted as a mere gossip rag.

9 | CAFÉ TROCADERO

BY MID-1933, MEANWHILE, state conventions were assembling to ratify the Twenty-First Amendment, which would bring the United States' failed Prohibition experiment to an end. As repeal drew ever closer with each state's ratification, Wilkerson decided that Vendôme needed to be the first establishment to legally import the finest wines and champagnes to Hollywood.

In September he boarded the ocean liner *Île de France* bound for Europe, carrying in his steamer trunk $60,000 and planning to search the continent for the highest-quality potables. The money represented all his profits from Vendôme—and, most likely, additional funds from friends back home who also wanted some of the good stuff they hadn't been able to get during Prohibition. While on the ship, Wilkerson bumped into two other passengers: Maurice Chevalier and Charles Laughton, Vendôme regulars who were considered Hollywood's finest epicures and wine connoisseurs. Wilkerson confided his plan to them, and they convinced him that there was no need to scour all of Europe; he could find everything he needed in France, the ship's first port of call. The two men gave Wilkerson the business card of and a letter of introduction to the president of a French wine syndicate.

When the ship reached France, Wilkerson met with the man and spent every penny he'd brought with him on his supply. Two months later, the freighter carrying Wilkerson's cargo arrived off the coast of San Francisco. Because Prohibition had not yet been repealed, port authorities would not allow the liquor to be unloaded, so it sat in the hold of the ship outside US territorial waters.

The state conventions would soon solve that problem, but Wilkerson faced another difficulty. Once he received the shipment, he would need a place to store it, with ample room and a stable temperature. He had experimented with underground storage at Vendôme Ranch, filling one hundred wine bottles with water, placing them in large wooden crates, and burying them in a ten-foot-deep pit. But he'd found that the heat, especially in the peak of summer, reached even to that depth. So he knew he'd have to find another way.

Someone informed him that La Bohéme, a roadhouse at 8610 Sunset Boulevard, had been shut down for liquor and gambling violations since early 1933—and that it had a wine cellar. The building was sitting abandoned, so when Wilkerson heard about the cellar, he broke a window and climbed inside to take a look. For the next week he checked the temperature in the cellar every day. He found it remained consistent, and he set his sights on the place.

Both the building and the land belonged to George and Francis Mont-gomery, who since the 1920s had owned the majority of the property on the Sunset Strip. Wilkerson made them an offer to buy La Bohéme. The brothers refused to sell but offered to rent the building to him instead. My father hesi-tated, wary of how the landlords could take advantage of him if he improved their currently vacant and dilapidated property.

But on December 5, 1933, the Twenty-First Amendment was ratified, and Wilkerson's inventory was released to him. With nowhere else to store the liquor, in January 1934 he reluctantly agreed to rent La Bohéme. Ultimately, what he anticipated would indeed transpire: as Wilkerson's ventures flourished, the brothers would raise the rent. "The Montgomerys were real SOBs," said Greg Bautzer. "They made Billy's life a living hell."

But for now he had the storage space he needed. He acquired a liquor license and began selling his inventory to eager customers at Vendôme. Wilkerson would become the most successful importer of fine wines and champagnes in Hollywood for the remainder of the Great Depression, taking monthly deliveries of hundreds of crates. He continued Vendôme's commit-ment to quality on the cuisine side as well, pilfering chef Felix Ganio and his crew from the Italian Pavilion of 1933 World's Fair; Ganio had been the personal chef of King Victor Emmanuel III of Italy.

But back at La Bohéme, things weren't running as smoothly. Wilkerson's insurance agent informed him that his premiums would double unless a tenant moved into the space upstairs from his wine cellar. He tried to rent it out, but the building was too rundown to attract any clients. He even tried giving the space away, to no avail. So he began considering the only other option available to him: making use of the space himself.

In 1934 the Sunset Strip was a 1.7-mile artery between Los Angeles and Beverly Hills surrounded by avocado groves and poinsettia fields. Wilkerson was struck by the fact that movie stars and other industry people traveled this route each day to and from work, and yet few businesses along the way catered to their particular needs. One evening he bumped into actress Kay Francis at a restaurant and listened as she complained that after a hard day on the set there was nowhere to go out without being hounded by autograph seekers and hysterical fans. She imagined a place with live music and dancing. Norma Shearer made the same complaint to Wilkerson. Naturally, he began to wonder why there weren't any nightclubs on the Strip grand enough to appeal to the industry's discriminating clubgoers. He decided in the empty space he had, he would start his own exclusive club.

Scratching together $5,000, he made a deal with a carpenter, an electrician, and a plumber to gut and renovate the abandoned roadhouse. He hired architect George Vernon Russell, agreed to pay for the materials his contractor, Bud Raulston, had to buy, and enlisted decorator Harold W. Grieve to completely revamp the interior. He asked all the workers to defer payment. Believing that a smart French-themed club would appeal to his intended customers, he ordered Grieve to create something reminiscent of Parisian sidewalk dining. Grieve, who later became known as "decorator to the stars," did not disappoint. In addition to the ornate chandeliers and striped silk chairs, the club had cream-colored walls and molding that boasted a hint of gold. This was Café Trocadero, and with its launch Wilkerson would usher in Hollywood's golden age of glamour.

How he came up with the name remains a mystery. According to Joe Pasternak, it was proposed by an actor named Richard Cortez—perhaps referring to former silent film star Ricardo Cortez. Regardless of who suggested it, the name was most likely taken from the famous Place du Trocadéro in Paris's 16th arrondissement, across the Seine from the Eiffel Tower.

Construction of the Café Trocadero dragged on for months. Wilkerson continually had to meditate on whether he should fold or move forward; this kind of soul-searching became one of his trademarks. Due to his gambling losses, by August 1934 the venture had run out of funds, and the construction crew threatened liens if they were not paid.

Legend has it that the following month Wilkerson was pacing the sidewalk in front of his uncompleted club with a $900 labor bill crumpled in his pocket when super-agent Myron Selznick drove past in his jet black Rolls-Royce. Wilkerson waved him down. "It's funny," Wilkerson recalled in a 1953 interview with the *Los Angeles Mirror*, "but while Myron was walking toward me, I had my next move figured out." The two men began to talk about the nightclub, and Wilkerson confessed he might never be able to open it—then asked Selznick if he might like to open the place himself.

Myron Selznick was painfully aware of his reputation as Hollywood's most notorious cheapskate. This likely was on Wilkerson's mind as he talked about the party Selznick could give—a way for him to discharge all his social obligations with one event. Next he gave the agent a guided tour, and by the time they reached the darkened wine cellar, the publisher was gently leveling his threat: if Myron didn't see fit to throw at least one party at Wilkerson's new club, the *Hollywood Reporter* would call him out as a freeloader.

Selznick, more than anyone, knew the power of a derogatory Tradeviews editorial, and he agreed to the publisher's proposal—funding an opening-night party to the tune of $6,000. Then he walked to his car, opened the glove compartment, and drew out his checkbook. "That check," noted the *Los Angeles Mirror*, "became the birth certificate to the Sunset Strip."

Just as he had done with Café Vendôme one year earlier, Wilkerson ran a series of provocative ads in the *Reporter* heralding the birth of Café Trocadero. On September 12, 1934, Selznick's party opened the nightclub. The event was a smash, and the place was packed with every major celebrity in town. A few nights later, on Monday, September 17, at 3:00 PM, Billy Wilkerson officially opened "the Troc," as it would be affectionately called. It was billed as the "West's first genuine Paris sidewalk café." At 8:00 PM that night there was a formal dinner dance at a hefty price of $7.50 per person—about $130 in today's funds.

But no one came.

A few guests who had been to the Selznick party and were devoted Vendôme patrons did show up—enough to garner mentions in the gossip columns the following morning—but they had little company. Partly to blame was the fact that Wilkerson's opening coincided with a hot-ticket event at the Hollywood Bowl, a performance of *A Midsummer Night's Dream*. The drought continued for several nights after that, however, Wilkerson pacing the floors of his empty nightclub dressed in his tails and spats. His tuxedoed waiters and busboys stood against the walls at attention, while four cigarette girls meandered through the empty space. The band played to an empty house. In frustration, Wilkerson instructed his maître d', Ralph Pauley (who also doubled as the assistant bartender), to put up the velvet rope and keep the band playing. "Tell everyone who comes or phones that the place is booked solid for two weeks," he said.

"That did it," said George Kennedy. "Within days, the place was jammed, with long lines outside the front door. Reservations were booked solid for weeks."

Café Trocadero included three main dining areas: the Louis XVI Room, which seated 50 and was reserved mainly for parties; the French-Blue Room, which seated 250; and the Main Dining Salon, seating 400. At the far end away from the foyer, steps descended to the powder room and to a less formal dining area: the Scottish Oyster Bar. The first of its kind on the West Coast, it was replete with hanging copper utensils and red-and-black plaid walls. "The Trocadero," remembered Joe Pasternak, "was the most beautiful place in the world."

Hatcheck girls in silk stockings, sheer aprons, and chic caps would greets arrivals in the main foyer, where a mural of Montmartre completed the illusion of continental elegance. "When they walked in the front door," said Tom Seward, "they were transported to Paris." The most coveted seats were those by the balcony, where lucky diners took in views of the city lights. "The Troc boasted the finest views of the city," said Seward. "No other place had them."

Wilkerson decided Café Trocadero would open only for dinner in order not to compete with his own Vendôme. The Troc quickly became the focus of evening activity in the film industry, and as at Vendôme, Wilkerson knew his clientele. He appealed to their snobbery by enforcing a strict dress code: suits and ties for men, preferably black tie (Wilkerson kept a closet full of coats and ties in different sizes for the underdressed), and for the ladies, lots of tulle and taffeta.

The Troc also charged the highest restaurant prices in the country. Chef Felix Ganio prepared a procession of expensive delicacies that included vol-au-vent, sweetbreads Toulousaine, breast of guinea hen under bell, and larded plates of beef forestiere, which, for an additional $9.00 (more than $150 today), patrons could wash down with a Château de Rayne-Vigneau 1901. And Seward observed, "We never served Italian food. Billy thought Italian food was the food of the poor."

My father imported another culinary concept from Europe: the doggie bag. The idea supposedly originated at the legendary Parisian restaurant Maxim's. Wilkerson not only adopted the idea at the Troc but raised it to an art form. The avid dog lover had elegant boxes designed for transporting leftovers to Fifi back home.

Wilkerson also provided not one but two bands so patrons could dance both during and after dinner. Harl Smith and His Continental Serenaders, and Ramon Littee and His Parisian Tango Orchestra belted out rumbas and jitterbugs and waltzes and tangos. The club frequently hosted theme nights, like its popular "Night in Spain," with decor appropriate to the theme and patrons who dressed accordingly.

My father's refusal to spare any expense gave some patrons pause—film choreographer LeRoy Prinz said of the sticker shock, "When you walked into one of Billy's places he took your socks off!"—but clubgoers were said to study the menus as if they were engaging novels. Seward credited the Troc with raising the standards for fine cuisine in Los Angeles. "Most of Hollywood at that time didn't know the difference between a filet mignon and a hamburger and a Coke," he said. "Billy changed all of that." Even the astonished Prinz ultimately had high praise for the Troc, saying that there was "no place like it on earth."

The Trocadero didn't just lay claim to providing the finest food, entertainment, and views in the city; according to the *Reporter*, it also boasted the finest wine list in the country. At one point, according to Tom Seward, this claim caught the attention of a young Guy de Rothschild, scion of the Rothschild banking dynasty. One evening while Wilkerson was dining with guests at his corner table, Rothschild marched in, sat down, and demanded to see the wine list. When it was produced, he dissolved into laughter, prompting Wilkerson to excuse himself from his guests and approach Rothschild's table to ask if there was something wrong.

Reportedly, Rothschild stabbed an index finger at the list and complained that it contained not a single selection from his family's famed wine estates. When Wilkerson assured him that they in fact carried *every* Rothschild wine, the scion proposed a challenge: for every bottle the host could produce, his patron would give him ten. "But first I want to see this vintage," Rothschild said.

Wilkerson nodded to his wine steward, and within minutes Guy de Rothschild's table was overflowing with bottles. As the steward headed back to the cellar, Rothschild yelled for Wilkerson to stop him. Wilkerson refused—a deal was a deal. Rothschild stood up and threw his napkin on the table. "It's impossible," he said. "That wine comes from my own private vineyard!" He stormed out of the restaurant. How Wilkerson was able to acquire these wines is unknown.

———

It wasn't the lavish accommodations alone that attracted all of Hollywood to the Troc. As with Vendôme, a powerful lure for actors, actresses, publicists, and photographers was knowing that patrons would be mentioned in the society pages and gab columns of the *Reporter*. Wilkerson sweetened the deal by ensuring that regular tables would be reserved only for the most famous celebrities— and for members of the industry's PR machines. Savvy press agents saw the value of having their up-and-coming talent photographed with established stars, and duly delivered them to the Trocadero's tables. The Troc even had its own house photographer, Hymie Fink, handpicked by Wilkerson. According to Edith Gwynn, many celebrities were petrified of Fink, who seemed to pop up everywhere; one long-standing joke among celebrities was that whenever they arrived home they checked under their beds to see if Hymie Fink was there.

Other local newspapers were soon staking out the Trocadero as well. Gossip columnists such as Louella Parsons (and later Hedda Hopper) would write their leads between bites of sweetbreads. Comedian Jack Benny reminisced that "dining at the Troc was better than paying an expensive publicist." Over the years, many A-list stars appeared regularly in all the papers for frequenting the Trocadero dining rooms, including Ida Lupino, Clark Gable, Bing Crosby, Fred Astaire, William Powell, Jean Harlow, Myrna Loy, Sonja Henie, Robert Taylor, and Tyrone Power.

Though publicity was certainly an aim, few of these luminaries were shy about how they enjoyed themselves, lending the club an atmosphere of both intimacy and exposure. Troc regulars developed their own ways of navigating the social scene. For instance, American-born socialite and spy Countess Dentice di Frasso (née Dorothy Caldwell Taylor) would usually arrive with a female friend in tow, and before leaving the club with a strange man, she would remove all her jewelry and turn it over to her friend for safekeeping.

Though movie stars frequently lost control after drinking one too many, another group of patrons were usually on their best behavior: the criminal element. Former bootlegger Joe Kennedy would dine exclusively at the Trocadero whenever he was in town. Prominent mob figures also frequented the Troc, including Wilkerson's Mafia ally Johnny Rosselli, future gambling ship proprietor Tony Cornero, and even the notorious Bugsy Siegel. My father's law-abiding patrons were thrilled to rub elbows with gangsters; as Tom Seward put it, "People like them only made the Troc seem more glamorous."

Sanctioned by the studios and their stars and spiced up by the mob presence, the club quickly became everyone's idea of a perfect nightclub. "The Troc became *the* place to see and be seen," said Seward. Booked weeks in advance, Troc reservations were as coveted in their time as Super Bowl tickets are today. It was said that many patrons saved up for months to dine at the club. "The Trocadero was at that time the finest club of its kind, possibly in the country," said Greg Bautzer, who in the latter half of the 1930s was just establishing himself as a Hollywood lawyer and man about town. "Whenever I could get enough money to go there, I would."

At a time before Visa and Mastercard, restaurant patrons ran monthly tabs. Customers may have had to pinch pennies to afford the Troc's prices, but my father had ways of ensuring that they paid their tabs on time. The *Reporter* would refuse to run press releases or review movies for industry figures as long as their Trocadero accounts were delinquent. For those who needed additional motivation, Wilkerson could threaten even worse consequences: permanent banishment from his club. To some patrons, this was worse than a death sentence.

For milder offenses, there was "Siberia," a seating concept first popularized at the Troc. Those who failed to pay their tabs on time, or who were merely unfashionable or unfamous, would be relegated to the back tables of the club, near the kitchen. Wilkerson also reserved his very best tables—those near the entrance—for those willing to pay extra to be noticed. Some people contend that Wilkerson created the very idea of ranking tables by location, pioneering it at Vendôme and popularizing it at the Troc, after which the idea spread nationwide.

The club's success didn't just revolutionize the restaurant business in Los Angeles; it also helped to refocus the industry around the Sunset Strip. Hollywood agents and publicists began to move their offices to the Strip; rather than race after clients all over town, they could simply oversee the action from their favorite table at the Troc. (The move also allowed them to take advantage of a tax loophole, since the Strip traversed unincorporated territory exempt from city business taxes.)

In its first twenty-four months, Café Trocadero grossed $3.8 million, making it the most successful nightclub in Depression-era America. Some in town were baffled that a trade paper publisher with little restaurant experience had reached such a milestone so quickly. But Wilkerson's friend Harry Drucker explained his abilities well. "He knew about it all. Billy knew how to find out about the restaurant business," Drucker said. "He knew about what's going on in the kitchen and so forth. He could switch from a publisher to a restaurant owner to a waiter. He was like a Jekyll/Hyde character. He had so many facets."

10 | THE SHAKEDOWN

EVEN AS THE END of Prohibition opened up new business opportunities for Billy Wilkerson, it cut off his criminal associates from a vital source of income. As ratification of the Twenty-First Amendment loomed, organized crime knew that its stranglehold over the U.S. liquor trade was about to come to a swift and definitive end. Though gangsters would still control other vice trades—gambling, narcotics, and prostitution—the impending loss of the proceeds from illegal alcohol sales meant they had to cast their nets in search of new revenue. They turned to an untapped market that seemed to hold the riches of El Dorado: the movie industry.

Until this point, organized crime had largely ignored the film trade. "Prior to 1930," Greg Bautzer said, "organized crime in the movie industry didn't exist." Since then, Handsome Johnny Rosselli had established some connections and done some favors for industry insiders like my father, Joe Schenck, and Harry Cohn, but he'd mainly seen this as a path toward a legitimate career as a Hollywood producer. Now he and his associates began to take another look at the business's potential for criminal exploitation.

The studio bosses smugly believed their businesses were impervious to mob infiltration. "It never even entered their minds," noted Tom Seward. They did vaguely suspect that Wilkerson had mob connections, and some even speculated that his Catholic faith gave him an inside track on the shadier members of the flock. (According to George Kennedy, my father's generosity to the Church did indeed open doors; whenever he made a donation to Blessed Sacrament Catholic Church in Hollywood, parish priests were all too eager to make introductions on his behalf.) But such connections remained unproven—and besides, the moguls were worried less about the damage a gangster could do with a tommy gun than about the trouble Wilkerson himself could cause for them with the *Hollywood Reporter*'s reviews and editorials.

It was a crucial oversight. Even as Wilkerson made life miserable for the studio heads through the *Reporter*'s coverage, he was helping the Mafia gain a foothold in their industry. As future *Reporter* staffer David Alexander put it, "Organized crime came to Hollywood through Billy." By the mid-1930s, he was ushering mob bosses into his venues with the grace and warmth of a maître d', and if a member of the crime underworld was looking for a favor, he could always find it in my father's office.

A frequent visitor to Wilkerson's office was Johnny Rosselli; according to Kennedy, he and my father had met there often from 1930 on, usually to vent their frustrations more than to concoct any specific schemes. My father, for instance, was continually grousing about his desire to get even with the studio bosses who had extinguished his studio dream. But as Prohibition neared its end, Rosselli came to Wilkerson with a major proposal: they should work together to take over the Hollywood unions, then use them to shake down the studios.

To Rosselli it may have been a way for the Mafia to replace its illegal liquor operations, but for my father it was an ideal opportunity to finally strike a blow against the studio moguls. In addition, Kennedy claimed, Rosselli gave Wilkerson a guarantee that if their scheme went south, the publisher would do no jail time. It was more than enough to spark his interest.

Before long, their preliminary discussions had morphed into a concrete plan. One night in 1934, Wilkerson was playing a private card game at Joe Schenck's Beverly Hills home. He confided to his friend that he was forming a syndicate with Johnny Rosselli, and asked if Schenck might be interested in joining them. According to Kennedy, Schenck immediately offered his assistance but made it clear he had no interest in sharing in the monetary proceeds. Schenck simply hated his fellow studio heads and imagined that if the scheme caused them enough grief, they might be willing to sell their assets to him at rock-bottom prices.

Each man brought to the table a vital component for enacting the shakedown scheme. Rosselli contributed Mafia muscle and influence, with a to-do list that included importing "enforcers" from back east. Answering directly to Rosselli, they would infiltrate the unions and continually threaten the studios with strikes if they didn't pay them off. Schenck, meanwhile, would cozy up to his fellow studio heads, positioning himself as liaison between them and the restive unions. His job was to quietly nudge the moguls into paying up, which he did by explaining that doing so was the only way to avoid nasty and costly production disruptions. Finally, Wilkerson, as the syndicate's head, would use the *Reporter* to keep the pressure on the movie brass.

My father had a habit of leaving the door to his office open so that he could bark orders throughout the day, so at one point George Kennedy overheard a meeting of the conspirators, in which Rosselli joked that the three of them would have the industry surrounded, drawn, and quartered in no time. "They don't stand a chance, Billy," Rosselli said confidently.

At the time, Kennedy didn't appreciate the significance of the gangster's comment or understand what he and Wilkerson were planning. As the publisher's secretary, he overheard a lot of requests for favors, screaming matches, and jokes about wanting someone knocked off, so he took everything with a grain of salt until it all made the news. He wasn't the only one in the dark. Initially, the only people who knew who was really behind this new syndicate were the masterminds themselves. Even today, the most common explanation of the shakedown attributes it to gangsters Willie Bioff and George E. Browne, under the direction of the man who succeeded Al Capone as head of the Chicago Outfit, Frank "the Enforcer" Nitti. But in the late 1930s and early 1940s, George Kennedy, Greg Bautzer, and others in Wilkerson's camp would begin to learn about his schemes, and discover the central role played by the trio of men they called the Hollywood Syndicate and others later referred to as the Hollywood Outfit. Still, even when the scheme became public, their involvement would be kept secret, possibly for the trio's own protection. "All the books give credit to everyone else," Kennedy told me, annoyed. During my many interviews with him, he was adamant that a scheme of such scope and sophistication could have only been orchestrated by men with connections at the highest levels of the movie industry: Rosselli, Schenck, and Wilkerson.

Despite Rosselli's assurances that the industry was helpless to resist them, Wilkerson wanted to see tangible proof of their scheme's effectiveness. The mobster was eager to oblige. It was at this point that he brought Willie Bioff and George E. Browne into the conspiracy.

Bioff and Browne were two of Rosselli's go-to enforcers. They'd met while selling "protection" to chicken dealers on opposite sides of Chicago's Fulton Street, and instead of engaging in a turf war, they decided to form a partnership known as B&B. Browne, the less colorful of the two—more bookkeeper than ax wielder—was also the business agent of the area projectionists' union, Chicago Stagehands Local No. 2. Rosselli ordered the duo to channel their energies away from shaking down chicken vendors and toward extorting the union's employers. As a field test of the syndicate's Hollywood plot, B&B would target prominent Chicago movie palace chain Balaban & Katz. The company was a subsidiary of Paramount Pictures, and within a few years one of its founders, Barney Balaban, would become president of Paramount. The conspirators understood that attacking a business of this caliber would send a chilling message to the other theater and studio owners.

Within a few weeks, Bioff and Browne had successfully extracted $20,000 from the chain, by getting the union to demand a pay raise for its projectionists and then accepting a bribe to quash it. It was more than enough proof that the scheme would work; the Hollywood shakedown was given the green light.

Rosselli summoned Bioff and Browne to Los Angeles to take over the Hollywood craft guilds. His first order of business was to get George Browne elected president of the national projectionists' union, the International Alliance of Theatrical Stage Employees (IATSE). IATSE also controlled many of the motion picture crafts unions, including those for the electricians, carpenters, set painters, and plumbers. In Hollywood, it was known as the Stagehands Union.

Having previously scuffled with IATSE, Rosselli knew its weakness. The previous July, during the uproar over industry pay cuts, the union had staged a strike against all the studios. The studio owners were caught flat-footed and assembled the Producers Association to entertain any and all ideas to combat the disaster. Columbia Pictures' Harry Cohn volunteered to take care of the problem, and called on his friend Johnny Rosselli to do whatever it took to end the strike. Handsome Johnny and his men teamed up with the International Brotherhood of Electrical Workers (IBEW). The well-organized counteroffensive burst through picket lines, taking the strikers' jobs and keeping the studios running. Within days, the strike was broken. IATSE, once the most powerful union in Hollywood, lost nearly all its muscle and was ripe for a takeover.

By June 1934 the time for that takeover had come. Rosselli ensured that the fix was in, and Browne ran unopposed for union president. As soon as his election was official, Browne appointed Willie Bioff as his personal representative. This allowed Rosselli to oversee all union operations in Los Angeles, without exposing him or the other members of the Hollywood Syndicate to scrutiny. Whatever they needed from the union, Browne and Bioff would see it done.

With its new, Mafia-backed leadership, IATSE again became a force to be reckoned with. The syndicate knew that if it called for a strike, no film in Hollywood could go into production. But Rosselli had another idea of how to put the arm on the studios, by turning one of their greatest advantages into a liability.

Though much of the studios' leverage came from the fact that they owned their own theater chains, it left them particularly vulnerable if business in the theaters themselves was disrupted. Thus, Rosselli wanted Bioff and Browne to issue an ultimatum: either the studios pay them a substantial sum, or they'd order a projectionists' strike. With no projectionists, films could not be shown, and tickets could not be sold. To avoid such a ruinous outcome, Rosselli expected the studios to part with 50 percent of their total profits.

But the idea of demanding such massive payments right off the bat made my father uncomfortable. "Mr. Wilkerson," Kennedy later learned, "thought that was way too ambitious." Wilkerson cautioned up front that this would raise too many eyebrows, but the overconfident gangster assured his partner otherwise. Still, Wilkerson lobbied to begin with a much lower percentage and to annually increase the amount. To appease his nervous friend, Rosselli finally acquiesced to a starting amount Wilkerson thought appropriate—enough to keep the studios in line but not so much as to raise suspicion. This start-up "fee" would be $50,000.

To begin with, on November 30, 1935, the syndicate called a strike on more than five hundred Paramount theaters from Chicago to St. Louis. At nine o'clock that night, all projectionists walked out and every theater went dark. The success of that strike led the syndicate to threaten a nationwide strike if theater owners failed to comply, and fearing disaster, the Hollywood studios paid up—just as Rosselli had predicted they would.

But tension soon arose between Rosselli and his enforcers. The pugnacious Bioff grilled his boss about why certain studios had been excluded from the shakedown. Of course, Schenck's most recent studio venture, 20th Century Fox, was strictly off limits. So too was Columbia Pictures, out of deference for the close friendship between Rosselli and Harry Cohn. Indeed, Rosselli and Cohn both lived in the ritzy Garden of Allah Hotel on Sunset Boulevard and were often traveling companions. They were even said to wear identical pinkie rings, which they had exchanged to honor their bond of friendship.

Though the precise list of omitted studios is unknown, it may also have included MGM, since Joe Schenck's brother, Nicholas, ran its parent company. In any event, Rosselli was adamant that the list was nonnegotiable, and ultimately Bioff backed off.

The omissions must have also chafed my father, who despised Cohn and disapproved of Rosselli's friendship with him, and considered MGM's Louis B. Mayer his nemesis. But even if two of his enemies remained out of reach for the time being, he was certainly happy to be inflicting so much pain on the other studios, to the tune of $50,000 a year.

Wilkerson, however, wasn't really interested in the financial damage. After all, as Kennedy explained, "The vast amounts of money the studios really possessed were untold. It's fair to say that they were rich beyond counting." Unlike Schenck, my father had no hope of bleeding them dry or buying them out. "Unless you were a Carnegie or a Mellon," said Kennedy, "nobody could buy the studios out." For Wilkerson, the key to bringing down the moguls was *power*, and now he not only oversaw an influential trade paper but also had a hand in a Mafia operation with its own leverage over the studios. This new source of power would prove essential to his rise. As his longtime friend Alex Paal later put it, "Billy became a kind of Hollywood don."

Wilkerson's influence over the mob's extortion plot, though, had its limits. Before long, another party to the scheme would start to realize how wealthy the studios really were, and he would not be so willing to ignore money for power.

11 | THE BREAKUP

WHILE WILKERSON, Schenck, and Rosselli were coming together to form the Hollywood Syndicate, another of my father's partnerships was deteriorating. His relationship with Edith had been strengthened by their shared struggle to establish their newspaper and lift themselves out of poverty, but with those goals achieved and his attention now divided between the *Reporter*, his restaurants, and his shakedown plans, Billy began to drift away from his wife.

Edith remained focused on the paper, where she wrote most of the editorial copy and, always innovative, introduced the first gossip column in a daily film trade publication. Her feature The Lowdown appeared on Mondays, Wednesdays, and Fridays, and her column The Rolling Reporter published on Tuesdays and Thursdays. In the evenings, she would return to their Beverly Hills home to prepare dinner for her husband, but he showed little gratitude for her hard work. When he got home, he would sit and read the paper, eat, then sit and read the paper some more. Edith nicknamed him "Sourpuss" and begged him to show her some attention, but to no avail. "The more successful Mr. Wilkerson became," George Kennedy said, "the more he outgrew Edith. He was always too tired, getting home from the office and the clubs."

Edith was also troubled by her husband's presumed infertility. Though she never discussed children with her husband, she yearned to have a family. In fact, said Kennedy, "most of Mr. Wilkerson's marriages were plagued by their inability to have children."

A final issue of contention arose between the couple when Edith's sister, Helen, mysteriously disappeared. "They looked everywhere for her," Kennedy remembered. "But she just vanished from the face of the earth." Edith blamed her husband, certain that her sister had been murdered by the New York loan shark her husband failed to repay back in 1929. Tom Seward and George Kennedy both thought Wilkerson took Helen Goldenhorn's disappearance as a warning; though they never heard further discussion of the matter, Wilkerson did make full repayment of the loan shortly thereafter. "It just doesn't make sense why he wouldn't have taken care of that," said Seward. "He knew how these people operated. He would have had more visits from people to collect the debt. Billy was the kind of guy who didn't like looking over his shoulder all the time."

With all this hanging over their marriage, before long the couple had stopped speaking to each other. Then the yelling at the office began.

In June 1935 Kennedy overheard a particularly notable screaming match in Wilkerson's office. According to the secretary, Wilkerson accused Edith of having an affair with a musician at the Café Trocadero. The knock-down, drag-out fight finally ended when Edith yelled, "You know, it really is no wonder why nobody can love you. You make it impossible for them!"

Unfortunately, Wilkerson's accusation was true. Starved of affection, Edith had run into the welcoming arms of a charismatic performer at the Troc. The revelation of their affair had instantaneous consequences: that same night, the musician arrived for work only to discover that he'd been replaced.

During these tumultuous times, Kennedy found himself more and more frequently in the unenviable position of playing intermediary between the feuding spouses. A few days after Edith's lover was sacked, she handed Kennedy a letter addressed to her husband. She made her instructions clear. "Make sure Sourpuss reads it!" she said.

Kennedy walked the letter into his employer's office and presented it to him, along with Edith's instructions. Kennedy watched from his office as his employer sliced open the envelope and unfurled the contents. It was twelve pages of double-spaced type, on reporter's copy paper readily available in the office, clearly a first and only draft bearing just a few corrections. Nagging, screaming, and even an affair hadn't worked to get Wilkerson's attention. Now Edith employed the skill that had always served her best, laying into her husband in sizzling prose.

"I want to be free," she began, insisting that she wasn't telling him anything he didn't already know. "I want to be free of the tension, the strain, the awful emptiness of living with you." She'd tried to make it work, she said, but now realized such efforts were futile:

> It is impossible with someone like you who puts a yard-stick on love and everything else in life—who would dole out his kisses according to the number of socks that have been mended that day—or who would judge the value of someone's help by the number of hours labor put in, instead of by the quality and actual value of that help. . . .
>
> A long time ago I pleaded with you to preserve the one thing that holds people together in marriage—togetherness. I pointed out to you that it was more important to us than any money you might make from the enterprises which you undertook. You certainly didn't undertake them for any reason concerning me. I have never in my life been extravagant or made any demands of you—I like comfort and nice things, yes . . . but you could never in your life have been made to feel that you had to "make a lot of money" to please me—so therefore it is merely that you had a choice to make—work or me. And you chose work.

"I hope it brings you happiness," she wrote, then added, "I want to be happy too." But she was looking for "a kind of happiness that you don't know and probably can't conceive of. Life can be so lovely, so exciting . . . so warm and full of meaning. I have known that feeling and I shall know it again. I would never know it with you." Though she knew that, in his own way, Billy loved her deeply, "it would be better perhaps if you have loved me a little less and seemed to love me more." It was a distinction she did not expect him to understand: "A lot of men don't know that it takes more than a nice little home and three meals a day to make a wife happy. That I guess, accounts for all the sex-starved, cheating wives in the world. But I don't mean to be one of them."

She went on to detail a recent incident that had opened her eyes to the depths of her husband's selfishness:

> I have watched you "manipulate" since the day we came out here, admired you for some acts, held you in slight contempt for others . . . I have watched you scheme, juggle accounts and chisel—

but I never in this world thought you would chisel me! But you did, Billy—and when that happened, I suddenly saw you as I had never seen you before . . .

I refer to the night about seven weeks ago, that you came home and informed me that you had bought me shares of the Reporter with my share of the insurance money—and then managed to chisel me out of the shares! I realize it's the way you've "worked" around here for years—I realize that your lust for possession (that's all your entire life is built on now) and your determination to get everything for nothing (at which you've been fairly successful) had gotten you to the point where you would even stoop to chiseling me! You are a past master at the "taking candy from a baby." . . . You are a past master of taking advantage of a situation to take advantage of people, whether you realize it or not. . . .

I used to listen to you say "I know I'm right"—and believed you! But now I know better. Billy—when a man gets to the point where he won't listen to anybody—when he becomes ruthless, and lies and lies to cover up his own mistakes—there's something wrong—something wrong with the man himself—not with everybody else in the world! . . . Either your success has done something to you—or you yourself, are too small, too unworthy, to merit or hold it!

Edith warned Billy that he was in danger of losing everything he had built—particularly if he continued to alienate the people around him who were capable of restraining his worst impulses. Pointing out others whom he'd recently wronged—from a department manager whose authority he'd undercut to the Trocadero musicians caught up in the firing of her lover—she offered some parting advice:

For God's sake, get wise, before your stubbornness costs you too much! Before you pay too much for the wrong things you do that are always getting you in jams. I trust people and have never been gypped in my life. You trust nobody—you take the attitude that everyone is trying to get away with something with you—and you are always getting gypped! And you always will, until you act like a human being instead of a madman!

Oddly, she offered no complaints about her husband's gambling problem. It's not clear whether he'd managed to conceal the extent to which it still plagued him, or whether she had her own reasons for not bringing it up.

Finally, she presented her demands for their separation. On the advice of "a man who is a good friend of both of ours—someone you respect," she insisted it was only right for her to keep the house. Her financial demands were modest, she said ("If I had to go to a court of law to fight for it, I could probably get a lot more"), and included a raise in her *Reporter* salary to fifty dollars a week, and fifteen shares of stock in the paper. "I figure that I can draw a hundred dollars a week against what that stock would represent at the end of a year, and live on that," she wrote. "My salary I would try to save or put toward an annuity or something."

She cautioned him against quibbling over the proposed settlement, which she argued was the bare minimum required to meet her needs. "I must have people to my home as they have me to theirs, I must buy gifts galore throughout the year, and I must be comfortable—and there is no reason why I shouldn't be!" The terms "are more than fair," she argued, "and you, who so dearly love to get off cheap, should be very gratified."

> Don't make me fight for what I know is right—I don't want to hate you and I don't want to fight and have nasty publicity and be forced to say and do the things I would have to do to you . . . it wouldn't be fair—and it is not necessary. If you will have your lawyer draw up an agreement calling for the things I've stipulated, I will sign it and Daddy can arrange with someone (I've already asked him) to get our divorce quietly and without any publicity in Yucatan within five weeks. Please give me your answer within a few days or I shall have to go to bat alone—I cannot continue like this—and I won't. And please have the chivalry and good taste to move out.

This letter provides a unique window into the world of Wilkerson's troubled married life. "It's remarkable," Kennedy later recalled, "for the fact that it graphically shows someone who was put through the Wilkerson meat grinder. Most of us were. But here it was on paper." According to the secretary, Wilkerson calmly read his wife's letter, then set it aside and returned to his paperwork, registering no emotion. "Ice ran through Mr. Wilkerson's veins when it came to soon-to-be ex-wives."

Nonetheless, the missive had the intended effect: on August 7, 1935, after four years of marriage, the couple finalized their divorce in Mexico. Edith had demanded stock in the *Reporter* against which she could draw $100 a week, but Billy made a shrewd counteroffer: lifetime alimony of $800 a month. Edith agreed, choosing a steady income over an ownership stake in the newspaper she'd helped to build. "I called her up," Joe Pasternak remembered, "and said, 'You made the worst deal in the world. You threw your entire life away for a lousy $200 a week.'"

But in many ways her life remained the same. She continued to write for the *Reporter* for the next thirteen years. At some point (early editions of the paper were never digitized, so it's hard to determine exactly when), she opted to take credit for her work, adopting the pen name Edith Gwynn, a variation on her maiden name of Goldenhorn. Her column The Rolling Reporter was retitled The Rambling Reporter and eventually became one of the industry's most read features, rivaling even the work of Louella Parsons and Hedda Hopper, considered the most popular Hollywood columnists of the day.

To many people, the fact that Edith remained at the paper was a sign that despite her razor tongue whenever the subject of her ex-husband came up, she never really got over him. "She wanted to be close to him" was Kennedy's theory. And according to him, Edith made it a solemn ritual to phone each new Wilkerson bride to congratulate her. "Welcome to the club," she would cackle sarcastically.

Edith herself never remarried, and never even had another love affair. After retiring from the *Reporter* in 1948, she could have continued to enjoy a career as a prominent writer and columnist but instead refused all offers from other publishers. She returned every advance check, thrusting out her beautifully manicured hands and shouting, "Do you see these hands? Do you see these hands? These hands will never touch a typewriter again!"

For the rest of her life, she lived alone in the house she and Billy had shared. She kept it exactly as it was the day he walked out, with the same furnishings, a 1930s candlestick phone and refrigerator, and photographs of their married life on display. She became an alcoholic and a recluse, never rising from bed before noon, curtains permanently drawn against the sunlight. When she did greet visitors, it was in her negligee with a Bloody Mary in one hand.

"It was eerie," Joe Pasternak recalled. "When you walked into her house it was like walking back into 1932. Everything was the same. It was as though Billy had just walked around the corner to post a letter." As Kennedy put it, "She became a character straight out of a Dickens novel."

On her deathbed in the late 1980s, Edith slipped into her favorite negligee and put on every article of jewelry Wilkerson had ever given her. Two gardeners found her dead on January 1, 1988, but stripped her of the jewelry before calling the coroner. Ultimately the theft was discovered and the gardeners were charged.

Right up until her death, Edith would periodically phone George Kennedy to demand that he return the angry letter she had written to her husband so many decades earlier. Somehow she was aware that he had retained possession of it—a fact Kennedy denied whenever Edith asked. "I knew she would destroy it," he explained. "My guess is that she regretted ever writing it."

12 | SUNDAY NIGHT AT THE TROC

CONSIDERING WILKERSON'S MULTIPLE DIVORCES, his gambling problem, and his reputation for profanity-laden outbursts, many considered his religious devotion to be out of character. But throughout his turbulent life, he continued to view the Catholic Church as his spiritual protector, and he remained forever grateful and loyal. Though he never partook of Communion or went to confession, he attended Mass every Sunday and donated profusely to the Church. It's estimated that over the course of his life Wilkerson contributed what today would be the equivalent of $7 million. In response, the Church conveniently forgave his colorful lifestyle. As he jokingly told a friend, his largesse was "the price of my train ticket to heaven."

But the prospect of buying his way to salvation wasn't the only reason he gave so freely to Catholic causes. One element of the Church in particular had a way of provoking his generosity. "Mr. Wilkerson was always a soft touch for nuns," George Kennedy remembered. Though Wilkerson was repelled by beggars and hated to be accosted on the street for money, nuns often arrived unannounced at his office in search of donations, and he rarely refused their visits. Said Kennedy, "Whenever they came to the office he always broke down." It was perhaps part of a more general weakness he had for those who approached him in a spirit of humility. "If you were contrite and said your mea culpas," said Kennedy, "Mr. Wilkerson would do anything for you."

Joe Pasternak witnessed the same tendency. "With some people," he recalled, "he had a soft streak, like nuns. He hated to be soft. He would come undone around nuns. He wanted to be strong and powerful."

103

One hot August afternoon in July 1935, Wilkerson was making the twelve-mile drive back to his Hollywood office from Trocadero Ranch, the latest name for his mother's home in Van Nuys, when he noticed a building with a cross on top. Recognizing it as Catholic, he pulled over to investigate. Inside he found a nun in a tattered habit on her hands and knees scrubbing the floor. He asked her what the place was, and she told him it was an orphanage for boys, one that would soon have to close for lack of funding.

The woman turned out to be Reverend Mother Regina of the Poor Sisters of Nazareth. The orphanage was called Nazareth House. Mother Regina explained to Wilkerson the specifics of its plight and the dire fate that awaited the boys who lived there. The publisher was so moved, he drove back to Trocadero Ranch and instructed his ranch foreman to send a truck to the orphanage with fifty gallons of milk and dozens of crates of eggs.

"We were praying for a miracle," remembered Mother Regina, "because anything short of that would not save us. That miracle was Mr. Wilkerson."

From that moment on, Wilkerson personally took charge of Nazareth House, organizing a California charitable corporation for the Poor Sisters of Nazareth of Los Angeles. Whatever they needed, he would help to provide. "He would look up from his desk," remembered Mother Regina, "and the first words from his lips were always 'What can I do for you, Sister?'"

The orphanage, remembered Bautzer, "was one of Billy's favorite charities, or maybe his only charity. He was forever putting the arm on me and all the rest of his friends to make the contribution." And the publisher's fundraising drives were not limited to his friends. Wilkerson had no qualms about soliciting his enemies. As Bautzer explained, "Billy used to be brutal about that. He'd call up L. B. Mayer, and say 'Sending Sister Theresa over. I want you to be generous.'"

He also promoted film premiere benefits, financed a swimming pool and other facilities for the orphanage, and every Christmas sent over dozens of turkeys, pairs of shoes, and toys. "One day he dropped by and presented us with the keys to a brand-new car," said Mother Regina.

While brainstorming clever ways to fund Nazareth House, he had a stroke of brilliance—a way to involve the Café Trocadero in fundraising efforts without having to close its doors to paying customers. Restrictive local blue laws prohibited dancing and drinking at public venues on the Sabbath, and for this reason the clubs in Hollywood, including the Trocadero, were closed on Sundays. But the ever-resourceful Wilkerson had discovered the loophole: the archaic laws did not apply to nonprofit charity events. He could open the Troc every Sunday for a Nazareth House fundraiser.

But what sort of fundraiser should it be? Wilkerson saw another opportunity in the fact that no other Hollywood venue at the time hosted an amateur night. He could provide a unique opportunity for Hollywood newcomers to perform to packed houses of industry notables—as Tom Seward put it, "A nobody could audition for Selznick or Zanuck"—and in return the Troc could present a show without having to pay any major talent. Thus, the event known as Sunday Night at the Troc was born.

Wilkerson knew that his idea was a low-risk venture, but he initially saw little upside, either; it was simply a convenient way to raise a bit of money for his charity. According to Seward, however, it very quickly "became the hottest ticket in town." From the moment the plan was announced, reservations were booked weeks in advance, with some patrons even flying cross-country to attend. Amateur night set Café Trocadero apart from all its competition, and would serve to define the club for as long as Wilkerson owned it. "Sunday Night at the Troc," Bautzer mused. "It was a big kind of event in the town. Why, I'd make a reservation weeks in advance."

Though the event welcomed all comers, it was not an open mike. Like aspiring amateurs of later generations on *Star Search* or *American Idol*, performers had to audition for their chance to be discovered. Wilkerson himself oversaw the process; he was said to be able to look at someone, talk to him or her, and recognize in a moment whether or not that person had talent.

But even with such a gift, as the event grew ever more popular Wilkerson realized that he needed help managing the auditions. He roped in a talent agent who was introduced to him by Johnny Rosselli, a man with an interesting past named Victor Orsatti. Orsatti was a former bootlegger with connections to both Rosselli and Jack Dragna. For years during Prohibition, he had supplied MGM fixer Eddie Mannix and his studio with booze. Mannix introduced Orsatti to his boss Louis B. Mayer, who immediately took a liking to him. The studio head was famous for telling the young bootlegger, "You're in a dying business. Get out while the getting's good."

It was Mayer who encouraged Orsatti to become an agent, one who would ultimately represent some of the biggest stars in Hollywood, including Judy

Garland, Betty Grable, Edward G. Robinson, and directors Frank Capra and George Stevens. He's also credited with persuading figure skating champion Sonja Henie to move to Hollywood and become an actress after the 1936 Winter Olympics.

At first, Orsatti and Wilkerson jointly presided over the Troc's amateur night auditions. Orsatti would screen the talent, but Wilkerson still made the final call. As talent night became a well-oiled, lucrative machine, the publisher delegated more and more of the process to Orsatti, trusting the agent's instincts, though he continued to insist on final approval. "Billy made all of the final selections," said Seward.

With Orsatti's help, Wilkerson became known as Hollywood's first major talent scout. If a performer genuinely impressed him, that person would earn repeat performances, which in turn made more of an impression on agents looking for new talent to sign. In this way, my father was responsible for launching a number of stellar careers. Because no complete list of amateur night performers has survived, we'll never know how many future stars got their start on the Trocadero stage. But in a 1960 interview with *Hollywood Close-Up*, Wilkerson took credit for catapulting a number of performers to stardom via Sunday Night at the Troc, including Mary Martin, Tony Martin, and Martha Raye. It's been said that outside the studio system, Billy Wilkerson discovered more movie stars and Hollywood talent than anyone else in the industry.

Not everyone who took the Troc's stage was bursting with talent. Albert "Cubby" Broccoli, producer of the James Bond franchise, recalled in his autobiography that "on lesser nights, when some of the acts would be truly terrible, Billy Wilkerson would bring his famous 'hook' into play." A holdover from vaudeville and burlesque days, the hook was a long pole with a curved piece at the end, designed to yank untalented performers offstage by the neck and into the wings mid-song or mid-joke. Wilkerson kept his in the Troc's closet and frequently and unceremoniously dispatched it to extract acts that belly flopped. Broccoli recalled a night when a top mandolin player from New York refused to exit the stage despite a restless audience. An infuriated Wilkerson, having had enough, shouted to the Trocadero manager, "Get the hook and pull that sonofabitch off the stage!"

To introduce the new talent, Wilkerson hired a Chicago comedian by the name of Joe E. Lewis. Lewis had been a marquee name, arguably the Robin

Williams of his day. At the apex of his popularity, while working at a mob-owned nightclub in Chicago, a rival club (also mob-owned) offered him twice the money. Lewis accepted. A few nights later, he was ambushed by his ex-employer's henchmen, who carved out his mouth with a knife. Lewis almost died, but after much rehabilitation, he regained the ability to speak, only to discover that no one in Chicago would hire him. Friends and business colleagues convinced him to reinvent himself on the West Coast. In Hollywood, Lewis auditioned for everyone but was universally rejected. His final stop and last hope was the Troc.

Lewis was not an unknown commodity to Wilkerson; he had seen the comedian perform during his Chicago heyday and knew he could draw in customers. When the desperate comedian begged Wilkerson for a shot, promising he could pack the house, Wilkerson gave him a chance. He paid him $200 a week, a far cry from the thousands he had commanded during his heyday in Chicago, and it was rough going at first. Lewis had lost his rhythm, and Wilkerson would have been justified in letting him go, but instead he guided Lewis back into the spotlight. His pep talks worked. Lewis at last regained his facility, and starting in 1936 he'd play to capacity crowds at the Troc for fifty-seven consecutive weeks, a Hollywood nightclub record.

Wilkerson discovered more than new and neglected talent inside Café Trocadero—he also found the next love of his life. In early September 1935, just one month after Wilkerson divorced Edith Gwynn, Vic Orsatti was on a date at the Troc with twenty-year-old Rita Ann "Billie" Seward. Billie was a model and film actress under contract to Columbia Pictures and had sung for a while with Ben Bernie's Orchestra. Vic introduced Billie to Billy, and according to Tom Seward, Billie's younger brother, Wilkerson was immediately smitten with the young blonde. They dated for just a few weeks before he asked her to marry him. On September 30, 1935, the couple eloped to Las Vegas.

Wilkerson wanted a palatial estate of his own to share with his new bride, and the following month he purchased almost four acres of rolling landscape in Bel-Air, at 10425 Sunset Boulevard. He reenlisted the team that had given life to his Trocadero vision—architect George Vernon Russell and contractor Bud

Raulston—joined this time by designer Doug Honnold, to create the home of his dreams. Homesick for his Tennessee boyhood and sensing he would never see his native soil again, Wilkerson wanted the design to reflect his southern heritage. At a cost of $150,000 (more than $2.5 million today), the team created an enormous mansion in the style of a French colonial plantation. Wilkerson affectionately referred to the sprawling acre of green lawn that stretched to the property line on Sunset Boulevard as his cotton field. The property was surrounded by open green fields to complete the nostalgic vision.

Inside, the first floor featured a living room, a dining room, a guest bedroom with bath, powder room, and dressing room, a butler's pantry, and a butler's bedroom and bath. There was also a wood-paneled den/library with a full wet bar, where Wilkerson would spend much of his leisure time. And there was a full-sized kitchen with a restaurant-sized icebox, its multiple doors of varying sizes spanning an entire wall. Two enormous wine cellars, each ten by twenty feet and sealed with thick metal vault bank doors, filled the basement. After a series of thefts from the wine cellar at the Troc, Wilkerson began to store his most prized vintages here.

On the second floor was a master bedroom suite complete with dressing room and bath, a living room, and a guest room and bath. Through the closet of the guest bedroom was a hundred-foot storage attic. In the master bedroom, Wilkerson insisted on installing a two-inch metal plate inside the wall at the head of his bed to serve as bulletproof protection. During a 1975 remodel, it would take contractors three days to remove that plate; they replaced it with a wall-to-wall plate glass window.

Over the five-car garage and laundry room were the servants' quarters—living room, two bedrooms and bath, and an adjoining patio area. The property also had a swimming pool, two bathhouses, a steam room, a professional tennis court, and a tennis pavilion with another full wet bar and a built-in outdoor grill. The tennis court was the first of its kind in Bel-Air: sunken for protection from the wind.

Construction of the mansion was supervised by Wilkerson's new brother-in-law, Tom, who lived in the servant's quarters until it was completed. Seward had previous experience in the field, having worked in construction for his uncle during the Depression for eighty dollars a week. That "was a fortune back then," he admitted, but when my father offered him fifteen dollars a week to come work for him, he jumped at the chance. "I wanted to be in the film business," he said, "and Billy was my ticket."

Seward quickly worked his way up the ranks to become my father's right-hand man. "Tom would come to play a significant role in the running and management of all of Billy's restaurants and nightclubs," said Bautzer. "He looked after all of those places as if they were his own." According to Kennedy, who watched their partnership unfold, "A great deal of the success of Mr. Wilkerson's clubs and restaurants was because of Tommy."

After he had successfully run his boss's restaurant empire for a time, said Seward, my father also put him in charge of all the business and advertising at the *Reporter*. Seward was even called in as a movie reviewer when extra hands were needed. For each new Wilkerson enterprise, Seward would manage the building, permits, and payroll. "Billy would get the ideas and I would do the work," Seward recalled.

Seward proved to be such an invaluable asset that he would remain in my father's employ for a total of seventeen years, far outlasting Wilkerson's marriage to his sister. If George Kennedy was my father's faithful watchdog, Seward became his shepherd.

13 | THE GAMBLER

WHEN TOM SEWARD FIRST went to work for Billy Wilkerson's empire, he soon discovered his new employer's overriding obsession. From the moment Wilkerson opened his eyes in the morning, he was preoccupied with gambling, planning his entire schedule around visits to card tables and racetracks. My father worked hard to keep his addiction private, and for the most part he succeeded, but his wives, his fellow gamblers, and a few trusted employees knew the truth.

According to Seward, by the later 1930s Wilkerson was gambling every day (except Sundays, when he was at church). Seward said he went to the track with his boss to keep him company, but watching him take a beating was painful. He recalled that Wilkerson often bet $500 on every race. George Kennedy, too, was astonished by his boss's recklessness; Kennedy was barely earning $100 a week, while his employer was blowing thousands at the track. Wilkerson was never without a pair of dice in his coat pocket, and a deck of playing cards was never far from reach. At restaurants he rolled the dice on tabletops to determine who picked up the check. Even at his own restaurants, he'd require guests to pay if they lost.

Wilkerson's weekend gambling trips to Joe Schenck's Agua Caliente resort in Mexico had only recently come to an end. He'd been a frequent visitor there despite the risk it entailed. "Those were the days that if you drove a nice car to Caliente, the Mexicans would steal it at the border," Seward said. In 1934, after he lost two V16 Cadillacs to Mexican border guards, whenever he was planning to visit Agua Caliente he traded cars with Kennedy and drove his secretary's modest Ford across the border.

But the excursions ceased when President Lázaro Cárdenas outlawed gambling in Mexico in 1935. Reportedly, Cárdenas wanted to be cut in on the resort's action, but Joe Schenck refused, and the president decided to teach the movie boss a lesson in Latin politics. Schenck forever regretted the decision, which cost him a fortune.

Fortunately, Wilkerson was deeply involved in establishing gambling opportunities much closer to home. While his primary reason for opening the Troc had been to have a place to stash his hooch, the club also became a front for illegal gambling. In the back room, patrons could find all-night, high-stakes, no-limit card games such as poker and gin rummy. Attendance was by invitation only, and the minimum buy-in was $10,000. Clearly, participation in these games meant one had been admitted into the uppermost echelons of Hollywood society.

The cigar smoke–filled back room hosted such notables as theater owner Sid Grauman, Charles Skouras of Fox West Coast Theaters, Joseph Schenck and Darryl F. Zanuck from 20th Century Fox, Warner Bros.' Jack Warner, MGM's Eddie Mannix and Irving Thalberg, Universal's Carl "Junior" Laemmle, and mega-producers Sam Goldwyn and David O. Selznick. Chico Marx, who had a gambling problem, was also frequently present, as was iconic American composer Irving Berlin. "There was no finer card player than Irving Berlin," Seward remembered.

But it was the studio brass whom Wilkerson was most happy to have at his tables. Not only did facing off against the high-rolling moguls help to satisfy Wilkerson's gambling addiction, but he also knew instinctively that it was one of the only ways to get them all in a room together. His goal was to create an atmosphere in which the studio bosses could air their grievances over turf disputes, smooth ruffled feathers, and swap assets and talent in lieu of cash. While in the front room of the Trocadero drunk actors and actresses rumbaed the night away, in the back room the movie titans were trading them.

Wilkerson himself lost thousands playing against the studio bosses, but those losses bought him a front row seat to their business deals. According to those closest to him, he was able to cull invaluable inside information in their unguarded moments—information he would later be able to use against them.

He even pursued his quarry to their private poker games, held weekly at the home of either Joe Schenck or Samuel Goldwyn. Attendees were handpicked by Schenck and Goldwyn and, like the Trocadero games, included many of the studio brass. But unlike Wilkerson's backroom games, at which the highest-value poker chip was $5,000, the Goldwyn/Schenck games were played with $10,000 and $20,000 chips. "You had to be rich to gamble that kind of cash at those games," recalled Seward. "Only the biggies would be there." Wilkerson rarely missed a game.

My father regularly lost so badly at the Goldwyn/Schenck games that he long suspected one or more of the bigwigs of cheating. He turned to his old friend Raoul Walsh; the director possessed an encyclopedic knowledge of both card games and card tricks. "He thought I was kind of a riverboat kind of card boy," Walsh recalled. Wilkerson strong-armed Walsh into teaching him some sleight-of-hand maneuvers. Kennedy noted that they didn't help. "He still took a beating."

Decades later, in the early 1950s, reports would begin to surface from some of his former poker buddies that Sam Goldwyn had indeed been an inveterate cheat. "If Mr. Wilkerson knew the truth" at the time, Kennedy insisted, "he would have taken the revolver from his waistband and shot Goldwyn. He hated people who stole money from him."

———————

Even excluding the private games, Wilkerson's gambling operation wasn't the only one in town. Clubs all over the city boasted illegal gambling dens, and casinos disguised as supper clubs had lined Sunset Boulevard even before my father opened his high-end establishment. Some of the clubs had been around since the 1920s, when Al and Lou Wertheimer, mob-connected bootleggers who had run Detroit's Purple Gang and were associates of Al Capone's Chicago Outfit, moved from Detroit to Hollywood. There they worked cover jobs as producers for Joe Schenck, but their real job was running Schenck's gambling operations. The Wertheimers, along with fellow gangsters Milton "Farmer" Page, Eddie Nealis, and Nola Hahn, made up what the Hollywood gaming industry called "the Gambling Syndicate." The syndicate developed a track record of success with gambling in California, co-owning and servicing the games at many clubs, including the Clover Club on Sunset and the Club Continental, formerly known as Airport Gardens, on Sonora Avenue in nearby Glendale, California.

According to Seward, however, these clubs weren't merely Wilkerson's rivals; he had a piece of their action as well. It was Wilkerson who had imported the Wertheimers' partner Nola Hahn from back east, via Johnny Rosselli. And the other members of the syndicate took their orders from Hahn. "Finding the group employment was solely his responsibility," Seward said. In fact, Wilkerson owned a stake in the Clover Club and several of Hahn's other gambling ventures.

What few knew was that the games in Hahn's casinos were fixed. As Seward explained, "[Hahn] put magnets under the roulette wheels, and the dice were shaved." The Clover's casino became a favorite of Harry Cohn and Joe Schenck, Seward added; they regularly dropped between $10,000 and $20,000 per night at the tables.

Wilkerson was also involved in expanding another illegal trade to Hollywood: prostitution. In the hills just above Sunset Boulevard were nestled ritzy bordellos affiliated with the supper clubs, and he would supplement his gambling and restaurant operations by ensuring that working women were on standby at each of his venues. It was likely an essential ingredient in his success, a key way of demonstrating that, as future *Reporter* employee David Alexander put it, "there wasn't anything Billy wouldn't do for a high-paying client."

The biggest obstacles for the purveyors of vice were the annoying police raids. The Troc and the Clover both had the advantage of being located in the unincorporated Sunset Strip, an area policed not by the LAPD, which tended to be intolerant of gambling and prostitution, but by the more lenient Los Angeles County Sheriff's Office. As Kennedy explained, "The sheriffs were much easier to bribe."

For them, the primary purpose of a raid was to ensure front-page coverage in the local papers the next day; as Seward explained, "The cops needed to look good . . . like they were doing their jobs." But it also sent a message to club owners: pay off the police or risk being shut down. Newcomers to the scene usually received a friendly visit from beat cops; if no payoff was forthcoming, a formal raid soon followed, in which the stingy club owners might find their equipment destroyed, their proceeds pocketed, and their establishment shut down.

Hahn was not a newcomer in need of a warning, but he had an ingenious system in place in case he was targeted anyway. If word of a raid came in, tables folded into walls, and nailed to the bottom of each table was artwork on a wooden panel, which blended into those walls. He had built chutes leading to the basement into which both money and chips could be tossed. In the basement those chutes were camouflaged as commercial water receptacles. Hahn prepped his staff to usher patrons out a back door into an alley, having advised the patrons in advance that in the event of a raid, any money in play on the tables would be lost.

Indeed, Hahn regularly staged *fake* raids, in which trusted associates dressed up like policemen and herded frightened patrons out of the building—thus allowing the gangster to scoop up all the money in play. "Hahn was the guy who pioneered the fake raid," noted Seward. "You probably couldn't get away with something like that today with all the surveillance cameras and all."

At the Trocadero, sophisticated raid precautions never became a necessity. We don't know how much Wilkerson doled out to law enforcement, but it was apparently sufficient, as the Troc's clandestine backroom card games went undisturbed.

———————

Still, the pitfalls of illegal gambling were considerable for business owners and gamblers alike, so my father began to see the appeal of being involved in a *legal* gambling market. In 1936 he decided to purchase a small hotel in Monte Carlo, and approached Joe Schenck for a loan. Because Schenck thought Wilkerson's proposal was stellar, he happily advanced him $75,000—in exchange for a share of the business.

Wilkerson traveled to the south of France with the cash literally in his pocket. Two weeks later, he telephoned Schenck with a sorrowful confession. He had never made it to the realtor's office. Instead, he had gone straight to the famed casino at Monte Carlo, where he spent two days and lost every penny. "Joe Schenck worshipped Mr. Wilkerson," said Kennedy. "Of course he forgave him."

The incident perfectly illustrates the precarious line my father always walked between his talent for creating successful businesses and his willingness to risk everything on the turn of a card or a roll of the dice. In business, Wilkerson was bold but methodical, laying out a plan and carefully considering every angle, and his daring efforts were often met with unparalleled success. But none of that clear-headed thinking was evident in his gambling. He would dive into a bet without thought, relying heavily on prayer and a lucky rabbit's foot he carried on his keychain. Long ago the fur had been worn off by continued rubbing, and the remaining sinews and bones were polished with wear. They scratched the lining of his pants pocket, creating the illusion that luck could still be found there. But it never was. Because of Wilkerson's uncontrollable obsession, he often rode a roller coaster from success to failure.

It was a ride taken by many in the film industry, including other chronic gamblers such as Joe Schenck, Sam Spiegel, David O. Selznick, and Mike Todd—not one of whom built a lasting empire. Many of those I interviewed over the years strongly believe that Wilkerson could have amassed one of the largest fortunes in American history, if only he'd invested his money instead of gambling it away. On the other hand, if he hadn't been attuned to the gambling world, so many of his greatest opportunities might never have materialized.

14 | HOLLYWOOD'S BIBLE

GAMBLING ALONGSIDE THE STUDIO moguls wasn't the only way Wilkerson was extending his reach into the domain of his hated enemies. By the mid-1930s, he was working many angles to compete with them on their own turf, and in so doing to increase the power and the profile of the *Hollywood Reporter*.

Another source of inside information was the studio publicity heads, whom Wilkerson loved as much as he loathed their bosses. Like everyone else in the industry, Wilkerson was keenly aware of their importance within the studio system. "Their job," said Greg Bautzer, "was to essentially mitigate disasters. They had enormously broad powers."

To safeguard the reputations of their respective studios, publicity departments functioned as arbiters of morality, inserting themselves into the professional and private lives of all studio employees, particularly actors, who were considered studio property. "If a studio didn't like your choice of boyfriend," said Tom Seward, "out they went. They were the true gatekeepers of the studios."

According to George Kennedy, their ability to run damage control extended much further. "They took care of things that needed fixing," he said. If studio owners were the bosses of their own mafia, the publicity departments were their henchmen, with license to harass and silence anyone under contract to the studio and to take measures to see that their mandates were obeyed. They put entire municipal police departments on their payrolls to take care of such vital matters as erasing records and even people.

Two of these henchmen were Harry Brand, head of publicity at 20th Century Fox, and Howard Strickling, his counterpart at MGM. Both men formed immutable bonds with Wilkerson, and while they reported to their bosses, they also reported directly to my father. Their reasoning was that the publishing tycoon was likely to get breaking news before they did, so it was in their best interests to keep on good terms with him, to lessen the chances that he would print something that could erupt into a scandal.

Strickling secretly dined with Billy Wilkerson at least once a week. "Howard would bargain with Billy over what he should run," said Bautzer, "and most times the two men would reach an agreement." The MGM executive became one of Wilkerson's closest friends—ironic, since his boss Louis Mayer was the publisher's greatest nemesis.

Wilkerson had a similarly warm relationship with Mayer's former head of production Irving Thalberg, known as Hollywood's boy wonder. When Thalberg died on September 14, 1936, at age thirty-seven, Kennedy recalled that Wilkerson wept uncontrollably at his desk. As the entire industry paused to pay tribute to the mastermind behind MGM's early successes, in an unprecedented gesture, the *Reporter* devoted its entire front page to Thalberg. The headline read, HOLLYWOOD IN GLOOM. "From the minute the word was broadcast that Irving Thalberg was dead," the lead piece went on to say, "the whole production industry seemed to have stopped. In every nook and corner, in every studio, in every office, men and women laid aside their work to discuss and mourn the passing of their leader."

But Wilkerson's connections to the publicity heads provided him with more than warm feelings. Whenever Wilkerson was personally in trouble, he could call in a favor, ranging anywhere from getting girls for clients to calling off a police or fire investigation.

———

Wilkerson, of course, was also the master of another type of Hollywood power, the kind wielded by prominent gossip columnists such as Walter Winchell and Louella Parsons. Unlike the studio tycoons, these columnists owned no part of the industrial entertainment complex and possessed no authority to hire or fire people. Rather, their power was mythical and theoretical, but it was undisputed. Studios could create talent, but only "the gossips" could insure their longevity. A few flattering lines could rescue a floundering career, while a jab in print could reduce movie stars to quivering blobs begging for mercy and forgiveness.

Celebrities who refused to confess their indiscretions to the biggest gossip columnists of the day were subject to the crushing weight of their criticism. They were "like a pit bull mauling an innocent bystander," Kennedy said. They extinguished promising careers as easily as if they were blowing out a candle. Even a counterattack by the appropriate studio publicity department usually failed to repair the damage. Once gored by one of the gossips, the wound was usually fatal. "Everyone in the industry read and cowered at their columns," said Kennedy.

In this age when gossip columnists dominated Hollywood, Wilkerson became their undisputed emperor. While the *Reporter* conveyed hard news in an unabashedly candid style, my father knew it was gossip that sold papers— and the *Reporter* had plenty of it. Because Wilkerson published his own paper, owned restaurants where celebrities cut loose, and had highly placed connections throughout the industry, he was able to eclipse the competition. Even Louella Parsons, and by the end of the decade her rival for reigning gossip queen, Hedda Hopper, quailed at Wilkerson's censure and kowtowed to him, because he knew how to get the valuable information they needed. "They were wise enough to stay on Billy's good side," remarked Seward. And Walter Winchell—the man whose gossip machine would one day send super-star Josephine Baker into exile at the peak of her career—admitted on several occasions that Wilkerson was the most powerful man in Hollywood.

The *Reporter*'s eye for scandal still regularly provoked the studios into pulling their ad support, so Wilkerson continued to refine his techniques for squeezing as much ad revenue out of his clients as possible. David Alexander, who joined the *Reporter* sales staff in 1936, remembered the paper juggling so many ad scams that they were hard to keep up with.

One of Wilkerson's most inspired techniques was to sell the same piece of advertising to multiple clients. Usually this took the form of a full-page charity ad that printed only the name of the charity, not the sponsors—which meant Wilkerson felt free to sell it to as many advertisers as he could, without telling them they were sharing the buy. "The same ad would be sold as much as a dozen times," said Alexander. "You couldn't get away with that today."

Another of Wilkerson's most lucrative schemes was the *Reporter* annual edition. Once each year, as *Time* reported in the mid-1940s, the *Reporter* produced "a heavy, slickpaper yearbook . . . and invited clients to advertise." The annual was almost totally devoid of editorial content. "It was mostly just a book full of ads," noted George Kennedy. "That was it." The *Reporter* continues to produce similar special editions to this day—for instance, its annual Power Lawyers issue, or its special award season issues filled with "For Your Consideration" ads.

For Wilkerson, the annual was produced for one ingenious purpose: to suck advertising dollars from clients the publisher deemed lagging in their contributions to the daily edition. "Publisher Wilkerson," wrote *Time*, "has almost overdeveloped an ancient publishing technique: that of rewarding advertisers in direct ratio to the extent of their advertising." Wilkerson sent out "suave circulars" in which he wrote, "Naturally, there never has and never will be any penalty for anyone not advertising, but if you can see your way clear, particularly right at this time, my organization and myself will appreciate it." No pressure, but if a studio refused to buy in, Wilkerson ordered a complete editorial blackout on all their material, from declining to run their press releases to withholding film reviews. As *Time* put it, "Those who decline to appear in the advertising columns are very likely to be missing from the text."

George Kennedy confirmed this scheme, adding that the only coverage non-advertisers could expect was an unflattering Tradeviews column. Movie executives, who dreaded more than ever what an editorial tongue-lashing from the *Reporter* would do to an expensive production, acquiesced to the shakedown. Remembered Alexander, "That was the one hedge we had against bad reviews shutting off ads."

Similar pressure was brought to bear on the *Reporter*'s non-studio accounts. Outside publicists eager to have their press releases run in the *Reporter* made sure that all their clients (usually actors) regularly advertised their upcoming appearances on stage and screen. In this way, the *Reporter* served not only as a scandal sheet but also as a sort of vanity publication.

———————

Thanks to Wilkerson's multipronged approach to amassing power, by 1936 the *Hollywood Reporter* had become more than just a thorn in the studio moguls' sides; it was, in many people's estimation, the most powerful trade paper in the country. As *Hollywood Close-Up* magazine later put it, "The paper had become Hollywood's bible." It also had a more colorful nickname, thanks to the film executives who read it first thing each morning while seated on the commode: "the toilet bible."

Close-Up magazine went on to say:

> It was said, and was frequently true, that a producer often first learned he'd been fired when he read it in The Reporter.
>
> Exhibitors would frequently refuse to book a picture if The Reporter panned it.
>
> But to receive the accolade in one of Wilkerson's Tradeviews was regarded as a tribute almost tantamount to something of an Oscar.
>
> A "break" in The Reporter was considered more valuable than a full-scale feature or review in The NY Times.
>
> The stars particularly, but in general everyone trembled over an item in The Rambling Reporter column. Erring husbands feared that column more than their wives.

"By '36," Tom Seward remembered, the studios "were openly courting Billy." My father's Tradeviews had become the most widely read column in the business, capable of launching careers or decimating them. And studios were so petrified of bad *Reporter* reviews that they'd begun showing Wilkerson screen tests before signing actors. By this point, as Greg Bautzer put it, "When you got a call from somebody at the *Reporter*, or even from Billy, you goddamned well answered it."

15 | THE *LONDON REPORTER* TO SUNSET HOUSE

WITH THE *HOLLYWOOD REPORTER* enjoying such tremendous success, Wilkerson decided the time was right to launch a sister publication. It would be identical to the original in both format and content but based in London instead of L.A.

From the time he secured his Fortnum & Mason franchise in 1933, my father had been enamored with London, seeing it as a burgeoning film market. He was convinced that by 1940 the movie industry there would be the equal of Hollywood's, and the city would need a trade paper to cover it. So in January 1936, with characteristic fanfare, he launched the *London Reporter*.

The *Reporter* set up offices at 154 Wardour Street in London's busy West End, though the paper would be printed at 83 Sunbeam Road. Wilkerson exported his gifted but temperamental news editor, Frank Pope, to London to oversee the operation, along with a handful of other members of the Hollywood staff. One month into prelaunch preparations, however, Wilkerson summoned Pope back to Hollywood. "He was too valuable to have in London full-time," remembered George Kennedy.

Wilkerson replaced Pope with Frank Tilley, whom he had stolen from the sales department of RKO Pictures. Under his supervision, the first edition of the *London Reporter* rolled off the presses on Wednesday, March 18, 1936. "We believe that in a period of five years," the departed Frank Pope wrote in the paper's first Tradeviews column, "that [London] will be of equal importance to Hollywood and, in a slightly longer period, the world's greatest production center."

Initially, most of the *London Reporter*'s ad buys consisted of congratulatory messages from Wilkerson's Hollywood clients. But Wilkerson soon learned that the British advertisers had a different attitude toward advertising than their American counterparts. While the Americans were used to being pursued and even badgered for business, in those days the British were offended by such hard-sell tactics. "They found it distasteful," remembered Radie Harris, who later became the *Hollywood Reporter*'s Broadway correspondent and spent many years cultivating British contacts for her column Broadway Ballyhoo. The Brits were used to providing advertising support without being asked—a system that depended on gaining the support of an old boy network and made sales difficult for newcomers, especially foreigners.

Wilkerson knew he could not count on his Hollywood advertisers to support his London operation long term, but he had little patience for what he called England's "smoking jacket rules." Desperate for local ads, he printed and reprinted his advertising rate card, each time dramatically slashing his prices. The tactic didn't work, and within a few months of its launch, the *London Reporter* was floundering. "Billy was in trouble," said Seward. "So much money had been invested, and bills couldn't be paid."

Seward and Wilkerson happened to be in London when a constable stopped by their Wardour Street offices to hand them a courteously worded summons. Wilkerson was asked to appear before a magistrate to explain why he had paid neither his office rent nor his printing costs. "They were very polite about the whole matter," remembered Seward. "They just didn't throw you into the slammer like they do here if you forget to pay a parking ticket."

By the end of July, after just five months in operation, Wilkerson decided the situation was hopeless, and the final edition of the *London Reporter* was printed on Wednesday, July 29. Wilkerson vacated the Wardour Street offices and fled England, missing his court date and failing to address any of his debts. He knew that returning to England could mean imprisonment.

Back home, the publisher blamed the failure of his London enterprise on the British, and resented them for running him out of the country. From that point on, he fiercely curtailed any news items or press releases having to do with British film production. "Billy hated the British after that," remembered Harris. "Any chance he got, he attacked them in print."

It would be thirteen years before his view of these events softened. In 1949, he finally returned to England to face British justice. The court, having become more lenient in the intervening years, imposed a £5,000 fine on the publisher. With his debts settled, he was contacted by British industrialist J. Arthur Rank, founder of the Rank Organization, who had launched his own film empire one year after the *London Reporter*'s collapse. Rank had seen the trade paper fail, but he admired Wilkerson and saw the paper's potential. He urged the publisher to give it another shot.

Wilkerson was blunt. "Once bitten, twice shy," he told the film magnate. The *London Reporter* would not be resurrected.

Back in 1936, however, as Wilkerson's London paper was swiftly failing, his original Los Angeles headquarters was undergoing a rebirth. By this point the *Hollywood Reporter* had once again outgrown its offices, but this time Wilkerson did not want to move into another existing building. Instead, he wanted a headquarters designed to his exact specifications, a place where every aspect of his publishing empire—from production to printing to distribution— could be housed under one roof. "The idea was that we could do everything ourselves," said Seward, "and not farm it out like we had been doing." And they would do it all without a change in address, erecting a new two-story office building directly behind the *Reporter*'s current offices at 6715 Sunset Boulevard.

For this project, my father once again hired architect George Vernon Russell, who had designed both the Café Trocadero and his Bel-Air estate, and decorator Harold Grieve, who had created the interiors at the Troc. The job was not just to design and build the new headquarters but to renovate the previous *Reporter* offices to accommodate two additional business ventures. Hoping to once more corner an untapped luxury market, Wilkerson told Russell and Grieve his plans to introduce Hollywood's first high-end barbershop and adjoining haberdashery.

At the time, most men wore suits and hats, and many American business-men paid daily visits to barbershops for shaves, manicures, and facials. But Wilkerson had done his research and knew that no other establishment offered wealthy men the opportunity to meet both their clothing and their grooming needs in one location. He wanted to build a barbershop perfectly suited to delivering a full spectrum of services, from towel wraps to facials to haircuts to manicures, and a haberdashery so well appointed it would attract well-to-do clients off the street. In May 1936 Russell and Grieve presented Wilkerson with their plans for his dream. "Billy was over the moon," recalled Seward.

For the exterior facade, Wilkerson demanded a particular type of black Italian marble. "It was beautiful," recalled George Kennedy, "but the upkeep was a nightmare." The problem was that the marble was designed for *interior* surfaces. "Exposed to the elements, we were calling the polishers to clean the front every other month," Kennedy said. "That became expensive."

The haberdashery lobby boasted fifteen-foot ceilings trimmed with elegant birch crown molding and supported by six large oak veneer columns. Each door was like "a palace doorway," Kennedy recalled. Harold Grieve installed wall-to-wall parquet floors, and chandeliers hung from the ceilings. A mammoth fireplace dominated the west end of the lobby, where clients could sit and enjoy a cigar. Exquisitely lit display cases offered shirts, ties, and men's cologne; wooden poker chip cases and decks of playing cards in elegant wooden or leather holders; and silk bathrobes and smoking jackets. All the cabinetry storing the inventory was custom made by hand from the finest woods.

In the exclusive seven-chair barbershop, banks of overhead fluorescent lights gave barbers the perfect illumination for their work without glare to distract clients. To quiet the din as the barbers and their customers made their way to and from the seven stations, Wilkerson installed cork floors, a pioneering feature. "No other barber shop in the country had cork floors," said barber Harry Drucker.

It was as an employee in Wilkerson's new barbershop that Drucker, who would ultimately become celebrity barber to movie stars and presidents, entered the publisher's world. The two men had met in New York City in April 1936, when Wilkerson was in town to drum up business. He stayed at the Waldorf Astoria, and one morning he visited the hotel barbershop for a trim, facial, and manicure and happened to sit in Drucker's chair.

During Prohibition, Drucker had run a successful barbershop in the Bronx whose clients included major players in New York's underworld, including Bugsy Siegel and Meyer Lansky. With the repeal of the Eighteenth Amendment, many of Drucker's regulars suddenly had no cash. "The money they made from alcohol all dried up," Drucker said. "They weren't spending like they used to. It was a real one-two punch." Without this vital gangster income, Drucker had begun making cutbacks, eliminating one barber at a time until he was manning the shop on his own. He finally gave up and sold the shop in 1936, going to work at the Waldorf Astoria. Wilkerson was his very first customer.

The visitor from California made an immediate impression on the barber. "Mr. Wilkerson looked very sharp. That's the kind of man he was all the time."

When the barber finished taking care of him, Wilkerson said, "You've given me one of the finest haircuts and shaves I've ever had. What's your name?" Drucker told him, and when Wilkerson asked when he took lunch, the barber said he could go anytime. Wilkerson took him out to an elegant restaurant to tell him of his dream of opening a first-class barbershop back in Hollywood. "Mr. Wilkerson was always a very direct man. He never pulled any punches. You knew exactly where you stood with him," Drucker said.

My father asked the barber what he thought about a combination haberdashery and barbershop, and Drucker said there was no money to be made in the barber business, but that "the barber business would create traffic for the haberdashery."

"That's right," Wilkerson said, as if he already knew the answer. "Thank you anyway." The two men shook hands.

"And that was that," said Drucker.

Five weeks later, Drucker got a letter from Wilkerson asking him to move to Hollywood and to bring more barbers with him. Suspicious, the barber phoned a friend who was well connected in the film capital and asked about Billy Wilkerson. When he learned how powerful Billy was, he told his friend, "That's all I want to hear." He rustled up five other barbers and their families, and a month later they arrived by train in Hollywood. "It was a big responsibility for Mr. Wilkerson," said Drucker. "He had to find housing for the barbers and their families."

But if there were any doubts in the publisher's mind, they were dispelled the moment in the summer of 1936 when he opened the doors of the barbershop and haberdashery he called Sunset House.

"We gained momentum like nobody's business in that shop," remarked Drucker. "It was the finest barber shop in the world. We had the finest clientele in the world." But according to the barber, Wilkerson remained true to the assessment both men had made in New York: he didn't expect the barbershop to make money; his sole purpose was to bring something special to the community.

For example, he wanted his employees to stand out from the average barber, who has a reputation for talking too much. On the cash register, Wilkerson placed a sketch of a man sitting in a barber's chair with the message OUR BARBERS ONLY SPEAK WHEN THEY'RE SPOKEN TO. "It was a lovely touch," remembered Drucker.

Drucker found one incident particularly memorable. A client identified only as "Mr. Walker" arrived one day, and according to Drucker, Wilkerson was very concerned that this man be well taken care of. He called down to the shop from his office on the second floor of the new building, and told Harry he wanted Walker to receive first-class service.

"We always give everybody first-class service," Drucker replied. "We had a system of shaving styling, for instance, that nobody else knew how to do."

After Drucker got through with "Mr. Walker," the client walked upstairs to see Wilkerson, and later Wilkerson told him the client had raved that Drucker was the finest barber he had ever met.

"Well," remembered Drucker, "Mr. Wilkerson came down, his face was so happy, you have no idea. But he didn't make a dime on it."

We don't know who this mysterious "Mr. Walker" actually was. Out of all my interviewees, Harry Drucker was the most reluctant to provide the names of the individuals mentioned in his anecdotes. George Kennedy called Drucker "the picture of discretion," noting that he went so far as to concoct code names for clients who preferred to keep their real names off his reservation ledger. Some of these anonymous individuals were probably celebrities, while others, "Mr. Walker" among them, were likely participants in organized crime. As commonly happens with barbershops, Sunset House quickly became a magnet for the underworld, patronized by such crime luminaries as Willie Bioff, Johnny Rosselli, and Bugsy Siegel. "It became the meeting place for the Hollywood crime people," noted Kennedy.

Bugsy Siegel, for instance, had first come to Hollywood in 1933, hoping like many of his counterparts to reinvent himself. Now that Drucker was also in town, his former Bronx client sought him out. Kennedy remembered Siegel's vanity as being off the charts. "He panicked every time he got a pimple and came running to Sunset House."

One time when Siegel and another member of an organized crime faction were in the shop at the same time, a fight broke out. Harry Drucker again refused to disclose the rival's name, but he spoke about the argument, which quickly escalated into a screaming match. He told me that it "silenced the entire barbershop."

"Apparently it was a dispute over turf," said Kennedy.

Drucker recalled that Siegel, still draped in an apron, face full of shaving cream, flew out of his chair, snatched the razor from the barber's hand, and lunged at the other man, shouting at him to get out. When Drucker saw the other man slide his hand inside his coat, he intervened, issuing a stern, uncharacteristically foul-mouthed warning to both of them: "Take your fucking business outside!" He pointed to the door. "This is a class joint. From now on, only one of you is coming in at a time. You're not disturbing any more of my customers. Do I make myself fucking clear?"

Drucker relayed the incident to Wilkerson. According to Kennedy, the publisher was furious. Knowing Siegel answered to Johnny Rosselli, he phoned his Hollywood Outfit partner and ordered him to get his man in line. The publisher told Rosselli he would take no more chicanery from Siegel.

Problems at the haberdashery, meanwhile, were less explosive but more insurmountable. Wilkerson had appointed a man named Jerry Rothschild to run that half of the Sunset House operation. We know little about Rothschild's previous work experience or how he came to my father's attention, but whatever his past, Wilkerson dispatched Rothschild to London to purchase the finest men's clothes his budget allowed. As Drucker recalled, "Mr. Wilkerson wanted something extraordinary in the way of men's clothing. He didn't want average merchandise." And he trusted his employee to comply with those instructions. "Mr. Wilkerson," said Drucker, "was the type of man when he hired somebody, he gave you all the power in the world. He didn't interfere with your business."

But Rothschild ignored his boss's orders. Instead he went to New York. There, through a contact in the garment district, he purchased twice the inventory he could have gotten in London for the same money. No one knows whether Rothschild was simply trying to be cost-efficient, or whether his garment district connection kicked back a portion of the funds for him to pocket. In any event, the manager returned to Los Angeles quite pleased with his purchases, and assured his employer that he would be pleased as well. But a few weeks later when the merchandise arrived, Wilkerson took one look at it and said, "You didn't go to London, did you?"

"It was amazing," remembered Drucker. "He knew just by looking at the clothing that it was inferior."

Rothschild sheepishly admitted he had not. As Drucker recalled, "Rothschild was a nice man, a very fine gentleman, but timid. Mr. Wilkerson on the other hand never, ever compromised." My father proclaimed that with clothing of such low quality, Sunset House would go out of business in three months. He fired Jerry Rothschild, called auctioneer Ben Bail, and auctioned off the entire inventory.

Thus, Sunset House, like the *London Reporter* before it, became a casualty of one of my father's favorite business maxims: "Close on the first loss." Whenever his emotions interfered with his creativity, he was apt to change his mind at the drop of a hat. As Drucker observed, "Most smart people are impatient, restless, especially when you're naturally emotional. You become patient when you have nothing to do. Smart people become impatient—impatient with imperfection, with mediocrity. Mr. Wilkerson was like that. He felt it was a waste of time to deal with somebody who knew less. He was a perfectionist. He couldn't stand mediocrity."

But according to Drucker, this wasn't simply an emotional impulse; it was a smart way to do business—to know when an endeavor was beyond hope of recovery. It's one thing if "the blueprint is done and you follow through on the blueprint, and something happens beyond your control," the barber said. "But if you disregarded the blueprint, that's it. When you open up a place and it starts going bad and you're trying to cure it, it's like curing a cancer.

"The haberdashery would have never succeeded in Hollywood. Beverly Hills, yes."

The barbershop, unable to carry the expense, closed three months later. According to Wilkerson's associates, the failed ventures cost Wilkerson in the neighborhood of $250,000. The publisher got Drucker a position as a studio barber at the new Republic Pictures, founded in 1935, and found employment in town for the other barbers Drucker had brought along from New York. Even Rothschild went on to start his own men's clothing store in Beverly Hills.

After all the inventory and furniture had been sold, Wilkerson rented out the space in the front of the *Reporter* building to a glamour photographer, the first in town to take nude portraits of women. And at that address, George Hurrell ultimately blossomed into a celebrated studio photographer whose portraits of movie stars came to define Hollywood glamour.

16 | DAILY LIFE AT THE *REPORTER*

THOUGH SUNSET HOUSE WAS the flashy public face of Wilkerson's 1936 expansion efforts, it was the new building behind it at 6715 Sunset Boulevard that would serve as the backbone of his empire for decades to come. Housing both editorial offices and an on-site print shop, it would remain the headquarters of the *Hollywood Reporter* until 1988—a span of more than fifty years.

This also meant that for decades, the *Reporter* offices were at the center of my father's daily routine. Like his business plans, his day-to-day life was guided by careful consideration and discipline, and his routine seldom varied.

Each day he woke up by 7:00 AM in his Bel-Air mansion and made his way to the master bathroom, his coterie of dogs at his heels. Wilkerson loved poodles, all variations of the breed, and he usually had five or six at a time. "He had an uncanny love of canines," remembered George Kennedy, "and to my mind, they came before everyone else, including women." Added Greg Bautzer, "Dogs were Billy's real religion." They all bore European names, like Pierre and Igor, but he also gave them nicknames. (In later years, for instance, his small beige poodle Pierre, who was incapable of controlling his bladder in the house, was aptly dubbed Pee-Pee.) Wilkerson would parade his dogs with their pom-pom cuts and fashionable Parisian collars through the *Reporter*'s corridors as if they were royalty.

In the mornings, however, they would settle down on the bathroom floor as their master took a ten-minute shower and then shaved with a straight razor. By the mid-1930s, he'd replaced his bushy waxed mustache with a manicured pencil-thin version. As he shaved, the mirror would have shown him a slim, darkly handsome man with a ruddy complexion, about five feet five inches tall. Many who knew him described him as possessing rugged good looks, with drooping lips and basset hound eyes. Once his mustache was perfect, he massaged Vitalis into his scalp and combed his dark hair, usually parting it slightly off center. The immaculately coiffed publisher then doused himself with Carnaval de Venise cologne.

Exiting the bathroom and entering his walk-in cedar closet, Wilkerson dressed in one of his countless tailored double-breasted suits, adding a flamboyant silk tie. "Billy always wore expensive suits," said *Reporter* employee Vic Enyart. This is how he dressed seven days a week—no one remembers ever seeing Billy Wilkerson slumming it. *Time* described him as looking like "a Central Casting Corporation gambler." In all, Wilkerson spent a minimum of an hour getting dressed and ready for his day.

His preparations complete, he donned a silk bathrobe instead of the suit jacket over his shirt and tie, then descended the mansion's grand staircase, reminiscent of a Hollywood set. In the dining room he sat at the end of long mahogany dining table, tucked a linen napkin under his collar, and pushed a buzzer under the table to alert the kitchen staff that he was ready to eat.

The morning menu never varied: one soft-boiled egg emptied into a clear glass cup and mixed with butter, salt and pepper, and a shredded biscuit. As he ate, he perused the current issues of the *Reporter* and *Daily Variety*, placing the two side by side and counting all the ads, back to front. He never read the editorial content. On a pad of paper to his right he tallied ads and made notes. After breakfast the staff cleared the table and brought him the phone, and he placed his first call of the morning to his advertising department. The screaming began. "Those calls came every morning at 9:00 sharp," said advertising staffer David Alexander. "Billy would be furious we didn't get ads *Variety* had gotten."

After this call, Wilkerson phoned George Kennedy. The secretary typically offered his boss a laundry list of suggestions, to each of which Wilkerson robotically replied, "Throw it out."

After his phone calls, Wilkerson returned to his closet and parted the wall of suits to reveal a small brown wall safe, from which he retrieved his watch, a ruby pinkie ring, and his alligator wallet, which was divided into two compartments. One contained singles, fives, tens, and twenties. The other contained $2,000 in hundreds. Kennedy noted that whenever a ten or twenty went missing from his wallet he'd notice it right away—but, ironically, if a hundred disappeared, he'd never realize it.

"He was always a cash man," said Joe Pasternak. Wilkerson avoided credit, considering cash the only reliable way of buying oneself out of a bad situation.

Finally, Wilkerson slipped out of his robe, slid into his coat, and usually was at his desk at the *Reporter* forty-five minutes later. The publisher's office was on the second floor of the new building, and Kennedy had instructed the switchboard operator to alert him when Wilkerson was on his way up. When he got word, he walked into his employer's office and turned on the desk lamp.

Kennedy then went to the adjoining bathroom, where a small white refrigerator sat. Inside, lined up like soldiers, was row upon row of Coca-Cola bottles. "There must have been about fifty of them in there," recalled David Alexander. Kennedy opened one of the bottles and placed it on Wilkerson's desk, along with the daily progress and financial reports. Besides delivering memos and fielding phone calls, Kennedy would provide his employer with a steady stream of Coca-Colas throughout the day.

Wilkerson's dull olive green wood-paneled office measured twenty-five feet by fifteen feet. A door opposite Kennedy's door led into another corridor; Wilkerson called it his escape door, through which he could make a hasty exit if an undesirable visitor showed up unannounced. Parked next to that door was a chair that had once been used by a British grenadier; upholstered in thick tuck-and-roll green leather, it was shaped to accommodate the soldier's giant bearskin hat. On the adjacent wall was a fireplace, and opposite the fireplace a beige couch sat against the wall. There was no artwork hanging above the fireplace or on any of the walls, just two small sterling silver–framed portraits of Wilkerson's mother on the mantel. The floor was hardwood, with just one area rug beneath Wilkerson's desk in the center of the room.

That desk dominated the room like a museum exhibit. He'd had it custom-built for his new office, a huge, solid oak partners desk with kneeholes on both sides. But reflecting his longstanding suspicion about partnerships, the drawers only opened on his side. The other side was a facade.

"Mr. Wilkerson's drawers were three feet long," Kennedy laughed. "I could never find anything in them. They were a mess"—a jumble of strings, candy, loose rubber bands, scrap paper, old postcards, and worn photographs. "He would call me into his office and ask me to find something in his drawers, and I never could."

The top left drawer was sacrosanct. There he kept the plate of the earliest childhood photo of himself, which according to Kennedy he viewed from time to time. In the top center drawer, just behind the pen and pencil holder, he kept a Colt service revolver, and under his desk, suspended from two brass hooks for easy access, was an ornately carved, colorfully painted Mexican piñata bat. (As someone whose life had been threatened numerous times, Wilkerson was a firm believer in self-protection.) The desk also held a silver cigarette lighter, a large ashtray that always seemed to be full, a black metal penholder, and three candlestick phones. Kennedy recalled Wilkerson gripping the telephone stand in one hand and bringing the mouthpiece directly to his mouth whenever he was shouting at someone. "When it was a screaming wife, Mr. Wilkerson always held the earpiece well away from his ear," Kennedy added.

Wilkerson's day would have run more smoothly if he'd been able to have one more phone installed—in his office bathroom. For years, he'd been plagued by bowel problems, and at home he had a small custom-made table in front of his commode where he could chain-smoke and read the sports pages while he waited for nature to take its course. But in the office he had more to do than simply pass the time, and in the 1930s bathroom wall phones were nonexistent. For a long time, Kennedy had to knock on the bathroom door to alert his boss to an urgent call. "Frequently," said Kennedy, "Mr. Wilkerson would be wiping himself on the way to his desk to answer the phone and struggling to pull up his pants." To quell his secretary's nagging, Wilkerson eventually had the telephone company install a thirty-foot cord that extended all the way to the toilet, and daily he screamed at his secretary from the toilet to bring him his ringing phone.

Next to the bathroom door was a single curtainless, translucent window that provided the room's only natural light, a single beam that shone onto the publisher's desk. In the center of the desk was the room's only source of electric light, a silver desk lamp that illuminated only the area directly beneath it. Aside from these two light sources, Wilkerson's office was a dark cavern where he spent nearly all his waking hours.

———————

Being summoned to Wilkerson's dark office was not something the *Reporter* staff looked forward to, as it generally meant the staffer in question was about to receive a severe dressing down. "If Billy called you up to his office," said David Alexander, "and didn't ask you to sit down, that meant he was going to chew your ass out." People claimed that when Wilkerson roared in his office, the lights throughout the entire building flickered. Indeed, many staff believed that if he was quiet for too long, something was seriously wrong.

To reach the publisher's office on the second floor, one had to climb a long flight of stairs, which Wilkerson's staff dubbed "the 39 Steps" after Hitchcock's 1935 thriller. While making the ascent, "the suspense was terrible," recalled Broadway columnist Radie Harris, who would start writing for the *Reporter* in 1940. "I never knew what I was being called up for. Nobody did."

Fortunately for Harris, she worked for the paper out of New York and paid only two mandatory annual visits to the *Reporter* offices in Hollywood. Even so, the teetotal columnist confessed to throwing back two straight scotches whenever she had to climb the 39 Steps. "It was the only way I could face Billy," she said. Wilkerson was keenly aware of Harris's popularity, but he made no secret of the fact that he himself was not a fan of Broadway. "He never gave praise," Harris remembered, "but liberally doled out criticism." The fact that he made her climb the stairs to meet with him may itself be a sign of the low esteem in which he held her—since Radie Harris had a wooden leg.

At other times, however, Wilkerson did not confine his outbursts to the privacy of his office. Two or three times a week he appeared in the newsroom to rail in front of an audience. "With arms flailing," said Kennedy, "he cursed out all and sundry" for reasons that were not apparent to anyone, then would "be over it in five minutes." These "performances" prompted Wilkerson's staffers to label him with affectionate but mocking nicknames; David Hanna, a staff writer who was also a great opera buff, dubbed him "Mad Margaret," after the character in Gilbert and Sullivan's opera *Ruddigore*.

Some *Reporter* staffers began emulating Wilkerson's hectoring style, including David Alexander, who would ascend to head of the *Reporter* sales department in the early 1940s and remain in that position until Wilkerson's death. One day Wilkerson called Alexander to his office and told him he didn't understand why he was so rough with people, and Alexander let him know he'd learned it all from his boss. "A smile crossed Billy's face," Alexander recalled.

"Once he brought up and dealt with a point, that was the last of it. He never brought it up again."

It was one of many instances in which Wilkerson's temper ended up rebounding on him. One day someone had the misfortune of having his car break down in the publisher's driveway, blocking access to his home. Seeing the raised hood, Wilkerson didn't stop to find out who was behind it. Instead he began to deliver a most profane lecture. When a tall man emerged from the car dressed in black and sporting a white collar, Wilkerson was shocked to silence. He spent the next few weeks apologizing to the priest.

At ten o'clock every morning, Wilkerson began tapping out his front-page editorial—a daily column of between three hundred and seven hundred words—on the typewriter that sat on a stand to the right of his desk. While Tradeviews was certainly written in my father's voice, I don't believe he was responsible for every word of every column. After all, he was not a reader or an investigator; it's doubtful that he took time out of his busy schedule to dig through sources or chase down leads. His editorials contained so many deeply sourced gems that I strongly suspect they were farmed out to his editorial staff, which included a crack researching and reporting unit. My guess is that the staff writers, who knew his politics and the subjects of interest to him, presented him with outlines or even complete editorials that he then rewrote in his own voice.

At ten thirty, he called Kennedy in to take dictation, which he always gave while sitting on the toilet. The shy secretary with poised pen and steno pad sat on the opposite side of the partially opened bathroom door. Kennedy vividly recalls those dictations being punctuated by his employer lifting one cheek at a time to "rip off the most tremendous farts." Said the secretary, "I knew instinctively that that meant he was beginning a new paragraph."

When lunchtime rolled around, Wilkerson might head to Vendôme, but otherwise he always ate at his desk, bringing food from home in a brown paper bag that he stored with his Cokes in the refrigerator. The man who served some of the finest food in the country ate sardines out of tin cans, which he spooned onto saltine crackers. To supplement the fish, his cook sometimes prepared sandwiches. "They were mostly things like tuna and chicken sand-wiches," Kennedy remembered, though Wilkerson's favorites were deviled egg sandwiches.

After lunch he took a catnap on the beige couch opposite the fireplace, and afterward he often headed out to the track—either Del Mar or Santa Anita, where he had private boxes. Knowing Wilkerson's predilection for heavy gambling, the tracks donated the boxes, since they knew they could easily underwrite the expense. Apart from a few key personnel, like Kennedy, no one at the office knew about these afternoon excursions. "They believed he was absorbed in meetings or at private screenings at studios," said Kennedy.

Wilkerson often returned to the office from the track to take care of out-standing and pressing matters. By the time he left for the evening, the neat piles of documents Kennedy supplied had become a snowstorm of paper that swirled across the surface of his desk, and a series of empty Coke bottles had gathered on the right-hand side of the workspace. It was left to Kennedy to tidy up the desk at the end of each day.

After work, Wilkerson never missed an afternoon visiting his mother. He'd sold Trocadero Ranch in 1936 and bought her a house at 1311 June Street in Hollywood, close to his Sunset Boulevard office. Despite his devotion to her, their visits were far from harmonious. "They couldn't stand the sight of each other for very long," recalled Kennedy. People recalled that the moment Mary saw her son walking up to her house, she began to scream at him, and the screaming continued unabated until he left.

"It was violent love-hate," remembered my mother. "They fought like cats and dogs every time they saw each other. She yelled and screamed at him, reminding him that he was a no-good son of a bitch just like his father for pissing his profits away at the craps table. She was the only woman he would take any shit from."

Despair over her son's vices had driven her from the Catholic Church years earlier, but she had another religion now: she was a snuff dipper and drank a fifth of whiskey every day. Each day as he left her house, she'd scream from her porch, "And don't forget my friends!" He knew exactly what she was talking about: Mary insisted on a daily delivery of snuff and booze.

The request embarrassed her teetotal son, so he delegated the task to his secretary, who daily arrived at Mary's front door with a brown paper bag. As

Kennedy remembered it, "She got pretty vocal after a couple of stiff ones. She wasn't a fall-down drunk, but she did have a sharp tongue."

Following his afternoon visit with Mary, my father headed home. In the early days of his empire, when his other businesses still required his direct supervision, he showered and changed into his tuxedo, then headed out to the Trocadero or one of his subsequent restaurants or nightclubs. There he remained until closing, coming home around 2:30 AM.

17 | FRIENDS AND ALLIES

MY FATHER'S SCHEDULE was a hectic one, but he still took time away from work to entertain his many friends. Throughout his life, he hosted Sunday barbecues at his Bel-Air estate, where anyone from John Wayne to Howard Hughes might be seen poolside or on the tennis court. Wilkerson felt comfortable with all manner of people, from European aristocracy to attorneys to barbers and cooks.

The attorney who was closest to Wilkerson was of course Greg Bautzer, who according to George Kennedy came into his orbit in 1937, a year after he graduated from law school at USC. Bautzer was young, tall, and handsome, with the build of a football quarterback, a head of curly blond hair, and perfect white teeth (which were actually dentures), and he set out to build a reputation as a Hollywood socialite lawyer. He made a hard-target list of the movers and shakers in Hollywood, and one of those he zeroed in on was Wilkerson. He followed the publisher everywhere, hustling after his account.

According to legend, when Bautzer learned that Wilkerson was currently represented by superstar lawyer Max Fink, he found a mole in Fink's office. His inside source—"probably a secretary he flirted with," Kennedy theorized—fed him information on Wilkerson's appointments. Bautzer would wait at the elevator and ride with Wilkerson up to Fink's office. After establishing a connection, Bautzer made my father an offer: he would provide him with legal services for six months for no fees, on the condition that if Wilkerson was satisfied, Bautzer would become his attorney—at half the rate he was paying Fink.

My father decided to test the young lawyer out by giving him the task of resolving his traffic violations. Wilkerson had a complete disregard for the rules of the road and was constantly ticketed for bad driving, especially for speeding. He was prone to shearing off the car doors that unsuspecting drivers had opened after they parked. Sometimes he hit unattended cars and kept driving, never leaving behind a note. (A few years later, in 1942, he would rack up nine hit-and-runs in a single year.) Wilkerson's heedlessness continually landed him in hot water with judges, who were infuriated by this blatant disregard for authority. But Bautzer jumped at the opportunity to prove himself, and he managed to get every legal summons dismissed. This so impressed Wilkerson, he fired Fink and turned all his business over to Bautzer—whom he nicknamed "Choppers" after his pristine smile.

Despite his charisma, intelligence, and drive, Bautzer was not without his shortcomings. According to my mother, he was a mediocre trial lawyer, but his courtroom failures were outweighed by his ability to make deals, which would often be cemented at my father's clubs and restaurants. He would remain Wilkerson's main legal counsel until the publisher's death.

———————————

Billy Wilkerson didn't just surround himself with shrewd go-getters, however. Every king needs a jester, so he also commanded a retinue of colorful characters who bowed to his every whim.

Two of his most fervent disciples were Alex Paal and Joe Rivkin. Paal was a bald, short, pudgy Hungarian screenwriter, film producer, and *Vogue* photographer whom my father unflatteringly nicknamed "Meatball." "Whatever it was about Meatball," observed Kennedy, "he always kept Mr. Wilkerson in stitches. He knew how to tickle his funny bone."

Joe Rivkin, a talent agent and man about town, was a faithful follower from the early 1930s to the end of Wilkerson's life. Because he was Jewish, he was sometimes the target of Wilkerson's less than enlightened views about ethnicity. According to Rivkin, one morning the two were breakfasting at the publisher's house when Wilkerson blurted out, "Let's get that Jew nose cut off." Never mind that it was a Saturday, Wilkerson roused George Kennedy from his day off and ordered him to comb through every business directory to find a surgeon. Kennedy was instructed to say that it was an emergency and that money was no object. Later that morning, Rivkin found himself seated in a plastic surgeon's chair, with Wilkerson directing the procedure.

Like many people in my father's life, Rivkin didn't hold such prejudicial behavior against him. To them, Wilkerson's charm cast a spell that made insults and slights seem like terms of endearment. Said Rivkin, "There was nothing to forgive. That was Billy and that was why we all loved him."

And despite any anti-Semitic tendencies, Wilkerson certainly lent a hand to many Jewish friends and associates who were struggling. For instance, though not a fan of Broadway in general, Wilkerson was a champion of Broadway playwright Norman Krasna and had instigated a number of favorable write-ups in the *Reporter*, boosting Krasna's career immeasurably. Conspicuously grateful, Krasna shipped the publisher numerous gifts over the years, including a wicker-colored Rolls-Royce.

Once, a large wooden crate from Krasna arrived at the publisher's office. Wilkerson sent George Kennedy down to the pressroom to fetch a crowbar, and while he looked on, Kennedy uncrated a cubist painting of a fractured still life. Wilkerson propped the painting up against his sofa and asked what the hell it was. Kennedy was very knowledgeable about art, having spent time in Gertrude Stein's Paris salon, so he told his employer it was either a Braque or a Picasso. "For a period," Kennedy said, "their styles were identical."

"Send this piece of shit back!" Wilkerson barked. According to Kennedy, "Mr. Wilkerson was no art lover. It later turned out to be a Picasso, worth a lot of money."

Another devoted Wilkerson follower and great beneficiary of his generosity was Albert "Cubby" Broccoli, who worshipped Wilkerson and was especially enamored with his Café Trocadero. "He went every chance he got," said Tom Seward. "He would have lived there if he had the chance."

Young Broccoli was gainfully employed at a major studio, and likely had mob connections through a cousin, shady talent agent Pasquale "Pat" Di Cicco. Even so, nightly dining at the Troc was cost prohibitive, so he approached Seward, who was the manager at the time, to ask him for a job. "He was hardly waiter material," remembered Seward. The heavyset Italian was over six feet tall and built like a linebacker. It just so happened, however, that Seward was looking for a bouncer, and Broccoli fit the bill. And so, in exchange for a food and liquor tab, Cubby Broccoli became the Troc's unofficial doorman, and ultimately Seward grew dependent on him. Over time Broccoli let his fists become his spokesman. "Cubby never backed down from a fight," remembered Seward.

According to E. J. Fleming's *The Fixers*, on December 21, 1937, Broccoli went too far. Comedian Ted Healy, former partner of the Three Stooges, was at the Troc celebrating the birth of his first child, and when the festivities became a little too boisterous, Seward signaled Broccoli to escort the inebriated Healy outside. It should have ended there, but Healy launched into a vitriolic rage and began taunting Broccoli, which amused arriving customers. Broccoli, in the company of his cousin Pat Di Cicco and film star Wallace Beery, escorted Healy to the Troc's rear parking lot; there were no witnesses as to what happened there, but the following morning Healy died of head injuries.

Knowing he could spend the rest of his life behind bars, a panicked Broccoli phoned Wilkerson to plead for help. "Billy had a soft spot for Cubby," said Seward. And because I grew up sitting on Cubby Broccoli's lap, I can vouch for that soft spot myself.

Wilkerson wasted no time in contacting MGM publicist Howard Strickling, who was more concerned about saving the reputation of Wallace Beery, a major star at MGM, than he was about a friend of Wilkerson's. Still, with Wilkerson's help, Strickling fabricated a story that drunken college students had attacked the comedian, and Broccoli and his accomplices were never charged.

Ted Healy's ex-wife, Betty Brown, an MGM contract player, was not so satisfied with the story being told. She insisted publicly that the investigation surrounding Healy's death was a sham. To throw off the scent, Wilkerson published her complaint in the pages of the *Hollywood Reporter*, but her contract with MGM was mysteriously terminated, and she never again worked in Hollywood.

After that, Cubby stopped serving as a bouncer at the Troc, but he continued to play a shadowy role in Wilkerson's life. Many sources have said that Broccoli did "favors" for the Hollywood Don, but precisely what those favors were no one seemed to know. "He took care of things for Billy," remembered Seward. "Cubby was always a phone call away." According to him, Broccoli was rewarded for services rendered with valuable connections to other Hollywood luminaries in Wilkerson's inner circle, including Greg Bautzer and Joe Schenck, who went on to help Broccoli with his career in the movie industry.

My father also maintained veiled connections to Broccoli's cousin Pat Di Cicco. According to Seward, the agent was in fact a Mafia underboss who apparently answered to Charles "Lucky" Luciano. Di Cicco also became infamous for using his paramours as punching bags, including his wives Thelma Todd and Gloria Vanderbilt. After the latter endured repeated beatings, the Vanderbilt family apparently paid off Di Cicco to the tune of half a million dollars to keep him away from the young heiress.

Wilkerson and Broccoli would fall in and out of touch, sometimes not seeing each other for years at a time. After one such interval, a few days before Christmas 1947, Wilkerson stopped by a Christmas tree lot in Beverly Hills to buy a tree and found a disheveled, down-on-his-luck Broccoli working there. According to Broccoli, he told my father he wanted to get back into the film business. After the two had finished tying the tree to the roof of Wilkerson's Bentley, the publisher said, "Stop by my office."

Right after New Year's Day 1948, Broccoli recalled, he showed up in Wilkerson's office. My father picked up the phone and called one of his industry connections, and before he knew it, Broccoli was back working in the film business. By the early 1950s, he was a producer with his own production company based out of London, Warwick Films.

He enlisted Wilkerson's help again while preparing to shoot Warwick's first feature, *The Red Beret* (a.k.a. *Paratrooper*). Knowing that it couldn't get distribution without a top star, Broccoli set his sights on Alan Ladd, at the time one of the biggest box office draws. He asked the Hollywood Godfather to arrange an introduction. Wilkerson agreed, and Ladd was attached to star, but another hurdle came with his efforts to shoot the movie in color. By this point, Hollywood was well into the transition from black-and-white to color films, and the most widely used process was Technicolor. All the major studios had the film-processing giant booked solid, and without a firm commitment from Technicolor, Broccoli was sunk. Knowing how much Wilkerson despised film industry monopolies, he once again leaned on his old friend.

Instead of calling Technicolor through regular channels, my father contacted Dr. Herbert Kalmus, the inventor and owner of the process, and politely asked him to accommodate the young producer. Reportedly Kalmus told him they were booked solid for eighteen months, but in return, Wilkerson warned Kalmus that he faced the wrath of the publisher's pen if Technicolor continued to show favoritism to the majors. "That they were making no room for anyone else outside the studios was bad PR for Technicolor," Seward explained. It was a compelling argument; as Broccoli wrote in his autobiography, Kalmus "gave us the valuable commitment we needed."

As a token of their gratitude to Wilkerson for intervening, Broccoli told me, he and his Warwick Films partner Irving Allen bought the parking lot next to *The Reporter*, which Wilkerson had been renting, and handed him the deed.

In the early 1960s, the film producer again called Wilkerson. He knew of another producer named Harry Saltzman who had purchased the rights to a series of spy novels by English author Ian Fleming. Broccoli was convinced a film adaptation of the books could become a big success, but he was reluctant to enter into another partnership; Saltzman was apparently eager to take on a producing partner but lukewarm on the Bond project. Broccoli asked Wilkerson if the opportunity was worth pursuing.

My father asked one simple question: "What does it have?"

"Spies and girls," replied Broccoli.

"It'll be a hit," Wilkerson told him.

Broccoli entered into a partnership with Saltzman, and in 1962 they released *Dr. No*, the first James Bond film, which became an international sensation. The rest is, of course, history.

To the end of his life, Broccoli was long on praise and affection for Billy Wilkerson. In his autobiography, published posthumously two years after his death in 1996, he wrote that Wilkerson's "influence in the industry extended far beyond his power as the publisher of the *Hollywood Reporter*." The producer was less forthcoming, though, when it came to the indiscretions he may have performed on behalf of Wilkerson and others. Whatever they were, Broccoli, like many in Wilkerson's life, took his secrets to his grave.

Another of the highly placed friends whom Wilkerson called on to aid Cubby Broccoli's career over the years, and whom Broccoli in turn likely assisted with shady "favors," was film producer, business magnate, and celebrity aviator

Howard Hughes, who later became the head of RKO Pictures and the wealthiest man in the world. There is no record of exactly how Wilkerson and Hughes first met—Hughes was no fan of the track or all-night poker games—but an educated guess is that they met at one of Wilkerson's restaurants in the mid-1930s. Hughes became another of Wilkerson's closest friends and staunchest allies.

Hughes's leading-man looks and six-foot-four frame were diminished the moment he opened his mouth: he possessed a nasal speaking voice that some found grating. He had moved to Hollywood in 1927 with his new bride, Houston socialite Ella Rice, with the intention of making movies. His good looks and open checkbook quickly catapulted him onto Hollywood's A-list, and he wined and dined movie stars at the best tables in town, including Vendôme and Café Trocadero. But at heart he was a private person, and very few could claim to know him well. Wilkerson was one who could, and the two became confidantes. "Billy was a very, very good friend of Howard's," remembered Bautzer.

Like many great friendships, Hughes and Wilkerson's was symbiotic. Wilkerson had Hollywood at his fingertips, while the much younger Hughes, constantly on the lookout for promising talent, needed Wilkerson's industry know-how and inside information. "The motion picture industry was the basis for their relationship," Bautzer said.

Wilkerson, in turn, could count on Hughes's wealth to keep the *Reporter* afloat whenever an advertising shutdown or gambling shortfall threatened the company's survival. He would squeeze ads out of Hughes for the color processing plant the magnate owned, and later for the airline TWA, which Hughes assumed ownership of in 1939. In Wilkerson's times of greatest need, an infusion of up to $25,000 would arrive, usually in the form of a check for a year's worth of prepaid advertising in the *Reporter*. "That would shake *Daily Variety* up," Seward recalled, "because they never got a dime out of Hughes."

My father was possessive of the contributions his wealthy friend made toward the business, as star salesman Vic Enyart discovered when he sold Hughes a couple ad pages for his color processing plant. Wilkerson "wrote the check for the commission on the two pages," Enyart recalled. "In the early days, Billy wrote all the checks out himself." Wilkerson was about to hand the check to Enyart when he changed his mind. "No, I can't pay you commission on that," he told Enyart. "That's my account."

Naturally, the salesman protested. Wilkerson relented and turned the check over to Enyart, who ran out the back door, got into his car, and drove straight to the bank. There he discovered that Wilkerson had already stopped payment. A furious Enyart drove back to the office and quit. A few days later Wilkerson called him and told him he would give him another check. "So I went in," said Enyart, "Billy handed me another check, and I went back to work again."

As obstinate as Wilkerson could be to his employees, he was always deferential toward Hughes. Ever grateful to for the bailouts, beginning in 1936 he offered the aviator a standing invitation to vet any issue of the *Reporter* before it went to press. It was an arrangement Hughes himself had insisted on; he detested seeing anything about himself in print, even favorable editorials. As Seward explained, "Hughes was a publicity recluse. He got upset about anything we printed about him. He would go to any length to kill it." And that hatred of publicity led to him becoming an unofficial editor of the *Hollywood Reporter*.

First Hughes would telephone to ask whether there was anything about him in the paper that day. If he decided there was reason for concern, he would arrive at the pressroom around eight o'clock as the paper was being put to bed. "He was the only unauthorized personnel Mr. Wilkerson permitted in the pressroom," remembered Kennedy. He would appear at the pressroom entrance, always dressed in black—"Hughes was queer for black," the secretary observed. The pressmen had received strict instructions to hold the presses while Hughes reviewed the plates in search of references to himself. Tom Seward often spoke with Hughes during these nocturnal visits. "He was always very subtle," Seward recalled. "'How's everything,' he'd say. 'What's new? Any news?'"

Hughes also paid frequent visits to the publisher's Bel-Air residence, calling ahead to make sure Wilkerson wasn't entertaining company. According to Bautzer, sometimes Hughes called the Troc and told Wilkerson he wanted to stop by to see him for a minute. After the club closed for the night, the two would meet at the Bel-Air estate and talk until the early hours of the morning.

Even during the workday, my father might be interrupted by a phone call from Hughes, regardless of where he was or what he was doing at the time. Wilkerson could be enjoying a private screening at one of the studios only to receive a call from his friend. Hughes had memorized the number of every public phone in central Hollywood, so the publisher would hang up, stroll outside to a public phone, and wait for Hughes to call him back there. The two often chatted on the phone for more than two hours at a time.

According to Kennedy, Hughes sometimes called the office and blurted out something like "Meet me at the corner of Sunset and Gower at 3 AM." Hughes rarely slept, but because my father cherished routine, the prospect of having to stay awake past three o'clock in the morning for a meeting brought out the worst in him. "Mr. Wilkerson would hang up the phone with Hughes and wail, 'Oh, God, God, God, this fucking Hughes is nuts!'" Kennedy said.

"Hughes would always meet you at some corner under some sign or clock," Tom Seward recalled. "You'd wait there for hours and then he would come whizzing by in a 1924 Chevy. He was quite a character."

Sometimes he would ask my father to stand under the pylon of Crossroads of the World, the shopping mall a block from the *Reporter* offices, at 2:00 AM. Kennedy said my father often stood there chain-smoking for hours before Hughes's nondescript black Chevy sedan arrived. The driver, usually a new face, would drive halfway downtown, deposit my father in the middle of nowhere, then drive away. Thirty minutes later, an identical Chevy sedan would pull up and collect Wilkerson. This time Hughes would be in the driver's seat.

Often the two men drove and talked all night, and then Hughes would drive my father back to Crossroads of the World. Then my father drove home to shower, shave, and change his clothes. Without any sleep, he would be back at his desk by 9:00 AM.

At other times it wasn't my father's late-night company Hughes was interested in. The publisher would receive a call from his friend, who would confess that he was lonely and wanted to meet some girls. Knowing Hughes's tastes in the opposite sex, Wilkerson would find four or five well-endowed women eager to be "discovered," seat them at a special booth in one of his restaurants, and invite Hughes to stop by to inspect them. Hughes would sidle in through the back door to be seated where he could see his prospective dates without them being able to see him.

According to Seward, if the women met with Hughes's approval, the aviator would set them up in rented homes, which he visited regularly. During these trysts, he would usually request that the woman remove her bra, then sit and stare at her breasts for ten minutes before leaving. In return for indulging this peculiarity, the women were given a house to live in, a chauffeur-driven car, singing or acting lessons, and a budget for wardrobe and food. My father's calculation was in some ways similar to theirs: in exchange for Hughes's financial support, he was willing to oblige, even enable, his outlandish demands.

Eventually, another of the publisher's friends would take over the job of Hughes's main procurer of women. According to George Kennedy, one evening when Hollywood agent Walter Kane was down on his luck, he called Wilkerson and threatened suicide. Wilkerson immediately dispatched Kennedy and Joe Rivkin to Kane's apartment. They got there in the nick of time and removed the service revolver from his hand. Wilkerson then phoned Hughes, who was a mutual friend, and told the mogul that Kane needed a job. After that, Hughes employed the agent as his chief procurer. Kane would attempt to take his own life at least once more, in 1947; his suicide note expressed deep gratitude for Wilkerson's friendship—as well as that of Greg Bautzer, whom he unexpectedly named as his sole beneficiary. But Kane again survived, and ultimately proved himself so useful as Hughes's procurer that in the 1960s the magnate made him director of entertainment at the Sands Hotel in Las Vegas.

In many ways, Billy Wilkerson had less in common with Hughes than with another titan of American business, William Randolph Hearst. Both were known by their first two initials, "W.R." Both were newspaper bullies who stubbornly championed their pet causes. Both valued a good story, even if that story had to be manufactured. And although Wilkerson's news organ was a mere speck compared to Hearst's empire, Wilkerson and the publishing goliath shared a professional as well as personal relationship that would endure until Hearst's death in 1951. If a rivalry existed, they kept it between themselves.

In fact, Hearst's respect for Wilkerson went far beyond publishing. The newspaper tycoon sought Wilkerson's counsel on matters from movie stars to state taxes. Like Wilkerson, Hearst was ever the seer, and as early as 1935 he was predicting runaway film production (more films being produced out of state) because of restrictive California state taxes. On occasion, Wilkerson sat at the Hearst dinner table in San Simeon, California. Along with a dozen other guests, he would ride the bumpy private train up to Hearst's so-called castle and stay the weekend.

Despite the men's similarities, however, their personalities weren't entirely compatible. In private, Wilkerson made no secret of his loathing for the San Simeon trips. "Mr. Wilkerson said Hearst was a fussy man," said Kennedy. "Everything had to be just so." The host demanded that his guests rise early and participate in daily physical activity. No sportsman, Wilkerson employed elaborate subterfuges to avoid tennis games and long hikes. While Hearst and his other guests dashed off for a swim or to knock out a game of badminton, Wilkerson looked for hiding places until dinnertime. But he found even Hearst's dining arrangements challenging. Unless sitting poolside at home, Wilkerson would never serve guests hot dogs on paper plates with ketchup bottles in full view the way Hearst was apt to do.

Always the gracious host, my father could also be tremendously generous to his friends; Greg Bautzer called him "one of the most generous men I ever knew." For those who were beneficiaries, his largesse had a way of overshadowing his faults and defects.

He did, however, have a tendency to recycle presents. On occasion it got him into trouble, if he failed to remember who had given him the gift in the first place. Hotshot publicist Russell Birdwell once bought Wilkerson a stunning Steuben glass vase, but Wilkerson thought it so hideous, he ordered Kennedy to rewrap it. Unfortunately, when it came time to regift it, he returned it to Birdwell. "Billy, looks like we shop at the same store," Birdwell quipped.

And there was a dark flip side to his generosity as well. Once Wilkerson washed his hands of someone, whether associate, colleague, friend, or wife, that person was never the same. Think of Edith Gwynn, living the remainder of her life in the home she and her ex-husband had once shared. Misfortune awaited those who ended up on my father's bad side; he was just as eager to punish his enemies as reward his friends.

That's what syndicated columnist Sheilah Graham discovered after she took a swing at Café Trocadero in the January 6, 1936, issue of *Hollywood Today*, writing, "Not even the doubtful pleasure of rubbing elbows with Louis B. Mayer can compensate for the high prices charged for rather inferior food." While the slight against Mayer was greeted with radio silence from the studio boss's office, Wilkerson declared open season on Graham. The failure of the *London Reporter* a few months later only further stoked his resentment of the British-born Graham, and from then on he rarely missed an opportunity to attack her.

In fact, more than three years later when the columnist was on a lecture tour, Wilkerson phoned his Kansas City correspondent Jack Moffitt, asking him to cover Graham's lecture there. He then asked Moffitt to send him the notes via special delivery, and he incorporated them into a scathing editorial published on October 27, a few days after Graham returned to Los Angeles:

> The two junkets, headed by prominent motion-picture columnists, now visiting various key spots throughout the country—Louella Parsons and Sheilah Graham—are having a good and very bad effect on this picture business.
>
> Miss Parsons will, unquestionably, do the business good . . . she should be commended and thanked and helped. . . . But the case of Sheilah Graham is another thing altogether.
>
> Sheilah Graham got $200 for a one-night stand at the Kansas City Woman's Club. The studios could have paid her two thousand to stay in Hollywood, and made money. The lecture was a dirt-dishing session that left none of the movie mighty unsmeared. Even Shirley Temple and her mother were exposed as having their hair dyed in Sheilah's shellacking. The nocturnal pastimes of an adult star were hinted at with Groucho eyebrows and streamlined innuendo . . .
>
> Miss Graham's speaking tour was arranged by her newspaper syndicate, the North American Newspaper Alliance, which serves a very important group of newspapers through the U.S., each of which gets quite a bit of motion picture advertising. Hollywood, its players, producers, writers and directors should tell Miss Graham they won't countenance her further "dishing" to the ticket buyers on this "lecture tour" and the industry should remind her papers such "dishing" is NOT CRICKET.

According to Graham's son, Robert Westbrook, Graham had returned to Hollywood heady from her tour, but reading Wilkerson's editorial plunged her into a pit of despair. (She would insist in her autobiography *Beloved Infidel* that Moffitt had not even attended her lecture.) Clearly the article had hit its mark. "The woman who could dish out criticism," George Kennedy observed, "couldn't take it herself."

Reportedly Graham complained to her paramour, writer F. Scott Fitzgerald, who vowed to defend her honor. He raced to Schwab's drugstore, bought a copy of the *Reporter*, and after reading the piece, telephoned another literary giant, John O'Hara, and announced that he wished to challenge Wilkerson to a duel. "I want you to be my second," he allegedly told O'Hara. O'Hara refused to participate, trying to convince Fitzgerald that dueling was out of fashion, even illegal. Eventually Fitzgerald set off for the *Reporter* offices without him, asked the receptionist where Wilkerson's office was, and barged past her and up the stairs. There he found Kennedy at his desk. Fitzgerald shouted that he wanted to see Wilkerson. The frightened secretary told him the publisher wasn't in.

Fitzgerald pounded Kennedy's desk and insisted the secretary find him, that he would not leave until he did. Kennedy remembered that the writer's breath reeked of alcohol. (It was no secret in the literary world that Fitzgerald lived out of the bottle.) He closed his office door and phoned Wilkerson while the author paced outside in the hallway "like a caged tiger," as Kennedy put it. The secretary told Wilkerson what was going on and cautioned him not to return to the office. Wilkerson took the advice.

To humor Fitzgerald, Kennedy told him he had delivered the message and that his employer would be returning. For the next hour Fitzgerald paced outside the office, seething and continually asking what was taking so long. At last Fitzgerald stormed off ("presumably for his regular stool at the bar at nearby Musso's," as writer Cecilia Rasmussen put it) and the matter seems to have died down.

But Sheilah Graham had learned how dangerous it was to make an enemy of Billy Wilkerson. By all accounts Wilkerson was a loyal friend, but if he didn't like somebody, he saw to it that they were uncomfortable. "I think Billy lived by kind of a creed," said Bautzer. "'Never forget a friend, never forgive an enemy.' I think it could be summed up in that way. He really did live like that."

18 | THE STARMAKER AND LANA TURNER

IN ADDITION TO SERVING as a wish-maker and favor-granter for many in the movie industry, Wilkerson also had a knack for smoothing out the turbulent careers of Hollywood stars. Actors and actresses were under constant pressure to serve the studios' interests both at work and in their off hours, and when they had personal problems or needed career counseling, few of them felt comfortable going to their bosses for advice. "There wasn't anyone they could talk to," remembered MGM's Howard Strickling. "Marching into Louis [Mayer]'s office and asking for personal advice just wasn't done." Therapy was not yet a fashionable solution, so what was a star to do?

Many of them turned to Wilkerson for guidance. One performer who did so was James Cagney, by the mid-1930s a marquee name at top of his game but also well known as a hell-raiser. He'd been aptly dubbed "the Professional Againster" and frequently clashed with his boss, Jack Warner, over pay and studio demands. This led to the actor's being ejected from the studio on more than one occasion. Few studio heads worried about cutting talent loose in those days. "It didn't matter who they were," noted George Kennedy, "even if they were box office draws."

One day when Cagney was shown the studio gates, he immediately drove over to the *Reporter* offices. According to Kennedy, who witnessed the event from his office, the star of *Angels with Dirty Faces* realized he had gone too far with his Warner Bros. bosses, and he got down on his hands and knees in front of Wilkerson and sobbed into the publisher's pant cuffs, pleading with him to intervene on his behalf. He promised to behave in the future.

151

"Shame on you," Wilkerson admonished Cagney. "You're one of the studio's biggest grossers. You go back to work and be a good boy." Afterward Wilkerson phoned Jack Warner to tell him the actor had reformed, and Cagney was reinstated the following day.

Women in the industry, in particular, knew they could come to Billy Wilkerson with their troubles. He would listen to them instead of trying to trade favors for sex—something that set him apart from the studio moguls. While the bosses outwardly posed as high-minded, well-behaved gentlemen, they all made widespread use of the infamous casting couch. According to Tom Seward, who would briefly work for the studios in the 1940s, auditioning actresses were rated based on how compliant they were.

Twentieth Century Fox's production head, Darryl F. Zanuck, behaved particularly egregiously. Wilkerson knew Zanuck had constructed a small room adjoining his office, one that housed a single bed. According to those who knew him well, every afternoon at four thirty the production chief informed his staff that he would be out of the office; in fact he was "auditioning" actresses in his private room. Seward recalled that Harry Cohn at Columbia did much the same thing; before Cohn had sex with one of his girls, Seward said, he "opened her mouth with a pencil and inspected her teeth, like he was sizing up a horse."

Wilkerson did not engage in such sleazy encounters—though for a man who procured women for Howard Hughes, this could not have been simply a matter of moral integrity. Instead, it reflected the fact that my father was scrupulous about avoiding personal scandal. "He was careful about his image," Kennedy said. "He knew the value of credibility in his business." Though reckless at the racetrack and the poker table, he was delicate and careful in his sex life, and he never engaged in any extramarital affairs. His intentions may have been largely self-interested, but by drawing such a stark distinction between himself and the womanizing moguls, he gained the respect of the women who came to him for help.

"We [women] knew he would listen to us," said Lana Turner of the man who set her on the road from anonymity to superstardom. Indeed, my father's role as starmaker to Turner is probably the best illustration of his influential and complicated relationship with the women of Hollywood.

Most days at *Reporter* headquarters, according to George Kennedy, Wilkerson would give ten or twenty minutes of dictation, then mysteriously disappear from his office for half an hour. The rest of the staff believed that their employer was simply taking a break from his work; only Kennedy was aware that he was headed out for a specific purpose: to visit Currie's Ice Cream, a block away on the corner of Sunset and Highland, where he would scope out the young female patrons. Kennedy knew that his employer was addicted to looking at young girls, though he left it at looking.

Wilkerson had chosen an ideal spot for his pursuit. This Currie's location was known not only as a purveyor of mile-high ice cream cones but also as a popular hangout for the coeds of Hollywood High School, which was catty-corner across the street. Wilkerson wasn't alone in his admiration of the young ladies of Hollywood High. At 3:00 PM each day, Errol Flynn parked his convertible outside the school to stare at the teenage girls in their pleated skirts filtering out of the main doors. "Jailbait," he is said to have muttered under his breath. Wilkerson was, however, less conspicuous than the movie star, and he spent many happy days sitting at the counter of Currie's eyeing the girls.

One balmy January morning in 1937, not long before a break between classes across the street, Wilkerson strolled into Currie's, parked himself at one end of the counter, and ordered his requisite Coke. Five minutes after he sat down, the young women began drifting in. In a group of three coeds seated at the far end of the counter, he noticed one in particular, a young chestnut-haired girl. Decades later Wilkerson told my mother how stunning Lana Turner had looked that day. "She was magic," he said. "She had a quality all her own that was unforgettable."

Wilkerson motioned to the Currie's manager and nodded in Turner's direction, asking who the girl was. The manager told him she was a regular named Judy. When Wilkerson asked for an introduction, the manager approached Judy and gestured toward Wilkerson. In Turner's recollection, she was nervous, since she had cut her typing class. "At first I thought he was someone from the principal's office," Turner said when I interviewed her in 1974. When she inquired why he wanted to meet her, the manager told her it was OK, that he was the gentleman who owned the *Hollywood Reporter*. He was, the manager explained, a "very important man." Wilkerson walked over to her, produced his business card, and asked if she would like to be in pictures. Fifteen-year-old Judy Turner told him she'd have to ask her mother.

A few days later, young Judy arrived at the publisher's office with her mother, Mildred, in tow. The older woman told Wilkerson they wanted to take him up on his offer, and he gave them a letter of introduction to talent agent Zeppo Marx. In short order, Marx had asked director Mervyn LeRoy to order a screen test. When Wilkerson saw the test, his hunch was confirmed—Turner was magical onscreen. LeRoy had Judy change her name to Lana and in 1937 cast her in her first film, *They Won't Forget*. When Turner began to receive fan mail addressed to "the girl in the sweater," everyone knew that she had connected with the audience just as Wilkerson predicted she would.

"Billy could recognize people right away," remembered Harry Drucker. "Lana Turner. There's an answer for you. He went into a coffee shop, looked at her, and says, 'This girl's got something.' That's it. That's the way he did everything." From that moment, her world was forever changed. "There's no question that the most remarkable thing about Lana's career was her discovery," said Greg Bautzer. "It became the most important event in her life."

It was also a pivotal moment in the mythology of Hollywood, capturing the collective imagination like no superstar origin tale before or since. As Mervyn LeRoy put it, "Her discovery became the stuff of legend." It was the prototypical Hollywood Cinderella story, with my father's letter to Zeppo Marx serving as the glass slipper that transformed young Judy Turner's life. Almost overnight the myth that film stardom was reserved only for the elite few was shattered: if a schoolgirl just minding her own business, sipping a Coke at a counter, could be plucked from obscurity and catapulted into the celebrity firmament, it could happen to anyone.

Closer to home, the discovery had another unintended consequence. Hollywood high school girls stampeded to Currie's, eager to be discovered by the mysterious man who had found Lana Turner. School authorities were baffled as to why so many girls were cutting classes and swarming the ice cream parlor. When the owner of Currie's placed a metal plaque on the seat Turner had occupied on the morning of her discovery, the frenzy only increased. The manager even made the mistake of pointing out Wilkerson to the waiting girls. No longer able to discreetly observe them, he was ultimately forced to abandon his regular visits.

Nevertheless, Currie's quadrupled its business over the next few years, and by the early 1940s the owner closed his franchise and retired to Florida. With the original pilgrimage site gone, it left an opening for someone else to attract the latest crop of young wannabe actresses. At Schwab's Pharmacy, located more than a mile from Hollywood High, owner Leon Schwab began to claim that Turner had been sitting at *his* counter when she was discovered—not by Wilkerson but by Mervyn LeRoy. "Schwab's made a fortune because of that claim," Kennedy recalled. "Nobody cared it wasn't true." Turner herself joked about the publicity the claim garnered: "I should own stock in Schwab's!" But others marveled at the incoherence of the revisionist tale. "If Lana was, in fact, discovered at Schwab's" while attending school some twenty blocks away, said Joe Pasternak, "she must have been a hell of a sprinter."

Few bothered to dispute Schwab's story, and by the time I interviewed her in 1974 even Turner couldn't remember the name of the venue where she'd first met my father. In her autobiography *Lana: The Lady, the Legend, the Truth*, published eight years later, she mistakenly claimed that she'd been discovered at the Top Hat Café, a.k.a. Tops Café, midway down the block from Currie's. Not only was the Top Hat Café not on the corner of Sunset and Highland, where all those interviewed recalled the discovery taking place, but it also boasted higher-end fare that few schoolgirls would have been able to afford.

Though my father's discovery of Turner made Hollywood history, his support of her career didn't end there. The *Reporter* mentioned her regularly, with Wilkerson himself trumpeting her stunning debut: "This young lady has vivid beauty, personality and charm," he gushed. Tom Seward, who dated Turner when she was still a teenager, said, "We always gave Lana favorable coverage."

Greg Bautzer, too, dated the young starlet, and in 1938, when he was twenty-seven and she was only seventeen, the two were engaged to be married. Their relationship couldn't survive the attorney's womanizing ways— Turner once received a call from Joan Crawford, who insisted that Bautzer was planning to leave his fiancée for her—but they remained close to the end of their lives.

Turner and Wilkerson stayed close as well, and the actress always looked back with affection on my father's proposal that day in the ice cream parlor. As Turner put it, "Other people over the years have been attributed with saying those lines. But it was Billy who said them, which I think is even more enchanting. God knows where I'd have been if I hadn't been at that time and place where he saw me."

Over the years some suggested that Turner had traded sex for the opportunity Wilkerson offered her, but everyone I spoke to agreed that he did no such thing. "He never went to bed with her," said Joe Pasternak, who then echoed George Kennedy's claims about how deliberately he conducted his personal life: "Billy was always careful about his image." According to Turner herself, he shepherded her to fame and fortune without so much as a hint of impropriety.

But for the rest of his life, every one of Wilkerson's wives would quiz him about whether or not he slept with Turner. In 1951, even my mother asked if he had gone to bed with her. His answer was classic Wilkerson: "No, but everybody else did."

19 | "HE'LL BRING US ALL DOWN"

IRONICALLY, WHILE WILKERSON BEHAVED as a gentleman with Lana Turner, careful not to damage his reputation as an upstanding family man, his marriage to Billie Seward was already falling apart. The pair were married just over a year and a half when, at the beginning of May 1937, she moved into a fashionable hotel and filed for divorce, citing incompatibility. "We can't get along," she told Louella Parsons in an interview, "so I thought it best to part now rather than continue to quarrel."

Problems for the couple had begun early. While Billie was aware of her husband's belief that they would not be able to conceive, she soon began to pressure her husband to adopt. He refused, and Billie began to drink. Her public displays of inebriation embarrassed him, which only increased the tension between them.

Her petition for divorce also charged Wilkerson with mental cruelty. According to Billie, her husband was cold and aloof at home and barely spoke to her. At other times he overpowered her with his shouting fits. When he forbade her to see friends, she'd had enough. But just when it appeared the marriage was finished, the couple reconciled, and Billie dismissed her divorce action.

Meanwhile, another partnership that had begun with great promise was also giving way to discord. The shakedown scheme masterminded by Wilkerson, Joe Schenck, and Johnny Rosselli had been successfully siphoning money from the studios: $50,000 a year from each of the major players, and half that amount from the smaller companies. Even their front men in the Stagehands Union, George E. Brown and Willie Bioff, were pulling in $50,000 a year for themselves. But the more money Bioff collected for his bosses, the unhappier he grew with his share of the take. According to Tom Seward, Rosselli told the gangster in no uncertain terms that he must honor their initial agreement.

Unfortunately, Willie Bioff was not the sort of man to take no for an answer. While some in organized crime, such as Meyer Lansky, took great pains to divorce themselves from Mafia stereotypes, Bioff was in many ways a cartoon caricature of a gangster. Pudgy, fond of large white snap-brim fedoras and wide pinstripe suits, he had a tendency to show up unannounced, accompanied by two bodyguards who squired him around in bulletproof limousines, and barge into people's offices.

Incensed at being rebuffed and seeing an opportunity, Bioff decided to go into business for himself. In late 1936, he began to secretly shake down individuals who were not on the Hollywood Syndicate's approved list. One of these targets was Jules Brulatour, distributor of Eastman Kodak film stock. In a scene straight out of a gangster film, Bioff confronted Brulatour and threatened to blow up his warehouse if he didn't pay up. Brulatour turned the tables and suggested instead that Bioff become his "purchasing agent." Bioff agreed, and in turn began to force the studios to pay him a 7 percent commission on all raw film stock. Over a two-year period Bioff raked in $230,000 from the Brulatour swindle alone.

For Bioff, however, this still wasn't enough. Around the same time, he summoned film company executives including Albert Warner, the vice president and finance director of Warner Bros.; Austin Keogh, vice president of Paramount; Hugh Strong, head of personnel at 20th Century Fox; and Leo Spitz of RKO to Manhattan's Warwick Hotel and demanded that they collectively pay him $2 million to ensure that the workers he controlled stayed in line. Though many of the bigwigs balked, Bioff was ultimately successful in quadrupling the annual studio take from $50,000 to $200,000.

Initially, Wilkerson, Schenck, and Rosselli were oblivious to Bioff's behind-the-scenes maneuverings. He continued to faithfully deliver the agreed-upon take from each studio, which was all that Rosselli required of him. The rest went into the union boss's pocket. But Bioff's avarice was not sated, and as his overinflated sense of power grew, he realized there was one substantial source of income he hadn't yet tapped: the syndicate members themselves. Since Bioff also controlled the restaurant unions, he set his sights on Wilkerson's restaurant business—according to Seward, he demanded half of his gross receipts. Bioff "clearly overstepped his bounds," Greg Bautzer said. "It was a classic example of power going to his head." Wilkerson refused to accede to the shakedown, and Bioff seethed.

Meanwhile, Bioff was also shaking down the members of his own unions. In 1937 he and Browne levied a 2 percent assessment on all IATSE members' wages. In response, a band of IATSE members retained an attorney to look into racketeering in the motion picture trade unions. On November 12, 1937, California State Assembly Speaker William Moseley Jones convened a hearing into the matter. The first day's testimony was anything but civil. IATSE representatives lobbed accusations of fraud and violence at the union boss, while Bioff's lawyers countered that the dissident unionists were Communist agitators. The next day, November 13, just before the hearing reconvened and Bioff was scheduled to testify, the hearings were abruptly and mysteriously called off. It would be another two years before anyone offered an explanation as to why.

Wilkerson, too, resolved to fight back against his rogue agent, running a story in the *Reporter* that spotlighted the Stagehands Union's attempts to take over the Screen Actors Guild. In retaliation, a furious Bioff decided to hit Wilkerson where it hurt. By this point Wilkerson was no longer running Vendôme, but Café Trocadero remained one of the centerpieces of his empire. The gangster called for a strike that would shut down the Troc.

The four-star restaurant business is a delicate endeavor, and even the briefest shutdown can spell an establishment's demise. At the news that Bioff was prepared to shutter his restaurant, Wilkerson went ballistic. According to George Kennedy, my father told Rosselli, "You gotta holster this piece of shit. He'll bring us all down." He even went so far as to suggest that Bioff be rubbed out.

Rosselli explained that he wanted his underling dead just as much as Wilkerson did, but killing a chicken vendor turned union chief would have reverberations all the way to the White House. Bioff had become too well known to the studio heads, and if he were murdered, it would likely trigger an investigation that would lead back to the trio's doorstep. Wilkerson was furious, but he had no option but to negotiate a cease-fire.

RKO's Leo Spitz served as intermediary, arranging for Wilkerson and Bioff to meet at the Santa Monica home of film producer Pandro Berman. It was there that Bioff angrily denounced Rosselli. "All your friends that you have working for you to try and get this matter settled won't do you a damned bit of good," the mobster reportedly growled. "That fellow Rosselli contacted me. I will chase that bastard out of this town. Who does he think he is, making a plea for you or anyone else?" Bioff wanted to give the impression that *he* was in charge of the shakedown scheme, not his boss Rosselli, whom he'd grown to resent. He had no idea that the man to whom he was ranting had conspired with Handsome Johnny to set up the scheme in the first place.

The gangster went on to forcefully explain that he would shut down the Trocadero unless its owner began coughing up 50 percent of its profits. And he added a new demand. From that day on, Wilkerson must refrain from printing any stories in the *Reporter* about IATSE, good or bad.

Wilkerson was leaving for Europe on business the following day, so to buy time, he gave in to the mobster's demands. He humbly asked Bioff's permission to leave without worry that a strike would be called on his restaurant while he was away. In return, he promised that when he came back from Europe, Bioff would receive cash based on the restaurant's receipts. "You can go to Europe," said Bioff, "on condition that you issue instructions that nothing good or bad will be published about the labor relations in the studios or about the international unit." In exchange, he promised, "none of your boys will be interfered with."

My father left for Europe as planned, but before he departed, he issued a strict edict to his editorial staff to run nothing about the movie unions while he was gone. While abroad, Wilkerson attempted to soothe Bioff's hurt feelings, buying him lavish handkerchiefs monogrammed with his name and bottles of rare wine. For Christmas 1937, he sent him a basket of liquor. Unfortunately, the *Reporter* staff back home thwarted his efforts to keep the peace, running an unauthorized story about IATSE. When Wilkerson learned about it, he immediately sent the labor boss a conciliatory telegram:

> For whatever mistake I have made I stand willing to do anything you dictate. I realize that it was an unfortunate set of circumstances occasioned by a new man at the news desk and a new man covering the union beat that the story got through. There was no intention not to take care of you as you have of me.
>
> Billy Wilkerson

But Wilkerson's efforts failed to pacify his enemy. One afternoon as Tom Seward was preparing to open the Troc for the evening, he was accosted by a giant of a man. According to Seward, the man's name was John M. Sargent, and he worked for Bioff as a representative of the cook's union in Los Angeles. Sargent threatened that if Wilkerson didn't comply with Bioff's demands, he would make the Troc's cooks walk.

Eventually, my father realized he had no choice but to play ball. From that point on, Bioff would appear at the *Reporter* offices at least once a month to collect envelopes of cash, his share of Wilkerson's restaurant profits. Kennedy estimated that each envelope contained as much as $20,000 in $1,000 bills—a staggering take, but probably not the 50 percent the gangster had demanded. According to the secretary, Bioff never asked for a paper accounting, and my father had the sense that the greedy labor boss was happy enough with his fat envelopes.

Even so, never content with the last scam, Bioff had also begun shaking down Joe Schenck. In November 1937 he'd planned to go after another name on the syndicate's no-go list, Harry Cohn and Columbia Pictures, but just as he was about to call a strike against Columbia, he had a sudden change of heart and decided instead to first go after Schenck and 20th Century Fox. Bioff had learned through an unknown informant of the private poker games held at Schenck's home. There the buy-in was $25,000 and as much as $200,000 was in play at any given time. The union boss also learned that Schenck kept a stockpile of cash, his "bank," hidden in a safe somewhere in his house—usually in the form of $1,000, $5,000, and $10,000 bills for his weekly games. Schenck's empire had far more meat on its bones than Wilkerson's, and that ignited Bioff's hunger.

In January 1938 he began to demand monthly payoffs of $100,000 from the film tycoon, accompanied by his standard threat: if Schenck failed to cough up, Bioff would issue an all-out strike against 20th Century Fox. Schenck, like Wilkerson, pleaded with Rosselli to do something, but again Rosselli argued that eliminating Bioff would put them all on law enforcement's radar screen. He assured his two partners that he was actively "taking care of the problem."

In private meetings with Wilkerson, Schenck expressed his doubts about Rosselli. He suspected that their partner was splitting the take that Bioff filched from the two of them. But Wilkerson insisted, "He wouldn't do that." Regardless, the irony was hard to miss: the men who'd dreamed up the Hollywood shake-down were now being shaken down themselves.

———————————

It was perhaps this bitter irony that prompted Wilkerson to get out of the restaurant business for the time being. After all, Bioff couldn't steal his Trocadero profits if he no longer owned the Trocadero. It's also possible, however, that Wilkerson was simply bored with the Troc; once a project reached its zenith, his interest almost always evaporated.

"Billy was a perfectionist," remembered Joe Pasternak. "Like I said in my book, once he attained perfection, he lost interest. One time he sold one of his restaurants right out of the blue, just like that, and I said, 'Willy, why did you do that?' He said, 'I'm bored with it.'" However, he had tried to maintain his interest in the Trocadero, remodeling the club three times at a cost of $271,000. At one point he hired Universal Pictures art director John Harkrider, who remodeled the club in black with neon, which *Time* described as "looking just like the inside of a Fridgidaire."

By 1938, however, Wilkerson was eager to rid himself of the Troc in the fastest way possible. He turned to one of his business associates, Gambling Syndicate member Nola Hahn. In addition to rigging games of chance, Hahn possessed a second unique skill: arson. He suggested that if Wilkerson wanted to quickly rid himself of the Troc, he could arrange an innocuous kitchen fire. In the aftermath, provided the club's insurance policy was up to date, Wilkerson could pocket the insurance money and sell off the club.

We don't know the month, but sometime in 1938 a fire gutted the Trocadero's kitchen. Although sheriffs investigated, it seems Hahn did his job well—perhaps too well. Nothing came of the investigation, but forever after, Wilkerson was haunted by the implications of Hahn's crime. If he could torch the Troc so easily and get away scot-free, how easily could he reduce the *Reporter* to ashes if Wilkerson ever got on his bad side? That same year he began to keep a complete set of *Reporter* printing plates and Linotype logos in a cardboard box at his home, stashed on the top shelf of his linen closet. He reasoned that even if he lost his factory and printing presses, armed with the plates and logos, he could put out his paper anywhere.

Later in the year, Wilkerson collected the insurance money and sold what was left of Café Trocadero to Nola Hahn for $268,000. But he secured one final condition of sale: Wilkerson's family and his guests could dine free at the club anytime. In addition, upon request, both food and beverages had to be delivered to his house and to his mother's home. Hahn imported the rest of the Gambling Syndicate to reopen the club with the intention of using it as a gambling den. Since Tom Seward owned a 20 percent stake in the Troc and had managed the club under Wilkerson's tenure, the Clover Club boys mandated that Seward resume those responsibilities for them. Petrified of gangsters, Seward not only refused their generous offer but gladly surrendered his 20 percent share without payment.

The club would continue under new management into the 1940s, but without Billy Wilkerson it wouldn't be the same. During his reign, some Hollywood historians contend, it had been not only the most successful nightclub of the Depression era but also the greatest. Even Wilkerson's own subsequent ventures, luxurious and successful as they might become, could never match the Troc's splendor—or its fame.

It was a year of endings for my father. Just months after he and Billie decided to give their marriage another shot, they separated for the last time. On May 9, 1938, their divorce was final.

Many years later Billie admitted that she and her husband were simply not a good fit; Billy had been much older than her, and hadn't accommodated her need to go out and have fun. She also told her brother, Tom, that when it came to sex, Wilkerson was strictly a missionary man. "Hop on and hop off whenever he wanted to," she said. But her simplest confession was also the most devastating: though she had admired and respected him, she said, she had never really loved him.

20 | WOMEN AND MARRIAGE

AS BILLY WILKERSON'S THIRD MARRIAGE reached its end, he retreated into a ritual he would follow for all of his divorces from this point on. He hid out at his office while an envoy, either Tom Seward or George Kennedy, supervised his spouse's departure from the Bel-Air estate. Kennedy remembers standing sentry over the years as one wife after another solemnly packed up. "I checked them in," he said, "and I checked them out." The publisher would remain in hiding until his envoy called him with the news that the withdrawal was complete.

Though my father and Edith Gwynn had fought bitterly over their divorce settlement, he did not ask Billie or any of his subsequent wives to sign a pre-nuptial agreement. Even so, he ended up paying them very little alimony. As Kennedy explained, "He was tough, and he had a good lawyer"—referring to Greg Bautzer.

And when my father was between marriages, Bautzer, the legendary ladies' man, served as his partner in debauchery. The lawyer would frequently room with Wilkerson in his Bel-Air mansion, and, as Kennedy recalls, the two happy bachelors "really swung through the trees."

Though faithful as a married man, as a divorcé Wilkerson let his libido run wild. "All Billy wanted was to get laid between marriages," said Joe Pasternak. (Pasternak also remembered him as "an ass man.") He would have had ample opportunity at his friend Joe Schenck's second home in Santa Monica. While Schenck used his home in Beverly Hills to entertain business associates and host his famous high-stakes poker games, his beachfront retreat on the Pacific

Coast Highway in Santa Monica was reserved for select male friends, Wilkerson included. There, decades before Hugh Hefner established the Playboy Mansion, the movie mogul supplied his guests with a bevy of young starlets.

Wilkerson would also retreat to Paris, accompanied by his friend Vic Orsatti. "If he didn't love America so much," Seward mused, "he would have lived in Paris, I think." But on his trips with Orsatti, Seward said, the agent was there for a particular purpose: it was Orsatti's job to line up all the bordellos the two bachelors would haunt. Wilkerson implicitly trusted Orsatti's instincts regarding the opposite sex. After all, he had introduced the publisher to Billie Seward, and over the years he would marry three beauties himself: actress June Lang, singer/actress Marie "the Body" McDonald, and model/actress Dolores Donlon. So when Wilkerson's marriage ended in 1938, he and Orsatti traipsed through the French capital, getting lost for days in its houses of ill repute.

During the 1930s and '40s, Paris was known for its themed brothels, and one of Wilkerson's favorites was an actual Pullman railcar transplanted inside a building, complete with the original sleeper compartments. Stewards dressed as conductors scurried down the aisles bearing trays of gourmet salmon and bottles of Dom Pérignon. Completing the illusion was an ingenious suspension device that rocked the carriage from side to side, simulating a train racing through the night.

Once the Paris bordello-hopping sated his sexual appetites and he returned to American soil, Wilkerson once again felt the urge to settle down. Like so many powerful men of his generation, he did not like being alone and was anxious to ensure that there was a woman waiting for him at home. And this meant taking another wife, since the morals of the time prohibited unmarried couples from cohabitating. As Bautzer put it, "In those days people didn't live together. That was unthinkable. You met them and married them. It wasn't like it is now."

But friends noted Wilkerson's pattern of jumping in and out of married life, and they urged him to rethink this approach. As Joe Pasternak explained, "Whenever he was seeing a girl, I would say," 'Billy, live with her, don't get married,' and he would say, 'I won't.' And then a couple of days later he would go up to Vegas and get married."

According to Joe Rivkin, whenever a woman took his fancy, a metamorphosis overtook him, and he pursued her with a vengeance. Romantic courtships were a Wilkerson specialty. Weeks of candlelit dinners followed by extravagant gifts found his victims falling helplessly under his spell. "He could turn on the charm like nobody you've ever seen," recalled Tom Seward. "He would move straight in for the kill like a Bengal tiger. It was truly fantastic to watch."

He met most of his prospective mates at his clubs and restaurants, but it remains unclear how and where he first encountered his next wife, the young model Estelle Jackson Brown, or "Brownie." They first became acquainted in mid-October 1939. As usual my father launched a whirlwind courtship, and the couple eloped to Las Vegas on December 12. Despite his staunch Catholicism, the publisher would never have a church wedding; Rivkin remembered that "the best it ever got was running away to Mexico or Las Vegas to a justice of the peace." This was unsurprising, however, given the Church's hostility toward divorce.

Soon after Billy and Brownie tied the knot, he reverted to his unromantic, withdrawn, moody persona. And Brownie certainly hadn't bargained for his combustible temper and demonic rages. "He was a very abrasive, impatient man," she recalled. All his wives experienced the same pattern; my mother's sister, Gloria O'Connor, would later remember my father as "'a bitter, nasty old man." It seemed that once the honeymoon was over—a period that usually lasted from a year to eighteen months—the man who lived for challenges quickly lost interest. "Even success bored him," commented my father's former brother-in-law Tom Seward. "This is certainly true of Billy's marriages."

Despite the lack of romance and attention, he saw his wives as his private property, demanding that they be in attendance when he returned home from work. They were required to play cards with him, mostly gin rummy, before dinner. Some of the women were excellent card players, and if their husband was on a losing streak, he accused them of cheating and banished them from the room and the game. According to all his wives, home life quickly degenerated into Billy sitting in his den for hours, either playing cards, reading the paper, or watching a ballgame or fight on TV. When he had to attend a social event, his wife was expected to play the role of escort. He and Brownie would travel to and from such events in a bulletproof Cadillac limousine, which he had ordered especially for himself and his fourth wife.

Other purchases were more personal. Usually after he had either berated or ignored his wife, Wilkerson would drive to the jewelry store and buy her an expensive bauble as a peace offering. (In later years, his preferred supplier

The signed 1958 studio portrait of my father found next to George Kennedy's body after his suicide. The inscription reads, "To George, with my affection, W. R. Wilkerson."

LEFT: Photo of Billy's father, William "Big Dick" Wilkerson Sr., taken from his Senate campaign button, circa 1904. RIGHT: Billy's mother, Mary Wilkerson, with a picture of her son, 1939.

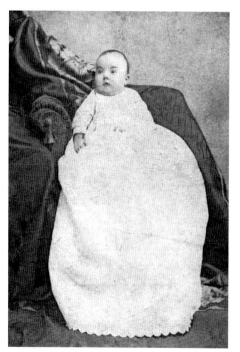

LEFT: The earliest known photo of Billy Wilkerson, a copperplate image taken when he was nine months old, Nashville, 1891. RIGHT: Billy at Mount St. Mary's Prep School, 1906.

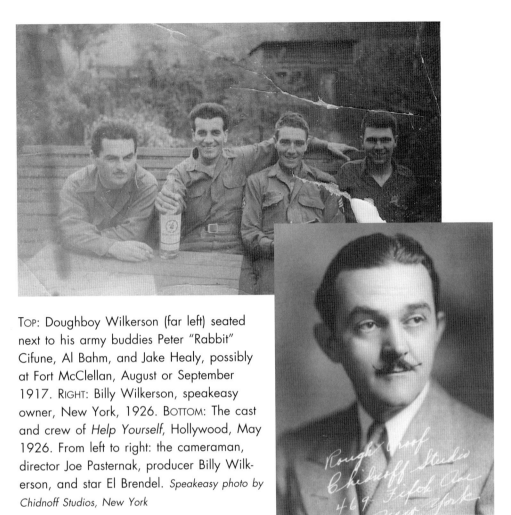

TOP: Doughboy Wilkerson (far left) seated next to his army buddies Peter "Rabbit" Cifune, Al Bahm, and Jake Healy, possibly at Fort McClellan, August or September 1917. RIGHT: Billy Wilkerson, speakeasy owner, New York, 1926. BOTTOM: The cast and crew of *Help Yourself*, Hollywood, May 1926. From left to right: the cameraman, director Joe Pasternak, producer Billy Wilkerson, and star El Brendel. *Speakeasy photo by Chidnoff Studios, New York*

THE Hollywood DAILY REPORTER

Vol. 1, No. 1   TODAY'S FILM NEWS TODAY   Wednesday, Sept. 3, 1930

INDIE REVOLUTION

TRADEVIEWS
by w. r. wilkerson

Here it is — we've been talking about it for weeks. What do you think of it? Going to give you all the news each day of the week. Not Hollywood chatter, but the news of the entire industry. On Saturdays (with the exception of Sept. 6th and 13th) the weekly takes the place of the daily. It will be an exhibitor proposition out and out. Unbiased reviews, plenty of exploitation, news and reports on equipment . . . everything to help the theatre owner and manager. If you like it tell us . . . and if you don't tell us. We want to know how it hits you.

•

Retrenchment in every corner seems to be the order of the day. Every studio affected. Theatre chains in a panic trying to make ends meet. Bankers yelling for a cut. Everyone gives a different answer. Terrific heat. Unemployment. Tom Thumb Golf. There is only one real answer. Poor pictures. Spot any house with a good attraction and you will not hear any excuses. Sound came too fast. The money rolling in caused producers to think they had the right formula. Wasn't so. That was curiosity money.

•

They are still saying that Franklin will go to New York to stay. We think if H.B. has his own say he will stay parked in L.A. Wouldn't you if your last year's check ran to better than $300,000 and were sitting back of the best theatre organization in the land? Why bring on new grief?

•

That old percentage thing is here. Exhibitors are squawking. Not about the percentage but the percentage with a guarantee. They're asking if they want percentage why not make it just that and not rope them with a guarantee along with it.

•

The word is around that Harry Sherman has a great picture in "Today." Bill Nigh directed and it is one of those rare things — an independent production.

•

The boys say there will be another squad given the air at the Fox studios in a day or two.

Schlessinger Backing Combination to Produce Features and Shorts with Guaranteed World Outlet
(Exclusive)

M.A. Schlessinger, the most powerful single individual in the motion picture industry who recently won the sound patent suit against Western Electric; owner of the DeForrest patents for sound; with his brother "I.W." controlling more theatres throughout the world than any other individual; head of the so-called South African Trust; producer and distributor of pictures throughout Europe, Asia, Australia and South Africa, tossed his hat in the ring of production and distribution of pictures in America on his arrival in Hollywood last week, thereby causing almost a revolution.

Schlessinger has called together every important independent maker of pictures and unfurled a plan for production and distribution of pictures that has left the indie producers

(Continued on Page 7)

PARAMOUNT ENTERS PHILA

Philadelphia. — Paramount-Publix took the first step yesterday in what may prove to be a major contest with the Warner interests, when it entered the Philadelphia territory with the acquisition of the local B. F. Keith house.

The theatre is to be operated on a de luxe first-run policy, in direct opposition to the Stanley-Warner house. Warners have previously been in complete control of the Philadelphia field, with Paramount-Publix following a hands-off course.

The B.F. Keith house has been obtained on a year's lease.

Hungary Kills Kontingent

Prague.— Hungary is stepping away from forms and customs of other Central European nations by doing away with its kontingent altogether and reducing duties.

The new rates are $375 for import certificates for sound films of more than 1500 metres and $157 for short films of less than 400 metres. There will be a supplementary charge of .07 per metre on sound films in addition to the above.

Milestone To Join Columbia

Lewis Milestone's next directorial effort will carry the Columbia label.

"Millie" has come to an understanding with the Columbia crowd after waiting months for Universal to take up their verbal option on his services for another after "All Quiet on the Western Front."

Big Three "Muscles In" With Old Percentage Gag

The big producing and releasing companies are finally to crash theatres with a percentage proposition for the exhibition of their product.

For years every argument on the sale of a picture finally reached the stage where the film salesman chimed in, "Will you play percentage?" and with that remark the exhibitor closed his desk for the night and bid the salesmen goodby. But if they are to run the product of the big three, Metro, Paramount and Fox, the coming year, they will have to play at least ten pictures on a percentage that will net the producer 25 percent.

The new contract from Metro, Paramount and Fox contains a clause for a flat percentage of 25 percent of the gross taken in by the house plus a minimum guarantee on at least ten pictures.

PAPERS TO BAN FILM PUBLICITY

Starting January 1, 1931, something like eight thousand newspapers throughout the country will ban movie press copy, or else charge for it by the line, if producers want it printed.

The N.E.A. has already voted to ban all free press matter. The Massachusetts Press Association has followed suit, and the edict affects all advertising agencies as well as movie space grabbers.

The News Associations contend that entirely too much gratis space has been given away, and further that enough publicity is sent via mail from Hollywood every week to fill the columns of all the papers in the associations.

Grainger Here Today

James R. Grainger, in charge of sales for Fox, arrives in Hollywood today from New York to look over Coast production. Grainger expects to stay in California two weeks before returning to the East.

Harley Clark Sees General Improvement

Showing assets of $30,444,121 and liabilities of $12,229,245, Fox Film's current report for June denotes a general financial improvement for the company, it is announced by President Harley L. Clarke.

In December, 1929, the current assets were $23,408,565.

The first issue of the *Hollywood Reporter*, September 3, 1930.

LEFT: Wilkerson with his editorial staff, Hollywood, 1936. RIGHT: Wilkerson's personal secretary, George Kennedy, shown here from his time in the service during World War II.

LEFT: *Hollywood Reporter* front page memorializing MGM's Irving Thalberg, with whom Wilkerson had a warm relationship, September 15, 1936. RIGHT: Hollywood Syndicate heads Billy Wilkerson and Joseph Schenck (center), head of 20th Century Fox, with Wilkerson's longtime attorney, Greg Bautzer, Hollywood, 1956.

As eager lunch patrons await entry to Vendôme, Wilkerson (left) dons a white waiter's coat and directs deliveries of food, Hollywood, 1933.

The Café Trocadero, Hollywood, 1934.

The Troc's main dining room, including a view of the bandstand, 1934.

The Hollywood Godfather has a long night at the Troc, 1934.

 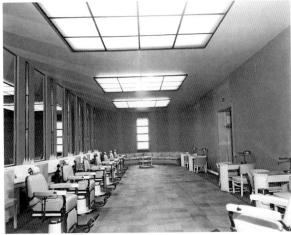

LEFT: Sunset House barbershop and haberdashery, Hollywood, 1936. RIGHT: The Sunset House barbershop, 1936.

LEFT: Ciro's front entrance, Hollywood, 1940. RIGHT: Ciro's main dining room, 1940.

LEFT: Restaurant LaRue main dining room, 1948. RIGHT: Restaurant LaRue, surrounded by a massive mudslide, Hollywood, 1950.

L'Aiglon's private dining room.

Aerial view of the partially completed Flamingo Hotel, Las Vegas, 1946. *UNLV Special Collections, Susan Jarvis, curator*

LEFT: Benjamin "Bugsy" Siegel's last photo, June 20, 1947. RIGHT: Wilkerson's bullet-proof 1939 Cadillac limousine—one of the many armor-plated vehicles he used for fear of suffering a similar fate.

Wilkerson hobnobs with Cary Grant at the Café Trocadero, 1936.

Godfather Wilkerson with Frank Sinatra, Hollywood, circa 1955.

Wilkerson presents a trophy to Marilyn Monroe on behalf of the citizens of Canton, Ohio, April 18, 1954.

Billy Wilkerson, best man at the wedding of Lana Turner and Bob Topping, with Mildred, mother of the bride, Bel-Air, 1948.

Billy and Helen Wilkerson at Lake Saranac, New York, 1912.

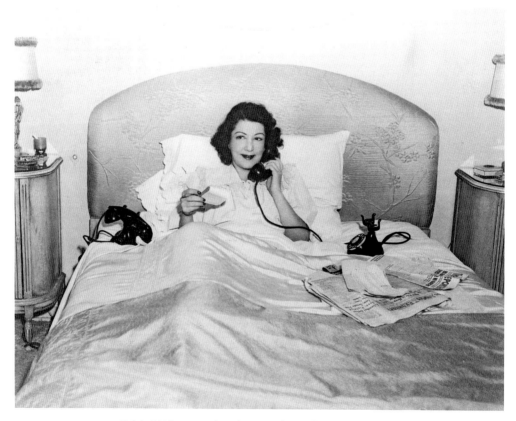

Edith Wilkerson, hard at work, Hollywood, 1932.

LEFT: Billie and Billy Wilkerson at Los Angeles Municipal Airport, 1935. RIGHT: Billy and Brownie Wilkerson on their way to their honeymoon, December 1939.

ABOVE: Billy and Vivian in Mexico City, 1946. LEFT: Billy and my mother, Tichi, in Cannes, France, 1952.

The Wilkerson mansion in Bel-Air, 1935. This view from the upper veranda shows the west lawn, bathhouses, swimming pool, and tennis court, and the open spaces beyond. *Photo by Fred R. Dapprich*

My father and mother at my birth, Santa Monica, 1951.

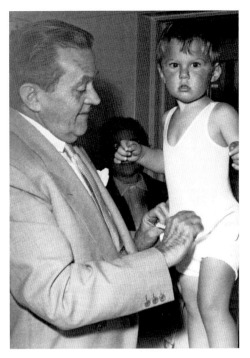

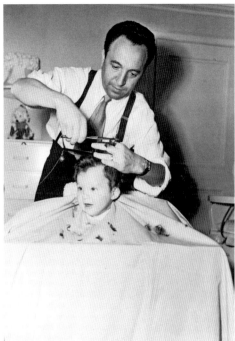

LEFT: My father and I, Bel-Air, 1953. RIGHT: I get my first haircut from Mafia barber Harry Drucker, Bel-Air, 1952. *Haircut photo by Alex Paal*

My sister, Cindy, and I at Howard Strickling's turkey ranch in Chino, California, 1957. *Photo by Howard Strickling*

Wilkerson whispers to his poodle Pee-Pee, Bel-Air, 1959. *Photo by Alex Paal*

My 1962 school photo, showing the uniform I was wearing when I saluted my father's empty bed after he passed away.

would be Ruser Jewels in Beverly Hills.) According to Kennedy, once they received the gift, all was forgotten; as he put it, "It was like a magic tonic." Just how much verbal abuse or neglect a wife had received was usually measured by the amount of jewelry the publisher showered her with. But neither Brownie nor her successors would garner the number of tributes a previous wife had amassed. "Edith got the biggest haul," Kennedy remembered.

Billy Wilkerson may not have been an ideal husband, but he was still a faithful one, continuing to abstain from any extramarital affairs. When he felt the need to escape from his domestic life, he turned instead to gambling, or he buried himself in his business endeavors. Kennedy, who saw multiple wives come and go, noted, "He simply gave it all at the office." Or, as Edith Gwynn put it to *Time* in 1944, "Y'know, Billy's real mistress is his work."

21 | JOE SCHENCK AND THE ARROWHEAD SPRINGS HOTEL

OVER THE COURSE OF 1939, as Billy Wilkerson went from swinging divorcé to devoted suitor and back to moody married man, he was also wrestling with big changes to his business empire. With Willie Bioff shaking him down, he'd sold Café Trocadero to Nola Hahn, and now his stake in Hahn's other clubs was also under threat. That's because, in January 1939, Earl Warren became California's new attorney general, and began to make good on his campaign promise to crack down on vice across the state. Warren's ascension marked the end of that magical period in Hollywood history when all the key ingredients were in place for businesses such as Wilkerson's to succeed: gambling, prostitution, fine dining, and superb entertainment. Immediately experiencing a dip in business, he began searching for new ventures.

His friend Joe Schenck, meanwhile, was in even more dire straits. The mogul continued making monthly payoffs to Bioff to avoid union action against 20th Century Fox, and the gangster insisted on receiving the money in cash. Schenck was increasingly finding this demand to be a burden. "Paying out a hundred g's in cash at a time," said George Kennedy, "that's huge money."

In early 1939 Schenck decided it was up to him to put an end to the financial plundering. One month, he presented Bioff with a Fox company check for $100,000, explaining that he had no cash on hand. Though the gangster expressed outrage, Schenck trusted his instinct that Bioff's greed would override his hesitation; he explained that Bioff could take the check now, or wait a week or two for him to round up the cash. Schenck's bet paid off: an incensed Bioff stuffed Schenck's check into his pocket and stormed out. The mogul understood that if Bioff deposited the check, it would be all the evidence the authorities needed to bring the gangster down. Of course, he knew he was also taking a risk—if the authorities began investigating Bioff, they might also discover that Schenck, Wilkerson, and Rosselli were the heads of the Hollywood Syndicate. Still, with his partners refusing to rock the boat, the studio head decided it had to be done.

The impatient union boss banked the company check, and when he did, Schenck immediately contacted federal authorities and proposed a deal. In exchange for his cooperation, he wanted no charges brought against him, and he wanted his role as informant kept confidential. He told the feds that he had been the victim of an extortion plot and had paid a bribe to Bioff to stop a strike against his studio. He described the payoff as a "loan" to the gangster, while Bioff would claim it was a commission check for Eastman Kodak film stock. To get to the truth, the FBI launched an in-depth investigation.

Wilkerson learned about the investigation and the check that had spawned it not from Schenck but from a connection inside the FBI, Agent Frank Angell. Angell, a young G-man who had begun his career in the Los Angeles Bureau in 1930, was awed by Hollywood glamour, movie stars, and the restaurants and nightclubs that peppered Dreamland. He was a devout Catholic, a parishioner of the same Blessed Sacrament Church that Wilkerson attended. Angell knew he would find Wilkerson every Sunday kneeling in a pew close to the altar, and he stalked the publisher at Sunday Mass, hoping for a meeting. When they failed to connect, he struck up a friendship with George Kennedy, who was also a Catholic and attended morning services five days a week. Not long after they met, Frank Angell and George Kennedy began attending morning Mass together and breakfasting afterward.

It was Kennedy who introduced the agent to Wilkerson. Having realized that his entanglements with organized crime left him vulnerable, the publisher jumped at the chance to connect with someone in federal law enforcement. "Billy was a smart man," said Harry Drucker. "A smart man covers all his bases." Angell was unaware of Wilkerson's criminal associates, and neither Rosselli nor Schenck knew about Angell. But the publisher knew just how to win the young agent's support. "FBI agents didn't make any money," Kennedy explained. "Frank was dazzled by Mr. Wilkerson's generosity."

When Angell informed Wilkerson of Schenck's exposure, the publisher blew a gasket. He called a meeting of the Hollywood Syndicate heads at Schenck's home in Beverly Hills, and there Wilkerson and Rosselli berated Schenck for his stupidity in not paying in cash. Why on earth had Schenck not consulted them first? Schenck contritely admitted to writing the check, but stressed that he had felt compelled to take matters into his own hands. What was immediately apparent to all three was that now that the FBI had opened an investigation into Bioff's activities, their original shakedown scheme was also in danger of being discovered.

Sacramento County district attorney Otis D. Babcock also learned of the FBI investigation, and it became a subject of the grand jury probe he convened to investigate alleged corruption in the California legislature. On April 4, 1939, the grand jury disclosed that two years earlier, when California State Assembly Speaker William Moseley Jones launched and then mysteriously canceled the inquiry into Bioff's shakedown of his own union members, Jones's law firm had received a payment of $5,000 from IATSE. In retrospect, the legal retainer looked a lot like a bribe. The Sacramento grand jury also learned about the $100,000 Joseph Schenck had paid to Willie Bioff, and it duly subpoenaed the mogul. When lawyers questioned him on the record about the check, the movie chairman again characterized the payment as a "loan," but left out the additional details about an extortion plot that he'd provided to the feds on condition of anonymity, which only fueled the grand jury's suspicions.

As the investigations continued, Schenck and Wilkerson met again at Schenck's home to discuss the options. The normally jovial Schenck worried that even if he testified under oath that he had been a mere pawn, a victim of extortion, as he'd told the feds he was willing to do, they could still charge him with bribing a union leader—a felony. Wilkerson began to grow paranoid about his own exposure, questioning Rosselli's promise that he would not do jail time. He apparently even broached the idea that they could both come clean, turning state's evidence against their coconspirators. For now, however, they chose to bide their time and see what the investigation would turn up.

As they waited for the other shoe to drop, Schenck also enlisted Wilkerson's help with a more conventional business dilemma. Along with William Paley, head of the CBS radio network (and later the architect of the network's early television success), Schenck had recently purchased and was in the process of completely rebuilding the Arrowhead Springs Hotel in San Bernardino, California. In the days before freeways, the property was a remote mountain resort more than three hours from Hollywood. It had been losing money for years, but the new owners hoped to turn its fortunes around with an injection of Tinseltown luxury. Schenck asked Wilkerson, who'd had so much success with exactly these sorts of efforts, to join the project as consulting manager.

My father was skeptical. To him the prospects of the Arrowhead Springs seemed limited, and most of his friends and business associates agreed. Little about the place seemed enticing, particularly since it was so far away.

But Wilkerson felt an obligation to his friend Schenck and decided to accept the offer—on one condition. So that he would be in a position to make all decisions necessary to make the renovation a success, he wanted to lease the hotel with an option to buy. He also suggested a time limit of one year; if, at the end of that span, he'd successfully revived the Arrowhead Springs, he could purchase it from Schenck and Paley. Eager to see their business succeed, the two men accepted Wilkerson's terms, and in October 1939 Wilkerson leased the building.

The new lessee began by bringing in the finest restaurant staff he could import from Hollywood. He also upgraded the menu—though, alas, the specifics remain a mystery, as does so much about the operation of the resort. What is known is that on December 16, 1939, the new Springs opened with a celebrity-packed gala, which Tom Seward remembered as "beyond successful."

The gala put the Arrowhead Springs on the Hollywood map, and Wilkerson followed it up with a whole string of similar events. He advertised heavily, extolling the six-story mountain resort's scenic virtues and the chilled champagne that awaited visitors, and Paley and Schenck were awed as they watched patrons flowing through the doors.

———————

Schenck could only do so much celebrating, however. Back in Los Angeles, around the same time as the Arrowhead Springs reopening, a federal grand jury launched an investigation into racketeering, restraint of trade, and particularly income tax evasion in the film industry. Schenck was again called before the grand jury to explain his $100,000 "loan" to Bioff. This time he testified that he had been the victim of extortion, vulnerable because he'd been eager to avert a strike by the Stagehands Union. The members of the grand jury didn't buy it—to them the check was irrefutable evidence of collusion between the studios and the unions.

What's more, prosecutors, with the help of the IRS, had discovered that the mogul had never paid taxes on his massive gambling profits. Alf Oftedal, the lead prosecutor in the case, was intelligent enough to realize that once Willie Bioff's thuggish tactics were put on display before a jury, it would be easy for them to see Schenck as a helpless victim of the gangster's schemes and find him not guilty. By charging him with tax evasion, Oftedal was confident Schenck would agree to a plea bargain. So in early 1940, both Schenck and Bioff were indicted for income tax evasion, with the hopes that the studio boss would make a deal to put Bioff and any other conspirators away on more serious charges.

But Schenck made no immediate move toward a plea. Again keeping his options open, the mogul stayed silent and prepared to go to trial.

———————

Whatever my father thought of his friend's legal troubles and the danger that he, too, might be caught up in them, it didn't stop him from pursuing new illegal opportunities. As the Arrowhead Springs Hotel's popularity grew, Wilkerson began hosting infrequent backroom card games there, managing the risk by only inviting carefully handpicked players who could be trusted to exercise maximum discretion. (It's unknown whether he'd planned to use the hotel as a gambling front all along, or whether the idea evolved as the resort grew more popular.) Unfortunately, news of the illicit card games quickly spread, and scores of Wilkerson's former patrons who missed the Trocadero's backroom games began to flock to the Arrowhead Springs. For them, it was an irresistible lure: a weekend of relaxation in the fresh mountain air, an evening of fine dining, dancing, and entertainment, followed by a quiet card game and a comfortable hotel bed. The isolated location lulled everyone into a false sense of security.

Wilkerson was caught by surprise and soon was unable to keep up with demand. Although a dedicated gambler, he knew little about the management of the games, so he contacted the old acquaintances who had done the job in Hollywood, particularly Nola Hahn and his associates who had made such a success of the Clover Club. In exchange for a percentage of the gaming operation's profits, the Gambling Syndicate set up shop in San Bernardino.

Some believe Wilkerson would have been better off exercising restraint, but now, lured by the card tables, he was once again immersed in the world of organized crime—even as the state attorney general was spearheading a crackdown and one of his closest friends was about to go on trial for his criminal connections. Others recognized, however, that this was a world Wilkerson had always known and would never shy away from. As Greg Bautzer put it, "Billy had dealt with organized crime all his life. He felt comfortable around these people." So he was happy to concentrate on running the hotel while Hahn and company procured gambling equipment, managed the casino, produced their own bank, and provided for the operation's security.

At the time, one of the prerequisites for a successful illegal gambling joint of this size was a long driveway with posted lookouts. The Arrowhead Springs possessed precisely such an invaluable feature. The gaming operation, located at the rear of the hotel facing the mountain, boasted a full complement of table games and other gambling equipment, including a hefty repository of dice, cards, and chips. The area was accessible by invitation only, kept off limits to the majority of hotel guests. But those who were invited gambled quite enough; Wilkerson was raking in a bundle.

Hahn miscalculated, however, posting no lookouts at the *rear* of the hotel. He assumed it was safe because it was wedged up against the side of the steep mountain. When Lake Arrowhead authorities became aware that there was gambling going on, they exploited this vulnerability. "It turns out," said Tom Seward, "that they had been staking out the place for months."

In late 1940, in a scene straight out of a western, a mounted posse of US marshals rode down the mountain on horseback and entered the rear of the hotel. Zealous axe-wielding deputies smashed tables and gambling equipment before carting off gamblers in handcuffs. Thanks to the intervention of Johnny Rosselli and MGM's Howard Strickling, Wilkerson escaped formal charges, but he decided he'd had enough of illegal casino gaming and returned control of the Arrowhead Springs to Schenck and Paley.

The decision turned out to be fortuitous, as one year later, when America became embroiled in World War II, gas rationing put severe restrictions on drivers. As Tom Seward put it, "Had Billy still been involved with the Arrowhead Springs at the onset of the war, chances are he would have lost his shirt. With gas rationing, people weren't doing much driving, and I think nobody would have come. Within weeks the hotel would have probably gone dark."

Once again, he'd escaped serious financial and legal consequences for his shady business ventures. But as Joe Schenck's trial loomed, he must have wondered whether his luck would hold out.

22 | CIRO'S

DURING THIS PERIOD, WILKERSON continued to make frequent visits to Monte Carlo, where he would spend his nights gambling—after dining at a bistro called Ciro's. No photographs or other records of this restaurant survive, but friends say Wilkerson was so taken with the elegant establishment that when he decided to get back into the nightclub business at the end of the 1930s, he re-created his own version of Ciro's in Hollywood.

The new Ciro's was erected on the former site of the Club Seville at 8433 Sunset Boulevard on the Sunset Strip. Architect George Vernon Russell and decorator Tom Douglas oversaw its construction. Wilkerson heavily supervised his architect, who produced a sleek, sophisticated facade, while Douglas was given free rein to create interiors that starkly contrasted with Russell's work. The decorator unleashed a riot of color and texture, with red silk sofas, ceilings painted a matching red, and walls draped in heavy ribbed silk dyed pale pastel green. Flanking the bandstand, Douglas installed bronze columns and urns to serve as light fixtures. It was, as George Kennedy described it, "a feast for the eyes."

To drum up publicity, Wilkerson planned three separate opening nights: a party for friends and invited guests only on Monday, January 29, 1940; a preview opening for critics and gossip columnists the following night; and the public opening on Wednesday, January 31. Appealing to his prospective customers' snobbery, he also ran daily ads in the *Reporter* reminding his readers that "everybody that's anybody will be at Ciro's" and dubbing the restaurant "America's Smartest Supper Club." "That was it," said Joe Pasternak. "The minute those ads appeared, everybody had to go to Ciro's. From the moment they started running in the paper, there was a line outside the club."

Six weeks after the opening, comedy megastar W. C. Fields was featured in another full-page ad in the *Reporter*: "I want to tell you that everyone in my party the other night and myself expressed the opinion that they had never tasted finer food or received such meticulous and friendly service in their lives."

Among those who contributed to Ciro's fine service in its early days was maître d' Louis Cantoni, who had worked at the original Ciro's in Monte Carlo. Ultimately, however, the Frenchman's titanic ego clashed with Wilkerson's. "Cantoni felt like he owned the place," said Seward. "At every corner they were locking horns. I was sure it would come to blows." By June 1940, Cantoni was summarily shipped back to Monte Carlo and replaced by Pancho Alliati, who would remain the nightclub's maître d' as long as Wilkerson owned the place. Seward remembered that Pancho became a legend. "Everyone loved Pancho. He was as charming as they come and efficient. He really knew how to work the door."

In the kitchen was former Vendôme and Trocadero chef Felix Ganio. While he, too, clashed with Wilkerson, the owner respected Ganio's talents, and the chef consistently proved himself. The nightclub offered fare from a multitude of different menus; sadly, only two from the Wilkerson era survive. One dinner menu offered petite marmite à la française, filets de sand dab au Chambertin, gigot d'agneau roti, caneton à la bigarade, pommes rissolées, courgettes à la provençale, salade de saison, cerises melba, and café noir. Another included frivolité de Ciro, consommé soubrette, poussin à la diable, filet mignon petit duc, pommes au four, épinard en branche, salade California, poire Alma, and demitasse.

Ciro's opened its doors at 7:00 PM, and Emil Coleman's orchestra took the bandstand at eight. There was no cover charge until ten. On Saturday evenings the club hosted formal dinner dances. "Ciro's wasn't as loud or as noisy as the Troc," remembered Kennedy. "The Troc was deafening." Focusing instead on refinement and intimacy, the new, smaller establishment was more in keeping with the mood of a nation on the verge of entering World War II.

Carefully tailored to the wartime environment, Wilkerson's latest venture became a gold mine. Everyone celebrated everything at Ciro's: benefits, birthdays, post-premiere parties, promotions. The club played host to such screen royalty as Lana Turner, Marlene Dietrich, Judy Garland, Jimmy Stewart, and Clark Gable. Even the reclusive Howard Hughes was a regular.

Johnny Rosselli was continually badgering Wilkerson to host backroom card games at Ciro's as he had at the Trocadero. While discreet gambling in the back room of a nightclub would provide less of a target for law enforcement than his complex Arrowhead Springs operation, my father had grown tired of navigating the hazards. Ultimately, however, he decided that the risks were manageable, particularly in so small a club, and the backroom games returned.

Though quiet and discreet by Wilkerson's standards, Ciro's nevertheless had a dark side. In the main dining room, fistfights were surprisingly commonplace. At Ciro's, it wasn't my father's gangster clientele who misbehaved; the intimate club became a well-known meeting place for those conducting clandestine affairs, and when an irate husband, wife, or lover discovered his or her unfaithful partner there, fisticuffs would break out as the other patrons looked on. "The fights at Ciro's were part of the attraction of going there," said Joe Pasternak.

It became such an issue that Wilkerson had to employ Golden Gloves fighters as busboys so they could double as bouncers and unceremoniously eject the unruly through the front door. To further discourage bad behavior, Wilkerson installed a spotlight that illuminated the two steps descending into the club's main room—no one arrived unseen. At closing time, staff immediately removed canisters of powerful cleaning agents from the maintenance closets and, in a well-choreographed ballet, removed bloodstains from the carpeted floors.

The gangsters, meanwhile, not only behaved themselves at Ciro's but were always quick to come to the Hollywood Godfather's rescue. One afternoon while Tom Seward prepared the bar for the club's opening, he was confronted by a man named William G. Bonelli, who was a member of the State Board of Equalization and in charge of controlling the sale of alcoholic beverages. The man told Seward he was going to cite him for serving alcohol to minors.

"I wouldn't be so stupid to jeopardize revoking the Ciro's license," Seward insisted, but Bonelli jabbed an index finger into Seward's chest and told him he would do as he pleased. Seward instinctively replied to the shove with an uppercut, laying the official flat. "Unfortunately there were no witnesses," Seward lamented.

A few afternoons later, while Seward again prepared Ciro's to open, he received a hand-delivered notice to appear in court. The charge was assault and battery on a state officer. Ciro's was also cited on the underage alcohol service charge. Seward began pacing, and Johnny Rosselli, who was in a corner booth playing cards, noticed and called him over to ask what was wrong. Seward told him it was nothing, but Rosselli's partner chimed in, "If he's asking, you tell him!" Rosselli introduced his partner as Benny Siegel—better known, to his own displeasure, as Bugsy. "That was first time I met Siegel," Seward said. "At Ciro's." He told the men the whole story.

Siegel stood up, walked into the lobby, and went into one of the two phone booths, where he placed a call. He returned, looked at Seward, and told him to forget about the subpoena. And, indeed, the authorities never contacted him about the matter again.

Bugsy Siegel was also a tremendous fan of Ciro's itself. When he was awaiting trial for murder in 1941, he refused to eat jail food and had the club deliver its food to his cell. And Virginia Hill, Siegel's paramour, frequently rented Ciro's for parties, counting $5,000 in $1,000 bills into Wilkerson's hand and telling him that if he had any other events scheduled for the evening she wanted, it was too bad.

Other customers were less free with their money. As at the Troc, regular Ciro's patrons received monthly tabs, payable in full on the tenth of each month. Those who did not pay on time risked their credit being permanently suspended. Among those with delinquent tabs who were forced to pay in cash were Jimmy Ritz of the famed Ritz Brothers; Mike Romanoff, owner of legendary Romanoff's restaurant in Beverly Hills; and legendary film producer Jerry Wald.

Ciro's was also notable for its technical innovations. Not only did it boast the first soundproof phone booths in Hollywood, but Wilkerson had additional phone jacks installed at every dining booth as well. If a patron sitting in a booth wished to make a call from his table, the steward would bring a phone to him and plug it in. The steward also brought a phone log to keep track of the booth, the caller, and the number called, as well as the time of the call and its duration. "Everything had to be recorded," remembered Seward.

The steward was instructed to visit the table every five minutes to monitor the progress of the call, and he would monitor long distance and collect calls especially closely. When the patron hung up, the steward collected both the phone and the log and added the phone charge to the patron's check or monthly tab. If the steward failed to turn in a slip, he became personally responsible for the charge, which was deducted from his paycheck.

Despite Ciro's enormous success, by 1942, with the club still at its zenith, Wilkerson had lost interest. He once again summoned Nola Hahn and ordered a kitchen fire. Hahn handled the arson in his typically masterful fashion, and neither the insurance company nor the fire department found any evidence of wrongdoing. Pocketing the insurance money, Wilkerson first leased and then sold the club to entrepreneur Herman Hover, who helmed it until 1959.

23 | TRIALS

WHILE BILLY WILKERSON entertained movie stars and gangsters at Ciro's, Joe Schenck was on trial for tax evasion, with prosecutors still holding out hope that he would make a deal with them that revealed collusion between the Mafia and the studios. During his trial, Schenck did not offer any new information, but when he was convicted in April 1941, the feds gained a new form of leverage: Schenck's sentence. He faced not only three years behind bars but also the revocation of his US citizenship.

The thought sent the Russian-born mogul into a panic. Nothing was more horrifying to immigrants of that era than deportation to the country from which they had fled. Faced with this new threat, Schenck agreed that in exchange for a reduced sentence he would reveal the inner workings of the extortion scheme. He agreed to testify against Willie Bioff and Bioff's partner George E. Browne, and snitched on all his fellow studio heads. In exchange his sentence was reduced from three years to eighteen months.

But Schenck remained loyal to Wilkerson and Johnny Rosselli, carefully omitting any mention of their involvement. So even though he quickly made good on his agreement to testify against the conspirators, and Harry Warner of Warner Bros. offered his own testimony that filled in some of Schenck's intentional gaps, the government still didn't reach a clear understanding of the extortion scheme. According to Kennedy, in the end they never did.

It was not for lack of trying. Based on Schenck's and Warner's testimony, a federal grand jury issued subpoenas for all the major studio heads. Despite the other moguls' clear involvement with Bioff's shakedown, the government was only able to make the case against 20th Century Fox. In fact, the only proof that the shakedown ever occurred was Schenck's $100,000 check. "There was no paper trail," said Seward, since the studios "made their payoffs in cash. The scheme would've worked had that idiot Bioff not turned on Billy and Joe. That was a huge mistake."

On May 23, 1941, George Browne, Willie Bioff, and five other conspirators were indicted for extortion and tax evasion. Schenck hoped the investigation would end there, but according to Seward he naively underestimated the union boss's determination to stay out of prison. The moment he entered a jail cell, Bioff phoned US attorney Boris Kostelanetz and offered to deal. In exchange for Bioff's testimony against the others involved in the shakedown, the government agreed to drop all charges against him—and to let him keep the money he'd stolen since the inception of the scheme. The authorities would even place him into the federal witness protection program.

With the deal negotiated, Bioff told the feds everything. He named everyone he knew who was involved in the extortion plot, including every studio head who had diligently made payoffs, and even admitted on the stand that his ultimate goal was to own half of all the studios. He also squealed about Schenck's private poker games, giving the authorities the size of the pot as well as the names of the attendees, including my father.

Fortunately, Bioff didn't know enough to finger Schenck and Wilkerson as the brains behind the Hollywood Syndicate; he could only name the one syndicate head from whom he'd taken his orders: Johnny Rosselli. Bioff did know that Handsome Johnny and my father were friends, though, so Wilkerson had some fear for his personal safety. To protect himself, in 1942 he paid gangster Tony Cornero $6,500 for his custom-built, pale-blue bulletproof Cadillac.

As for Schenck, he still had to serve his eighteen-month sentence on the original tax-evasion charges. In May 1942, he was transferred to a minimum security prison in Danbury, Connecticut, where he promptly phoned Wilkerson and pleaded with the publisher to help him get out as soon as possible. According to Kennedy, Wilkerson promised to do all he could and fiercely lobbied for a second sentence reduction on Schenck's behalf—taking his request directly to the head of the FBI, J. Edgar Hoover.

It's not clear how or when Wilkerson's relationship with J. Edgar Hoover began, but they probably first met during one of Hoover's many visits to the West Coast. No correspondence between the two men or photos of them together survive, but according to several people with whom I spoke, they enjoyed a cordial if formal relationship, bonded by shared interests including a mutual hatred of "Reds" and an obsession with the ponies. When Hoover was in Los Angeles, he attended the track as Wilkerson's guest in his private box. The FBI director also seems to have turned to the publisher when he needed an informant on Hollywood affairs; for instance, in early 1940, the agency asked my father to find out what he could about a woman named Hilda Kruger, an aspiring actress in Hollywood suspected of being a German spy. (Wilkerson, in turn, sent Greg Bautzer to seduce her.) Despite Wilkerson's colorful and often shady life, an FBI Freedom of Information Act search conducted in 1992 revealed surprisingly little about him; it seems likely that Hoover's fondness for Wilkerson was reflected in the sparseness of his FBI file.

In any event, Wilkerson clearly felt comfortable enough with Hoover to turn to him in Schenck's hour of need. The publisher also lobbied for a presidential pardon, a plea helped by the fact that Schenck had made a hefty contribution to Franklin D. Roosevelt's Democratic Party. While it may be mere coincidence, after serving just four months and five days of his eighteen-month sentence, Schenck was released from prison in September 1942, and shortly thereafter returned to 20th Century Fox as head of production. He'd receive his full presidential pardon a few years later, from FDR's successor, Harry S. Truman, on October 26, 1945.

––––––––––

Wilkerson's efforts over the summer of 1942 may have helped his friend escape more prison time, but there was nothing he could do to salvage another personal relationship. His marriage to Brownie had lasted nearly three years—nothing short of a miracle. But by July 1942, Brownie had had enough of her husband's jealousy, temper tantrums, and acidic criticism. She fled to Reno to sit out the necessary six weeks to establish residence in order to obtain a quick Nevada divorce. That divorce was finalized on August 13, 1942.

As he adjusted once more to unmarried life, he was also dealing with the absence of his personal secretary. The Japanese had attacked Pearl Harbor the previous December, provoking the United States' entry into World War II. In June, George Kennedy had marched into his employer's office and announced that he'd decided to do his part for the war effort—he wanted to enlist. Lest Wilkerson think it an impulsive decision, Kennedy insisted that he had been mulling it over for weeks, and when his employer told him he couldn't risk losing him, Kennedy explained that though he was flattered, he'd made up his mind. Wilkerson agreed to think it over.

My father knew if Kennedy enlisted, he would be shipped to the Pacific and would likely see active duty. Not daring to risk losing his right-hand man, for three days after Kennedy told him of his plans, Wilkerson made phone calls and pulled strings. His secretary ended up as a captain in the Coast Guard. "Mr. Wilkerson got me shipped out to a remote outpost in Alaska that dealt in supplies and munitions," recalled Kennedy. "The only action I saw was drinking and fucking."

During Kennedy's time in the service, Wilkerson clearly missed his secretary. "He wrote to me on a weekly basis," Kennedy remembered. "They were all in longhand, keeping me abreast of all the news at the paper. I knew how busy he was and for him to take the time to write me was a big deal." Wilkerson displayed the same tenderness in letters he wrote to Kennedy on another occasion, while traveling in Europe and overcome by his gambling mania. He poured out his heart in intimate correspondence, which Kennedy kept for the rest of his life and shared with me in his later years. I will always regret that I did not make copies of these letters; after his death, his family destroyed practically all of his correspondence, and I was unable to save these vital records of the two men's fondness for each other.

———

When Tom Seward learned that Wilkerson had granted Kennedy's request to enlist, he followed suit, but my father was adamant that he could not spare him. At this point, Wilkerson was still convinced that he would never have children, and without the ability to produce an heir, he'd toyed with the idea of adopting Seward and naming him his successor.

Bautzer talked him out of it. "It was a bad idea," Bautzer remembered. "What if he wanted to legitimately adopt an infant in his marriage? With Tom already a legal son, that, I would imagine, would put a great strain on his marriage."

Regardless, a headstrong Seward told Wilkerson in no uncertain terms what to do with himself and went off to war. Because of a medical deferment, Seward could not get into the military and instead went to work for Lockheed, servicing US military aircraft overseas. According to Kennedy, this decision led to a bitter falling-out between the two men.

Ultimately my father and his ex-brother-in-law mended fences. In May 1944, when Seward returned to Hollywood on leave, Wilkerson offered him a partnership in his empire—against Bautzer's advice. This included an interest in the crown jewel, the *Reporter*. Seward accepted. On July 1, 1944, they entered into the partnership, with Wilkerson contributing assets valued at $372,000 and Seward committing to a gradual buyout worth $228,000, and both men agreeing that Wilkerson would own 62 percent and Seward 38 percent of the publisher's kingdom.

Once their signatures were dry and Seward was back at work in Wilkerson's empire, Seward discovered that his new partner was a changed man. My father was now peering over his shoulder and micromanaging him, and before long Seward had had enough and decided to take a job at MGM as an assistant director.

That job lasted less than six months. "I hated being on location in the middle of a desert trying to get people to do their jobs," Seward said. "It wasn't glamorous at all. The actors were the worst. I learned what prima donnas they could be." After much cajoling, Wilkerson convinced Seward to return to the fold.

———

Greg Bautzer, too, spent the early 1940s contributing to the war effort, learning to pilot blimps for the US Navy. So he probably directed Wilkerson to another attorney when, in October 1943, the publisher was subpoenaed to testify in New York at the extortion trial of Johnny Rosselli and the other Hollywood shakedown conspirators who'd been fingered by Willie Bioff. Although Bautzer may not have been able to advise Wilkerson directly, it was at this point that he first became aware of his client's involvement with the shakedown. As Bautzer calmly observed, "On occasion Billy got himself into some pretty bad jams." With a trace of annoyance, the suave attorney added, "Most often of his own doing."

On November 25, Wilkerson gave his testimony in the case. He was asked about the gifts he'd given Bioff back in 1937, and about a Tradeviews column in which he'd stated that Bioff was the type of man for whom IATSE ought to be grateful. He was asked if he'd published these flattering remarks out of fear. "No," he testified. "I thought he was doing a pretty good job for the IA." The publisher did admit to making one deal with the union boss: when he guaranteed that the *Reporter* would not publish news about IATSE or studio labor relations in exchange for Bioff calling off a strike at the Trocadero. However, he neglected to mention that he'd also made regular cash payments to the union boss.

He couldn't confess his full involvement in the scam, of course, but the extent to which he held his tongue probably has to do with how much Joe Schenck's conviction for tax evasion spooked him. Wilkerson had struggled with his own tax problems ever since his Manhattan speakeasy days. He hated paying income tax, and employed many schemes to hide his assets. Because of this, by 1943 he had been under federal scrutiny for years. As the US Board of Tax Appeals wrote, "Wilkerson's life has been a successful though precarious one." He knew that taking the stand against Bioff ran the risk of opening that can of worms, and his goal on the stand was simple: to distance himself as much as he could from the scandal. This meant providing as little information as possible.

On December 30, 1943, a verdict was reached. Johnny Rosselli and five other defendants were convicted of extortion. Each received a ten-year prison sentence.

Based on the research I have done over the course of forty years, I believe that Billy Wilkerson escaped his own prison sentence because his friend Johnny Rosselli offered himself up as a sacrificial lamb. By accepting blame for the scheme himself, and allegedly calling in favors from his government contacts, Handsome Johnny made good on his long-ago promise that Wilkerson would never serve jail time if their shakedown went bad.

Before Rosselli went to prison, he made my father one more promise. He would, he said, kill Bioff, the man who had brought down the Hollywood Syndicate.

24 | RESTAURANT LARUE

BARELY TWO YEARS after losing interest in the successful Ciro's and selling it off, Wilkerson was again contemplating a return to the luxury dining market. He hadn't found any renewed enthusiasm for the business in the intervening years; he simply realized how much demand there was among the Hollywood elite—not for the club itself, which remained in business under its new management, but for the card games Wilkerson had hosted in its back room. Practically everywhere Wilkerson went, he bumped into former patrons who begged him to open a new establishment and bring back the games. When he confided in Joe Pasternak that he was weary of the work involved in running even an intimate nightclub like Ciro's, Pasternak suggested he open a small restaurant instead.

He thought about the idea for some time before finally leasing a space across the street from Café Trocadero's original site, on the corner of Sunset Boulevard and Sunset Plaza Drive, in early 1944. Investing $44,000 in the project, he again enlisted decorator Tom Douglas and architect George Vernon Russell to work their magic. From Russell he wanted a round building that would complement the corner lot, while he gave Douglas no instructions other than to do what he always did so beautifully. Like Ciro's, the new venue was a feast for the eyes, with an ebony and red leather bar where patrons patiently waited to be seated in the main dining area, which featured pistachio-and-cocoa-striped booths. The overflow tables on the French terrace were surrounded by flower boxes.

RESTAURANT LARUE | 187

While this new place was smaller even than Ciro's, it had all the classic hallmarks of a Wilkerson establishment. Instead of a big band or an orchestra blasting patrons onto the dance floors, here an accordionist and a violinist would play softly. Wilkerson named it Restaurant LaRue ("*la rue*" being French for "the street") to conjure the intimacy of a Parisian sidewalk bistro.

Legend has it that one of LaRue's most important hires came directly from Paris as well. Whenever Wilkerson visited the French capital, he had a habit of walking all over the city at night before turning in. During one visit, he was apparently strolling the Champs-Élysées when he stopped at an outdoor café for a cigarette and a Coke. A young couple sat across from him. For some reason, the lovers ordered a single orange. The waiter produced it on an elegant white plate, and Wilkerson was riveted as he watched him peel it with "the grace of an artist," as George Kennedy put it. The publisher was struck dumb by the sight, but when he found his voice again, he asked the young waiter, Bruno Petoletti, to come to Hollywood to become LaRue's maître d'.

"Mr. Wilkerson recognized talent right away," said Harry Drucker. He hired four-star chef Orlando Figini and paid him an extravagant $175 a week. Wilkerson even paid his dishwashers $7 a day, an excellent wartime salary. He also relaxed his male-only server rule. "I was one of Mr. Wilkerson's first waitresses," remembered Grace Bouliance, who had been Wilkerson's hatcheck girl at Ciro's.

My father was unwilling to relax another discriminatory hiring policy. Black employees were nowhere to be found in his dining rooms or kitchens—or his print operations, for that matter. In his views on race, Wilkerson was a product of the Old South: thoroughly intolerant but publicly polite. He paid lip service to the talents of African American performers and athletes but viewed black people as better suited for menial roles such as cotton pickers or cabin stewards than for work in exclusive venues such as his. On this point he would remain regrettably consistent to the end of his days.

The ongoing war effort meant that LaRue had to deal with the federal government's strict regulation of the food supply, which included both rationing and price controls. Nevertheless, Wilkerson knew that it was high quality that made his restaurants special, and he pushed back against the government's insistence on austerity as much as he was able. When Restaurant LaRue launched in April 1944, *Time* called it "the fashionable place to dine" with a decor that was "chi-chi like crazy." One of his secret weapons was royal squab diable at a pricey $2.25. "People couldn't get enough of it," said Seward. "Billy made a killing."

Even though wartime gas rationing prevented Angelenos from going out as regularly as they once had, Hollywood's royalty immediately flocked to the latest glamorous haunt, squeezing into a space that accommodated just 280 customers. Hundreds more were turned away at the door. Before long its tables were known for the celebrities who occupied them: the Humphrey Bogart Table, the Ronald Reagan Table, the Clark Gable Table. Restaurant LaRue became an even bigger magnet for organized crime than Wilkerson's previous establishments. Bugsy Siegel, Virginia Hill, and Mickey Cohen were regulars.

LaRue's patrons likened its atmosphere to elegant home dining. While in his previous establishments Wilkerson had drummed up publicity by encouraging photographers to swarm his celebrity guests, here he went out of his way to insulate the clientele from media scrutiny. He was also careful to discourage the culture of fisticuffs that had come to define Ciro's. In stunning contrast to that club's nightly dustups between illicit paramours and angry spouses, at LaRue all the customers were on their best behavior. One patron described the venue this way: it was as if the dust from the wings of a mythical butterfly had drifted onto diners, mesmerizing them.

In its first ten weeks of business, LaRue grossed $109,000. After that the restaurant's weekly take averaged $14,000, an astounding figure in WWII-era America. But once it was up and running, Wilkerson had little to do with its day-to-day operations. He left that to Bruno Petoletti and Orlando Figini. "Mr. Wilkerson made Figini and Petoletti partners," George Kennedy said.

During the war, LaRue opened for lunch from 11:30 to 2:00 PM and then, because of strict blackouts, started serving dinner at 4:30 and wrapped up before sunset. Immediately after dinner service ended, busboys cleaned tables and Wilkerson himself locked the doors. Then came the exclusive event for which he'd reentered the restaurant business in the first place.

Hidden behind accounting books in LaRue's small office at the rear of the bistro, my father kept a rack of chips and sets of cards and dice. Each night, he hosted discreet card games with no more than six invitees, which would last until dawn.

Away from LaRue, Wilkerson's own gambling addiction continued to consume him. Wilkerson's employees were sworn to secrecy about those Friday afternoons when their boss took the business payroll and staked it all at the track—often only to lose it. Some of his loyal staff even agreed to take temporary pay cuts to cover their boss's losses. They said they always knew he would make good later on. As George Kennedy explained, "There was a lot of hand-wringing over it. But everybody stood by Mr. Wilkerson."

Though Kennedy wouldn't be officially discharged from the service until the following year, by 1944 he was apparently back at work at the *Reporter*. It's unknown whether he was there to help out while on leave from the military, or whether my father had pulled some more strings to bring him back to Los Angeles more permanently. In any case, he found himself deeply involved, as he had been prior to joining the war effort, in managing his boss's gambling losses. He remembered, for instance, that the Bank of America branch that held both the publisher's personal account and the *Reporter*'s account—the only bank Wilkerson had commerce with—often called the secretary to ask which obligations it should honor first, the payroll or the gambling debts.

In addition, only Kennedy and Tom Seward knew that often when their boss was away on "business trips," he was in fact traveling out of town to gamble. After Earl Warren initiated his crackdown on illegal gambling in California in 1939, the state's compulsive gamblers had grown more likely to seek legal gambling elsewhere. At the time, the only state that had legalized gambling was Nevada—it had been legal there since 1931. Most of Nevada's gambling activity was centered in the north, around Reno and the state capital of Carson City. But Wilkerson was drawn to a town some four hundred miles to the south: Las Vegas.

My father enjoyed the variety of gambling options Vegas offered; if his luck was down at one casino, he simply roamed to the next. "When I feel the table turn cold," he once said, "I leave the casino." Many mornings he chartered a plane from Los Angeles Municipal Airport, flew to Vegas, and spent hours at the casinos, making or losing between $10,000 and $20,000 before returning home. If he was particularly unlucky, he played through the night hoping his luck would change.

When Wilkerson ran out of money on one of these trips, he would phone Kennedy and instruct him to go to Bank of America, where the publisher had a line of credit. The branch manager would hand Kennedy an attaché case. The faithful secretary then took the next available flight to Las Vegas and handed over the case. "I lost count of how many cases I delivered to Mr. Wilkerson. And I knew I wasn't carrying Christmas cards," he said. Indeed, these shipments sometimes contained as much as $50,000 in cash.

At times, Wilkerson was as reckless about getting to and from the casino as he was about spending money once he got there. Though he'd normally charter a plane to Las Vegas, he sometimes made the three-hundred-mile drive instead, gas rationing and the desert heat be damned. Heedlessly speeding along in his Cadillac convertible, he chain-smoked the entire way, never crushing cigarettes in his ashtray but simply tossing them out the window.

Once when returning from Las Vegas, a lit cigarette he tossed landed in the backseat, which caught fire. My father never noticed the black smoke billowing from the back of his car—he never used his rearview mirror. His car was spotted racing through Baker, California, at over a hundred miles per hour, with a long plume of smoke trailing behind. The fire department was alerted and gave chase. Believing the red lights, horns, and sirens had nothing to do with him, he accelerated to get out of their way, and after a sixty-mile chase the fire department finally overtook him. When he saw that his car was on fire, he leaped out and let the firemen do their job.

Kennedy told me my father had a difficult time convincing the judge that he hadn't known his car was on fire. (He claimed that his rearview mirror was broken.) He also had no driver's license, and after a search was found to possess $14,000 in cash, which he explained were his winnings from gambling in Vegas. Exasperated, the judge asked my father if he thought he was a law unto himself, but he did let him off after imposing a hefty $750 fine.

On another occasion he and his disciple Joe Rivkin took a long winter road trip to Reno. Rivkin recalled that the publisher almost killed them both, because he was driving his Bentley "like a lunatic." Rivkin was furious. "I told Billy that if he didn't slow down, to let me out and I'd walk to Reno."

At one point the Bentley hit a patch of black ice and the car spun 360 degrees, skidding to a halt at the edge of the road. The two men emerged shaken into the blistering cold, and saw that the front wheels had stopped just few feet from a cliff that plunged hundreds of feet into a gorge below. "We knew we were lucky to be alive," Rivkin said. "I remember really letting Billy have it, 'Have I made my point now?' I screamed at him." In no hurry to resume the journey, the two men stood in the freezing cold for quite some time, smoking cigarettes.

———————————

Back in the casinos, Wilkerson frequently found himself staring into deep chasms of debt. When he couldn't get hold of cash to place a bet, casino owners regularly gave him lines of credit for whatever the amount wagered and lost, since he had a reputation for honoring his gambling debts. In 1940, for example, his daily markers had never totaled less than $500 a day and frequently ballooned as high as $27,000. He would write IOUs or marker slips on anything that came to hand—scraps of paper, table napkins, receipts—so long as he never had to leave the table. Kennedy remembered receiving frantic phone calls from the bank asking for signature verification on these questionable documents. "They used to drive the bank crazy. They would go nuts trying to figure out what these doilies with large dollar amounts written on them were." On one occasion the branch manager called Wilkerson's office to verify an IOU for $23,750 that appeared to be written on toilet paper. Kennedy asked if the document bore Wilkerson's signature and when the branch manager confirmed that it did, Kennedy told him he had best honor it.

At other times Wilkerson's friends bailed him out with timely loans; Howard Hughes and Joe Schenck in particular continued to come to the rescue by advancing him funds under the guise of prepaid advertising. He also turned to his mother for financial assistance. For more than a decade, Mary Wilkerson had continued her Depression-era habit of keeping all her money hidden away in old coffee cans; she also remained extremely frugal, owning only a few dresses that she wore until they were threadbare and refusing to replace anything in her home, from carpet to roof, unless absolutely necessary. Since her son paid all her expenses, she saved every penny he gave her in those coffee cans, and she would hand them over to him when he confessed his gambling losses—which he always did, despite the discomfort such announcements caused her.

Mary never bailed out her son without a good scolding, though—usually accompanied by the throwing of crockery. She hated that he gambled, as much as he hated that she drank; most of their arguments revolved around those very subjects. "Each had no tolerance of the other's vices," observed Kennedy. "In this respect, they were a match made in heaven."

Of course, my father wasn't always dealing with losses. Like most gamblers, he did have some big wins every so often. He'd hit it big in the "Match of the Century," the November 1, 1938, horserace in which Seabiscuit met War Admiral at Pimlico Race Course in Baltimore, Maryland. War Admiral was the favorite, but Wilkerson wagered $20,000 on Seabiscuit. His return is unknown, since the odds varied depending on the bookie, but he made a killing.

And once in a while he had periods of monk-like abstinence from gambling. Kennedy saw this as a type of self-flagellation, penance for the unfathomable losses he had racked up. Seward recalled weeks at a time when Wilkerson didn't touch a deck of cards or set of dice. "I thought it was a miracle," he said. But these periods were always short lived, and usually a domestic dispute or business disappointment would plunge him back into the next binge. Between 1930 and 1945, even in good years, he never lost less than $150,000 (more than $2 million today). Those who knew him were amazed that he managed to avoid bankruptcy.

Fortunately he possessed both the psychological resilience and the material resources that allowed him to weather his staggering losses. He almost always had his own restaurant where he could dine in luxury free of charge, and studios eager for a good word from the *Reporter* would send him a steady stream of generous gifts, from large tins of beluga caviar (one of his favorites) to season baseball tickets. The studios also flew him first class to film junkets and sent limos to the airport to pick him up and carry him to gratis rooms in luxurious hotels. At times, Kennedy recalled, even his clothing and cars were complimentary. And his ability to lose vast amounts of money and keep on going, no worse for wear, was a sign of prestige among the Hollywood elite. As Kennedy explained, "The mere fact that you could afford to blow that kind of cash indicated in some way that you were a mover and a shaker."

But by 1944, Wilkerson's ability to absorb his losses was being severely tested. And his last-ditch efforts to find a solution to his addiction would inspire the Hollywood Godfather's most ambitious project: building his own Las Vegas casino.

25 | THE FLAMINGO

BY JULY 1944 Billy Wilkerson's gambling losses for the year were nearing $750,000 (more than $10 million today). The amount had exceeded the *Reporter*'s annual profits four months earlier; by this point it was swallowing up a substantial portion of the publisher's gross receipts. Those privy to the numbers felt it was only a matter of time before Wilkerson's gambling crippled both him and his businesses. It was an especially ominous development for my father's new business partner, Tom Seward. "I watched Billy gamble my future away," Seward said. But Wilkerson continued to deny that he had a problem.

By the fall, Wilkerson's gambling debts had ballooned to $1 million, and still he relentlessly gambled on, wagering every penny he could raise. Kennedy remembers everyone holding their breath. "I went to Mass every morning and prayed," he said.

Before long, Wilkerson was unable to pay important business bills, and one after another, major vendors halted shipments of paper, ink, and other vital supplies. When the *Reporter* was able to arrange shipments, they arrived COD. The rising debts also forced Wilkerson into compromising situations that even the ethically flexible publisher would've previously found unseemly. If he was unable to pay his markers at the poker games, he bartered away *Reporter* advertising (though Joe Schenck always forgave such debts). By November 1944, the financial situation simply became too dire for even Wilkerson to ignore.

At the time, there were no organizations devoted to treating compulsive gamblers; gambling addicts had to fend for themselves. Finally recognizing his gambling as an affliction rather than a hobby, he began to search for a cure. One night over a private dinner with Joe Schenck at the mogul's Santa Monica home, he poured his heart out. His friend offered this advice: "If you are going to gamble that kind of money, be on the other side of the table. Build a casino. Own the house."

For the next several days, Wilkerson pondered Schenck's advice. It was true that if he owned his own casino, he could gamble there in relative safety, as any money he lost to the house would actually still be his. In fact, he'd long toyed with the idea of starting his own gambling place. But he had no desire to repeat his disastrous experience running the Arrowhead Springs Hotel. If he opened another major gambling venture, this time it would have to be legal.

He considered breeding thoroughbred horses to compete at the local tracks but eventually rejected this idea as too risky, since he knew little about thoroughbred breeding and training other than the fact that frequently horses were doped and bets at the tracks were rigged. He briefly flirted with starting an operation in Cuba; in the years before the Communist revolution, the island nation offered not only legal gambling but also tax-free profits so long as the income remained undeclared in the States. But Cuba was a long way from Hollywood, and doing business under a foreign flag could be tricky. So he turned instead to his favorite venue for legal gambling in the United States: Las Vegas, Nevada.

Las Vegas's renaissance had begun in 1940 with the arrival of a few blocks of small, rustic hotels decorated in a charming dude ranch motif. A series of casinos affectionately known as "gambling halls" or "gambling shacks" occupied Second and Fremont Streets. The following year, Tom Hull had built El Rancho Vegas, the first combination hotel, casino, and showroom. Energized by a booming wartime economy, Vegas was poised to welcome defense workers and soldiers, and by early 1945 it would be home to ten neon-lit hotels and thirteen casinos.

By December 1944, Wilkerson had identified the first step in a plan to stem his gambling losses by owning a Las Vegas casino. He started by taking over the El Rancho Vegas, paying then-owner Joe Drown $50,000 for a six-month lease. But he didn't plan to simply run someone else's casino for long; he had bigger goals in mind.

His long-term plan was to attract not just die-hard gamblers like himself but the snobbish Hollywood crowd more generally. From the start, he recognized that even an establishment like the El Rancho would have trouble tempting the denizens of Beverly Hills into crossing the searing desert. Even he, a gambling addict, hated the desert, and he knew that apart from gambling Las Vegas had little to offer. The weather was unpleasant and the scenery unmemorable. The rustic casinos and hotels couldn't hold a candle to the accommodations in Monte Carlo. At night, sleeping poorly, Wilkerson recognized how much his addiction had consumed him, that he had visited and revisited such an inhospitable place just to partake of its gaming opportunities. However, he also saw an upside to the town's isolation: if he could convince people to visit, the lack of distraction would likely encourage them to spend more time at the tables.

Although my father's vision was still unformed, he knew that an attractive venue would require a sizable piece of land. In January 1945, on a taxi ride with Tom Seward from the El Rancho to the small Vegas airport, Wilkerson spotted a FOR SALE sign on a large lot containing dilapidated shacks and a crumbling motel sign. "Take that number down," he barked at Seward, pointing at the phone number on the FOR SALE notice. He didn't care that the land was several miles out of town; the important thing was that it was big—thirty-three acres. As Wilkerson would learn, it belonged to Margaret M. Folsom, a small hotel owner down on her luck. One month later, in mid-February 1945, Wilkerson dispatched Greg Bautzer, fresh out of the navy and still wearing his uniform, to Vegas to negotiate with Folsom. The publisher himself would stay behind the scenes for the time being; as a known Vegas high roller, he couldn't reveal his involvement without inflating the asking price.

Bautzer learned even more about Folsom. She was a widow who had moved to Vegas from Hawaii, where she'd operated a successful bordello. She had no lawyer, nor did she want one, preferring to handle all her own business. After an entire day and night of tough negotiating, Folsom sold Bautzer the property for $84,000.

Still wanting to keep his plans under wraps, my father instructed Bautzer to ensure that the lot continue to be known as the Folsom property. Wilkerson conveyed the down payment of $9,500 via a generic customer's check from one of the casinos rather than drawing from his personal account. And the deed was not even recorded until nine months after the sale.

When Wilkerson's purchase did become common knowledge, many felt that he had made a mistake in buying land so far from Vegas's other hotels and casinos. Friends and colleagues dismissed the entire venture as a crazy risk.

But Wilkerson was pleased with how his plans were proceeding. He knew he wouldn't have been able to buy such a large lot in the middle of Vegas, and he believed that the remote location would further distinguish his new creation from the less imposing businesses in town. It would also help him avoid direct conflict with the other casino owners, several of whom had become good friends of his, and none of whom welcomed the competition.

Still, as George Kennedy put it, the established operators had cause to feel threatened. Those familiar with my father's track record knew that he possessed both the means and the talent to duplicate his Hollywood success in their town. They began to worry about what a grand Wilkerson property could do to disrupt their small but steady flow of customers.

Wilkerson decided that his new resort would need to house all his passions under one roof. It would be a gambling mecca, a luxurious home away from home, and an insulated universe of fine dining, high-quality floor shows, and outdoor activities. By early April 1945 he had summoned George Vernon Russell and Tom Douglas to his Hollywood office to outline his vision.

He planned to build the largest hotel in Las Vegas, five stories tall with 250 rooms. The El Rancho, which was currently the largest, had only 110, and the Last Frontier only 107. Wilkerson's new hotel would also be far more luxurious, with elegant accommodations designed to attract an upscale clientele. He instructed Douglas and Russell to pay close attention to the bathrooms, modeling them on those in Parisian hotels, each with a sunken bathtub and something rarely seen in America—a bidet. He also wanted a spa and health club like those in the German resort town of Baden-Baden, where weary gamblers could relax with mineral baths and massages. Steam rooms and a gym would be available as well.

Wilkerson wanted to set aside space within the hotel for ten retail stores, which would carry internationally renowned brands such as Cartier and Chanel. He recruited four top chefs from Europe and planned multiple options for refreshment: a café, a bar/lounge, and a restaurant along the lines of LaRue. The gigantic showroom would be based on the one in Paris's Moulin Rouge, while its nightly floor shows would be modeled after those at another Parisian cabaret—the Folies Bergère, a Wilkerson favorite. A nightclub would offer dancing and sophisticated after-dinner entertainment by popular bands and other top-flight live acts.

As for the casino itself, Wilkerson explained to his architect and designer that he wanted a palatial environment that would encourage gamblers to lose themselves completely in the thrill of the games. He spoke openly about his own compulsion, explaining to Douglas and Russell that when he gambled, he hated to be disturbed or interrupted; he lost all track of time and the outside world ceased to exist. He confessed that his own lost weekends were the inspiration for his luxury resort. Isolation, seclusion, and privacy were, he understood, key factors in the addicted gambler's quest, and he was keen to foster them through the casino's design.

The layout he had in mind was radical for the time. It would place the casino at the hub of the hotel, ensuring that no guest could enter or exit without passing through the casino. Wilkerson also believed that natural light interfered with a gambler's concentration, so he insisted that the casino floor would have no windows; "Never let them see daylight," he told Russell and Douglas. There would be no wall clocks, and the lighting would be permanently dimmed. In the gambler's mind, it would always be night, and time would pass unnoticed.

My father also emphasized comfort within the casino. Prior to this point, most gambling tables had hard, straight wooden edges, "very much like kitchen tables but covered in felt," remembered Kennedy. Wilkerson asked that his tables be custom designed with curved edges and leather-padded cushioning around the sides. He also felt that standing diminished the pleasure of the game, so he mandated chairs and stools at every table. Above all, the casino had to be a gambling palace, matching the elegance and sophistication of Monte Carlo or Casino d'Evian. Evening dress would be black tie.

As usual, once he had expressed his desires, Wilkerson gave Douglas and Russell a free hand. They would be responsible for replicating the success they had repeatedly achieved for him in Hollywood. Many onlookers thought he was asking for the impossible. Transporting the glamour and romance of Paris to Hollywood was one thing; hauling it out to the middle of the desert was quite another.

To assist them with the effort, the publisher hired Eduardo Jose Samaniego, in his opinion the finest landscaper in the world. Tasked with designing the hotel's exterior spaces, Samaniego submitted drawings that included a thirty-foot waterfall and acres of land overflowing with exotic plants and flowers—all of which would be transplanted from Los Angeles. Other amenities outside the main building would include private bungalows, a swimming pool, courts for tennis, badminton, handball, and squash, and a nine-hole golf course—the first course at any Vegas hotel. For the more adventurous there would be a trapshooting range and stables housing forty-five horses.

Samaniego's designs and Wilkerson's other plans demanded an enormous amount of fresh water. Fortunately, the nearby Boulder Dam (soon to be renamed the Hoover Dam) promised a limitless supply. A more daunting environmental issue was the intense heat, which abated only during the winter months. In most Vegas hotels, electric ceiling fans churned the unbearable hot air through the room, while a few employed swamp coolers, primitive precursors to air-conditioning. "They were noisy, wet, and damp," said Herb McDonald, recalling his days as the assistant general manager of the El Rancho Vegas. Wilkerson decided his would be the first hotel in America to offer modern air-conditioning technology—the desert would at long last become habitable.

All things considered, the new hotel was a truly massive undertaking, of the sort no one before Billy Wilkerson had even dreamed. And as always, his vision was elitist, a playground for the wealthy and the powerful. As Kennedy recalled, "Mr. Wilkerson was unconcerned with the casual, local gambler. He was building the resort for his Beverly Hills clients."

Usually Wilkerson named his projects long before they reached completion, often drawing inspiration from his travels. Searching for a suitably exotic designation, and thinking of one of his favorite nightspots in New York City, the Stork Club, he recalled another species of bird, magnificent and pink, that he'd seen on a trip to Florida. What better namesake for an establishment that shared these creatures' beauty, grace, and elegance? He could even import the birds themselves to strut across an artificial lake on the hotel grounds. Wilkerson commissioned Hollywood graphic artist Bert Worth to design the logo for the venue now that he'd arrived at its name: the Flamingo Club.

––––––––––

Wilkerson knew no gambling operation could succeed without the same kind of skilled and experienced professionals he had found in Hollywood. From croupiers to cashiers to lookouts and undercover security guards, he sought quality. "Mr. Wilkerson's steadfast philosophy had always been 'You get what you pay for,'" said Kennedy. "He believed that if you hired and bought the best, you got the best. It was that simple." As he had with Bruno Petoletti and Orlando Figini at Restaurant LaRue, he locked in key personnel by bringing them aboard as silent partners. Such profit participation was usually so lucrative that few hires had serious thoughts about leaving.

Unfortunately, Nola Hahn's ability to run an ambitious gaming operation had been called into question by the catastrophic failure of the Arrowhead Springs Hotel. So this time Wilkerson looked to new recruits to manage the Flamingo casino: Gus Greenbaum and Moe Sedway, the Nola Hahns of Las Vegas. "Casino wizards," remembered Seward. Greenbaum was an Arizona bookmaker with a police record but a reputation of being highly skilled at casino management. Sedway was a loyal associate of crime boss Meyer Lansky who had been making trips to Nevada on the mob's behalf for years.

In 1945 the two men were running Vegas's El Cortez Hotel and had made a particular success of its gaming operation. Wilkerson had first approached them back in February, and Sedway initially expressed skepticism. He felt Wilkerson's vision was too grand and his property too far out of town. But Wilkerson stressed his ability to attract high-society clientele and argued that they, not the locals, would bring in the big money. "The Boys," as Wilkerson affectionately referred to Sedway and Greenbaum, were entranced by his enthusiasm and accepted his offer.

No one knows what percentage Wilkerson offered for their participation in running the gaming, but for a slice of the profits and a silent partnership, they agreed to manage and operate the entire casino and assume total responsibility for the games. They also agreed to help procure all necessary permits. It was an effective match, with Sedway and Greenbaum contributing their vast knowledge of casino management but relying on Wilkerson's flair for creating glamorous successes.

George Vernon Russell and Tom Douglas also did not disappoint. Russell drew up magnificent plans for the mammoth complex, and Douglas created detailed designs for interiors with glittering chandeliers, fine woods, polished mirrors, and costly marble. The upholstery would be plush and elegant, gilt and velvet.

But as the plans grew, so did the budget. Completion estimates totaled just under $1.2 million. Although Wilkerson accepted this figure, he did not have the ready cash to invest, so as much as he loathed borrowing, he approached

Bank of America. Normally banks clamor after high-profile businessmen like Wilkerson, but the risk-averse bank declined to lend him the full amount, politely reminding him that in 1944 they had extended him a line of credit of $200,000 that he had used to cover gambling losses. "They were aware of Mr. Wilkerson's gambling," said Kennedy. "Naturally, they were wary about risking a large sum they may not get back. That he was an extremely successful businessman didn't matter. A gambler was a gambler to the bank."

Bank of America eventually agreed to finance the publisher's dream to the tune of $600,000—if Wilkerson put up his successful businesses as collateral. He approached Howard Hughes for an additional $200,000; Hughes thought he was crazy to have anything to do with the Nevada desert, but advanced him the requested funds without question, under the pretext that it was a year's worth of prepaid advertising in the *Reporter*.

The impresario was still $400,000 short. With characteristic confidence, he decided to make up the difference at the gaming tables. Over two nights in April 1945 he risked $200,000. By the end of the second evening, it was gone.

He asked Russell and Douglas to scale down the plans to accommodate a smaller budget, and the two substantially modified the blueprints to exclude the hotel; the new designs would include only a casino, restaurant, and café. Optimistic as ever, Wilkerson predicted that the casino, once in full operation, would bring him the necessary funding to add a hotel and the rest of the missing amenities.

For months, Wilkerson had talked enthusiastically about his project. Then, suddenly, conceding that his gambling had gotten the better of him, he decided that remaining involved in the Flamingo's construction would only aggravate his habit. Fearing for his financial safety, he vowed never to return to the source of his temptation and officially turned the Flamingo over to Sedway and Greenbaum, explaining his reasoning in a letter:

> I have become convinced that Las Vegas is too dangerous for me. I like gambling too much, like to shoot craps and drive myself nuts and the only way I can defeat it is to keep away from any place that has it. And that is what I'm going to do.

Some of Wilkerson's friends believed he was merely using this latest gambling binge as an excuse to bow out of an already overwhelming operation, but

Las Vegas had genuinely become Wilkerson's nemesis. Having lost close to $10,000 in a single afternoon on July 13, 1945, he wrote, "I was so disgusted with myself." On July 14 he lost another $5,000 at the Last Frontier.

It was the wrong time to be losing cash. He had gambled away $60,000 set aside for the acquisition of badly needed new printing presses for the *Reporter*. The alternative was to finance the equipment, something he was adamantly opposed to. The publisher also owed Moe Sedway $5,000, but he persuaded him to deduct this debt from the $9,000 he still had invested in the Flamingo property; aware of Wilkerson's addiction and hoping to prevent the project's land being lost as a result, Sedway had agreed to cover any debts Wilkerson incurred in exchange for a bigger slice of casino profits and ownership in the land. By early September, Wilkerson had gambled away his remaining ownership in the property, and on September 15, 1945, he deeded the land to Sedway.

In his letter turning over control of the project, Wilkerson suggested that his original plans for a combination casino and hotel had been overambitious and that the costs of building and operating such a venture would be prohibitive. But he also stressed that the scaled-back, casino-only plans would be "rich, sufficiently big and could be built economically and when opened, few if any would try to create something in opposition to you." He assured Sedway and Greenbaum that no one was in a better position than they were to accomplish this. In closing he added:

> I want you to know that I will be happy to be of any service that will not take me to Las Vegas. I can be of much help to you here in talent, in seeing that you get a good crew for your dining room and kitchen and other things which I would be delighted to do. It's my impression that you will be much better off without me.

After Wilkerson washed his hands of the Flamingo project, however, "the Boys" did not proceed with it on their own. Despite Wilkerson's blessing and encouragement, they were content with their success at the El Cortez. And alas, within days of throwing in the towel, Wilkerson was back at the tables in Las Vegas, gambling like a man possessed.

Fortunately, Joe Schenck still had faith in the Flamingo's potential, and he appealed to his friend to reconsider the project. In another abrupt about-face, in November 1945 Wilkerson repurchased the Flamingo land from Moe

Sedway. Just how Wilkerson procured a new cache of discretionary capital remains a mystery, but a good guess would be that it came from either Schenck or from Johnny Rosselli. It's also not clear how much Wilkerson paid Sedway or if he continued to retain Sedway and Greenbaum's services, but in late November, nine months after he purchased Margaret Folsom's land, Flamingo Club construction began.

The project was officially under the control of W. R. Wilkerson Enterprises, and the builder was Bud Raulston, who began by bulldozing the two dilapidated motel shacks. Within six weeks, foundations were laid for the kitchen, bar, and dining room, a basement was excavated, and the piping was completed. Soon, all the main girders for the building's shell had been erected. Nearly a third of the construction, based on the modified blueprints (which excluded the hotel), was complete before Wilkerson ran into unexpected difficulties.

By the end of 1945, World War II was over, which meant that labor was plentiful. But thanks to the wartime restrictions, building materials remained scarce. When they could be obtained, they were astronomically expensive. Wilkerson had already sunk $300,000 into the operation, and between his gambling losses and additional debts to Moe Sedway, he owed a grand total of just under $400,000. In a last-ditch attempt to raise the additional capital to complete construction, Wilkerson turned once again to Lady Luck, staking $150,000 of his remaining $200,000 at the gaming tables. He lost it all.

Next Wilkerson turned to Hollywood. The studios were constantly building and dismantling movie sets; he offered bargain-basement advertising rates in the *Reporter* in exchange for surplus lumber and metal. According to Tom Seward, the publisher even went so far as to threaten not to review key movies unless the executives agreed to provide him with supplies. With this combination of incentives and threats, he succeeded in cajoling several studio heads into donating materials from their backlots.

But these scavenged supplies added little real value to the construction effort, and by early January 1946 the project had ground to a standstill. Dismayed, he paid everyone off in cash and left the Flamingo's skeleton to lie beached in the hot, empty desert.

Just as Wilkerson was reaching the end of his financial tether, Moe Sedway was bringing the Flamingo project to the attention of his boss Meyer Lansky.

Sedway saw it as a unique opportunity for their syndicate to expand operations in Las Vegas, and he predicted that the postwar demand for entertainment would be enormous. According to his calculations, hordes of gamblers from every state in the union would soon be flooding Las Vegas. They could either prepare for this massive influx or lose out to the competition.

At first Lansky did not share Sedway's rosy opinions about the future of gaming in the Nevada desert. He hated the heat and believed it would keep visitors away. Lansky had pictured Wilkerson's operation as a modest casino and nightclub and doubted whether it would be enough to draw the crowds Sedway described. But when Sedway told him of Wilkerson's original plans for a grand hotel/casino, Lansky began to change his mind. He decided to make the publisher an offer he couldn't refuse.

For well over a month, the building site stood quiet as Wilkerson teetered on the brink of abandoning his dream. Then, in February 1946, Wilkerson and Bud Raulston were touring the site when an expensively dressed man drove up and introduced himself as G. Harry Rothberg, a businessman from the East Coast. In truth, Rothberg and his brother, Sam, had made their fortune trading liquor during Prohibition, when they'd been the largest and most powerful distributor of black market liquor in the state of Illinois. After Prohibition, Sam continued to create the brew at a new plant in Pekin, Illinois, under the banner of the American Distilling Company, while Harry owned and operated its New York–based distributor.

Rothberg told Wilkerson and Raulston that he represented a firm in New York that wished to invest in the Flamingo Club. He and his associates knew that Wilkerson was broke, and they were willing to help him complete his Las Vegas venture—including his abandoned plans for an attached hotel. In exchange for funding, Wilkerson would retain a one-third share in the project and the contractual promise that he would continue to call all creative shots. When the hotel/casino became operational (no later than March 1, 1947), Wilkerson would be its sole operator and manager; all others would be silent partners.

Rothberg asked how much capital Wilkerson needed to complete the project. Without hesitation, Wilkerson told him: $1 million. Rothberg didn't blanch; he told Wilkerson if the deal went through, he would be advanced the full amount, with a guarantee that he "would not have to put another dime of his own money into the project."

Rothberg was charming, and he flattered Wilkerson by telling him he was the only man suited to completing this task. Wilkerson said he would take the offer under consideration. But he hesitated. The deal meant that he would be handing over two-thirds ownership in his latest venture to unknown parties, a big price to pay. He also wondered how Rothberg knew so much about his plans and finances, since he had never put out the word that he was looking for a partner or that he was short of funds. He had no qualms about outside investors who put up cash in exchange for a slice of the pie and then got out of the way, but he was wary of meddling partners who might interfere with his business and negatively affect his balance sheets. He already had a turbulent new partnership with Tom Seward, and he wasn't sure he needed another.

But Rothberg's deal, giving him creative and managerial control and a substantial cut of the action, seemed to promise acceptably silent investors. Ultimately he was amenable to all Rothberg's terms save one: he demanded that he retain complete ownership of the land. Exactly why he insisted on this one change is a mystery. Some have speculated that he planned to use the land as a money source, either arranging for the hotel to lease the land from him or taking out loans against the property. In any event, Rothberg consented to the modified agreement. "Billy, after a considerable amount of soul-searching on it agreed to go ahead and accept the deal," Bautzer said.

On February 26, 1946, Rothberg and Wilkerson signed a contract. Once he had Wilkerson's signature, Rothberg vanished; he would not appear again for more than a year. But the investors he represented quickly made good on their side of the bargain. Though some accounts suggest that Wilkerson received his completion funds later in the year, in fact it was in early March that W. R. Wilkerson Enterprises received the agreed-upon $1 million to complete the Flamingo Club—which the publisher, once again pursuing his original vision, renamed the Flamingo Hotel.

Wilkerson had been right, however, to question the motives of his new mystery investors. Harry Rothberg had organized them under the direction of Meyer Lansky, and they consisted of both polished businessmen and career criminals. The Flamingo was the group's first major investment in Las Vegas, and with a million dollars at stake, it was also by far their boldest and riskiest venture. These were not the sort of people to leave such a major investment unsupervised.

With a year to meet his deadline, Wilkerson happily resumed construction, but the ink on the contract had been dry no more than a month when Moe Sedway and Gus Greenbaum visited the construction site, bringing with them a loudly dressed character who enthusiastically presented himself to the publisher as his new partner. My father was already acquainted with the man—and his notorious temper. It was Bugsy Siegel.

26 | BUGSY SIEGEL

THE RELATIONSHIP BETWEEN BILLY WILKERSON and his new inves-
tors was delicate. He'd long been involved with gangsters, of course, but in the
past he'd entered into such relationships deliberately, with the confidence that
he'd be protected by loyal partners such as Johnny Rosselli. This time, he'd been
taken by surprise and forced into business with underworld figures with whom
he'd previously had few dealings, who hoped to use his high-profile reputation in legitimate business circles to front their criminal activities. To save
the Flamingo, he'd signed a deal with the devil; decades later, Mayer Lansky
biographer Robert Lacey observed, "Billy Wilkerson inadvertently became the
midwife who delivered the eastern Mafia to Las Vegas."

Wilkerson was particularly shocked to learn that Benny Siegel was his
new partner. He'd complained to Handsome Johnny years earlier when the
gangster attacked another customer at Sunset House with a razor, and it wasn't
an isolated incident of violence. Siegel had a reputation as a dangerous bully,
prone to sudden outbursts that some likened to epileptic seizures. The slightest
provocation could ignite his temper and provoke him to acts of homicidal rage.

Harry Drucker, who'd had to quickly de-escalate the Sunset House incident,
recalled that in fact Siegel rarely got angry, "but when he did, he really let go."
Greg Bautzer remembered the gangster's face darkening when he got upset,
his blue eyes turning slate gray. And George Kennedy said that "Mr. Siegel
was not the sort of man you got angry. Even worse, he never forgot why you
got him angry. It gave new meaning to the word *grudge*."

It was not merely a problem of impulse control. Siegel worked hard to cultivate the image of a cutthroat gangster, distinguishing himself by his ruthless ability to make good on threats uttered in anger. "Anyone who knew Siegel took his threats seriously—or was wise enough to," Bautzer said. He viewed murder as a convenient solution to problems that would not go away on their own.

But Siegel had another side to his personality. Many were familiar with his warm, easygoing charm; he was typically attentive and vibrant—a flamboyant dresser—and sometimes even boyishly innocent and reserved. Since coming to Hollywood in 1933, he'd fallen in love with the Sunset Strip nightlife and sat at the best tables in all the top Hollywood venues. He was especially smitten with the film industry and mingled with the stars at celebrity parties. He even rubbed shoulders with Jack Warner and Joe Schenck, and quickly established himself as a playboy on par with Howard Hughes.

Siegel's sources of income during the 1930s and '40s remain a mystery. They were said to be prodigious, including takes from racetracks and race wire services in the neighborhood of $20,000 a month. He also owned a piece of the Clover Club, and it was rumored that he'd owned a small percentage of Joe Schenck's now-shuttered Agua Caliente resort. From time to time the gangster was even known to play the stock market (without success). And while Siegel referred to gamblers as "suckers," his gambling addiction rivaled Wilkerson's.

At one stage, Siegel briefly flirted with the idea of becoming a movie star like his boyhood friend George Raft. Naive but ambitious, he financed his own glossies and screen test. But his ego prevented him from starting at the bottom of anything, so seeking work as an extra was out of the question. He knew he had only to ask his connections in the industry for help, but his pride prevented him from doing so, and the gangster's film career never got off the ground. For the most part Hollywood regarded him as a failure. Little of what he did during his sojourn was noteworthy.

The studio gates may have stayed closed to Ben Siegel, but Hollywood's bedrooms opened their doors to the gangster. The town was fascinated with gangsters, and such stars as Betty Grable, Lana Turner, and Ava Gardner, as well as millionaire Countess Dentice di Frasso, often were seen being squired around town by Siegel. He often was mired in very public romantic drama, which peaked when he got involved with Virginia Hill, a plump aspiring actress from Alabama. Few could see what attracted the charismatic gangster to the vulgar Hill, but according to Hill herself, her lock on Siegel was based on her ability to arouse and satisfy his sexual needs (she would say as much under oath at the Kefauver hearings of 1950–1951). Siegel also recognized himself in Hill—they both were streetwise and stubborn.

Siegel's notorious love life earned the ire of his gangster colleagues who advocated anonymity in their professional lives and stability in their domestic lives. These colleagues were quick to note that Siegel was a married man and urged him to keep a lower profile. He did not.

Siegel's publicity-shy associates were further embarrassed by his violent temper tantrums. He was considered a loose cannon rather than a clever entrepreneur like his friend Meyer Lansky, and he did not possess Lansky's brains or uncanny business acumen. While Siegel's power and influence have never been in dispute, he was never in the league of mob figures like Lansky or Rosselli.

Siegel's notoriety had become impossible to ignore by 1942, when he went on trial for the November 1939 murder of mob informant Harry Greenberg. The case attracted widespread public attention, particularly in Los Angeles. When George Raft testified for his friend, crowds flocked to the courtroom. Siegel's preferences in jail were also a hot topic at Hollywood's society parties. Not only did he demand to eat Ciro's food in his cell, but he was even allowed female visitors and was granted leave for "dental visits" that were, in truth, conjugal visits. Shortly after the trial began, the two main witnesses against Siegel and his accomplice, Frankie Carbo, suddenly died. On February 5, 1942, the district attorney, stripped of his case, dismissed all charges against Siegel.

The gangster was a free man, but he remained unable to escape his ignominious reputation. It clung to him, as did his hated nickname, Bugsy, an ugly reminder of a thuggish past. He'd come to Hollywood in search of legitimacy and respectability—and now, in 1946, Wilkerson's Flamingo project offered him a second opportunity to reinvent himself.

Siegel had first visited southern Nevada with Moe Sedway in the 1930s. On Meyer Lansky's orders, the men had been sent to explore the possibilities for expanding their operations, but like Lansky, Ben Siegel ended up at a loss to understand what anyone would want with the place. He fled for the klieg lights and glamour of Hollywood, making his home in Beverly Hills while Sedway stayed behind in Vegas. But shortly after Wilkerson brought Lansky and his associates into his construction efforts, the mob boss began to pressure Siegel to represent their interests to Wilkerson. (Many believed that Siegel was actually involved in the Flamingo before this, as early as mid-1945, but his name does not appear on any documentation prior to February 1946, nor did Wilkerson mention him or any other controlling influence in his 1945 letter that temporarily turned over the Flamingo project to Moe Sedway and Gus Greenbaum.) At first, Siegel wanted no part of an operation that meant forsaking his comfortable Beverly Hills nest and Hollywood playboy lifestyle, but Lansky insisted. Ultimately Siegel acquiesced.

Despite his initial shock, Wilkerson did likewise. After all, he'd never personally run afoul of Siegel's temper, and Siegel had been a tremendous fan of Ciro's and Sunset House. The publisher was even well acquainted with Siegel's brother, Dr. Maurice Siegel, who was a studio doctor at Columbia Pictures. And ultimately he chose to set aside any misgivings he may have had—with Siegel in particular or with the Mafia's uninvited participation more generally—to keep construction on track. "It was Billy's decision to concern himself with the eventual outcome and success of his project rather than on connections his business associates might have had," Bautzer said.

———————

Unlike Wilkerson, Siegel had never built anything before, so in the beginning of their partnership he deferred to my father on everything. Indeed, Siegel went overboard to win the publisher's approval, charming his way into his office and showering Wilkerson and his staff, especially George Kennedy, with lavish presents. "Wanting to see Mr. Wilkerson, he always came to the office with gifts," Kennedy recalled. "Mr. Wilkerson got a lot of clothing. I got mostly silk neckties. He was always extremely cordial in his dealings with Mr. Wilkerson. A real gentleman. He could charm the wrappings off a mummy. And whenever Mr. Wilkerson needed something done, Mr. Siegel saw to it immediately."

Throughout the spring of 1946, Kennedy recalled, his employer and Siegel met almost daily at the publisher's office at the *Reporter*. Wilkerson gave Siegel simple tasks and welcomed suggestions from the gangster. Siegel's connections enabled Wilkerson to obtain black market building materials, ending the problematic postwar shortages. Wilkerson's mood improved as he saw his dream getting back on track. One afternoon in late March, Siegel and Wilkerson were visiting the construction site in Las Vegas, and Wilkerson was talking about a future day when hotels would be lined up and down the road as far as the eye could see. Siegel asked him why anyone would want to come to this godforsaken city. Wilkerson explained, "Because of people like me. People will endure almost anything, go anywhere, where there is legal gambling."

My father worked hard to get his inexperienced partner up to speed. "Siegel did not know a bidet from a Bordeaux, much less marbles from Italy," said Tom Seward. "Billy showed him everything." Wilkerson shipped Siegel off to his architects, builders, and decorators, who patiently schooled the gangster. Colin Russell, son of architect George Vernon Russell, remembered that "Siegel would sit in my father's office for hours soaking up all the information." "The reality is that Siegel became Billy's errand boy," commented Bill Feeder, a Wilkerson friend and *Reporter* employee.

From the start, however, the partnership was colored by Siegel's Jekyll-and-Hyde personality. On one Saturday morning, for instance, George Kennedy was the beneficiary of the mobster's tender side. Siegel was meeting with Wilkerson in his office as usual, and the secretary was taking notes. At around eleven thirty, Kennedy received a call letting him know that his elder brother, Harry, was dying. Kennedy asked to be excused. Three hours later he returned, grief etched upon his face. Siegel immediately asked him what was wrong. "There was genuine concern in Mr. Siegel's voice," Kennedy remembered.

When he told Siegel and Wilkerson that his brother had died in his arms and requested the rest of the day off, my father responded in typical Ebenezer Scrooge fashion, reminding his employee that there was simply too much work to be done around the office to let him go. Kennedy retreated from his boss's office, but Siegel followed him into the corridor and withdrew from his pocket the thickest roll of $100 bills that Kennedy had ever seen. With tears in his eyes, Siegel pressed the entire roll into Kennedy's palm and insisted he take it. Touched, Kennedy thanked the gangster but refused the generous offer.

Siegel's dark side was also in evidence. Once in the spring of 1946, Wilkerson called a late-night meeting in Vegas with Siegel, George Vernon Russell, and Tom Douglas to complain about a member of the building crew who was doing substandard work. "The guy was building doors so that they opened all the wrong way," Kennedy recalled. The men stood around a table reviewing the blueprints in an unfinished room of the Flamingo, next to a small room

Siegel had converted into a makeshift gym where he lifted weights. Wilkerson vented his frustration over the crew member's errors: "This guy's driving me nuts. I wish to God someone would take care of him!"

In a voice from a different world, Siegel said, "I'll take care of him, Billy." A panicked Wilkerson quickly cried, "Shit, no. Not like that!"

As time went on, the gangster's respectful admiration for Wilkerson began to dissolve into jealousy. This is hardly surprising; Siegel rarely allowed himself to be outdone by anything or anyone, so being the subordinate party in a teacher-student relationship quickly wore thin. Siegel began to feel intimidated and paranoid, increasingly resentful of Wilkerson's talents and vision. "Siegel did not want to be *like* Billy," Seward explained. "He literally wanted to *be* Billy Wilkerson."

The problems started quietly. Siegel began making decisions without consulting Wilkerson, informing work crews that the publisher had put him in charge and ordering changes that conflicted with the blueprinted plans. "Mr. Wilkerson would give an order, then Ben Siegel would reverse it," Kennedy recalled.

Wilkerson was understandably furious. When he confronted the gangster, Siegel sheepishly apologized, but once the publisher's back was turned, he resumed the same behavior. At one point my father attempted to remind Siegel of his ownership stake in the project: "For every buck you put into this deal, thirty-three cents is mine," he said, laughing.

"Mr. Siegel didn't like that," Kennedy remembered. "That wasn't the way you talked to Ben Siegel."

Siegel progressed from subverting Wilkerson's authority to outright denying it. According to Kennedy, whenever his employer was asked about Siegel's role in the project, the publisher called him a silent investor and a "helping hand." But one day syndicated newspaper columnist Westbrook Pegler approached Siegel and asked him to describe his role in the project. He exploded, giving the columnist an earful. "This is my fucking hotel!" Siegel shrieked. "My idea! Wilkerson has nothing to do with it! Do you understand? Nothing to do with it!"

Soon, the mere mention of Wilkerson's name sent Siegel into a red-faced, fist-pounding rage. If anyone asked about Wilkerson's participation in the project, Siegel would angrily refer to his partner as something tantamount to a mere workman. As his mind diminished Wilkerson's importance, it inflated his own. He began to see himself as Las Vegas's gambling czar.

Siegel's behind-the-scenes interference began to slow the project's pace, and in an effort to keep construction moving smoothly, Wilkerson agreed to a compromise: management of the project would be divided, with Siegel supervising the hotel portion, while Wilkerson retained control of the casino and everything else. The publisher felt that if Siegel made a mess of the hotel, he could still salvage the project. Once more, he trusted that the casino and the other attractions would eventually bring in enough cash to allow him to finish off the hotel.

Siegel asked Wilkerson to find him his own architect and contractor, further splitting the construction project in two. With little or no communication between the two men after that, the operation fell into disarray. Siegel became drunk with power, and within a month he had spent all the funding allocated for the hotel portion. He stridently demanded more from Wilkerson's budget. Again Wilkerson refused.

"Siegel was out of control," recalled Bautzer. "Where Billy was sticking to his budget, [Siegel] was not." According to Kennedy, "Mr. Wilkerson knew he was dealing with a lunatic at that point."

Wilkerson's only hope was to alert the powers behind Siegel to the situation. He reasoned that if they could be convinced to remove Siegel in time, he could ensure the venture would be a success. But by May 1946, Siegel had begun to gain the support of the wary syndicate members, persuading them to let him take the helm with assurances that under his control there would be no changes and that Wilkerson would not be eliminated from the creative process. With his appeal to higher authority cut off, my father saw no way to maintain control. So when Siegel offered to buy out the publisher's creative participation with corporate stock—an additional 5 percent ownership in the operation—he accepted the offer.

On June 20, 1946, Siegel formed the Nevada Project Corporation, naming himself as president. The law firm Pacht, Elton, Warne, Ross & Bernhard in Los Angeles handled the incorporation, naming the original directors of the corporation. The directors were N. Joseph Ross (Siegel's Beverly Hills attorney), Siegel himself, Moe Sedway, and original front man G. Harry Rothberg. The corporation defined everyone else, including Wilkerson, as a mere shareholder. Although the publisher retained a considerable stake in the project and still owned all the land, the incorporation heralded the end of Wilkerson's creative participation and the beginning of Siegel's reign. From this point on, the Flamingo was a syndicate-run operation, and any friendship that remained between Siegel and Wilkerson was at an end. By early July they were no longer speaking.

After cementing his power, Siegel could not get rid of Wilkerson fast enough; he never again consulted him. He fired all Wilkerson's on-site associates and staff, replacing Tom Douglas and George Vernon Russell with contractor Del Webb and architect Richard Stadelman. Webb and Stadelman were well qualified for their new positions—Webb, for instance, was a prominent real estate developer who'd recently become co-owner of the New York Yankees—but Siegel showed poorer judgment with another staffing choice. He delegated responsibility for the property's interior decorations to his girlfriend, Virginia Hill.

Wilkerson, meanwhile, was still in line to manage the hotel, but that was something he couldn't do until the syndicate finished building it. Stripped of all control over that process, the publisher left it in Siegel's hands and headed back to Hollywood.

27 | THE CRUSADE

WILKERSON'S RETURN TO HOLLYWOOD hadn't been preceded by a long absence; he'd been dividing his time between Los Angeles and Las Vegas while overseeing the Flamingo's construction. And during his days in L.A., he'd been busy with more than meeting with Bugsy Siegel in his *Reporter* office. For one thing, after a matrimonial sabbatical of more than three years, the fifty-five-year-old publisher had been searching for a new bride.

One evening at LaRue in February 1946, he met a twenty-seven-year-old, slim, dark-eyed model and actress named Vivian DuBois. As he had done with others in the past, Wilkerson immediately decided she was the woman for him. On May 9, the two eloped to Las Vegas.

Vivian was an avid tennis player who pursued her love of the game at every opportunity. Whenever she and Billy went to Vegas, he holed up in a casino and she sought tennis partners, mostly people her own age. While he was "taking care of business" in cavernous casinos, Vivian played on the sun-drenched courts. After all, there would be no upside to playing cards with her husband. "When I won at cards," she confessed, "he accused me of cheating."

One day Wilkerson took a break from the tables and found his wife at the tennis court surrounded by a bevy of young men. Already infamous for turning different shades of red whenever one of his wives talked to another man, he was incensed and ordered her off the courts. When she yelled back at him, asking what she was going to do with her time instead, he told her he would give her credit in every casino in town. Vivian did not share her husband's love of gambling, but she agreed to play at the tables next to him. When she won an average of $15,000 a session, it only further infuriated her husband. Tom Seward recalled Wilkerson's jealousy "because the one thing he couldn't do"—win at the tables—"his wives could."

When Vivian was overcome with boredom, she sneaked back to the courts, only to be discovered again, at which point Billy unceremoniously whisked her back to Los Angeles. Vivian recalled that "many enjoyable weekends in Vegas ended that way."

But things got worse for her when my father lost control of the Flamingo construction and returned to Hollywood in search of his next major project. The crusade he launched next would prove so controversial that not even his new wife would be spared the blowback.

Some historians, including *All American Mafioso* author Charles Rappleye, maintain that Billy Wilkerson ignited his "Communist witch hunt" as a smoke-screen, a way to cover up his involvement with organized crime. Certainly, by 1946 he had more to hide on that count than ever. But a more likely explanation is that he was returning to his long-term objective: to get revenge on the studio bosses and destroy their unfair movie monopoly. If he exposed the studios' creative talent as Communists in the pages of the *Reporter* and demanded they be drummed out of the industry, he'd be striking a blow at his enemies' ability to make money. "Billy wanted to clobber the studio owners," Joe Pasternak explained. Convenient targets such as their writers "just happened to be in the way." And if his campaign, the first of its kind, proved successful, he'd raise his own profile and that of his paper, proving once and for all who really held the reins of power in the film capital.

Wilkerson's chosen target demonstrates once again his remarkable sense for what scandals would capture the attention of the public. In postwar America, fear and hatred of Communism were on the rise. Communist Russia's brutal dictator, Joseph Stalin, had ended World War II by gobbling up the nations of Eastern Europe and bringing some 100 million more people into the oppres-sive grip of the Soviet Union. At home, Stalin initiated "purges" of his political enemies and butchered his own people. The horror that Americans felt over Communism's rise is not unlike the fear that gripped later generations at the rise of ISIS. And Wilkerson had no compunction about appealing to people's growing anxiety in order to sell newspapers.

But my father's opposition to Communism was not merely a cynical ploy. Since his eye-opening visit to Russia in 1921, his own hatred of its political system had only grown. He was horrified that the United States and its allies had done nothing to stop the Soviet Union from drawing the Iron Curtain around Eastern Europe, bartering away multiple nations in exchange for Stalin's support against Hitler and the Axis powers. George Kennedy articulated the disgust that many Americans such as Wilkerson felt at their country's inaction: "The Allies did nothing. Fighting the war in Europe was all for nothing." Stalin's takeover, he said, "was just as bad as Hitler's invasion of Europe."

Wilkerson's early support for Hollywood's trade unions had also given way to a deep mistrust, as he came to see them as a stalking horse by which Communists would inject their poisonous ideology into the industry and the nation. He was especially suspicious of the Screen Writers Guild, with which he had clashed as far back as June 1938, when guild president Dudley Nichols took out a full-page ad in the *Reporter* and Wilkerson's Tradeviews column actually offered a rebuttal to its claims. By 1946, like many conservative Republicans, the publisher had come to see even the Democratic Party as a leftist threat to the American way of life. And like others in Hollywood's right-wing minority, he'd begun to worry that liberals were taking over the industry. By arguing against the creeping spread of Communism, Wilkerson was angling to become the spokesman for and conscience of a Hollywood faction that dared not speak publicly. As Greg Bautzer put it, "Billy's stance was politically popular at that time. Many people felt the same but were not as vocal about it."

Wilkerson's religious beliefs played a part as well. He saw Communists as godless, and like so many Catholics of his day, he believed that atheism was derived from the devil and was the natural enemy of humankind. Communism and its attendant atheism was, to him, a disease infecting his beloved movie industry that needed to be stamped out. (Indeed, the subject so disturbed him that by the time I was a child in the mid-1950s, it was a forbidden topic of conversation at our family dinner table; when my mother did discuss it with my sister and me, it was always in the car on a side street parked a mile away from our house.)

As he contemplated whether to begin naming names, however, my father knew that it was a risky stand to take. Many in the industry were already disturbed by his politics, and more and more critics perceived him as a man willing to throw the little guy under the bus. If he started attacking industry insiders for their politics, advertisers might withdraw their support, and some readers might boycott the paper. He understood the dangers, but he also knew if his gamble paid off, he would be seen as Hollywood's conquering emperor.

During one of his late-night drives with Howard Hughes, he spoke openly about his plans and his fears. Hughes could actually help him with both. Beyond worrying about advertiser and reader backlash, Wilkerson was also concerned about what would happen if he called someone a Communist who could show that he or she had no such associations. The *Reporter* had been involved in numerous libel suits in the past, and he was wary of leaving himself open to more. Any accusations would have to be based on reliable information from the most highly placed sources. Fortunately, Wilkerson knew that Hughes had powerful connections at the FBI and elsewhere in the government. So he made the business magnate a proposition: if he could convince his government contacts to hand over a list of names and other details identifying Communists within the movie industry, Wilkerson would print them on his front page.

An attack on Communists was perfectly in line with Hughes's politics, and as a film producer he'd also had his differences with the studio bosses. Hughes loved nothing better than settling old scores, and he was delighted that Billy Wilkerson would be slaying his dragons for him. He agreed to reach out to his connections.

One may wonder why my father didn't look for dirt from his own government sources. But Agent Frank Angell had resigned from the FBI the previous year, establishing his own private investigation firm in Hollywood. (For the next five years, the *Reporter* would be his one and only client.) Wilkerson could always have called on fellow anti-Communist J. Edgar Hoover—but he knew that Hughes had stronger connections and was likely to get information more quickly.

Sure enough, during another late-night drive, Hughes handed Wilkerson a sealed manila envelope. The next morning at his desk, Wilkerson sliced it open and found an extensive typewritten list from the FBI of all current and former members of the American Communist Party employed in the entertainment industry. "Mr. Wilkerson was as giddy as a schoolboy," recalled George Kennedy.

As my father's lawyer, Greg Bautzer advised him against publishing the information he'd received. But when Wilkerson refused to change course, Bautzer recalled, he suggested a way his client might skirt libel laws: instead of directly accusing someone on the list of being a Communist, he could reframe it as a question. Even that would be potent enough to brand the subject with the charges. And so was born a question that still echoes with significance all these decades later: "Are you now or have you ever been a member of the Communist Party?"

On the eve of launching his editorial campaign, my father did something thoroughly out of character: he went to confession. In George Kennedy's thirty years of service to Wilkerson, he had never before and would never again be aware of an instance in which his employer paid a visit to the confessional. But in this moment, apparently, Wilkerson feared for his immortal soul: Would his campaign against the Communists be considered a forbidden act of retribution? "In the eleventh hour he agonized over it," Kennedy said. "I guess he needed spiritual confirmation."

The afternoon of Saturday, July 6, 1946, Wilkerson knelt in the claustrophobic confessional. In the confessor's compartment was the pastor of Blessed Sacrament Catholic Church, Father Cornelius J. McCoy. McCoy knew Billy Wilkerson well; after all, he was a generous benefactor, and the church had honored him with a bronze wall plaque bearing his name. When the parishioner spoke to begin his confession, the priest immediately recognized Wilkerson's voice and expressed his surprise. My father explained his predicament, and there was a long silence. Finally, the pastor burst out with his response: "Castrate those Commie sons of bitches, Billy!"

The very next day Wilkerson's partner in the endeavor, Howard Hughes, was piloting an experimental aircraft of his own design when he crash-landed in Beverly Hills. He was nearly killed, and the accident would haunt him for the rest of his life. But Wilkerson's plans continued uninterrupted.

On Monday, July 8, Wilkerson published his initial anti-Communist editorial, a general warning about the spread of Communism in the film industry. "Mr. Wilkerson was prepping the public for the names that would follow," said

Kennedy. For the next three weeks, his editorials continued in the same vein. Finally, on Monday, July 29, in a column headlined A VOTE FOR JOE STALIN, Wilkerson came out swinging, printing the names of eleven officers of the Screen Writers Guild whom he accused of being "avowed Leftists and sympathizers of the Party Line." These were the first names on what would eventually become the infamous Hollywood blacklist: Dalton Trumbo, Maurice Rapf, Lester Cole, Howard Koch, Harold Buchman, John Wexley, Ring Lardner Jr., Harold Salemson, Henry Meyers, Theodore Strauss, and John Howard Lawson.

Louis B. Mayer was one of the first people to call the publisher that morning. According to Kennedy, he was furious. "Frankly, I don't give a shit what these sons of bitches do on their own time," Meyer shouted, "but you printing it is bad for business." Harry Cohn likely conveyed much the same sentiment—as a later accused writer, Walter Bernstein, explained, "If you could make a buck for Harry Cohn, being a Communist or a Republican didn't mean anything to him." Other calls followed; Kennedy remembered the switchboard lighting up like a Christmas tree with complaints.

Scores of people called to warn Wilkerson that by writing these editorials, he was biting the hand that fed him. Instead, according to Kennedy and Seward, the *Reporter*'s circulation soared. Delighted, the publisher continued his blitzkrieg, taking closer aim at the individual people on his list.

On Monday, August 19, 1946, Wilkerson called out Lester Cole, the first-ranked vice president of the Screen Writers Guild:

> We would like to ask Mr. Lester Cole . . . "Are you a Communist? Do you hold card number 46805 in what is known as the Northwest Section of the Communist party, a division of the party made up mostly of West Coast Commies?" . . .
>
> Cole is a member of the League of American Writers, the American Peace Mobilization, the Hollywood Anti-Nazi League, the Hollywood Peace Forum and Fourth Writers Congress, and many other organizations labeled as Communistic fronts. He, with John Howard Lawson and many other reported Communists and fellow travelers, attempted to defeat Jack B. Tenney, chairman of the Fact-Finding Committee on Un-American Activities in California back in 1942. He has been a contributor to a Communist publication. He was reported to have been one of the chief "yellers" at President Roosevelt

to stop the deportation of Harry Bridges, Communist West Coast labor leader. During the period when Hitler and Stalin were pals and loved each other with a non-aggression pact, Cole chairmanned a meeting held at the Hollywood Chamber of Commerce, at which Theodore Dreiser answered Howard Emmett Rogers, who criticized Hitler's ruthless bombing of women and children on the British Isles, with: "If they (the Germans) did away with every man, woman and child in England tonight, this would be a better world."

So again we ask the question of Lester Cole, first vice president of the Screen Writers Guild: "Are you a Communist? Are you a member of its Northwest Division, assigned to that special group known as Branch A of the writers' section and do you hold card number 46805 in the Communist party?"

The next day, in an editorial headlined RED BEACH-HEAD! Wilkerson took aim at John Howard Lawson, founder and original president of the Screen Writers Guild. The fusillade continued on Wednesday, with Wilkerson referring to Lawson as "the first commissar of thought planted by the Communist Party in the motion picture industry."

Wednesday's editorial, headlined HWYD's RED COMMISSARS!, also skewered Writers Guild secretary Maurice Rapf ("Are you a member of the Communist Party and do you hold Party Book No. 25113?") and treasurer Harold Buchman ("Are you a Communist? Are you a member of the Party's Northwest Section . . . and do you hold Communist Party Card No. 46802? Also, were you not a member of the Young Communists League?"). Expanding his original list of alleged Communist sympathizers, Wilkerson also called out the political activities of the guild's current president, Emmet Lavery; its third-ranked vice president, Oliver H. P. Garrett; and its executive secretary, William Pomerance.

The publisher even viciously questioned the religious faith of Emmet Lavery, a fellow Catholic. Wilkerson claimed that Lavery's religion made him "an ideal front man for the Guild's Communists" and asked, "Is he a dupe or a dope? Is he a starry-eyed liberal who has been conned into thinking the Comrades really believe in the Brotherhood of Man? Or is he an opportunist who is trying to work both sides of the street?"

The editorial ended with a call to action: "This, fellow Americans, is the record of the leadership of the Screen Writers Guild—an organization that seeks to control the greatest medium of thought in America—motion pictures! Is our industry going to let them get away with it?"

But that was by no means the end of the story. Wilkerson pressed the attack in Thursday's column, MORE RED COMMISSARS, in which he harpooned two more men on his original list, Dalton Trumbo and Ring Lardner Jr., and two additional guild members, Gordon Kahn and Richard Jay Collins. His takedown of Trumbo was particularly detailed:

> The Reporter, here and now, asks Trumbo to answer these questions: "Are you a Communist? Is your party name (or alias) Hal Conger? Are you a member of Group 3, Branch A of the American Communist Party? Are you the holder of Communist Party Book No. 36802?" . . .
>
> During Russia's invasion of Poland and Finland under the terms of the Berlin-Moscow pact, he vigorously opposed American preparedness and American aid to Britain. His book, "The Remarkable Andrew" (published in 1941 by J. B. Lippincott and Company), attacked lend-lease on the curious grounds that cooperation with the British was distasteful to the ghost of Andrew Jackson.
>
> At the time his book was published, millions of Jews were experiencing the niceties of Third Reich "civilization" in German concentration camps. Yet Trumbo dismissed appeals on their behalf as "British propaganda." But after Germany invaded Russia, he was quick to charge all critics of the Soviet system with "anti-Semitism."
>
> Trumbo appeared on the platform of the American Peace Mobilization, at a meeting held on April 6, 1940, to accuse President Roosevelt of "war mongering." The Attorney General of the United States later exposed this organization as "one of the most dangerous Communist groups in the country."
>
> In September, 1942, as a member of the National Federation for Constitutional Liberties, he signed an open letter to the President, denouncing the deportation proceedings being conducted against Communist labor leader, Harry Bridges. This group also was branded as Communist-controlled by the Attorney General.
>
> In the same year, Trumbo was a member of the committee which supported LaRue McCormack, an officer of the California Communist Party, in McCormack's campaign for the United States Senate.

On December 1, 1944, Trumbo was one of the sponsors and speakers at the first anniversary meeting of the American Youth for Democracy. One year before, this group had changed its name to "American Youth for Democracy," after previously having been known as "The Young Communists League."

Such is the record of "The Remarkable Trumbo."

Trumbo himself fired off a personal response to the publisher, questioning the genuineness of his accusations. The writer pointed out that the *Reporter* had given positive recommendations to the last three films he scripted (*A Guy Named Joe, Thirty Seconds over Tokyo*, and *Our Vines Have Tender Grapes*), and carried ads for the films as well—odd if Wilkerson considered their author a dangerous promoter of Communist ideas. "If these films contained any elements of communist propaganda," he wrote, "I cannot believe that you lack either the intelligence to detect them or the courage to denounce them. Your failure to do so indicates that your professed alarm . . . is insincere and without basis in truth." He continued:

> We live in a country founded upon the principle that a man's race, his religion and his politics are his private concern, protected as such by law. Any answer to your "questions," either positive or negative, would constitute an admission on my part of your right to assume the function of industry inquisitor. I deny that right, and have no intention of collaborating with you to establish it.
>
> Your piece on me is, in the main, a melange of inaccuracies, distortions and inventions. Coming from one who has testified in open court that he does not necessarily believe the editorials to which he affixes his name, this should surprise no one.

Though the letter would be included in later collections of Trumbo's correspondence, my father did not retain the copy he received. According to Kennedy, he immediately threw it away, thinking it unworthy of a reply.

But other rebuttals came swiftly on its heels, and some of them Wilkerson did see fit to answer. On Monday, August 26, Oliver Garrett wrote "An Open Letter to Wilkerson," and the next day, Wilkerson fired back at Garrett with an editorial headlined THE $600 QUESTION? Emmet Lavery responded to the

Reporter's attack on his politics and his Catholic faith, and on August 29, Wilkerson printed the letter in its entirety, all twenty-seven hundred words filling two side-by-side pages in the *Reporter*. The publisher insisted that "this letter is printed in full NOT because any law of the State of California could insist on such a printing but because The Reporter offered its columns to any of the members of the Screen Writers Guild who might see fit to answer some of the questions asked them in these pages."

Lavery's missive was painfully earnest:

> My life as a Catholic, until you chose to cast slurs upon it in your newspaper, has never been questioned by any editor anywhere in the world. . . .
>
> *I am not a Communist, and I never have been a Communist.*
>
> *I am not a member of the Communist Party, and I never have been a member of the Communist Party.*
>
> *I am a Roman Catholic, not merely one who pretends to be a Roman Catholic.*
>
> *I am, I believe, sincere and conscientious in the practice of my faith.*
>
> *I am not a front man for anybody and I have never been a front man for any Communists. . . .*
>
> *I have not gone along with any program which has taken the position that Roman Catholicism is immoral or idolatrous or that the Catholic priesthood is an agent of immorality.*

Wilkerson salivated at the opportunity to reply to Lavery's rebuttal, and did so in consecutive Tradeviews on September 11 and 12. He headlined both pieces MY DEAR MR. LAVERY. In the first, he began by reminding Lavery of the *Reporter*'s early support for Hollywood's writers—his belief that "the very foundation of ALL pictures, good or bad, was the story" and his editorials' advocacy for quality writing and improved salaries for writers. But his support, he said, was soured by the creeping influence of Communists within the Writers Guild:

> Of the writers we singled out to ask questions . . . NOT ONE has seen fit to answer. Why? We asked each of them if they were Communists. We asked some of them if they ever heard of party memberships in

the Northwest Section and of particular party numbers. No answers. We did not accuse you of being a Communist but asked you if you were a dupe or a dope. . . . You denied all. But still you head a Guild, many of whose board of directors are under question as to Communistic activities within and without the industry.

He ended the first part of his response by again questioning Lavery's Catholic faith:

Knowing that Communism as practiced by the Soviets is the greatest enemy of your Church, that they are destroying your Church wherever they can, murdering your priests, continually yelling at the Pope? If you ARE the Catholic that you claim, then you must be using your office to rid your Guild of any and all Red influence and at the same time do the greatest service to your Church.

And in the second segment, he contrasted Lavery's faith with his own:

I'm a Catholic, too, Mr. Lavery, maybe not as devout as you contend being; maybe not as highly deserving of testimonials as you, but I AM a Catholic, I go to church and at one time I was preparing myself for the priesthood. But as good or as bad a churchman as I am, I certainly would not tolerate the bedfellows—nor share their opinions, nor condone their actions, nor become a part of their organizations— that your record seems to indicate are yours.

Such strident views earned my father more enemies than just the men he was savaging. Many who had previously been neutral or even supportive were both furious and distraught that he was naming names. As one anonymous Wilkerson detractor put it, "Germany had Goebbels, and Hollywood had Wilkerson." Left-wing playwright Arthur Miller grew to loathe the publisher, and indeed that hatred was part of what inspired his 1953 play *The Crucible*, which drew haunting comparisons between the anti-Communist campaign in Hollywood and the seventeenth-century witch hunts in Salem, Massachusetts. Some loyal *Reporter* sponsors also began to withdraw their support. The Writers Guild alone revoked $50,000 in ad revenue as the man who had long been the writers' darling morphed into their public enemy number one.

But it was Vivian Wilkerson who bore the brunt of the attacks against her husband. Strangers approached her in the street and told her precisely how they felt about what he was doing. Before long she began receiving threatening phone calls, even anonymous death threats, at the couple's Bel-Air home. "It definitely rattled her," said Kennedy. "She couldn't feel safe at home. She came to the office and stayed there until Mr. Wilkerson left with her."

———————————

Not everyone was angry, however. To those on his side, Wilkerson's outspokenness was inspirational. Joe Pasternak said, "Billy was an honest guy, and an honest guy can't be a nice guy." And Harry Drucker remembered, "Billy was an American. He was against Communism."

Drucker recalled one incident in particular that exemplified his views on the subject. "Not to mention any names, but one writer came over to me and took me out to dinner. He said, 'Isn't this terrible how Billy Wilkerson is picking on people? You can't be free with someone like that.' And I said, 'Now wait just a minute. I wasn't born in this country. I came from the other side, from Russia. I know all about it. Gonna ask you a question. Were you born in this country?' And he says, 'Yes.' I said, 'Were you ever in Russia?' he said, 'No.' I said, 'OK, I see you're a writer, right?' and he says, 'Right.' I said, 'And before you make a picture you go through the script and you want to find out what it's all about, right?' and he says, 'Right.' I said, 'You call yourself a Communist yet you know nothing about it. If you want to do something good for this country you don't have to become a Communist. You could be a Republican or a Democrat and fight for the right."

Wilkerson himself had no regrets. He began to see himself as a holy figurehead, sword in hand, slaying Communists—a Christian driving out the heathens. His devotion to his anti-Communist campaign grew so deep it paralleled his devotion to Catholicism. Indeed, he pursued his task of routing out the Communist influence in Hollywood with such zeal, many around him grew unnerved. "Hating Communists became popular," said George Kennedy; in fact, as a staunch Catholic, he shared his employer's antipathy for godless

Communism. "But Mr. Wilkerson took it to a whole new level—he wanted to burn them at the stake. It was Biblical, almost apocalyptic." As Kennedy explained, "Mr. Wilkerson felt there were exceptions [that warranted] suspending free speech, and Communism was one."

But Kennedy also understood how others could get drawn into such radical politics. Once in the late 1930s, driven by curiosity, Kennedy himself had attended a pro-Communist meeting at the home of writer Peter Viertel. He remembered seeing at least fifty people in attendance. "I thought it would be an evening of coffee and cake and high-minded conversation," he said, "that sort of thing." He was disgusted to find that instead, he and the other newcomers were bullied into joining the Communist Party. Fledgling studio writers in particular were informed that they might have trouble finding work in the film industry if they refused to join.

Based on just these sorts of connections—years old, sometimes coerced, often tenuous—more and more of the working people of Hollywood would soon be branded as Communists. This despite the fact that Communism's influence over the film industry was extremely difficult to substantiate. Hollywood productions of the era included scores of anti-Communist films, but no films that incorporated Communist propaganda. As Kennedy noted, "Many tried hard to find any Communist subversion in the movie industry and could find none." Even the party's influence on the organizational level was questionable; Peter Viertel pointed out that "the Communist Party was active in trying to guide the destinies of the guilds and unions that were formed in the industry, and even in that arena they were unsuccessful."

Wilkerson's crusade, on the other hand, was an unqualified success. As he'd hoped from the beginning, the more anti-Communist red meat he published, the more he increased the popularity of the *Reporter* and his own profile within the industry. From this point on, the studio bigwigs "didn't exactly genuflect and kiss his ring," said Kennedy, "but you could sense the change in their demeanor."

Meanwhile, his victims' misfortune was growing as well. As the studios felt increasing pressure to respond to the anti-Communist outrage, the accused men and women would find their careers increasingly in jeopardy. It seems likely they would never have faced a blacklist if not for Wilkerson's inflammatory editorials. As Joe Pasternak put it, "If Billy had said nothing, printed nothing, the whole thing would have never happened."

28 | EXILE

AS BILLY WILKERSON'S ANTI-COMMUNIST campaign took off, the man who had helped make it possible was slowly recovering from his horrific plane crash. When Howard Hughes was well enough to receive visitors, Wilkerson and Tom Seward visited him in the hospital, where, in typical unabashed fashion, the publisher blurted out, "Serves you right for not wearing your chute." Wilkerson's friend Walter Kane had told him that the mogul refused a parachute.

According to Seward, when my father said that, Hughes burst into such a fit of giggles that his pain returned and he needed to be remedicated. "Hughes had a salty sense of humor," Seward said. He had seen Wilkerson roast his friend on more than one occasion. Howard Strickling remembered witnessing it as well, adding, "No one talked to Hughes like that except Billy."

Hughes would ultimately make a miraculous recovery, but he admitted to Wilkerson that he was in constant pain. The flow of pain medication he had been prescribed to lessen his misery became his best friend. In later years Hughes's drug addiction would be well known, but in those days it was one of Hollywood's best-kept secrets, one Wilkerson helped to keep.

Sadly, the drugs also caused Hughes to develop paranoid delusions, which grew so acute that he could no longer bring himself to dine openly in clubs and restaurant dining rooms. When he went out, he insisted on being seated in the kitchen, a spot to which few people were invited. At LaRue, Wilkerson had a small table installed and beautifully dressed and set for one, with a pristine white tablecloth, elegant silver service, a single rose in a crystal vase, and a napkin in a silver ring.

Wilkerson was struggling with his own source of chronic pain: the floundering Flamingo Hotel project, which was now firmly in the hands of the incompetent Bugsy Siegel. Though Wilkerson accepted that he no longer had any control over the project, he had not withdrawn quietly. Just a month after he was relieved of his responsibilities, on July 14, 1946, gossip columnist Walter Winchell shared a well-sourced scoop on his enormously popular radio program: "According to the FBI, a prominent West Coast racketeer is endeavoring to muscle a prominent West Coast publisher out of his interest in a West Coast hotel."

While Winchell named no names, few listeners had trouble determining to whom the blind item referred. They would likely have been surprised, though, to learn who had planted the item: it came from none other than FBI director J. Edgar Hoover, prompted by a call from Wilkerson himself. According to Tom Seward, after the Winchell broadcast, the FBI called Siegel in for questioning, and he predictably denied making any threats against the publisher.

By late July 1946, observers didn't need a blind item to know that the project was in trouble. It was evident to everyone except the man in charge that Siegel possessed neither his former partner's expertise nor the vision to pull off something of the Flamingo's magnitude. "He had no idea what he was doing," George Kennedy recalled.

As Siegel grew increasingly autocratic, the project's budget swelled even further. "Siegel just didn't want marble," said Kennedy. "He wanted the finest, most costly Italian marble there was." The site began to swarm with construction equipment and overflow with materials—all supplied through Siegel's connections. Carpenters, plasterers, and other workmen were flown in and paid handsomely, sometimes as much as fifty dollars a day.

Siegel decreed that each bathroom in the now ninety-three-room hotel would have its own private plumbing and sewer system at a cost of nearly $1.2 million. More toilets were ordered than needed. Cost: $50,000. Because of the plumbing alterations, the boiler room, now too small, had to be enlarged. Cost: $113,000. Siegel also ordered a larger kitchen. Cost: $29,000.

The main Oregon Building featured seventy-seven luxurious rooms, with sixteen fire exits. Siegel's extravagances included a lavish fourth-floor penthouse for his own private use. He ordered an escape hatch in the closet of his suite that led to an intricate labyrinth of secret passageways, which he'd use for smuggling women and gangsters into his room and for security in case he needed to escape. Although many of the staircases in the passageways led nowhere—they had been constructed in an elaborate attempt to confuse law enforcement—those who knew the layout could descend to the garage and a waiting getaway car in less than a minute. The steel ceiling beam crossing Siegel's living room was too low for the gangster, who kept hitting his head as he paced the carpet. He ordered it moved. Cost: $21,750.

The Flamingo's catastrophic cost overruns have always been attributed to Siegel, but his girlfriend Virginia Hill shares much of the blame. Siegel often left Hill in charge of the operation while he went on fundraising expeditions. When the mobster saw the heavy curtains Hill had ordered for the main lounge, he knew they were highly flammable, and he knew too that the nearest fire station was seven miles away. The drapes had to be returned to Los Angeles and treated for fire-proofing.

But by far the most stupefying cost was Siegel's frenetic building, destruction, and rebuilding. Once, after the builders had constructed a solid wall in the casino, Siegel demanded that they add an enormous plate glass window with a view of the pool. (This was also a radical departure from Wilkerson's vision of a casino without natural light or other distractions.) Siegel used so much concrete that any renovation became an ordeal; simply dislodging a banister in the casino taxed a battery of jackhammer operators for two days. Much later, during a remodel in the mid-1960s, it would take three days for a wrecking crew working with a giant iron ball to demolish a single wall.

Disgruntled unpaid builders and dishonest contractors also wreaked havoc. By day, trucks regularly delivered black market goods to the site, but by night those same materials were pilfered and resold to Siegel a few days later.

Siegel's checks began to bounce. One for $50,000 to his general contractor, Del Webb, was returned to Webb stamped INSUFFICIENT FUNDS. Siegel abjectly apologized and assured the contractor the cash would soon be in hand, but angered by Siegel's nonpayment, Webb ordered trucks full of materials, checked them onto the Flamingo site, and charged them to the corporation—then redirected them to a building project at another location. Nothing was unloaded at the Flamingo. Webb eventually settled for payment part in cash and part in stock.

Siegel's ignorance of responsible business practices extended even to the simplest dealings with his underlings. On one occasion, Siegel summoned architect Richard Stadelman to his penthouse suite at the unfinished Flamingo to discuss business. The gangster was lying in bed and rambling on and on. Stadelman noticed, with acute embarrassment, that the gangster was naked under the single sheet, beside an equally nude Virginia Hill. Not once did it dawn on Siegel that this behavior was in any way unusual.

Right in the midst of this turmoil, Siegel was preoccupied by the fact that the land beneath the Flamingo still belonged to Wilkerson. The mobster wanted possession of that as well. He had already obtained a portion of it shortly after seizing control of the project, agreeing on June 26, 1946, to buy half the property in exchange for an additional 5 percent stake in the Nevada Project Corporation. The land, still in Greg Bautzer's name, was quitclaimed and deeded to the Nevada Project on July 31. "Mr. Wilkerson believed he would make far more money owning a bigger share of corporate stock than asking for a cash buyout," Kennedy explained.

But Siegel brooded over Wilkerson's remaining land interest, and in early August he approached Bautzer and asked him to convince his client to sell his final parcel. In exchange, Wilkerson wanted an additional 5 percent of the corporate stock, and on August 22, the parties executed an agreement to this effect. Wilkerson quitclaimed and deeded his final parcel of land to the Nevada Project Corporation on November 27, 1946. Wilkerson's share of the project increased to 48 percent, making him the Flamingo's largest single stockholder, while Siegel now had what he wanted: full control over both the building and the land beneath it.

By this point, however, the gangster's senseless extravagances had become too egregious to overlook. As expenditures soared to more than $4 million (almost $50 million today), the syndicate that had backed Siegel's takeover of the project began to openly question his effectiveness. In November, Siegel's partners issued him a stern ultimatum: provide them with a full accounting of how he was spending their money, or the syndicate would cut off any future funding. The last thing Siegel wanted to do was produce a balance sheet, so instead, through Greg Bautzer, he began to pressure Wilkerson to sign for a bank loan to keep the project afloat.

My father, of course, knew that Siegel was in deep trouble. According to Bautzer, although Wilkerson had been cut out of the project, Gus Greenbaum tipped him off about the extent of the cost overruns. Through his attorney, Wilkerson reminded Siegel that he had both a signed agreement and Harry Rothberg's verbal assurance that he would not have to invest any more of his own money.

In turn, Siegel reminded Bautzer that the Flamingo was still his client's venture, too. If they didn't come to a new arrangement, the project might collapse into bankruptcy, in which case Wilkerson would lose his entire investment. He would probably also be blamed for the project's failure. Signing for the loan, on the other hand, meant pinning his hopes on the remote possibility of future success. Even for a seasoned gambler, this was a difficult call.

Against his better judgment, on November 29, 1946, Wilkerson signed for a $600,000 loan from Valley National Bank in Phoenix, Arizona. But because $600,000 was but a drop in the ocean of debt, Siegel also launched a relentless private fundraising campaign.

Suddenly, and very much against Wilkerson's advice, Siegel was in a hurry to finish the hotel, doubling his work force in the belief that this would ensure completion in half the time. But it was the costs, not the building, that began rising faster. Siegel paid overtime and even double time, and in some instances special bonuses tied to project deadlines were offered in hope of increasing productivity.

With the hotel still unfinished but work on the casino nearly done, Siegel moved the grand opening of the latter from the original date of March 1, 1947, to December 26, 1946. Siegel was hoping to bring in sufficient revenue from the casino to complete the hotel. "The casino was barely ready," Kennedy remembered. "Mr. Wilkerson was fit to be tied. He paced the floor, yelling at the walls, 'That motherfucker, what the fuck does he think he knows?'"

His fury was reason enough to break through months of radio silence: he called Siegel directly and warned him not to move up the opening date. The publisher argued that it would be business suicide. It was bad enough that Siegel would be opening the casino without any hotel rooms to accommodate the guests; that, at least, was a desperation move Wilkerson himself had considered resorting to when he was at the helm. But it was sheer idiocy to expect an elite Hollywood clientele to fly out to Las Vegas on the day after Christmas. Traditionally, people in the entertainment industry stayed home during the final two weeks of the year.

Ben Siegel dismissed Wilkerson's solemn warnings. He shouted into the phone, "I'm the one who makes the decisions!" Wilkerson hung up, stoically surrendering to total failure.

But he was not even close to discovering the true extent of his problem with Bugsy Siegel. *Reporter* employee Vic Enyart remembers the morning in December 1946 when he was in Wilkerson's office and his boss got a phone call from J. Edgar Hoover. "Billy, I remember, didn't say anything. He just listened, which was unusual for him. As he listened, I watched his face turn ashen. He said, 'Thank you' and hung up. 'That was Hoover,' he said to me, 'He's warning me about Siegel.'"

"Hoover had called Wilkerson to tell him of the possibility of a complete syndicate takeover of the Flamingo," said Bautzer, "and that his life might be in danger."

In later years, Bautzer said, Hoover would continue this helpful habit of alerting the publisher to potentially dangerous business contacts. But the warning about Siegel had come too late. At that point, any attempt to extricate himself from the project would jeopardize his entire investment.

So instead he decided to bolster his investment, by making sure the world learned about the Flamingo opening. He hired press agent Paul Price, and the two men began to formulate a massive public relations campaign for the gala. Their publicity materials included glossy prints of half-naked, well-endowed young women wearing seductive smiles, suggesting that plenty of action awaited high rollers even after they left the tables.

Wilkerson was in the middle of this campaign when Siegel summoned him to the Flamingo for a meeting. The exact date and time of this gathering is unknown, but according to Greg Bautzer, it took place just a few weeks before the opening. Present were two lawyers representing Siegel: Louis Wiener and Clifford A. Jones. At the time, Jones was also the lieutenant governor of Nevada. Although Wiener and Jones would later not recall attending the meeting, Bautzer insisted that they were there. Also accompanying Siegel were Moe Sedway and Gus Greenbaum, and Wilkerson attended with Bautzer. As my father's lawyer explained, "Billy owned 48 percent of [an investment worth] $6 million. He was dealing from a position of immense strength."

Bautzer vividly remembered that Siegel got straight down to business, opening the meeting by standing up and loudly insisting that Wilkerson give up his ownership interest in the corporation. Wilkerson responded by asking what he would be paid in exchange, and Siegel menacingly let him know he *wouldn't* be paid, and that he'd better have all his interest in hand. Wilkerson began to speak, but Bautzer stopped him. Taking care to use language the gangster would understand, he explained that his client had a legal right to the shares and didn't have to do anything with them.

Siegel explained the real problem: as part of his desperate fundraising campaign, he had oversold the investment, offering 50 percent more shares in the corporation than were actually available. If he didn't deliver the promised ownership stake to his investors in the East, he would be killed. He needed my father's shares to make up the shortfall. According to Bautzer, Siegel turned to Wilkerson and angrily said, "I'll kill ya if I don't get that interest."

At this point Bautzer stood and told Siegel to sit down and shut up, then ordered his client out of the room. He issued a stern warning to the gangster's attorneys: "You'd better shut this guy up, 'cause I'm gonna make an affidavit on the remarks Mr. Siegel has made at this meeting and who was present. I'm sending one copy to the district attorney of Los Angeles. I'm sending one copy to the district attorney of the county here in Las Vegas. I'm sending one copy to the attorney general. And I'm sending one copy to the FBI. And if Mr. Siegel is wise, or his associates here are, they'd better make sure Mr. Wilkerson doesn't accidentally fall down a flight of stairs. They'd better make sure he doesn't sprain an ankle walking off a curb, because that affidavit is going to be in the hands of those men, and I'm going to be prepared to testify like all the rest of you are going to have to testify as to the statements Mr. Siegel has made. So they'd better be goddamn sure Mr. Wilkerson enjoys a very long and happy life."

Siegel's attorneys told Bautzer to take it easy, that he had no need to file affidavits or involve district attorneys, but Bautzer insisted that was what he was going to do and stormed out.

Wilkerson and Bautzer left that meeting stunned at everything they had just learned. Siegel clearly had no intention of honoring any legal obligations, which meant Wilkerson's stock in the Nevada Project was worthless. As George Kennedy put it, "Mr. Wilkerson received toilet paper for his interest." And there was no doubt that if push came to shove, Siegel would kill anyone who got in his way.

As Bautzer and Wilkerson drove back to the El Rancho Vegas, where they were staying, Bautzer asked Wilkerson where he had gone after the lawyer ordered him out of the room. "To the john," Wilkerson answered. Some would later say that Wilkerson actually peed in his pants and had to go to the bathroom to clean up. Regardless, Bautzer took his words to mean that in that moment, he understood for the first time that his life was in danger.

Back at the hotel, the men conducted a postmortem and reviewed Wilkerson's options. They could give Siegel what he wanted, but while Wilkerson would most likely walk away with his life, he would forfeit his entire investment. The alternative was to stand firm against Siegel's outrageous demands, in the hopes that eventually the syndicate would replace the unstable gangster with someone who'd respect his rights as a shareholder. For the time being, however, Bautzer felt sure that Siegel's death threat had been made in earnest. He recommended that his client leave Las Vegas immediately, assuring him that he would handle negotiations in Wilkerson's absence. Then, while Bautzer wrote out the promised affidavits, Wilkerson ordered food and made travel arrangements. By the time room service arrived, the publisher had lost his appetite.

An hour later, Wilkerson departed. En route to the plane, he made a brief unscheduled visit to the Nevada State Police, where he applied for a permit to carry a concealed firearm. Bautzer did not know it yet, but his client had already decided to go into hiding.

Around midnight, Bautzer received a phone call from one of Siegel's lawyers, Nevada lieutenant governor Cliff Jones, proposing a meeting for the following morning. Bautzer told Jones he would not meet with Siegel again and suggested that the two of them meet one on one. Jones wanted Wilkerson to be present, but when Bautzer refused, the lieutenant governor acquiesced.

In the meeting the next morning, Jones confirmed that Siegel had oversold the project in order to raise completion funds. He also told Bautzer the syndicate had given Siegel an ultimatum. Jones wanted to know what Wilkerson's sellout price was. Bautzer told him he had no idea, but he would ask his client.

Meanwhile, however, Wilkerson had caught a flight to New York, where he boarded the *Île de France* bound for Europe. From Le Havre, he made his way by car to Paris, where he booked into the plush Hotel George V under a pseudonym.

Wilkerson's plan was simple: he would wait in Paris until things cooled down. He was certain that it would be only a matter of time before Siegel was fired and he himself was reinstated as the project's creative director. Thus he would retain his investment and could complete his hotel without interference.

While in exile, Wilkerson managed to create the illusion that he was still at his desk in Hollywood. He continued to write his Tradeviews column for the *Reporter*, either dictating it by phone or telexing it into the paper. He relied heavily on his Hollywood headquarters and the foreign correspondents' office for accurate field reports, but that had been common practice whenever he was traveling.

To support this subterfuge, he shunned all his customary pursuits in Paris, rarely went outdoors, and kept to himself even inside. If someone recognized him in the lobby, he told that person he was visiting briefly on business. If he was invited to dinner or for a drink, he politely declined, saying he was leaving early the following morning. His only indulgence was a daily walk to a nearby sidewalk café for a Coke and an English-language newspaper. Every Sunday, he made a single major excursion—a cab to Notre Dame Cathedral for Mass.

According to Kennedy, Wilkerson's whereabouts were kept secret from all but a few. When he finally made contact with his attorney, Bautzer was stunned that his client had dropped out of sight but not surprised to learn where he had ended up. Bautzer relayed the details of the meeting with Cliff Jones.

"He was reticent about selling," Bautzer recalled. "He said, 'Forty-eight percent of this deal is rightfully mine. Why the hell should I sell?'" The publisher briefly toyed with the idea of contacting Moe Sedway, but soon after Wilkerson's departure for Paris, Sedway had mysteriously disappeared.

Wilkerson decided to fight back the way he always had: in print. He began to run notices in the *Reporter* attacking the Flamingo project and revealing to the entire world that its true cost had soared to over $5 million. The negative public attention could not have pleased Siegel's more conservative Mafia partners such as Meyer Lansky.

Wilkerson spent a chilly Christmas in Paris. On the Flamingo casino's opening day, he sat alone in his hotel room eating dinner and reading the newspapers. Nobody from Wilkerson's camp attended the opening. A few days later, he received a call confirming exactly what he'd warned Siegel about: the opening had been a disaster.

To begin with, Siegel had managed to generate considerable confusion regarding the opening date itself. On a whim, he had decided that a weekend event would be more likely to entice the star-studded roster of guests he needed so badly to attend, and he thus sent out invitations for Saturday, December 28. Then he changed his mind again, and invitees were notified by phone that the opening had changed back to its original date, December 26.

If any celebrities were not too baffled to attend, arrangements had been made to fly them to Las Vegas. Prior to the Flamingo meeting and Wilkerson's decision to flee to Paris, the publisher had chartered two TWA Constellation airliners from Howard Hughes. Indeed, according to Tom Seward, Hughes volunteered his own services as a pilot to fly in a few handpicked celebrities, including Wilkerson, in his converted B-25 bomber. But at the last moment Hughes was called away on other business. Hughes sent both Wilkerson and Seward gold Piaget watches to apologize for his inability to attend—but in the end it didn't matter that he couldn't be there. On the evening of the gala, bad weather grounded all flights in L.A.

Despite the canceled flights and the incorrect invitations, a handful of celebrities did make it to the opening, driving to Las Vegas for the event. June Haver, Vivian Blaine, George Raft, Sonny Tufts, Brian Donlevy, and Charles Coburn were welcomed by a cacophony of construction noise and a lobby draped with decorators' drop cloths. Despite the fact that it was winter and the Nevada desert was known to turn cold, that day was unseasonably hot. The air-conditioning system repeatedly failed, leaving guests cursing the heat. Though only a few celebrities had shown up, the gala was jammed with curious Las Vegas locals, who stared in amazement at croupiers and dealers in their white ties and tails.

The contrast was stark between the hoped-for atmosphere of luxury and the shoddiness with which it had all been executed. Even something as simple as providing matches for the customers almost went completely awry. Thousands of Flamingo matchbooks had been printed, but they bore Wilkerson's name as manager, and Siegel ordered everything with Wilkerson's name on it destroyed. Fortunately, some brave soul realized that there was no time to reprint the matchbooks and suggested that a number be saved. Siegel hired a squad of women with black grease pencils to strike out the publisher's name wherever it appeared, and guests were spared a matchbook drought.

Wilkerson had much earlier arranged the opening night's entertainment, and things onstage went smoothly. The performers included master of ceremonies George Jessel, Jimmy Durante, Xavier Cugat and his band, Rose Marie, Tommy Wonder, and the Tune Toppers. All among the top stars of the day, they performed without a hitch. But the performance of the offstage talent was a different story entirely.

Siegel had decided to rely on the kitchen staff, chefs, waiters, and bartenders Wilkerson had recruited in Los Angeles. But these new recruits had yet to complete their training, and now they were being thrown into an unfamiliar working environment in an unfinished building. Their service prompted numerous complaints. The locals in particular were put off by the snobbish atmosphere, feeling insulted when asked to remove their cowboy hats and accustomed to being waited on by friendly, chatty waitresses instead of an all-male staff of formal waiters and aloof captains.

Siegel's dealers were poorly trained as well, which is partly to blame for the fact that the casino lost money on opening night. But another factor was the lack of adjoining hotel space, which meant that gamblers eventually had to take their winnings to another establishment.

Back in Paris, Wilkerson continued to lie low as his adversary's operation crumbled further. After two weeks in operation, the Flamingo's plush gaming tables were $275,000 in the red. Siegel couldn't understand what was wrong but speculated that the local desert folk were more cunning than his newly trained dealers, who had not "found their rhythm." In late January 1947, with no resources left, Siegel shut down the casino and blamed everything on Wilkerson.

The gangster still planned to reopen once the hotel was finished, but since the casino had lost money instead of making money, he was no closer to solving the problem of the project's skyrocketing costs. And he still needed Wilkerson's shares to satisfy the investors he'd defrauded.

In a series of phone calls to Paris, Bautzer pressed his client to sell his ownership interest, but Wilkerson remained resolute. First, he told Bautzer, nobody was going to scare him out of a business deal. Second, he was sitting on a potential windfall. He owned close to half of an investment worth more than $6 million, and he was eagerly awaiting Siegel's removal by the syndicate. But as weeks in exile turned into months and the gangster remained at the helm, Wilkerson began to feel increasingly unsafe. He started to wonder whether any business deal was worth the deprivations—the hiding, fitful sleep, and loneliness.

By mid-February, he came to the conclusion that the Flamingo would never be his, and he set his sellout price at $2 million. He also insisted on a signed document releasing him from all financial responsibilities and any other obligations to the corporation. Bautzer conveyed this offer to Siegel's attorneys, and while they agreed to the document releasing Wilkerson, they balked at the price and offered a mere $300,000. Wilkerson scoffed.

Concerned for his client's safety, Bautzer asked him to consider dropping the amount to $1 million, and after much cajoling, Wilkerson agreed. When Bautzer relayed the new amount, Siegel's camp countered with a final "take it and get out" offer: $600,000 (nearly $7 million today). Reasoning that the precise dollar amount was insignificant compared to the value of his life, Wilkerson finally accepted the deal.

But since both Bautzer and Wilkerson refused to meet with Siegel, the task of extracting payment fell to Tom Seward. In late February, he was dispatched to Las Vegas, where Siegel was just about to open the hotel. He had scheduled the opening for March 1, Wilkerson's original date. This time he was so determined to get it right that he had arranged a dress rehearsal. Seward was there. He sat next to Siegel in a booth surrounded by more gangsters: Meyer Lansky, a reemerged Moe Sedway, Gus Greenbaum, and Farmer Page. Siegel was clearly annoyed by Seward's presence, particularly because Wilkerson's business partner was there to collect money Siegel had only grudgingly agreed to pay.

Siegel turned to Seward, made a symbolic revolver out of his hand, and pressed it against Seward's temple. Seward recalled feeling the pressure of the gangster's fingers against his skull as Siegel whispered that if his partner were there, he would blow his fucking brains out. Seward was terrified.

But Siegel was called away to take a phone call, and once he was out of sight, Seward made his excuses to the other mobsters and hurried back to Hollywood empty handed. He told Bautzer he wanted nothing more to do with Siegel. He missed out on the second Flamingo opening, which was again plagued by myriad problems—with the service, the kitchen, and the plumbing—that drove guests to competing establishments.

Finally, on March 19, 1947, Siegel and G. Harry Rothberg signed a formal "Release of All Demands" absolving Wilkerson of any responsibilities to the Nevada Project Corporation. The document also promised to pay the publisher $600,000 for his ownership interest, half due in early May and the balance due three months later.

Wilkerson could breathe easier, but to Tom Seward, it was another affront. He'd done a lot of work on the Flamingo project, and in return Wilkerson had promised him a piece of the action. Seward, like his business partner, had been salivating at the prospect of owning a spectacular multimillion-dollar hotel. "I never saw a nickel," Seward lamented.

A week after the agreement was signed, Wilkerson returned to Hollywood from his Paris exile. Still uneasy, he made Tony Cornero's pale-blue bulletproof Cadillac his main mode of transportation. His trepidation was not unwarranted; Wilkerson had only been back at his desk in Hollywood for a few days when George Kennedy put through an urgent phone call.

Kennedy recalled, "Mr. Wilkerson asked me who it was. I said the frantic woman would not say, but I remember strongly suggesting he take the call and put it through to Wilkerson's private line."

The anonymous caller hysterically begged Wilkerson to leave town immediately. Her husband, newly paroled—"a good man" she said—had been contracted to kill him. She said she didn't want him "mixed up in any more trouble." She repeated her plea, then abruptly hung up.

Within forty-eight hours Wilkerson was heading back to Paris. As Bautzer put it, "There was every chance, of course, that it was a bluff. I asked Billy not to take the risk." (Fortunately, my father's jet-setting lifestyle made these repeated quick getaways easier to pull off; he knew how to live out of a suitcase, and always had two steamer trunks on standby in his attic.)

In late April, Wilkerson received confirmation from Bautzer that the Nevada Project Corporation had transferred the first of its two agreed-upon payments to his Bank of America corporate account. Reassured that the deal with Siegel was proceeding without difficulty, he spent the next two weeks in Paris doing the things he found most pleasurable: sightseeing, shopping, even visiting the Moulin Rouge. He even felt comfortable asking his wife, Vivian, to come and stay with him. She registered under the alias "Emma V." Together at night, they strolled the city's streets, enjoying the sidewalk café nightlife. Wilkerson had grown so comfortable, in fact, that his *Reporter* columns made no attempt to conceal his location; his daily Tradeviews were bylined from the French capital.

Bugsy Siegel, too, was growing more comfortable in his role; by mid-May, the Flamingo was at last turning a profit. But to his syndicate partners, it was too little, too late. With Siegel still refusing to provide a detailed accounting of his expenses, the syndicate had launched its own investigation.

By late May, Wilkerson was thinking of returning home for good when George Kennedy called him in Paris with a mysterious warning. Kennedy relayed the contents of an anonymous phone call he had received at the offices, advising him to tell his employer to remain in France until "it was over." The mystery male did not identify himself. "What was really spooky," said Kennedy, "was that the caller identified me by name." Kennedy theorized the caller was an emissary for Johnny Rosselli, who was still doing time for his part in the Hollywood shakedown plot.

Whoever it was, he was clearly looking out for Wilkerson's safety, so the publisher delayed his departure from Paris. Bautzer cautioned his client to remain in his hotel room, and Wilkerson went back into hiding. This time, however, Vivian stayed with him.

On the morning of Saturday, June 21, Wilkerson was out for his daily walk. He bought an English-language newspaper and sauntered to a sidewalk café around the corner from his hotel. After ordering a Coke, he unfolded the paper and took one look at the front-page headline. Without reading the rest of the story, he stood up and returned to the hotel. Waiting for him was a cable from Kennedy confirming the newspaper story. On the evening of June 20, as Benjamin "Bugsy" Siegel sat reading a newspaper in Virginia Hill's Beverly Hills rental house, an assassin riddled his body with a full magazine of bullets from a .30-30 military carbine.

On June 25, 1947, Billy and Vivian returned to the United States via the SS *Queen Elizabeth*. When Kennedy met the couple at Los Angeles Municipal

Airport, Wilkerson greeted his secretary in characteristic fashion. "What the fuck did you waste company money on a cable for?" he growled. "It made every fucking paper!"

———————————

No one knows exactly who orchestrated Siegel's murder and why. The most widely accepted theory is that Siegel's own partners killed him. They certainly had reason to do so: their investigation into Siegel's finances had confirmed that he was wildly out of control. There was no evidence of embezzlement, but he'd allowed crooked contractors and unpaid builders to swindle the operation, lost money to Virginia Hill's incompetence, and by the end oversold shares to outside investors by as much as 400 percent. The unenviable task of conducting a full accounting of Siegel's losses would fall to his successors, Moe Sedway and Gus Greenbaum, who took possession of the Flamingo mere minutes after the shooting. No one disputed their authority.

But would the syndicate have killed their bungling associate rather than simply replacing him, as my father expected them to? They'd already helped to *save* his life when his defrauded investors threatened to kill him; when Siegel called the meeting to demand Wilkerson's shares, Sedway and Green-baum were by his side. And despite their differences, Meyer Lansky and Ben Siegel had been boyhood friends, and it seems likely that the crime boss would have intervened to prevent the murder of a man he considered practically his brother. Lansky would have had particular grounds to argue for mercy given that at the time of his death, the Flamingo was finally showing a profit.

And there are other theories. Some believe that Siegel was murdered by a disgruntled associate from his bookmaking activities in California. Some place the blame on other Las Vegas business owners, who perhaps hoped that killing the head of the Flamingo project would head off the eastern syndicate's infiltration of their territory.

Tom Seward believed that Siegel's death was arranged by Virginia Hill, who wanted to be rid of her abusive boyfriend. Interestingly, at the time of Siegel's death Hill was not at home—she was in fact in Paris, just like Wilkerson. Some have theorized that Siegel sent her there to flush out Wilkerson's precise where-abouts so he could order a hit. But it is equally possible that Hill had wanted to put distance between herself and her boyfriend. Seward speculated that she had arranged his murder and then hightailed it to Paris to establish an alibi. But one could also imagine that a savvy woman like Hill knew there were other threats to her boyfriend's life—and simply didn't want to risk being killed alongside him.

To me the most plausible theory of Siegel's murder is that Johnny Rosselli stepped in to protect his friend Billy Wilkerson, perhaps even at the publisher's behest. George Kennedy already believed that Rosselli was behind the anonymous call warning Wilkerson not to return from Europe. Even while behind bars, the mob boss had sufficient underworld connections to end Siegel's threat for good. If my father did participate in or have prior knowledge of the plot to murder Siegel, it could have only been through Rosselli.

Wilkerson certainly faced scrutiny when police launched an inquiry into Siegel's death. FBI agents visited his Hollywood office unannounced and grilled him about his involvement in the Flamingo and the Nevada Project Corporation. The detectives intimated that Wilkerson knew more than he was telling them and implied a direct link between the publisher and organized crime. Wilkerson emphatically denied any such connections.

The FBI inquiry turned up nothing incriminating, but over the next few years, Wilkerson would receive several rude reminders of his entanglement with Siegel's death. The first of these happened in the early 1950s, as Wilkerson was driving up to Sun Valley, Idaho, for a week with his then-girlfriend: my mother, Tichi Noble. One evening during dinner, Virginia Hill entered the hotel dining room and hurried to Wilkerson's table, where she exploded at him, screaming that it was his fault—that it was because of him Siegel was killed.

People stopped eating as Hill shot accusations at Wilkerson. After working herself into a frenzy for what seemed like minutes, she violently slapped his face several times and stormed out. "The entire room went quiet," remembered my mother. "After she left you could have heard a pin drop."

Wilkerson never saw Virginia Hill again, but not long after, on March 15, 1951, she was a key witness during hearings into organized crime headed by Senator Estes Kefauver. In public testimony, Hill again pointed a finger at Wilkerson. "He is the one that got Ben into that Flamingo, and did everything bad to him," she claimed.

Though many speculated, one person who professed to know the truth about Bugsy Siegel's death was Moe Sedway's widow, Beatrice "Bee" Sedway.

In a 1992 interview, the former moll, who never went anywhere without a belly gun in her purse, told me she knew who had killed him but refused to talk. Since the statute of limitations does not apply to murder, she feared she could still be charged as an accomplice or an accessory to the crime.

Bee Sedway also asked *me* a question, wondering how my father had met his end. The matronly blonde widow said she was convinced that Wilkerson had exited life in the same fashion as Ben Siegel. She believed that a man with so many shady associates, some of whom had become enemies, could not have lived such a public life for so long without eventually meeting a violent fate. But she didn't know that he had Johnny Rosselli watching his back until the day he died. As for her own secrets, in true Mafia fashion, she took them to the grave, passing away in 1999 at the age of eighty-one.

She wasn't the only person I spoke to who refused to share knowledge of Bugsy Siegel. The same year I interviewed her, I talked to Richard Gully, who had been Jack Warner's personal assistant for a decade beginning in 1948. He had also been one of Siegel's close friends. Gully insisted to me that he never talked about Siegel to anyone—which struck me as odd, since he had in fact effusively shared anecdotes about the gangster with other authors and with many journalists over the decades. I don't know why he clammed up when talking to me; perhaps over time he had found that his connection with the hoodlum was a source more of embarrassment than of affection.

Ultimately, Siegel's story was both tragedy and farce. As Greg Bautzer observed, "This was not his business. Prior to the Flamingo, Siegel exhibited no experience in building anything. He was in way over his head." He concluded, "Siegel was not the right choice to head an operation like the Flamingo. He was a paranoid man who had no business masterminding a multimillion-dollar deal. I blame the principals associated with Siegel who let him get away with it as much as I do Siegel. The Flamingo wound up being the most expensive hotel ever built in the world at the time."

In the end, Siegel was never able to overcome his identity crisis. He remained bound by his gangster past and his own violent nature, and he was never able to grasp the legitimacy and the glamour he craved. Ironically, in death Ben Siegel finally earned the enduring fame he had so long thirsted for in life.

Under the stewardship of Moe Sedway and Gus Greenbaum, the Flamingo did finally prosper. The new managers departed from Wilkerson's elegant vision in many ways, first by dropping the formal dress code. "People running around in the middle of a hot desert in black tie and formal attire," remembered film director Howard Hawks, "it was preposterous. You only see that in movies."

The Flamingo became an egalitarian establishment where gamblers could relax and flirt with Lady Luck at prices affordable to almost anyone. It was just what the enterprise needed to succeed: in its first year alone, the Flamingo turned a $4 million profit.

Though the Flamingo didn't become the luxury destination he had imagined, in later years Wilkerson would be awed by how accurately he'd envisioned the rise of Las Vegas as a whole. The transformation of the sleepy desert community into a luxurious gambling mecca far surpassed even his most optimistic predictions. The stretch of land several miles out of town where he first broke ground became crowded with fabulous hotels, each one more outlandish than the last, all glittering monuments to Billy Wilkerson's passion for gambling.

29 | THE BLACKLIST

WHILE BILLY WILKERSON was distracted by Bugsy Siegel's death threats, his anti-Communist campaign was taking on a life of its own. Other publications began to take note of the *Reporter*'s rising popularity, and realized that there was money to be made by jumping on the Communist-naming bandwagon. As Tom Seward put it, "Ruining people's lives was big business. Anti-Communism sold papers." The *Chicago Tribune* had been the first major outlet to follow Wilkerson's example: from November 8 to November 22, 1946, the *Tribune* ran a continuous series of anti-Communist articles that added more fuel to the fire Wilkerson had ignited. Headlines screamed, BARE GRIP OF REDS ON FILM INDUSTRY. Other papers soon joined in the crusade.

From there the anti-Communist fervor spread to the federal government—specifically, the House Un-American Activities Committee (HUAC). As Peter Viertel recalled, the members of HUAC "were almost all political reactionaries . . . influenced and brainwashed by the yellow press." One year after Wilkerson first asked, "Are you now or have you ever been a member of the Communist Party?" that question began to echo through the halls of Congress, drowning out voices of reason. The outcry would reverberate throughout the nation for the next decade.

HUAC had been established in 1938, its official role to investigate Communist and fascist organizations that had become active in the United States during the Great Depression. But the committee also looked into the activities of other groups on the political left. Defenders of HUAC argued that it uncovered vital information that bolstered national security; critics charged it was a partisan tool bent on discrediting President Franklin D. Roosevelt's liberal New Deal programs.

Hollywood quickly became one of HUAC's targets, but the committee's early efforts garnered more punch lines than headlines. When a witness testified that Communist organizations were exploiting numerous celebrities, including young Shirley Temple, for propaganda purposes, Roosevelt's secretary of the interior, Harold Ickes, joked that HUAC had uncovered a conspiracy of dangerous Hollywood radicals being led by the ten-year-old star. Even Wilkerson himself was initially skeptical of the committee's efforts.

But after the war, as tensions escalated between the United States and the Soviet Union, HUAC was reinvigorated. And by September 1947, my father's scathing editorials had inspired the committee to take dramatic action. HUAC issued forty-three subpoenas calling prominent Hollywood figures to testify regarding the alleged Communist infiltration of the film industry. The list included many individuals whom Wilkerson had called out in print for their supposed Communist connections, including Lester Cole, Howard Koch, Ring Lardner Jr., John Howard Lawson, William Pomerance, and Dalton Trumbo. In fact, my father later received confirmation, from no less an authority on the federal anti-Communist campaign than Senator Joseph McCarthy, that HUAC had drawn names directly from his *Reporter* editorials. The committee also subpoenaed a number of others to testify against the alleged Communist infiltrators; these so-called "friendly" witnesses included Walt Disney, Adolphe Menjou, Gary Cooper, and studio bosses Louis Mayer and Jack Warner.

For the studio moguls, the congressional attention could not have come at a worse time. Box office revenues were on the decline from wartime highs, and with television viewership rising, the industry would find it even more difficult to attract an audience in the very near future. Labor unrest was rampant; just two years earlier, police had used nightsticks, fire hoses, and teargas to break up picket lines on the Warner Bros. lot.

Worst of all, the moguls' studio monopoly was under fresh attack. For years, they had successfully fought off legal challenges, despite the fact that their studio-owned theater chains and shady business practices gave them blatantly unfair advantages over unaffiliated theaters and independent movie producers. Thanks to accommodating federal officials, they'd managed to negotiate compromise agreements that allowed them to retain their theater holdings in exchange for relatively minor adjustments to their most egregious practices. But after a federal court ruling in 1946 made a mess of their most recent compromise, both the studios and the government appealed the case, known as *United States v. Paramount Pictures*, to the US Supreme Court. And now Hollywood was mere months away from having to defend its monopolistic practices before the highest court in the land.

At such a delicate moment, a rash of bad publicity about Communist infiltration could prove devastating to the industry. The movie bosses knew they needed to present a united front. On November 25, 1947, they checked into the Waldorf Astoria Hotel in New York City for a secretive two-day conference worthy of the Cosa Nostra. Every studio head and theater chain owner in America was in attendance, among them 20th Century Fox's Joe Schenck and his brother, Nicholas Schenck, of Loews; MGM's Louis B. Mayer, Warner Bros.' Jack Warner, and Columbia Pictures' Harry Cohn; Barney Balaban from Paramount; Dore Schary from RKO; and independent producer Samuel Goldwyn. Also attending was James Byrnes, formerly the secretary of state and briefly a Supreme Court justice, who was now special counsel to the Motion Picture Association of America. This was the only time the entire complement of industry brass had met all together in the same room.

Since no minutes or notes were taken, information on the meeting is hard to come by. But Wilkerson could rely on his friend Joe Schenck to let him know what transpired. According to Schenck, when the topic of HUAC's anti-Communism inquiry came to the floor, it was easy for most in the room to trace it back to Wilkerson's editorials. Harry Cohn raged, "Had that sonofabitch only kept his pen in his pocket, we wouldn't be dealing with this shit!"

Cohn and Mayer both thought they could alleviate the situation if only they had something to hold over Wilkerson's head; this suggestion caused an uproar of approval. "He once borrowed five grand from me," Cohn interjected. It's never been clear what Cohn meant by that, though Greg Bautzer suggested that Cohn was insinuating Wilkerson had taken some kind of bribe. (When Schenck relayed this morsel of information to Wilkerson, the publisher called Harry Cohn a liar in print and never again spoke to him.)

According to Schenck, he himself defended Wilkerson, saying that the publisher's editorials had created a diversion, a way to focus the conversation on something other than the studios' impending antitrust case. The other moguls saw the wisdom of changing the conversation, and agreed that it was time to embrace Billy Wilkerson's crusade.

The government had given them the perfect opening to do just that. Just one day earlier, Congress had cited ten writers for contempt. The so-called Hollywood Ten, which included initial Wilkerson targets Lester Cole, Ring Lardner Jr., John Howard Lawson, and Dalton Trumbo, had refused to answer HUAC's questions about their alleged Communist ties. The movie titans knew that they could demonstrate their commitment to the cause by throwing these men under the bus.

Some of the meeting's participants resisted the idea of firing their best writers. And one in particular, RKO's Dore Schary, expressed deeper misgivings. It seemed unfair, he thought, for them to condemn people who had done nothing but express their political and philosophical beliefs; he worried that they were starting something from which they would never recover. In the end, although Schary's concerns would prove prophetic, the assembled moguls decided to ignore them.

Within days of the conference, the studio brass issued a joint statement denouncing and disowning all the cited writers. In the "Waldorf Astoria Declaration," the studios agreed that not just the Hollywood Ten but anyone who had Communist sympathies or affiliations would be denied all opportunities for employment in their industry. They also extended an invitation to Hollywood's talent guilds to work with them to root out any "subversives." To many in the industry, it was a sad but unsurprising turn. Said screenwriter Peter Viertel, who would himself later be caught up in the anti-Communist dragnet, "These people, like all our leading industrials, were more inclined to be spooked by 'the Red Menace,' as they felt they had a lot to lose."

Thus, with the studios' support, Wilkerson's catalog of alleged subversives became a register of the permanently unemployable. This had not been his primary intention—he'd wanted to bring down the studio chiefs, and now they were finding a way to enhance their own standing by joining his campaign. But that didn't stop him from naming more alleged Communist sympathizers in the pages of his newspaper, even though he now knew he was signing their professional death sentence. "People dreaded getting out of bed in the morning to see if their names were in the *Reporter*," recalled Tom Seward. "The mere suggestion you were a Commie and you were finished."

The situation placed the *Reporter* staff in a difficult position. Many of them disagreed with their employer's politics, but they chose to keep silent. As George Kennedy recalled, "I had friends in the industry, good friends, whose lives were being ruined by what we were printing. They called me for help, begged me to intervene on their behalf, but I had to stand behind Mr. Wilkerson." At one point the publisher even considered clearing his own organization of anyone with Communist affiliations. He decided against it, but he did order Tom Seward to hold the *Reporter*'s film reviewers to their boss's hard-line conservative slant.

Nevertheless, it was Wilkerson's own rabble-rousing editorials that made his political stance most abundantly clear. Indeed, although the ever-expanding list of accused Communist sympathizers had been embraced by HUAC and the studios, it remained associated with the man who had first committed it to paper. To the Hollywood community, it would forever be known as "Billy's Blacklist," or simply "Billy's List."

30 | L'AIGLON

THANKS TO HIS ANTI-COMMUNIST CAMPAIGN, Wilkerson's publishing business was booming, but in another area of his empire, he was once again considering a retreat. Restaurant LaRue was still thriving, and after paying off what remained of his initial Flamingo loan from Bank of America, he had $25,000 of the syndicate's buyout left over to invest in new business ideas. But his conflict with Siegel had left him reluctant to pursue similar ventures in the future. As Greg Bautzer put it, "Billy wanted to retire from the restaurant, nightclub, and hotel business. He had had enough."

Thus, my father anticipated using the remaining settlement money to pay off some of his other business debts. Bautzer, however, lobbied hard for him to invest it in a new enterprise for the tax savings. Eventually, in late 1947, my father agreed to put all $25,000 toward a new nightclub.

This time he found a location not on the Sunset Strip but in Beverly Hills, on the southeast corner of Beverly Drive and Wilshire Boulevard. (It's unknown what business was previously at the site, but it would later be home to the successful Blum's Restaurant.) Wilkerson yet again hired George Vernon Russell and Tom Douglas to design the building, and gave Douglas a free hand with the interiors. Even before construction began, my father picked out the name that, like the Flamingo, reflected his penchant for exotic birds: L'Aiglon, French for "The Eaglet."

The new club's theme was also familiar. It was a French-style bistro, with Douglas's interiors evoking Montmartre. Wilkerson hired Romy Campagnoli as chef and rehired the popular maître d' from Ciro's, Pancho Alliati. A sixteen-piece string orchestra was the icing on the cake. In November 1947, L'Aiglon launched and became an instant smash.

Unfortunately, few photos of L'Aiglon survive, but we know its physical splendor was matched only by its cuisine. Almost immediately, L'Aiglon was grossing $45,000 a month, a staggering figure for a postwar restaurant in Los Angeles. Alas, the club was so extravagant that it needed to take in more than twice that amount just to break even; every month it was losing $64,000. Bautzer explained that "it was so successful, it went broke. People would come in for a salad and a cup of coffee and stay all night long listening to the orchestra. There was no turnover." In an effort to curb his overhead, Wilkerson began to cut the string section, one player at a time. As George Kennedy put it, "You could judge how well the place was doing by how many string players remained in the orchestra."

While L'Aiglon struggled to take off, Howard Hughes invited Wilkerson to accompany him on another maiden flight—that of his giant flying boat the *Hercules*. With metal in short supply because of the war, Hughes had been eager to show the US government that he could construct a fleet of military transport planes almost entirely out of wood. He'd constructed a prototype, but an unfriendly press dubbed it the "Spruce Goose," and a skeptical Congress demanded to see a demonstration. When a test flight was scheduled for November 1947, the aviation tycoon asked his friend to come along.

Wilkerson had an avowed fear of flying with Hughes. While he acknowledged that Hughes was an excellent pilot, he felt the aviator took too many chances and had one too many crashes on his résumé. "Generally," said Kennedy, "Mr. Wilkerson used the excuse that he was sick. Hughes was sympathetic to illness, being a world-class hypochondriac himself. It was an old standby excuse that always worked."

This time Wilkerson provided his usual excuse—but sent Tom Seward to the test flight in his stead. Seward and a number of journalists joined Hughes aboard the *Hercules* as he made a few taxi runs. Then Hughes ordered the majority of the press off the plane but instructed Seward to stay onboard. Seward was aghast at finding himself standing on the flight deck as Hughes briefly lifted the plane into the air on its first and only test flight.

When air travel didn't involve his reckless friend, Wilkerson was far less squeamish. Around this same time, Wilkerson and Seward were traveling to New York on business but arrived at the airport a few minutes late and were informed that their flight had already departed. Wilkerson was furious, but they did manage to book passage on a later flight.

Eighteen hours later, the two exhausted men checked into their hotel room, and Wilkerson went straight to bed. Seward couldn't sleep. He strolled to the corner to buy a paper before ambling off to a coffee shop. There he sat down, ordered, and opened the paper. "I thought I was going to faint," he said. The flight they had missed in Los Angeles had crashed, killing everyone onboard. Though Seward didn't recall all the details, this was probably United Airlines flight 624, which was flying from L.A. to New York City by way of Chicago but crashed in Pennsylvania on June 17, 1948.

Seward hastily canceled his order and dashed back to the hotel, where he shook Wilkerson awake and shoved the headlines in front of him. "I thought he was going to kill me," Seward laughed. "You fucking woke me up to tell me that?" the publisher growled. "For Christ's sake, let me sleep!"

If anything about commercial air travel troubled Wilkerson, it wasn't the prospect of dying in a plane crash—it was traveling in any conditions that were less than first class. "If he couldn't travel first class," said Joe Pasternak, "he didn't go at all. Traveling second class was like going steerage on an ocean liner for Billy."

Back at L'Aiglon, however, Wilkerson's commitment to luxury was bleeding the venture dry. As losses mounted and the string orchestra dwindled, the club's troubles were compounded by regular clashes between its chef and its maître d'. Two men of no small ego, Campagnoli and Alliati hated each other, and if one walked into the other's territory, a fistfight immediately ensued. Wilkerson hired Jack Seward, Tom's younger brother, to keep the two men apart, but it hardly mattered. Some nights Campagnoli hurled pots and pans at Alliati, yelling at him to get out of his kitchen. The maître d' responded by slinging those pots and pans right back.

By August 1948, just nine months after opening, the L'Aiglon orchestra had been reduced to one solemn violinist. Wilkerson made the decision to close the club's doors. As Pasternak put it, "Billy loved beautiful things, expensive things. He had incredible taste. He went out of business he was so good. That was L'Aiglon."

31 | *UNITED STATES V. PARAMOUNT PICTURES*

IN FEBRUARY 1948 the federal government's antitrust case against the Hollywood studios had gone before the Supreme Court. Attorney General Tom C. Clark argued that the studio system constituted an illegal monopoly, and that the only sure way to put an end to the studios' control of the market would be to force them to divest themselves of their theater chains. Industry lawyers, including former Supreme Court justice James Byrnes, countered that such drastic measures would destabilize an already struggling film industry, without lowering costs or improving choices for the moviegoing public.

Echoing the flag-waving appeal of the Waldorf Astoria Declaration, Byrnes also emphasized the role of Hollywood movies in promoting American values and confronting tyranny abroad. Filmgoers around the world, he said, were drawn to "the freedom of American life portrayed on the screen. Wherever there is a dictatorship, of the right or of the left, there is a ban on American pictures."

But the studios' patriotic posturing had little effect. On May 3, 1948, the Supreme Court, in a 7–1 decision with one justice not participating, ruled that the studios were indeed a monopoly. The justices sent the case back to the lower court, telling it to reconsider whether separating the studios from their theater chains was a necessary remedy.

Many accounts of the *United States v. Paramount Pictures* case treat the high court's decision as the end of the story—the moment when the breakup of the studio bosses' monopoly became inevitable. But, in fact, the moguls didn't immediately divest their theater holdings. They dove back into negotiations with the government, hoping that yet again they could wrangle a compromise that allowed them to keep their companies intact. In fact, Joe Schenck was downright optimistic: "I think the ruling means the end of the divestiture threat," he said.

But this time it would be different. To be sure, the studios faced a more organized opposition than they had in the past, including the non-studio film-makers of the Society of Independent Motion Picture Producers. But according to George Kennedy, it was Billy Wilkerson who struck the final blow against his enemies' unfair power structure—with the help of an old friend struggling to reintegrate into Hollywood high society.

———————

Johnny Rosselli had been sentenced to ten years behind bars for his role in the studio extortion plot. Fortunately, before Willie Bioff tore the scam apart, Rosselli had ensured that it included regular payoffs to his contacts within the government. When Handsome Johnny landed in prison, he put the screws to them: if he wasn't delivered from imprisonment as soon as possible, he would sing about those payoffs. It was a contingency of which Wilkerson was apparently aware; George Kennedy overheard a discussion of the matter in his employer's office. Kennedy said the gangster had kept careful records of the payoffs—at least, he claimed to have done so.

It's unclear whether this threat was a motivating factor, but on August 13, 1947, Attorney General Tom C. Clark approved the release of Rosselli and his confederates in the shakedown case, just three and a half years into their decade-long sentences. It was the earliest they could possibly be paroled, a fact that provoked a national scandal.

As a parolee, Rosselli was under too much scrutiny to immediately resume a life of crime, so he returned to Hollywood in search of legitimate employment. But he quickly discovered that the town's movers and shakers refused to return his calls. The man who'd once cavorted with movie stars and done favors for studio bosses was now perceived as a Judas who'd repaid their hospitality by shaking down their industry.

Even Rosselli's bosom buddy Harry Cohn at Columbia Pictures turned his back on the gangland boss. He showed up at Cohn's office asking for a job—after all, he had kept Columbia off the Hollywood Syndicate's list of extortion targets, and the company hadn't been touched even when Bioff went rogue. But Cohn refused to find him work at Columbia. The best industry job Rosselli could obtain was as an assistant purchasing agent for B movie outlet Eagle-Lion Films, which paid only fifty dollars a month. He was soon promoted to associate producer, but when his contract was up, the studio failed to renew it. As rejections and humiliations piled up, Rosselli stewed in his own rage.

Fortunately, he had one loyal friend he could still turn to: Billy Wilkerson. The first place Rosselli had eaten when he got back to Hollywood was Wilkerson's Restaurant LaRue, and now, as frustration over his situation became too much to bear, he headed to the publisher's office in the mood to vent.

According to George Kennedy, Rosselli showed up at *Reporter* headquarters one morning in quite a state. He ranted to Wilkerson about all the people in the film community who had benefited from his help prior to him serving time but were nowhere to be found in his hour of need. As Kennedy put it, "Rosselli loved Hollywood. When people were giving him the cold shoulder, he really took it hard." Kennedy recalled that Rosselli focused much of his ire on Harry Cohn, calling him "an ungrateful cocksucker" and screaming that he could have reamed Cohn's ass.

Wilkerson let his friend scream, then proposed a more productive course of action. The time was finally right, he decided, to bring down the studio tyrants who had rejected them both.

My father knew that the Supreme Court's decision in *United States v. Paramount Pictures* had left the studio heads in a precarious position. They were counting on their political muscle to convince the government to save their businesses, just as they had when they jumped on board Wilkerson's anti-Communist campaign, or sent a former justice to extol their patriotic devotion before the Supreme Court. But their lobbying relied more on lip service than on financial contributions. While some moguls aligned themselves with one of the political parties—Louis B. Mayer, for instance, was an outspoken supporter of the Republicans—there are no records to suggest that they contributed large-dollar donations to either party. The film bosses felt they owed the government no favors. It was a costly miscalculation. As Kennedy put it, "They never dreamed they would have to make payoffs to stay in business."

And now they'd made an enemy of a gangster who'd been paying off government connections for years. In the meeting in the *Reporter* offices,

Wilkerson suggested that Rosselli call on his carefully developed contacts within the Department of Justice and nudge them toward rejecting any compromise the studios proposed. If they were reluctant to do so, Rosselli should threaten to publicly embarrass the DOJ by publishing the details of his early parole.

They both knew, of course, that cutting off the chance for compromise would force all the studios to divest their theater chains—including 20th Century Fox. It would be a terrible double-cross of their friend and partner Joe Schenck, one that would cripple his business and wipe out a sizable chunk of his fortune. (Ironically, in the days of the Hollywood shakedown, Rosselli had given Schenck advice that would've helped him avoid this exact situation, suggesting that the mogul start making his own payoffs as "insurance" against government interference. Unfortunately, Schenck had recoiled at the idea.) Though torn between his love for his friend and greatest supporter in the film capital and his hatred of the studio monopoly, my father was committed to proceeding. "It was clear to me," recalled Kennedy, "that Mr. Wilkerson had given this a lot of thought."

Rosselli, too, considered the pros and cons. Wilkerson broke through his misgivings with a simple question: "Do you want your chance to get even with these sons of bitches?" The gangster agreed that he did. Finally, Wilkerson asked Rosselli to promise that the publisher's name would never be connected to the plot. Rosselli assured him he didn't even need to ask.

Rosselli quickly went into action, twisting arms at the DOJ. We'll never know for sure whether his influence was a deciding factor, but a compromise to save the studios' theater chains never emerged. Wilkerson's associates certainly believed that his plan had made the difference. "Using Rosselli to gain access to government," said Tom Seward, "that was Billy's genius." Still, with the government refusing to bend and the studios clinging desperately to the status quo, the situation remained at an impasse.

Then, in November 1948, another of Wilkerson's closest allies helped pierce the indecision. Howard Hughes, who had purchased RKO Pictures earlier in the year, announced that his studio would accept the Supreme Court's recommendation and voluntarily relinquish its theater holdings. The industry's united front was broken; within months, Paramount Pictures had also agreed to give up its theaters, and the rest of the studios were soon forced to follow suit.

Though film historians would later see this turn of events as inevitable, Joe Schenck suspected that someone had stacked the deck. He sensed that some player within the industry had influenced the Department of Justice to bring down the studio monopoly—he just didn't realize who. For his part, my father did not have the courage to tell him. Until the day he died, Schenck would never imagine that it was his two syndicate partners and closest friends.

In any event, the film tycoons' legs had been successfully amputated. Without the theater monopoly to prop them up, the studios' economic situation continued to worsen, and they struggled to hold on to their remaining sources of power. Over the next decade, they had less and less money to spend on long-term talent contracts, so more and more stars became free agents. To secure these performers for an individual film, studios would have to compete with one another and negotiate with the stars' increasingly powerful talent agents. And with no exclusive talent contract, studio moguls and publicity heads lost the ability to control every aspect of a star's private life. The movie stars who had prostrated before the studio bosses would now hold the reins.

In the late 1940s, of course, some of this was still in the future. But the writing finally was on the wall. When Wilkerson realized that the studio bosses were doomed, said Kennedy, he was jubilant. "It took Mr. Wilkerson nearly two decades," the secretary remembered. "But in the end, he destroyed them."

32 | "THAT WAS WHO HE WAS"

BY THE LATE 1940s Billy Wilkerson had broken his enemies' monopoly and proved himself the most influential voice in Hollywood. The studios no longer dared to retaliate against him by cutting off their *Reporter* advertising, and Wilkerson had finally assembled the funds to upgrade the paper's pressroom, a project previously thwarted by his gambling losses. The new first-floor print shop was as massive as an airplane hangar, with a freight elevator, a large cage-like contraption, that ascended to a second- and third-floor warehouse containing the *Reporter*'s paper and ink inventory.

And yet, despite his heightened stature and the paper's rising fortunes, he remained the same tightfisted and temperamental boss he'd always been. Much to the staff's fury, Wilkerson would routinely make morning rounds switching off desk lights, looking to save every penny he could. That included the light in his secretary's office; George Kennedy would wait until his employer was safely back in his own office before switching his desk light back on.

Employee paychecks were also a constant sore point. Instead of allowing his employees to share in the *Reporter*'s success, he stringently held them to whatever salary figure they had negotiated up front. This penny-pinching was especially galling since everyone now knew of his gambling excesses, not to mention his unwavering generosity to Catholic charities. "Mr. Wilkerson was stingy when it came to salaries," recalled Kennedy. "But that was who he was, and he never changed."

He was also the same man who'd once attempted to cancel his top salesman's commission check while he was on his way to the bank—he bitterly resented any sales commission that equaled or exceeded what he himself was earning. "As a matter of course, Mr. Wilkerson hated to sign any check over $300," Kennedy recalled. A few years down the road, on December 23, 1955, Wilkerson would make his discomfort very clear in a letter that accompanied the largest commission check ever paid to a *Reporter* staffer. The precise amount is unknown, but it was made out to top adman Vic Enyart. The letter read:

> My dear Vic:
> The attached is the largest single check ANYBODY has ever drawn at THE REPORTER during its more than 25 years of publication. I am glad for you to have it. It will make up for a lot of slow weeks you have had—slow, because I don't feel you have been giving it the hustle you should and I hope this check might inspire you to get out among your accounts more, work with them, and bring in the business you are capable of IF you give it the hustle.
>
> Merry Xmas!
> Billy

"He hated signing that check," said Kennedy, "just hated it. Vic deserved it, but the amount killed him."

Kennedy wasn't just a constant witness to his boss's stinginess; he also continued to bear the brunt of his employer's volatile temper. At times the publisher would hover over his secretary while he typed and yell, "Faster! Faster!" To get himself through a "Wilkerson Day," Kennedy had begun to take Benzedrine, and at home he drank. While his loyalty was never in question, his management skills suffered as his drug and alcohol use increased; his filing became increasingly sloppy and more and more phone messages went awry. He had no reason to expect his boss to turn a blind eye, as Wilkerson had always been merciless about his staff's vices.

Kennedy recalled one telling incident that had taken place years earlier. In the 1930s Wilkerson invited his young secretary to be a guest at one of his Hollywood clubs. Kennedy had a wonderful time—so much so that when he attempted to drive home, he realized he was too drunk to drive. He parked and curled up in the backseat to sleep it off. Unfortunately, he had parked his car in the direction of oncoming traffic and was picked up by police, handcuffed, and thrown in jail. In Kennedy's wallet, the police found his business card and phoned his employer. When they told Wilkerson what had happened and asked if he was willing to post bail, the publisher refused, telling them to leave him behind bars. "It'll do him good," Wilkerson apparently said. Kennedy spoke wistfully of the incident: "There's no one more intolerant of an alcoholic than a reformed alcoholic."

Wilkerson had grown no more lenient in the intervening years, so Kennedy's drug-induced errors earned him monumental tongue-lashings. By the 1950s, his addiction would worsen, leading to memory loss, and while he became adept at covering, he knew it was only a matter of time before his mountain of excuses was exhausted. When Wilkerson could tolerate no more, Kennedy was fired.

In fact, during the course of their three-decade-long relationship, Wilkerson fired Kennedy repeatedly. "Billy used to fire people just like that, but he hired them back. Kennedy was fired about ten times," Joe Pasternak recalled. "He always asked me back," Kennedy said. "He needed me and he knew it."

Clearly, though he never went easy on his secretary, their relationship was one of Wilkerson's most cherished, too important for him to end it permanently. Kennedy took pride in that fact. He also reaped some fringe benefits from the position: because all calls to Wilkerson came through Kennedy's office, those in search of access or seeking favors frequently showered Kennedy with lavish gifts. Nonetheless, the emotional whippings his employer subjected him to would scar him for the rest of his life.

Kennedy wasn't the only employee who turned to drugs in response to Wilkerson's rain of abuse. Mike Connolly, who would take over the Rambling Reporter gossip column after Edith Gwynn's departure in 1948, also fortified himself with doses of Benzedrine, and joined Kennedy after work to down Manhattans at Musso's.

Like Kennedy, Connolly was gay; by this point Wilkerson had hired at least a half dozen gay men for key positions in his businesses. Ironically, despite his disapproval of their orientation, they became his Praetorian Guard. "The gays at the *Reporter* were the most devoted people in Billy's life," said Tom Seward. "I think it was their devotion that finally won him over. They worshipped Billy."

But that doesn't mean he'd been cured of his intolerance. At his private dinner parties, Wilkerson would direct a litany of cruel mockery at his gay employees, getting up from the table and mimicking his secretary mincing about the office to the delighted howls of his guests. "Mr. Wilkerson had a streak of sadism a yard wide," said Kennedy. "It always got back to me, and it hurt."

———————————

Wilkerson also maintained his feud with bellicose news editor Frank Pope, who instead of being repeatedly fired would periodically resign in disgust after a particularly bitter row. A few weeks later, a contrite Wilkerson would rehire him—usually, in a break from his normal procedure, at a higher salary. There were times, however, when Wilkerson grew tired of these theatrics and initiated a search for a permanent replacement.

In one of these instances, a response came in from Adela Rogers St. Johns, who for decades had been the star female writer of newspaper mogul William Randolph Hearst. Perhaps getting wind of Wilkerson's job opening from their mutual acquaintance Hearst, she showed up at the *Reporter* offices and pleaded with the publisher to give her son Mac a test drive. St. Johns, according to Kennedy, was so persuasive that he hired her son without an interview.

Many times after visiting Mac in the newsroom, St. Johns would saunter upstairs to Wilkerson's office unannounced and unsolicited. There she poured her heart out to him for hours. As with the women of Hollywood who came to him for advice, or the nuns who relied on him for his charitable contributions, the hard-nosed publisher was uncharacteristically indulgent of her intrusions.

According to Kennedy, Mac St. Johns was "capable but colorless himself. Mr. Wilkerson was never really fond of him, I don't think. But he filled a need he had at the time." There were no loud clashes between the two men—but perhaps Wilkerson missed those confrontations, because St. Johns was soon let go and the editorship returned to Frank Pope. But whenever the battles between Pope and Wilkerson became insurmountable, once again Mac St. Johns was called in.

Eventually, though, Pope would be permanently replaced. In 1950 the role of editor passed to Don Carle Gillette, formerly of *Film Daily* and *Billboard*. Gillette would be the last person to hold the role during Wilkerson's lifetime.

Howard Hughes, meanwhile, still played the role of the *Reporter*'s *unofficial* editor, intervening to quash stories about himself or his business empire. He had even attempted to kill a Tradeviews editorial he disapproved of while Wilkerson was hiding in Paris from Bugsy Siegel. My father's absence had apparently cut off the normal channels Hughes relied on to quash stories, so he phoned Seward several times demanding to know where the publisher was.

At the time, even Hughes wasn't allowed to know the publisher's whereabouts, so Seward told him there was nothing he could do. Hughes called Seward again at 4:00 AM, begging him to kill the column on his own initiative, to no avail. It was printed in its entirety, upsetting Hughes terribly. Still, Hughes's fondness for the Hollywood Godfather meant there were no lasting repercussions.

But how had Hughes found out about the column in the first place? Wilkerson had long suspected that someone in his own offices was tipping off Hughes to pieces the *Reporter* was planning to run about him. It turned out Hughes did indeed have a paid informant on the staff. Seward eventually learned that Bill Feeder was on the payroll of both the *Reporter* and Howard Hughes, and realized that he must be Hughes's spy. But when Seward revealed his discovery, Wilkerson refused to believe him. "They were close friends," said Seward. "I guess acknowledging the betrayal would have been very hurtful."

Though he went to great trouble to keep friends and employees in his life, Wilkerson couldn't or wouldn't stop the procession of discontented wives. Vivian Wilkerson had endured death threats from both gangsters and her husband's political opponents, and through it all she had tried to be supportive of Billy. But like his previous wives, she learned soon enough what a Wilkerson marriage was like. "I found myself relegated to a mantelpiece like some trinket," she recalled. By late 1947 their marriage was unraveling, and on December 3 of that year, Billy found himself in domestic relations court in a predivorce hearing.

Before Judge Fred Miller, Greg Bautzer faced off with his client's wife. Vivian asked for $800 a month in living expenses, while Bautzer argued that $300 was enough. "Didn't you tell me you had clothes enough to last a year or more?" Bautzer asked. "Didn't you say all you needed was a raincoat, two pairs of low-heeled shoes and two or three sweaters?" Vivian countered by complaining that all her suits were too short. To the publisher's chagrin, the judge bowed to the demands of fashion and awarded her $600 a month.

Subsequently, though, the marriage lumbered on for another fifteen months. Then, on March 7, 1949, Vivian appeared in court again, testifying that her husband was prone to outbursts of jealousy that caused her to recoil in embarrassment. In Judge Benjamin J. Scheinman's courtroom, she spoke to his possessive behavior at locations near and far. "At home, he was always very moody. Wouldn't speak. Made scenes before groups of people. He was firing cooks all the time. He said I didn't know how to order." When the couple visited Belgium, "he made a scene in front of six of my friends because I was speaking French and he didn't understand the language." On a trip to Palm Springs, "we went there for two days, and because he said I was talking too much to a certain man, he hurried me home the first day."

Vivian's sister, Claudia LaGrave, also took the stand. She testified that Billy was overly critical of his wife. "She'd feel like falling through the floor because he'd make a scene about it. Mother was worried about her." Billy thought that her mother was concerned because Vivian, like Billie before her, had begun drinking heavily in public. Vivian told me that it was the death threats against them as a result of her husband's blacklist that had provoked her to start drinking more.

The couple reached an agreement giving Vivian alimony of $400 a month and an automobile. Finally, on March 14, 1950, their divorce was finalized. Once again, Billy Wilkerson stepped into bachelorhood.

33 | CLUB LARUE

SINCE GEORGE KENNEDY described gambling as the means by which Billy Wilkerson purged himself of success, it's no surprise that the publisher's recent victories also failed to quiet the lure of the card tables and the track. His compulsion was still out of control. But Wilkerson remained convinced that Joe Schenck's advice had been right—that he could take the risk out of his addiction if only he owned the house where he was wagering his money. He decided to take another crack at opening a Las Vegas casino.

After the twin catastrophes of the Flamingo and L'Aiglon, he swore off any more large-scale projects. He decided his new Vegas venture would be a quiet, out-of-the-way club that incorporated his two great loves—gambling and fine dining. He met with George Vernon Russell at Restaurant LaRue, and over dinner they drew a crude floorplan on a cocktail napkin. The new venture would comprise two modest-sized rooms: an elegant restaurant and bar, and a three-table casino where guests could enjoy blackjack, craps, or roulette without distraction. Wilkerson was fascinated by the idea of patrons getting up from the dining table to gamble between courses, an idea as novel as the Flamingo casino design had been. Hoping it would meet with the same success as his current Hollywood restaurant, he gave it a matching name: Club LaRue.

With an initial outlay of $135,000, he began construction in the spring of 1950. Again he hired Vernon Russell and Tom Douglas. Unfortunately, no photos of Club LaRue survive, but as with his other projects, the Wilkerson touches abounded. "It was a beautiful place," remembered Greg Bautzer. "Very

265

elegant but much smaller than his other places. I would venture to say it was half the size of his LaRue in Hollywood."

There is no record of whom Wilkerson hired to run the casino, but it certainly wasn't Gus Greenbaum and Moe Sedway, or any other associates from the Nevada Project syndicate. He still had hard feelings over how they'd handled the Bugsy Siegel debacle.

Club LaRue opened without fanfare in the summer of 1950, but from the beginning its life was troubled. According to Tom Seward, the publisher was again approached by the representative of a syndicate interested in his business. But unlike Harry Rothberg back in 1946, this new representative didn't offer a generous buy-in; he simply demanded that his syndicate be cut in on the club's profits. "They knew Billy could make *any* venture successful," Bautzer noted. "My guess is they probably weren't enamored about the competition." Wilkerson refused to play ball.

Immediately, anonymous patrons began to book large blocks of bogus reservations, ensuring night after night of an empty house. Shipments of food and supplies were hijacked, forcing the club to have replacements trucked in overnight at great expense. Some of the food orders were laced with laxatives; Seward suspected that members of the kitchen staff had been paid off. To further drive customers away, thugs hit the parking lot, harassing patrons when they arrived or robbing them as they were leaving.

Remarkably, Wilkerson diehards were undeterred and continued to patronize the place, but his casino management and the green casino staff were ill equipped to handle what happened next. "Mechanics" showed up at the tables, counting cards and swapping in shaved dice to outplay the casino. In its first two months of operation, the club lost $250,000. After four months, the losses totaled $480,000. Seeing no viable alternative, he closed the doors to Club LaRue in October 1950. He sold the property to new owners, who kept the restaurant and kitchen, which would eventually become the footprint for the Sands Hotel.

"They won," sighed Seward. "The big boys broke him. They came in and played him dry. Had Billy not gone in underfinanced, he probably could have weathered the losses and made the place a success." But Wilkerson had finally gotten the message: Las Vegas was never destined to be his. After Club LaRue he never built there again—or anywhere else, for that matter.

Though Club LaRue failed in a matter of months, its Hollywood namesake was by this point the longest running of all my father's entertainment ventures. Restaurant LaRue had stopped serving lunch after the war, but it was a premier destination for dinner and drinks.

Bartender Jimmy Dvorak, hired in 1946, was considered the best in town, and also the fastest. It's unknown where Wilkerson found Dvorak, but he was certainly a coup. "Dvorak had a remarkable memory for everyone's drink," remembered LaRue waiter Kurt Niklas. No sooner had a patron eased through the front door than Dvorak had his drink mixed. One of his secrets was that before the restaurant opened, he premixed all his drinks in gallon vats in an adjoining preparation room.

While LaRue had a reputation for serving some of the finest food in the United States, and Wilkerson often boasted that LaRue had the best of everything, it in fact sold some of the cheapest alcohol, unbeknownst to its customers or to management. In his preparation room, Jimmy Dvorak emptied out bottles of Jack Daniel's, refilling them with cheaper alcohol. "They thought they were being served the best alcohol," said waiter Niklas. "Instead they got low grade, like Gilbey's Gin." Many who realized what was happening believed Dvorak had a drinking problem and was purloining the high-end stuff.

Kurt Niklas was hired in 1950 straight off the boat from Germany. It was his job to serve Wilkerson dinner every night at the LaRue bar. He recalled that LaRue's owner dined early and left early. Wilkerson frequently tested the fare at all his establishments, and he was uninhibited about voicing his displeasure with either the food or the service, even in front of dining patrons. One evening, Niklas served his employer and Tom Seward dinner, but something about the meal displeased him. Although there was a full house, Wilkerson spat the food out into his hand, then slapped it on his plate. He summoned the chef and yelled at him: "Shit! What do you call this? Why can't you get this fucking thing right?" Seward recalled that the room fell into complete silence.

But since Wilkerson didn't drink, he never tested the liquor. Leaving such matters to his trusted celebrity bartender, he never discovered that Dvorak was pulling a bait and switch. As Niklas said, "Dvorak knew this and really took advantage of it."

One evening, the young waiter took it upon himself to challenge Dvorak's larceny. In response, the bartender ushered him into his preparation room and shut the door behind him. He violently pinned Niklas against the wall and threatened him: "Shut up and mind your own fucking business if you still want to have a job!" The customers, Dvorak argued, "never know the difference anyhow!"

Although Wilkerson was not aware of this particular scam, he certainly knew that his restaurant employees sometimes stole from him. "It's not that they're stealing," Wilkerson complained to Tom Seward. "Everyone knows they do in the restaurant business. What concerns me is how much they're stealing." Wilkerson did nab LaRue staffers whose thefts were less carefully concealed, such as those attempting to walk out the door with paper-wrapped steaks under each armpit.

The management had to be particularly vigilant against the theft of one item in particular. Restaurant LaRue became legendary for, of all things, its cookies. The restaurant made a daily batch—of what kind no one could recall. But Niklas did remember that they were so popular that the moment they came out of the oven, they were placed on a tray and deposited in the safe below the cash register, where they remained locked until the restaurant opened. "Anyone who dared help themselves, even try one," said waitresses Grace Bouliance, "got a good dressing down."

But one day Niklas decided to chance it. "I took one off the tray as I was passing by," he confessed. But head chef Orlando Figini saw him put it into his mouth and immediately approached to lay into him. "I was so embarrassed I didn't know whether or not to swallow the damn thing, so I wound up spitting it in his face. To this day I can't remember the taste!"

Fortunately, Kurt Niklas's restaurant career was not badly damaged. The young man whom Wilkerson helped get his start in America later became a restaurateur himself, opening the famous Bistro Garden in Beverly Hills in 1979.

Though Restaurant LaRue wasn't sabotaged by gangsters or crippled by its own extravagance, it faced a more elemental problem: Mother Nature. In L.A.'s torrential winter rains, mudslides would flow down Sunset Plaza Drive from the hills and choke Sunset Boulevard. For days, sometimes even weeks at a time, the mud chased away clients from all the establishments on the Sunset Strip. In part because of these perils, by 1953 Wilkerson was eager to unload LaRue.

On May 21, 1953, he agreed to sell controlling interest in the restaurant to his existing business partners, chef Orlando Figini and maître d' Bruno Petoletti. Wilkerson received $5,000 when the sale entered escrow, and another $25,000 within sixty days of closing. Petoletti and Figini tendered a promissory note for $60,000, the balance of the total sale price; they would have two years to pay this final amount and complete the sale.

Wilkerson insisted that while the final payment was still outstanding, he and a few people close to him would be permitted to eat at the restaurant free of charge and help themselves to supplies of food and beverages for home consumption. This arrangement lasted for more than a year, until in July 1954 Figini and Petoletti attempted to pay him the balance due. Suddenly, Wilkerson rescinded the sale.

"Mr. Wilkerson and his friends were enjoying the perks so much that they wanted to keep the party going," Kennedy explained. "If the milk's free, why buy the cow?" Incensed, Figini and Petoletti filed suit in superior court, claiming $35,000 in damages for Wilkerson's rampant freeloading. The trio settled out of court, and in August 1954 Restaurant LaRue officially changed hands.

With that, Billy Wilkerson was out of the restaurant business for good. Some have lamented how quickly each of his establishments came and went, with only Restaurant LaRue continuing under his ownership for more than a few short years. But like the gourmet meals they served, they were memorable precisely because Wilkerson offered them up only at the peak of their freshness. His legendary boredom, his insistence on abandoning every endeavor at the pinnacle of its success, ensured that no project outlasted its sell-by date. Had he held on longer, it seems unlikely that his venues would have attained the same mythical status.

Still, my father's restlessness had always kept him moving forward, searching for the temporary high of his next victory. So why not another gourmet eatery after Restaurant LaRue? Why not another casino scheme after Club LaRue? The truth is, by the early 1950s he was focused on other things. Wilkerson had entered into a new phase of his life, with a new wife and something he thought he'd never have: a family.

34 | THE NEXT CHAPTER

AROUND THE TIME HIS MARRIAGE to Vivian ended, Billy Wilkerson had begun making pilgrimages to Joe Schenck's beach house in Santa Monica, where he indulged his carnal urges with the young women his host kept on hand. On one such visit, however, a woman caught his eye who was not one of Schenck's eager starlets—she was a statuesque redhead busy with housework. Wilkerson inquired after her, and Schenck informed him that she and her sister were his new housemaids from Mexico. Their mother was Schenck's cook in residence. Wilkerson asked to be introduced, and before long Wilkerson and Beatrice Ruby Noble, better known as Tichi, began to date.

In early 1951, the twenty-four-year-old Tichi announced she was pregnant. When her sixty-year-old boyfriend asked who the lucky father was, Tichi replied, "You are."

Wilkerson was incredulous. Five childless marriages had reinforced his belief that he was sterile, while decades of dealing with unsavory people had primed him to expect a shakedown. He thought it likely that his girlfriend was lying in an effort to extract money from him, and he dispatched Joe Rivkin to Schenck's house to intimidate her.

As Tichi recalled it, Billy's messenger parked in front of Schenck's house, rolled down his car window, and hollered up to the second floor, "You good for nothing piece of Mexican shit! Go back to Mexico and fuck your own kind, you whore!" Tichi remembered the insults and expletives lasting for several minutes.

Next the publisher shipped his girlfriend off to a dozen doctors to make sure she was actually pregnant. In the 1950s, pregnancy tests involved drawing blood from the patient, injecting it into a live rabbit, and then euthanizing and autopsying the animal to look for changes caused by pregnancy hormones. As each test came back positive, Billy insisted on yet another. "I killed a lot of rabbits," Tichi recalled.

Even after he accepted that Tichi was really pregnant, he still refused to believe that the baby could be his. This was decades before the advent of DNA testing, so science offered no sure method to determine a child's paternity. Reaching her breaking point, Tichi screamed at Billy to get a fertility test. When his own test also came back positive, he was finally convinced.

"When Billy found out that he was going to be a father," said Joe Rivkin, "he was the happiest man in the world."

Wilkerson had vowed to Rivkin that he would never marry again. "Five wives is enough," he said. But on February 12, 1951, the couple wed in Phoenix, Arizona. It was quickly apparent to everyone who knew him that Tichi was a stabilizing influence in his turbulent life. "Out of all his wives," said Joe Pasternak, "Tichi was the only one who knew how to handle him."

One of the first issues on which she laid down the law was the treatment of my father's six prized poodles. Wilkerson's spoiled pets had long vexed his wives; "They looked so strange and futuristic," said his previous spouse, Vivian. "They looked more like walking bushes than dogs." My father always instructed his cook to prepare special meals for them, including steak, salmon, and even caviar. "Nothing was too good for them," remembered Joe Pasternak.

My mother's biggest problem was that they had total access to the house. She complained that they were everywhere, even in the master bedroom. "I couldn't stand it," she said. Her first decree was to exile the six dogs permanently from the bedroom at night. At first her husband resisted, but she adamantly refused to sleep in the same room with them, threatening to relocate to the guest bedroom if her husband did not comply.

He reluctantly caved but then built a zoo-quality kennel in the back of the house. Every morning as he toweled off from his shower, he would press an electric buzzer concealed behind the bathroom door, which signaled the kitchen staff to release the dogs from their cages. The herd stampeded through the hallways, thundered up the stairs, and finally reached the master bathroom, where they pounced on their master, greeting him.

Tichi was also not afraid to confront her husband regarding his reckless gambling. Billy considered her a good luck charm, so when they visited Las Vegas, he would ask her to stand next to him at the tables. Every time he won, he handed her the chips to hold on to. (He would also occasionally provide her with her own chips to play, but he became so jealous of her lucky streaks that he soon discontinued the practice.) Tichi deposited his winnings into the pockets of her maternity gown. "Pretty soon they would be full of chips," said Tichi. "Billy forgot about them." But every time her husband lost, Tichi would say, "That could have bought the kid a stroller" or "That could have bought the kid a playpen."

On October 4, 1951, Billy Wilkerson's fervent wish was finally realized. That's the day I was born at St. John's Hospital in Santa Monica, making him a father for the first time at the age of sixty-one.

When he arrived at the office from the hospital, he could barely contain himself. Columnist Bill Diehl vividly remembered the day. "Billy Wilkerson, publisher of the *Reporter*, married—and not a young man—burst in to say his wife, Tichi, had just had a baby. Both Mike [Connolly, the Rambling Reporter columnist] and I guffawed as Wilkerson exclaimed, 'And all those years, I thought I was shooting blanks!'"

The romantic story goes that after my birth, my father was inspired to quit gambling cold turkey. He did indeed give up his destructive hobby, but his motivation was not simply to provide a good example for his son. Once again, his gambling losses had opened up a chasm of debt; by the fall of 1951, he'd failed to pay enough *Reporter* bills that deliveries of paper and ink were sporadic and again arrived COD. In addition, the IRS had finally busted my father for unpaid taxes. Kennedy recalled that the feds put him on a budget.

My mother was terrified that they would have to give up their lifestyle, especially their excellent French cook, Juliette Sauvage, whose meals she had grown fond of. She knew the only answer was for Billy to get his addiction under control. "I made a deal with him," my mother recalled. "If he quit gambling, I would help him manage his finances."

Though he swore off wagering, he still always kept a deck of cards within easy reach, and he found ways to duplicate the social aspects of gambling. At least three times a week, he invited over Bel-Air neighbor Benedict Bogeaus, an independent film producer and owner of General Service Studios, to play gin rummy or poker with him. The two men played for toothpicks, which they kept in a silver box in the middle of the table. Their games always began civilly, but as they progressed, the players began to accuse each other of cheating. The sessions usually dissolved into screaming matches, after which Bogeaus would get into his car, hurl a stream of expletives about never wanting to see my father again, and speed away. A few days later the two men would be back at the card table as though nothing had happened.

Wilkerson had another outlet to replace his obsession with cards and horses: his passion for sports. He himself was never an athlete (despite owning the first sunken tennis court in Bel-Air and a majestic swimming pool), but he was a devoted fan, especially of boxing and baseball. Now, instead of ducking out of work in the afternoon to visit the track, he would frequently head to Gilmore Field (located at the future site of L.A.'s Farmers Market) to watch minor league baseball games featuring the Hollywood Stars.

Wilkerson was so passionate about baseball, he could rattle off all the batting averages of the major leagues as far back as 1905. "The only time he listened to the radio in his car was when there was a ballgame or fight on," said Kennedy. Sometimes he refused to get out of the car until the game ended. And at home, "when a game was on," my mother complained, "you couldn't keep him away from the TV."

Maybe it was partially out of financial necessity, but clearly fatherhood was changing Billy Wilkerson. No one remembered my father as a demonstratively affectionate person, but one day Kennedy witnessed a display of emotion from his employer that left a lasting impression. The secretary was attending a small dinner party at our house when my father learned that I had taken ill. He excused himself and summoned Kennedy upstairs with him. Seeing my condition, he ordered Kennedy to call the doctor, and he left behind his dinner guests to sit by my bedside until the doctor arrived.

"It was very touching," Kennedy remembered. "That's something I never forgot."

35 | THE PARTNERSHIP

FATHERHOOD MAY HAVE REVEALED a new side to Billy Wilkerson, but it didn't change who he was as the publisher of the *Reporter* any more than defeating the studio bosses had. To his employees, he was as stingy and mercurial as ever, and to studio heads and stars who met with his disapproval, he was merciless. Matinee idol Ronald Reagan twice charged into the paper's offices in a rage over negative reviews, on one occasion taking a swing at editor Don Carle Gillette only to slip and fall on the polished parquet floor before connecting.

But to the industry luminaries who still beat a path to his door, he remained the Hollywood Godfather, generous with advice and eager to grant favors. One icon who frequently reached out to Wilkerson for career advice was Frank Sinatra. According to George Kennedy, "He knew only too well the value of Mr. Wilkerson's support and the power of a good review in the paper."

By 1952, however, Sinatra's career was in the toilet. MGM had fired him, he and his agent had parted company, his television show had been canceled, and his record company had dropped him. He knew that if he was going to reclaim his fame, he needed to land an eye-catching movie role.

He found one in Columbia Pictures' upcoming production *From Here to Eternity*, based on James Jones's eight-hundred-page novel, which had been published the previous year to great acclaim. Sinatra was eager to play bullied protagonist Private Maggio. Over lunch at the Columbia commissary, Sinatra made his pitch to Harry Cohn, but the mogul was unconvinced.

Sinatra left that meeting and drove to the *Reporter*, where he found my father at his desk. Wilkerson never closed the door to his office so he could communicate with Kennedy as necessary, but the singer insisted on privacy. Out of respect, the publisher closed his door three-quarters of the way. Through that narrow opening, Kennedy heard the singer break down, citing the litany of woes he was suffering, making it clear to Wilkerson that the publisher was now Sinatra's only hope. Wilkerson told the crooner not to worry.

The next morning, my father summoned Harry Cohn's former friend, now bitter enemy Johnny Rosselli. Though the gangster would never regain the elite status he'd enjoyed in Hollywood prior to his imprisonment, he had not lost his power to intimidate. Wilkerson told him he needed to get his man Cohn in order and make sure he cast Sinatra in his upcoming film. Rosselli was more than happy to oblige. "I'll make it simple for this bum to understand," he said.

Meredith Harless, Louis B. Mayer's former assistant, confirmed what happened next: Rosselli made an unannounced visit to Cohn's office and made a threat it would've been hard for the mogul to misinterpret: he must either make Sinatra his star or prepare to meet his maker. The rest is history; *From Here to Eternity* catapulted Sinatra to stardom, winning him the Best Supporting Actor Oscar for 1953.

Wilkerson and Rosselli still made a formidable team, but by this same point, the publisher's partnership with Tom Seward was crumbling. Seward had helped turn my father's businesses into such well-oiled machines that by the late 1940s, he no longer felt obligated to stay late at his clubs to supervise and close. In return, however, Seward had watched in disbelief as his partner refused to stop appropriating income and capital from their partnership to pay off his gambling debts. "These were expenditures of very large sums," Seward remembered. "I didn't have to ask what they were. I knew they were from his gambling."

For years, he said, he contemplated suing my father for mismanagement. By June 1951 he'd worked up the nerve to demand an accounting of his partner's expenditures. In response, Wilkerson took over exclusive control of the business, attempting to force Seward out.

George Kennedy suspected that there was another reason why Seward's issues with Wilkerson came to a head when they did: it was around this same time that Tichi's pregnancy was announced. Now that Wilkerson had a child of his own on the way, Seward was no longer his heir apparent. As Kennedy put it, "Tommy saw the writing on the wall. He didn't need the roof to fall in on him."

Two months before I was born, on August 10, 1951, Seward filed suit against my father, charging that he had "grabbed sole control of everything, as though no partnership existed" and tried to "squeeze him out." These actions, the suit alleged, constituted a dissolution of the partnership. Seward demanded the appointment of a receiver for the *Hollywood Reporter* to oversee an accounting of the business, followed by its sale and the division of the assets between the partners. He also asked for $150,000 in damages (more than $1.4 million today).

For the first time in decades, Bautzer did not represent my father in court. He withdrew on ethical grounds, since he had been retained earlier by Seward and "questioned the propriety of aligning himself with one partner against the other." My father demanded that Max Fink, Seward's attorney, withdraw as well, since he had preceded Bautzer as the *Reporter*'s attorney. Judge Ellsworth Meyer upheld Fink's resistance to that demand.

Robert R. Ashton represented my father and petitioned successfully to have Judge Meyer removed from the case, citing bias. Unfortunately, Meyer was replaced by Judge Arnold Praeger, who according to Kennedy "had a real hard-on for Mr. Wilkerson. He viewed him as this bug-squashing tyrant."

Praeger certainly showed no deference to Wilkerson when, in March 1952, he issued a subpoena for all *Hollywood Reporter* corporate documentation and accounting ledgers, from the paper's inception to the date of Seward's petition. Praeger clearly wished to establish the *Reporter*'s true book value, while Wilkerson's goal was to reduce the amount of money he was at risk of losing to Seward by undervaluing the company as much as possible. Through his lawyer, he told the judge that no such files existed. Praeger threatened my father with contempt, telling him in no uncertain terms that he had until the following court date a week hence to produce all the subpoenaed material.

This placed Wilkerson in a bind. In fact, he had years' worth of corporate documents filed away in the *Reporter* offices. If he turned them over, not only would he be unable to hide the company's true value, but he'd be handing the court evidence of his underhanded business practices and unsavory associates. He decided to take matters into his own hands.

On Friday afternoon, after the rest of the *Reporter*'s staff had gone home, Wilkerson instructed Kennedy to light a fire in the publisher's office fireplace, something he had never done before. The fireplace had in fact been installed merely for decorative purposes. "Ridiculous building fireplaces in Hollywood," Kennedy mused. "It never gets cold."

From the second-floor storeroom, Kennedy transported boxes of records on a dolly he pilfered from the empty pressroom. One by one, he extracted the contents of each box, and he and my father fed them to the flames. Around the clock for the next two days, the men systematically incinerated twenty years of records. "We took shifts," Kennedy remembered. "One of us did the burning, while the other rested on Mr. Wilkerson's office sofa or went out to get sandwiches."

Before emptying out each box, Kennedy did a quick perusal of the contents. His conscience would not allow him to destroy certain items of historical significance, so he spared from the flames such papers as Wilkerson's legal contracts with the Nevada Project Corporation bearing Bugsy Siegel's signatures and Edith Gwynn's breakup letter. Kennedy managed to spirit these documents into his briefcase while my father was out picking up sandwiches. He then transported them to his Pasadena home, where he hid them within the pages of the books in his library. There they remained for decades, until he began to reveal them to me.

By early Sunday afternoon it appeared that everything had been destroyed, when suddenly the fireplace flue erupted. Smoke filled the office. Kennedy opened the only window, but it was useless. The smoke was overpowering, and he had to call the fire department.

After extinguishing the fire, the fire chief issued my father a citation. Zoning laws enacted since the office was built had rendered the use of the fireplace illegal, a fact that neither my father nor Kennedy had bothered to research prior to embarking on their office bonfire. My father knew the citation would make Judge Praeger wonder just what had happened to the subpoenaed documents he was unable to produce. He imagined the court, with his own credibility shattered, relying only on Seward to determine what his company was worth. He saw himself being charged with destroying evidence and led out of court in handcuffs.

He phoned Johnny Rosselli but couldn't reach him. Panic stricken, he called his old friend Harry Brand, publicity head at 20th Century Fox. He told Brand the truth, that he was being sued by his business partner and there was a very real chance Seward might be awarded a sizable portion of his empire. He confessed that he had burned evidence and knew this could prove incriminating. It was a compromising thing to admit to Brand as well, but Wilkerson's special bond with the studio publicity heads had not frayed. And even as the power of their studios was fading, they still held sway over local officials. Brand was sympathetic, and he agreed to help.

According to Kennedy, no one knew exactly what Brand did, but he succeeded in getting the fire department's citation rescinded. Indeed, he did his job so well that no record of the incident exists, other than Kennedy's recollection.

The next week, when my father came to court empty handed, he told Judge Praeger that he had done a thorough search but could locate no relevant documentation. According to Seward, he blurted out in court, "He's lying!" Max Fink pressed the judge, and Praeger, suspicious himself, issued a search warrant for both the *Reporter*'s premises and the Wilkerson estate.

During the search of our home, Tichi took me to her mother's house, where we stayed for three days while the police did their work. Kennedy, however, was there as they conducted their eerily silent attic-to-basement sweep. After overturning the entire house, they'd found not a single file pertaining to *Reporter* business for the years in question. Wilkerson's risky gambit had succeeded, much to Seward's shock and frustration.

The lawsuit moved forward, albeit slowly. Proceedings were delayed until May 1952 after my father provided Seward with a good-faith payment of $15,000. A further continuance until October 28 was arranged when my father agreed to pay Seward $20,000 "without prejudice." Finally, in late December, the two reached an out-of-court settlement. Seward agreed to dissolve their partnership without selling off the company, in exchange for an undisclosed buyout. Kennedy remembers the figure being $150,000, minus what my father had paid to date, and the two men never spoke to each other again.

By burning two decades of records, Wilkerson had succeeded in shielding a good portion of his financial worth from the court and his now ex-partner. But the lawsuit alone doesn't explain why he conducted such a comprehensive purge. After all, the court would not have been entitled to private communication between spouses, and yet without George Kennedy's intervention, Edith Gwynn's letter would also have been consigned to the flames. Maybe my father had a more personal reason for burning it all: he was now a family man, whose wife and son could be hurt and whose domestic contentment could be contaminated if the secrets of his past were ever revealed. Perhaps the court's subpoena had provided him with both the inspiration and the opportunity to erase the unwholesome parts of his history.

Further evidence of this revisionist impulse is the fact that my father began to extricate himself from many of his organized crime associations. Even Johnny Rosselli would fade from his life; he and my father rarely saw each other in his later years.

But Handsome Johnny never forgot the promises he'd made to the Hollywood Godfather. It took him a few more years to fulfill the vow he'd made to Wilkerson so long ago, just before he went to prison for the Hollywood Syndicate's crimes. On the morning of November 4, 1955, the syndicate's disloyal front man Willie Bioff—while in federal witness protection under the guise of a Phoenix, Arizona, retiree named William Nelson—climbed into his pickup truck with the intention of spending the day fishing. As soon as the mobster switched on the ignition, an explosion reduced him and his truck to fragments. When Wilkerson heard the news, he knew Rosselli had kept his word.

Rosselli's continued fondness for his old friend would come through in the condolence telegram he sent when my father passed away in 1962. Then, fourteen years later, on August 7, 1976, Johnny Rosselli was found dead himself in an oil drum bobbing in a Miami bay.

36 | THE SHADOW

IN LATE APRIL 1953 my sister, Cynthia Diane, was born, and my father's quest to reclaim his past from the darkness only intensified. Shaking off the fear of the stock market that had plagued him since the Wall Street crash of 1929, he founded Wilkerson Investment Inc. in an attempt to go legitimate; it proved a futile effort. A more enduring result of his quest was that he discovered a long-buried nostalgia for his childhood. As we grew from infants to children ourselves, he would hold forth endlessly at the family dinner table about those years, painting vivid pictures for us of his leaky red schoolhouse and his treks through the woods.

Family dinner hour was sacrosanct. Since my father sold Restaurant LaRue the year after my sister was born, he would always dine at home. He'd leave the office, pay his obligatory visit to his mother, and drive straight home, making himself comfortable at a small card table in the corner of his paneled den. There he chain-smoked and played solitaire until dinner time. Our family always dined punctually at 6:00 in our formal dining room—my parents sitting at opposite ends of the long mahogany table, my sister and I seated across from each other.

After dinner, he retired to the master bedroom, where he sat in his favorite reading chair and read the sports pages of a few newspapers. After the papers, he often watched the fights or a ballgame and was usually in bed by 8:30. By his bedside were his beloved Perugina chocolates from Italy and licorice from Blum's of San Francisco. Once he finished eating his bedtime treat, he deposited his dentures in a glass of water by his bedside and switched off the light.

Yearning for additional family time, my father began taking more and more time off from work to spend with us. He shared his love of travel by taking us on at least two trips abroad each year that for him were both business and pleasure. In spring, my father rented a villa in the hills of Acapulco where we spent three weeks. We summered in Cannes for an additional three weeks, occupying the same fifth-floor corner suite at the Carlton Hotel my father had always had. We made regular visits to Venice, Rome, London, Madrid, Paris, Tokyo, and Hawaii. As many as eight people traveled in our entourage, including nannies and tutors for us children. "No one could doubt Billy's devotion to his children," said Harry Drucker. "Never did I see anything like it."

In many ways, Wilkerson had settled into a kind of quiet domestic bliss. But one of the shadows of his past loomed larger than the others. From it he would never truly be free.

———————

In early January 1950, George Kennedy recalled, his employer had received a phone call from a member of the US Senate, congratulating him on the "fine work" he had done with his anti-Communist campaign. The caller was the junior senator from Wisconsin, Joseph McCarthy. Having won his seat in 1946, McCarthy was midway through an undistinguished first term and looking for an issue that would offer him a springboard onto the national political stage. Nothing cements power better than a scapegoat, so Wilkerson's Red-baiting editorials caught his attention. As Edith Gwynn put it, "Hitler had his Jews. And McCarthy had his Communists."

For the next three weeks, Kennedy said, McCarthy and Wilkerson exchanged a handful of phone calls, though the two never met in person. Then, on February 9, 1950, the senator followed in Wilkerson's footsteps, launching a campaign of his own.

In a speech in Wheeling, West Virginia, McCarthy proclaimed that he held in his hand a list of 205 known Communist spies within the US State Department. In reality, he was shaking a few rolled-up sheets of blank paper, but with those words the senator ingeniously tapped into the nation's reptilian fear. While Wilkerson had focused his campaign fairly narrowly, railing against the supposed threat of Communists within the movie industry, McCarthy turbocharged it, warning that Communism posed an urgent threat to the US government and to national security. McCarthy didn't have Wilkerson's gift for writing earth-shattering editorials, but his thundering oratory spread the publisher's gospel, boiling down the threat so it was easier for worried Americans to understand. Where Wilkerson's editorials posed questions about potential Communist ties, McCarthy offered a simple answer: all Communists were traitors.

The senator quickly became the public face of the government's anti-Communist inquisition. "Everyone was afraid of McCarthy," said Edith Gwynn. "No one would stand up to him." By the time he won reelection in 1952, the blacklists touched off by Wilkerson and HUAC had spread, now encompassing not only the entertainment industry but also the legal profession, academia, labor unions, the State Department, and the US Armed Forces. Some of the targeted individuals were indeed affiliated with the Communist Party, but numerous others were falsely accused. Some lost more than their jobs; they were deprived of their passports or even imprisoned.

Within the government, "loyalty-security reviews" became commonplace, and those deemed a liability often lost their jobs without ever learning who had accused them of wrongdoing or even what they'd supposedly done. Screenwriter Peter Viertel was among those flagged for review. A World War II veteran in the US Marine Corps Reserve, he was summoned before a military inquiry investigating his supposed Communist ties—in part because of a review published in Billy Wilkerson's newspaper. In the late 1940s, Viertel had written the film *We Were Strangers*, which was directed by the legendary John Huston. In its review, Viertel recalled, "the *Reporter* accused the movie of being pure Communist propaganda that was being foisted on the public by three well-known 'Reds,' John Garfield, Huston, and myself." At the time, Huston shrugged off the notice with a single comment: "Who cares what the *Reporter* has to say?" But Viertel learned the extent to which some people did care when the officers at his inquiry read the review out loud and grilled him about its accusations. Viertel wrote in his memoir *Dangerous Friends*, "That an old notice in a trade paper with a doubtful reputation for objectivity could be used as evidence seemed incredible to me."

Nonetheless, the screenwriter was fortunate enough to have been presented with the allegations against him, and he was able to counter them to the military's satisfaction. He thus escaped a military discharge—and the career-ending place on the Hollywood blacklist that would have accompanied it.

Others in the industry were not so lucky, as Billy's List continued to grow. Many exceptional careers were extinguished, and industry figures who refused to name names faced jail time. Some who were accused "confessed" in order to save their own careers, claiming to have been duped into attending discussions or seminars sponsored by the extreme left. Friends turned on one another. As Kennedy put it, "While the right wing in Hollywood was well organized, the Communist Party informed on its own."

Some were implicated by sheer innuendo or considered guilty by association. "The real victims of the blacklist were those who had the wrong last names or went to meetings just to pick up girls," said film producer Howard W. Koch. Another producer, Samuel Bronston, had attended no suspicious meetings but was simply the nephew of the late Russian revolutionary Leon Trotsky. "No studio would touch Sam because of his uncle," said Kennedy. Bronston made a film in 1945 and did not make another for more than a decade.

Just as egregious as the false accusations was the corruption that accompanied them. Bribery was rampant; for a fee, names could be removed from the blacklist. When actress Beatrice Straight was blacklisted in 1953, she paid a fixer $500 to remove her name from the list. The malfeasance extended all the way to the top. When playwright Arthur Miller was subpoenaed to testify before HUAC in 1956, committee chairman Francis E. Walters told Miller that he could get out of appearing if he persuaded his new wife, Marilyn Monroe, to be photographed with the congressman. After the newlyweds refused the request, Miller appeared before the committee, declined to name names, and was found guilty of contempt of congress in May 1957.

Though careers and reputations were the primary casualty of the blacklist, the quality of Hollywood moviemaking suffered as well. "There was a pall of fear over Hollywood," blacklisted screenwriter Paul Jarrico said. "It was the difference between films like 'Casablanca' in the '40s versus 'Pillow Talk' in the '50s. People were scared to make movies that said something."

From our vantage point, all of this may seem shocking, but at the time the supposedly liberal Hollywood establishment was silent on the injustices of McCarthyism. "Quite a few people were innocent of the accusations against them," said Peter Viertel. "That the slurs on the reputations of innocent people resulted seemed to bother no one."

One person who apparently had no regrets was Billy Wilkerson. The publisher was surprised and delighted that McCarthy had taken up his standard in Washington, and back in L.A. he continued his own crusade. He'd become Hollywood's go-to authority on anti-Communism—so much so, Greg Bautzer recalled, that by 1950 the studios were asking Wilkerson to vet potential employees for subversive ties.

Emboldened by his earlier successes, he next set his sights on one of the giants of the film world: Oscar-winning director Elia Kazan. Kazan's 1951 film *A Streetcar Named Desire* had shot both him and star Marlon Brando to fame. But early the following year, Kazan was called to Washington for what was supposed to be a confidential executive meeting of the House Un-American Activities Committee. There, hoping to escape being added to the blacklist, he confessed that he had joined the American Communist Party for a short time in the mid-1930s, while a member of the Group Theatre, a progressive theater collective in New York City. He refused, however, to accuse other Group Theatre members of Communist ties.

Though the HUAC meeting was meant to be confidential, Wilkerson learned of it from a member of the committee, Representative Harold Himmel Velde of Illinois, who was not only one of the publisher's strongest supporters but also a loyal informant. After Velde passed him the minutes of the meeting, Wilkerson printed the following story on March 19, 1952:

> Elia Kazan, subpoenaed for the Un-American Activities Committee session, confessed Commie membership but refused to supply any new evidence on his old pals from the Group Theater days, among them, John Garfield.

It was a scandalous revelation not just for Kazan but also for 20th Century Fox, for whom he had directed the just-released *Viva Zapata!* After reading the piece, Fox's production chief, Darryl Zanuck, phoned Wilkerson and read him the riot act. My father informed Zanuck that his source had also told him Kazan would soon be called to an open meeting of HUAC, from which his testimony would be made public. "Mr. Kazan," Wilkerson said, "should do the right thing. He should take out a rebuttal ad in the *Reporter* and preempt

THE SHADOW | 285

anything that is going to be made public." He followed that up with a threat: "If he doesn't, we will certainly do a piece on Mr. Kazan, and I'll tell Sokolsky [a popular syndicated newspaper columnist] to do a column. I'm doing Mr. Kazan a favor."

By this point Wilkerson had discovered that he could make additional profit by charging his victims to place rebuttal ads in his newspaper. Bautzer recalled him frequently boasting that the pages of the *Hollywood Reporter* were the best "confession booth" there was. When his victims called to complain about something derogatory printed about them, he would simply say, "Take an ad out."

Zanuck didn't take Wilkerson up on his offer, but Fox did pressure Kazan to cooperate fully with the committee or be consigned to the blacklist. So when he next appeared before the committee on April 10, 1952, the director caved, providing HUAC with the names of eight men associated with the same Communist group he'd joined in the mid-1930s, most of whom were friends he had worked with at the Group Theatre.

Soon thereafter the head of Wilkerson's sales department, David Alexander, called Kazan to once again pitch him on the idea of taking out an ad to tell his side of the story. According to George Kennedy, the director shouted indignantly, "I'm not giving that bastard a nickel." But he couldn't deny the value of what Wilkerson was proposing, so on April 12, he placed an advertisement in the *New York Times* called "A Statement by Elia Kazan" in which he defended cooperating with HUAC and urged others to follow his example.

By naming names, Kazan had succeeded in saving his career, but his reputation was irreparably tainted. The dark cloud would hang over him for the next fifty years. In 1999, when Kazan received an honorary lifetime achievement award at the Oscars, celebrities of the day joined surviving victims of the blacklist to protest. Blacklisted writer Abraham Polonsky went so far as to say that he wished Kazan would be shot onstage.

In the later years of his campaign, Wilkerson didn't just focus on higher-profile targets such as Elia Kazan. He also expanded his focus from targeting supposed anti-American influences to shoring up pro-American values. In early

1954, J. Edgar Hoover called my father to thank him again for his fine work in exposing Communists in America. Kennedy overheard him telling Hoover, "This must never happen again. America is a Christian country. It must be protected. There must be appropriate safeguards." That was the year my father decided it was time that the United States government recognize Christianity as the nation's official religion.

Wilkerson had always keenly desired to tear down the division between church and state. Not only were his anti-Communist efforts in part a religious crusade, but he had made a pitch for Christian values in his writings at every opportunity. Now he threw his support behind several of the pro-religious movements of the era: inserting "God" into the Pledge of Allegiance and adopting the phrase "In God We Trust" as the national motto.

The first of these goals was already close to being realized. On June 14, 1954—Flag Day—Congress changed the words of the Pledge of Allegiance from "*one nation, indivisible*" to "*one nation under God, indivisible.*" Two years later, on July 30, 1956, Congress passed a law declaring "In God We Trust" the US national motto. And a year after that, on October 1, 1957, IN GOD WE TRUST was printed for the first time on US banknotes.

It's unknown what behind-the-scenes role Wilkerson may have played in facilitating these campaigns, either on his own or via the powerful FBI director. But for the rest of his life he would crow that he had been responsible for officially making America a Christian nation. As IN GOD WE TRUST began to appear on all new banknotes, he bragged that he had permanently ended the division between church and state.

———

By the time Wilkerson began his pro-religion efforts, the anti-Communist hysteria was already starting to abate. Senator Joe McCarthy's grandstanding tactics had backfired when he accused the US Army of harboring Communists in 1954. Days of televised hearings followed, heavy on blustering accusations and void of any hard evidence, which exposed the senator to the American public, even many of his own supporters, as the bully he was. ("Have you no sense of decency, sir?" army lawyer Joseph Welch famously asked.) By December 1954, McCarthy had been condemned by the Senate for conduct unbecoming a senator. His Robespierre-like reign of terror finally at an end, he descended into alcoholism and died less than three years later.

Wilkerson's career, on the other hand, survived and even thrived as the blacklist era came to a close. Unlike McCarthy, Wilkerson had chosen both his targets and his words carefully, accusing people only of what he could prove based on verifiable information from the FBI. Of course, he still faced the threat of lawsuits from the people his witch hunt helped to ruin, but his careful planning protected him from most of their claims. While close to eighty targets threatened to sue Wilkerson for libel between 1946 and 1957, only eight actually did. And interestingly, all these cases targeted Mike Connolly's Rambling Reporter gossip column and not Wilkerson's vitriolic Tradeviews. The reviewer who called out Peter Viertel's film *We Were Strangers* had likewise left himself open to libel claims in a way his employer was always careful to avoid. "Looking back," mused Viertel, "I really don't know why neither John Huston nor I [decided] to bring a libel suit against the *Reporter* and the film critic who called us well-known 'Reds' in his review."

Suing for the most money was writer Garson Kanin, who brought a claim of $2,025,000 (more than $19 million today) against the paper on April 8, 1952. Neither it nor any of the lawsuits brought against Wilkerson ever went to trial. On the few occasions a complaint wound up in preliminary hearings before a judge, Greg Bautzer shrewdly argued that since a Communist organization was merely a political party, accusing someone of membership could not be considered defamatory. "Legally," he told the court, "you can no more sue someone for calling you a Communist than you can a dirty Republican."

And, of course, other wronged parties continued to resort to extralegal remedies. There were more anonymous death threats, and a few times my father was run off the road. Even the nonviolent encounters could be unnerving; complete strangers frequently approached my mother in public and told her she should do something to stop her husband. Her concerns over the family's safety spiraled into heated arguments at our dinner table, and shortly after my sister was born, she angrily demanded that my father move her and us children to Europe until the fervor passed. No one was going into hiding, he replied, assuring my mother she had nothing to fear.

He had certainly fortified our lives against outside threats. While we lived in a fairytale world, dining with movie stars behind the walls of an exquisite

Bel-Air estate, there were guns hidden throughout our house, mostly in drawers, and my father carried a belly gun in his waistband and Walter Kane's .38 service revolver in his glove compartment (the same gun George Kennedy had wrested from Kane's hand after his suicide threat). An Army .45 slumbered on top of his bedside night table, cocked, with the safety on. A second revolver was tucked under his mattress, and I myself discovered a third nestled alongside another .45 in one of my mother's hatboxes. My father also continued to drive bulletproof cars: deluxe Cadillacs, Chryslers, Rolls-Royces, and Bentleys.

Wilkerson may have faced legal and physical jeopardy as a result of his crusade, but he never truly reckoned with the human cost. Some historians believe that because of the national anti-Communist campaign, between ten and twelve thousand people lost their jobs, while others put the number at closer to fifty thousand. Hundreds were imprisoned. In Hollywood, Billy's List denied work to more than three hundred writers, directors, and actors. But the publisher would never apologize to any of the victims of the Communist witch hunt, and he never repented of the part he played. As Kennedy put it, "As far as I know, he never lost a night's sleep over it."

As I learned about my father's role in the blacklist decades later, I hoped to discover signs that this wasn't entirely true. I was relieved when George Kennedy told me that in 1957 J. Edgar Hoover asked him to spearhead an anti-Communist task force for the FBI, but he gracefully declined. If he was refusing out of a sense of regret, though, he never let on; he told Hoover that he declined the job only because he had too little time even to run his own empire. And he certainly showed no qualms the following year when J. Edgar Hoover presented him with a plaque commending his efforts in fighting Communism. It was mailed to *Reporter* headquarters, where he had it hung in the hallway outside his office.

In the late 1950s Wilkerson did make an effort to help one victim of the blacklist reclaim his career. Producer Samuel Bronston, the nephew of Trotsky who hadn't made a film since 1945, approached my father in 1958 to discuss his plight. According to my father's longtime friend Alex Paal, my father liked Bronston, and as long as he liked someone, he didn't care about his connections. "As much as Billy hated Communism, he knew it wasn't Sam's fault that his uncle was a Commie leader," Paal explained. "At some point Sam must have pledged his patriotism to Billy. At least that's my guess."

Wilkerson told Bronston in no uncertain terms that because of his family connection, he would never find employment on American soil, but after doing some homework, my father uncovered an opportunity abroad. The chemical giant DuPont had millions of dollars tied up in Spain that the government refused to release. He urged Bronston to approach the chemical giant with a proposal: Since it was likely DuPont would never see their money outside Spain, why not use the quarantined funds to make feature films there? Bronston did as my father suggested, DuPont bit, and by 1959 he was producing again, making big-budget epics like *El Cid* and *King of Kings* (both released in 1961).

Two years later, producer/director Otto Preminger made a grander overture toward one of my father's victims—and in doing so finally broke the blacklist. In January 1960 he announced to the *New York Times* that the screenplay for his movie *Exodus* would carry the name of blacklisted writer Dalton Trumbo. When no public uproar ensued, other filmmakers followed suit, and their exiled colleagues began to return to work. It was Otto Preminger's courageous announcement that finally silenced what had begun with Billy Wilkerson's pen.

In 1962, just a few days after my father was buried, my mother removed J. Edgar Hoover's plaque from the wall outside his office, carried it home, lit a fire in the fireplace, and fed it to the flames. Never mind that it was early September and L.A. was choked by a brutal heat wave. I remember her sitting on the couch, still as a statue, watching the flames consume that plaque until it was reduced to ashes.

37 | THE OLD DAYS

BY THE LATE 1950s, my father's health was failing. He smoked at least three packs a day of unfiltered Piedmonts, and on a bad day the number of packs rose well past that. His trademark was a lit cigarette dangling from the corner of his mouth while he labored at his desk, and no one recalls ever seeing my father without one. By 1956, he had started showing symptoms of emphysema.

At the time, the public was just starting to come to grips with the health dangers of smoking, but my father nonetheless suspected that tobacco was the cause of his ailment. Even so, "he couldn't quit," George Kennedy bluntly observed. My father's physician, Dr. Hans Fehling of Hollywood—who had previously *recommended* smoking to his type A patient as a way to calm his nerves—now suggested that he switch from unfiltered cigarettes to filtered Kents, and use a filtered cigarette holder. Unsurprisingly, his condition continued to worsen.

My father was also suffering the effects of his decades-long addiction to Coca-Cola. He consumed close to twenty-five Cokes a day. The same commercial Coca-Cola truck that delivered soft drinks to restaurants and vending machines drove up our driveway every week. The driver would unload stacks of wooden crates filled with glass Coke bottles, and by week's end, every bottle would be empty, back in those wooden crates. Not only had this addiction rotted his teeth, forcing him to rely by this point on a full set of dentures, but it left him with a nearly dead palate. He was unable to taste anything unless it was heavily laced with pepper. "Everything had to be spiced up so he could taste it," my mother recalled.

Though he frequently survived on canned sardines and deviled egg sandwiches, he loved to experiment in the kitchen, and his specialty was hot pepper soup. Our family cook, Juliette Sauvage, told me that he frequently dumped large amounts of pepper straight from the box into the broth. Whenever he made his special soup, the rest of the family politely pretended to sip it at the dinner table. Between spoonfuls, I took huge gulps of water. "You had to call the fire department after taking a spoonful of that soup," recalled my mother.

When I had my tonsils removed, my father paid me a visit in the hospital on his way into the office. He was carrying a thermos of hot pepper soup under his arm. "Just the thing to fix him up," he told my mother. She begged him to leave the thermos at my bedside and assured him I would eat it later, but he insisted that I have some while it was still hot. Fortunately my mother won that argument, and when he was gone, she mercifully poured it down the sink.

In June 1957, another cooking-related incident provided the earliest signs that my father was developing dementia. Late one afternoon he returned home from the office and marched into the kitchen, where he announced to Juliette that he wanted baked beans for dinner. That wasn't unusual. What was different were the specific cooking instructions. He demanded that Juliette place the unopened can of beans directly into the oven rather than pouring them into a saucepan. Baffled, Juliette warned him this was dangerous, but he was adamant, repeating the order before departing for the den and his regular pre-dinner game of solitaire.

Through the oven window, the kitchen staff monitored the can as it expanded. Juliette rushed into the den to deliver this news to her employer, who was visibly infuriated at being disturbed. He barked at her to call him into the dining room when the beans were ready to be served.

When the can began to buckle, Juliette ordered everyone out of the kitchen and followed the staff to safety. Moments later, the explosion, which could be heard throughout the entire house, sent the whole family, our cook, the maid, and the gardener scurrying into the kitchen, followed by my father, his reading glasses on his nose and a deck of playing cards in his hand.

I recall that the kitchen was unrecognizable. The explosion had shattered the small pane of thick oven glass before ripping the door completely from its hinges. A thick coating of baked beans darkened the entire room. It took the staff three days to clean up the mess. Even months later, we were still discovering beans and tin can fragments wedged between gaps and in the corners of the kitchen.

Despite his declining health, my father remained a formidable presence at the *Hollywood Reporter*. When a member of his editorial staff, Jaik Rosenstein, complained about his miserly salary after eight years of employment, the publisher summarily fired him. An inflamed Rosenstein threatened to start a rival trade paper, and when Wilkerson dared him, Rosenstein launched *Hollywood Close-Up* magazine. "It was comical," remembered George Kennedy. "He started his own paper for the sole purpose of getting even with Mr. Wilkerson. It was David and Goliath all over again."

But if Wilkerson was now the fearsome giant, he was determined to prove that no little guy could yet knock him down. In 1957, one of the newest additions to the *Reporter*'s sales force was called into his boss's office. Kennedy had brought this thirtysomething salesman to the paper, and the two men had a friendship outside of the office. But by this point it had become clear that he was inflating his commissions by putting a lot of bad credit on the books. Despite their friendship, Kennedy felt duty bound to report his chicanery to his boss. His friend "was doing a cha-cha with the books," Kennedy recalled. "My loyalty was to Mr. Wilkerson."

When the salesman showed up at my father's door, he was greeted by the dressing-down of a lifetime. The man endured Wilkerson's screams—then sank to the floor in a heap, eyes closed. Thinking his employee had fainted, he yelled for Kennedy, who bent down and pressed two fingers to the salesman's throat. There was a pause and Kennedy announced, "He's dead, Mr. Wilkerson."

What my father did next haunted Kennedy for the rest of his life. Enraged, he removed the piñata bat he kept under his desk and advanced on the corpse. As he was just about to take a whack at it, Kennedy restrained him, shouting at him to stop.

"But that bastard stole from me!" my father exclaimed. Kennedy removed the bat from his hand. He forcefully explained if the coroner found injuries on the body, Wilkerson was sure to be charged with homicide. The publisher composed himself, lit a cigarette, and instructed Kennedy to make sure the ambulance drivers carried the body out through the back. "No one who stole from Mr. Wilkerson was leaving by the front door," said Kennedy, "not even into the afterlife."

The coroner eventually determined that the salesman had had a preexisting heart condition and died of a heart attack, but because he was only in his thirties, word spread like wildfire through the office that my father had shouted him to death. "From that moment on," said Kennedy, "the offices ran in a state of terror."

If Wilkerson's work persona ever showed signs of softening, it was in response to growing signs that the Hollywood he knew, that he'd spent decades bending to his will, was slowly fading away. Since he first arrived in Los Angeles in 1930, Louis B. Mayer had been his most hated adversary. But when the mogul passed away on October 29, 1957, the publisher had a reflective moment. His next Tradeviews column paid tribute to Mayer's achievements:

> He was, of course, Louie B. Mayer [*sic*], who created the entire tradition of glamour in Hollywood, and had the administrative genius to organize stars, writers, producers and directors on such a vast scale as MGM, and to see that they made pictures, and then to be able to sit at a preview and tell how good they were, how they could be improved, and how much money they would make.

He even compared Mayer favorably to his long-departed friend Irving Thalberg, whose 1936 death had reportedly moved him to uncontrollable tears. "A lot of the glory accorded Thalberg, in fact," he wrote, "actually reverted to Mayer."

Wilkerson's friends were fading along with his enemies. Also in 1957, Joe Schenck retired from 20th Century Fox. He and my father remained weekly poker buddies into 1958, when the movie tycoon suffered a stroke. He never fully recovered.

My father also remained close with Howard Hughes, bearing witness as his eccentricities slid further into obsession and delusion. When I was a young boy, Howard Hughes was a frequent caller to our home. I used to watch him drive up our driveway from my second-floor bedroom window. It always took him several minutes to park his car, using an arcane ritual—back and forth and back and forth. He was obsessed about parking it as close to the courtyard wall as possible.

He always wore a tired grey Stetson, a black leather aviator's jacket, a white shirt untucked and unbuttoned at the collar, dark slacks, and an old pair of white sneakers with no socks. He entered through the kitchen door, but to avoid touching the handle, he tugged a white handkerchief out of his pocket and used it as a glove. Typically, a maid escorted him into the den, where he sat and waited in the dark room for my father. According to my mother, he removed his jacket and folded and refolded it several times until he got it just right.

As a young boy, however, I couldn't have cared less about our guest's strange habits. The day he presented me with a hand-painted wooden model of a TWA Super Constellation, he stole my five-year-old heart and kept it forever.

As Hughes's illness grew worse, he began imagining that his telephones were bugged, and also developed an intense distrust of Western Union. Whenever he wanted to send a message, it had to be hand-delivered by courier. As *Reporter* sales head David Alexander recalled, "That courier would many times travel round the world. If the package was to be delivered to Pakistan, for instance, the courier would go the long way around." And again my father helped him out. Whenever he traveled to Europe on business, he carried documents and correspondence for his friend.

Eventually the movie tycoon took to isolating himself in a tiny attic at the top of his headquarters at 7000 Romaine Street in Hollywood. His sanctuary had eight phones but no furniture except for a green canvas army cot, and the only illumination came from a bare lightbulb that hung from the ceiling. He called my father from there, impatiently dialing and redialing if he got a busy signal. When he finally got through he would growl, "Your line's been busy for the past hour, Billy!" Once after a Hughes phone call came in, my father snapped at Kennedy, "What does he expect? That I sit by the phone waiting for his fucking call?" But despite the understandable frustration, he clearly continued to cherish their friendship.

Hughes would remain a legendary eccentric and recluse for the rest of his life, never again appearing in public after 1958. By the time my father died four years later, Greg Bautzer had become the focus of his obsessive calls and odd demands just like my father before him. Bautzer served as Hughes's attorney, but some suspect that by this point he was also the magnate's only friend. In 1966, after selling his stock in TWA for an estimated $550 million, the man who had thought my father was crazy for building a resort in the Nevada desert plowed most of the proceeds into Las Vegas hotels. Hughes died on April 5, 1976.

Not every old friend could be as persistent a presence in my father's life as Howard Hughes, but he still looked back on them fondly. In a lifetime rich with accomplishments, one of my father's proudest memories was still discovering Lana Turner.

Since conveying Turner from Currie's Ice Cream to movie stardom some twenty years earlier, my father's reputation as a starmaker and friend to female performers hadn't waned. In a Tradeviews column in 1953, he'd predicted of Grace Kelly, "It won't be long before this attractive kid will be the Number One Box Office attraction in the world." Once again he was right. Even Marilyn Monroe frequently reached out to my father for advice. In fact, she would phone him just days before being found dead on August 5, 1962, though by that time my father was near death himself. Still, according to Kennedy, he always went out of his way to help the troubled actress.

He'd also kept in touch over the years with his most famous discovery. In 1948, Lana Turner asked him to be the best man at her fourth wedding, this one to Bob Topping. Flattered, Wilkerson offered his house for the ceremony. On April 27, 1948, Wilkerson's mansion was decorated with three hundred delphiniums, roses, gladiolas, daisies, and gardenias. My father hired the ever-shrinking string orchestra from his nightclub L'Aiglon and had fresh lobsters and five pounds of top-quality beluga caviar flown in from Boston. Turner had wanted a small wedding—twelve at the ceremony and seventy-five at the reception. The press was to be excluded. Studio policemen were brought in from MGM to surround the house. However, the press was soon swarming the property, trampling the lawns and the flowerbeds and invading Turner's intimate gala. The *Reporter* did get a special scoop, but the next day every newspaper in Los Angeles covered the wedding.

Turner gave Wilkerson a Vacheron Constantin watch with his initials engraved on the back to thank him for everything he'd done for her. It remained a sentimental favorite even a decade later.

Turner's marriage, on the other hand, didn't last. By 1958 she'd been divorced two more times and was dating mobster Johnny Stompanato. He was insanely jealous and abusive to her—a fact that would lead directly to his gruesome demise. The official story of how he met his end has gone down in Hollywood history, but according to George Kennedy, what really happened was even more sordid. Kennedy's version of events cannot be verified, but it offers an intriguing possibility: that in Lana Turner's hour of need, the man who launched her career intervened one last time to help save it.

As Kennedy's story goes, it was a rainy Good Friday, April 4, 1958, when a disturbing phone call came in to our Bel-Air residence from Lana Turner. Kennedy said that my father remembered her as being so distraught, sobbing and breathless, that she could barely speak. She was desperately trying to locate her former fiancé Greg Bautzer but couldn't find him. When my father asked if there was something he could do, Turner confessed that she had killed her boyfriend. Sobbing uncontrollably, she told my father that after Stompanato threatened her and her fourteen-year-old daughter, Cheryl Crane, she had stabbed the hoodlum while he slept. Now she didn't know what to do.

My father knew that even if the movie star had acted in self defense, her career could not survive the revelation that she'd killed a man. He instructed her that under no circumstances was she to call the police; instead, she should sit tight and do nothing until he reached Bautzer. Kennedy recalled that he successfully tracked the lawyer down and relayed Turner's message.

What happened next is particularly hard to verify. Bautzer was never one to talk out of school, and the following account did not come from him. But Kennedy said that my father later learned the details; the secretary theorized that either Bautzer took him into his confidence because of their close relation-ship, or Turner herself updated him on what transpired.

Apparently when Bautzer rang Turner, he gave her the same advice Wilkerson had: stay put and don't call the police. His next phone call was to defense attorney Jerry Giesler. Giesler was Bautzer's idol, a legal magician who had won acquittals for most of his celebrity clients, including Robert Mitchum on drug charges, Errol Flynn for statutory rape, and director Busby Berkeley for murder after a drunk driving accident. He also represented Bugsy Siegel in his 1942 murder trial.

According to Kennedy, Giesler made his way to Lana Turner's palatial rental house on Bedford Drive. He surveyed the crime scene, then counseled Turner that her teenage daughter, Cheryl, should take the fall for Stompanato's murder. His thinking was simple: a jury was more likely to be sympathetic toward a young daughter defending her mother than toward Turner for defending herself. Geisler then restaged the murder to remove any evidence of the actress's guilt. "He rigged everything," Kennedy insisted, "but that's what his clients were paying him for."

Regardless of what really happened behind the closed doors of Turner's home, by the time the police arrived on Bedford Drive, not a drop of blood could be found either on the victim's body and clothes or on the carpet of her spotless pink bedroom. No usable fingerprints were found on the knife. Cheryl Crane confessed to the police that when she saw her mother being assaulted, she grabbed an eight-inch kitchen knife and buried it in the gangster's abdomen.

After an inquiry, the coroner concluded that Turner's daughter had acted in self-defense. She was never charged with the gangster's murder, though the remainder of her adolescence was troubled. The media, of course, followed the case intently, but they ultimately seemed satisfied with the official explanation, and the moviegoing public forgave Lana Turner for her poor choice of paramour.

Which means that if Kennedy's recollections are accurate, Billy Wilkerson, the consummate Hollywood newsman, was sitting on an exclusive story far more valuable than a celebrity wedding: a superstar actress killing a man and then letting her own daughter take the blame. If so, he chose never to run it, valuing an old friendship and an acting legacy he'd been instrumental in creating over the latest scandalous scoop.

38 | CURTAIN CALL

AS A YOUNG BOY, I spent every chance I could with my father. When he returned from the office, my mother always told me not to disturb him—that he wanted to be left alone. Still, that never stopped me. I would play cards with him, sitting on opposite sides of the green felt card table, where he taught me old maid and go fish.

As my father's dementia progressed, however, I would no longer find him in the den with his cards before dinner. Instead he would return home from the office, gather together his beloved menagerie of poodles, and sit and talk to them in his favorite reading chair for hours.

By this point he'd also allowed the dogs to befoul our once-elegant home. One of them had developed a bladder infection when I was very young; it was then that the small beige poodle Pierre became known as Pee-Pee. Following its lead, within a few weeks all the dogs began baptizing every inch of carpet and curtain in the house. Everywhere the outlines of urine stains turned the champagne-colored carpets into strange floor maps, and within a year they had turned a hideous yellow. Cigarette burns from my father's careless chain-smoking added to the effect. My mother nagged incessantly, but she couldn't convince him to order new carpeting and drapery or even fumigate the house to rid it of the cloying stench of urine and stale cigarette smoke. People stopped coming to visit.

By the late 1950s, my mother had reached a breaking point, and began a systematic extermination campaign against the creatures she held responsible for her misery. Later she explained to me her feelings of suffocation, with which I sympathized, but I always wished she had arrived at a more creative solution, perhaps finding the poodles new homes and telling my dad they had

298

CURTAIN CALL | 299

passed away while he was at the office. Instead she began to crush high doses of aspirin with a mortar and pestle and secretly mix it with the dog food; one by one, the dogs died.

My father was heartbroken and puzzled, but he never sought autopsies, which certainly would have revealed the truth. When one particular dog died, he was so distraught that Greg Bautzer gave him a Pekinese puppy. "It turned out to be a piranha," said George Kennedy. The puppy attacked anything that moved, and after three weeks of chaos, my father called his secretary in despair to come remove the dog. When Kennedy arrived, my father ushered him into the library and pointed to the dog hiding behind the sofa. Kennedy reached behind to gently ease the animal out, but it bit his hand. He retrieved a pair of heavy-duty gardening gloves from his car and, after a dramatic struggle, finally apprehended the dog, deposited it in the backseat, and took it to the pound. The number of dogs in the house continued to dwindle; ironically enough, by the time my father died only prime offender Pee-Pee would remain.

Like his dementia, my father's emphysema was becoming more worrying. When Dr. Hans Fehling's cigarette-focused advice fell short, another doctor, whose name is lost to us, prescribed a more radical therapy than a filter. Once a week, before the Coca-Cola trucks pulled up, Abbey Rents began delivering three large canisters, two of oxygen and one of helium, to our home. The large green bottles were parked in the corner of the master bedroom behind a purple divan. When my father returned home from the office, he would remove his jacket, loosen his tie, and lie down on the divan. For the next twenty minutes he lay prone with a mouthpiece inserted into his mouth. I remember watching him heave at those tanks, the needles on the dials jerking between numbers. Even then I realized that their twitching represented life itself.

My father bitterly complained about the treatments. After a few deep inhales, he would dissolve into a violent fit of coughing, his wheezing some-times growing so dire that on a few occasions my mother called an ambulance. "It was just all that good air going down," his doctor assured her. Inevitably, once the treatment was over and my father lit up a cigarette again, the fits miraculously stopped.

The helium portion of the treatments brought a hint of comedy to these tragic scenes. The gas transformed my father's gravelly growl into a high-pitched squeak. Many times during one of these treatments, he would have to take an important phone call—usually from one of the studio heads, who thought they were the victims of a prank. "Of course this is Billy Wilkerson," my father would insist. "Who the hell do you think it is? What? I sound like Mickey Mouse? What the fuck are you talking about?"

As his emphysema progressed, scheduled treatments were no longer enough; he would lapse into convulsive fits of coughing and would need an immediate treatment to alleviate them. Abbey Rents supplied my father with a portable version of his home apparatus so he could continue to travel: two large, black, hard-shelled cases, one that housed the regulator mechanism and the other miniature tanks. These followed us all over the world. In the summer of 1959, we arrived in Cannes for our yearly stay but learned that the airlines had sent my father's oxygen kit on to Frankfurt, Germany. Without the tanks, there was no way to soothe his coughing fits; watching him endure them was agonizing, like witnessing a diver trapped underwater without air. When it all became too much for my mother, she frantically called the front desk for an ambulance. A medical unit responded with oxygen.

Besides the medical issues, my father's chain-smoking also raised safety concerns. It was not uncommon to discover a lit cigarette my father had forgotten still burning on the edge of a countertop, its ashes drooping precariously over combustible carpets. In the 1950s, many houses in Los Angeles burned to the ground because of unattended cigarettes, and many smokers perished in bed when they fell asleep with a lit cigarette in hand. We all worried about that, and despite my mother's ardent pleas and lectures, my father continued to smoke in bed.

As stubborn and frustrating as my father could be, his own mother was even more of a challenge for the family to deal with. As George Kennedy noted, "Mr. Wilkerson and his mother were cut from the same cloth, but his mother won the door prize." Grandma Mary was decidedly unfiltered after she'd downed a few whiskies, and would give those around her a piece of her mind.

My father had been forced to ban her from his dinner parties for exactly this reason, restricting her to family dinners.

She only visited us once a month—as frequently as my mother could stand being with her. Grandma Mary, in turn, was no better disposed toward my mother than she'd been toward any of his other five wives; she once confided in George Kennedy that none of them were good enough for her "Willie." She kept her distance from me and my sister as well.

By the late 1950s she was nearly ninety years old but still fiercely independent. She insisted on doing all her own gardening. Billy would arrive for his afternoon visit to find her on the roof of her house pruning trees, and he would scream at her to come down. She would scream back that she was busy. On one occasion, concerned for her safety, he called the fire department. When they emerged on the rooftop, attempting to reach her, Mary beat them on the heads with the end of a gardening tool.

Then, in the spring of 1959, while we were on vacation in Acapulco, my father received a cable from Kennedy letting him know that his mother had fallen off the roof and broken her arm and hip. He returned to Hollywood while we remained behind in Mexico.

After the accident she was bound to a wheelchair, immobile and unable to tend her garden. She never visited our house again, and she plunged into a deep depression. "She would sit in her wheelchair on her front porch all day waiting for the four o'clock visit from Mr. Wilkerson," said Kennedy.

On April 19, 1960, we were on vacation in Honolulu when my father received a call from George Kennedy. His mother had died at age eighty-eight. Once again he immediately flew back to Los Angeles alone. There he learned the true circumstances: his mother had committed suicide—something I wouldn't learn until ten years later, when Kennedy finally revealed the family secret.

It was Kennedy who'd been charged with watching over Mary while we were on vacation. My father told him to make sure she had enough groceries, but Kennedy noticed she wasn't eating. When he asked her why, she told him she'd had enough of life. Kennedy knew Mary to be blunt, but he didn't know what to make of that comment.

Her intentions became horribly clear when he checked in on her again on April 19 and found her slumped over in her wheelchair. "She waited until Mr. Wilkerson was out of town, and then she just stopped eating," Kennedy explained. "She lived alone, so it was easy."

After my father returned home, his secretary accompanied him to the mortuary, and the two men in their dark suits stood over her open casket. Kennedy watched my father break down, crying so hard he had to hold on to the side of the casket to steady himself. "He was inconsolable," he said. At the funeral, attended only by my father and Kennedy, my father laid a simple spray of white roses on the silver casket, which was interred at Holy Cross Cemetery.

When we finally returned from Hawaii ourselves, we came home to a broken man. My father had ordered that Grandma Mary's house be left untouched, and for months he visited it alone every day after work just as he had while she was alive. No one knows what he did there, but he certainly made no effort to clean it out. Only after his own death would that finally happen.

Many people saw the change in my father after his mother's death. "He lost his will to live after that," said Kennedy. "Oh sure, he came to the office every day, but his heart wasn't in it."

Perhaps that's why, around the time he turned seventy in September 1960, he decided it was time to retire. Over the years, according to Greg Bautzer, he had periodically floated the idea of selling the *Hollywood Reporter*, but never with the intention of actually going through with it. "He got, every once in a while, a free appraisal of what somebody else thought it was worth by the offers." This time, however, he was serious. He put out word that the *Reporter* was for sale.

In short order, a deluge of offers poured in. One of them came from TV host Ed Sullivan, which wasn't a surprise, since at one point a few years earlier my father had considered offering him the editor's desk. Bart Lytton of Lytton Industries, a financier the *L.A. Times* later called "brash, colorful and controversial," also made an offer. Ultimately my father made a deal with Walter Annenberg, who owned *TV Guide* and the teen magazine *Seventeen*. Said Bautzer, who negotiated the deal, Annenberg was interested in the *Reporter* because "it would be a great source of information for his various publications." My father agreed to sell him the paper for $3.5 million in cash (nearly $30 million today), surmising that this would be enough for retirement and to take care of his family.

But when my mother got wind of the deal, she became hysterical. She believed that selling the paper would leave us destitute, particularly since she feared my father would begin gambling again. She pleaded with her husband not to "sell our future away." With tears running down her face, she approached my sister and me and begged us to intervene. "Please go talk him out of it!" she sobbed. "Please!"

We found our father sitting in his favorite chair in the master bedroom reading a newspaper. Obeying our mother's request, we began to plead. He lowered his paper and blurted, "But we'll be making millions!'" Whether it was our pleas or our mother's threats of divorce, the Annenberg deal evaporated.

My father still could have retired without selling the paper, delegating the role of publisher to someone else. But as long as he was the owner, he insisted on going into the office every day, even though his energy was failing him. "He sacked out on the couch and napped the first thing when he got in," Kennedy recalled.

He also made a point of carrying on our family traditions, though his worsening health made that more difficult as well. Just before Christmas each year, my father would buy two new cars. Drivers conveyed the gleaming new vehicles up the driveway and drove the older models away. The type of vehicle never varied: he bought a Chrysler Imperial for himself, always in handsome jet black, and a beige Cadillac Eldorado for my mother. But one night in the summer of 1961, my father announced at the dinner table that he had ordered a different color Chrysler this year. When my mother pressed him, he smiled impishly and told her he'd ordered one in light purple.

A week later—still months before Christmas—a shocking pink Chrysler Imperial was delivered to our home. The driver handed my mother the keys and was about to leave in his chase car when my mother stopped him and insisted her husband hadn't ordered this car. Both the color and timing made no sense, she explained. But the salesman unfolded the paperwork and pointed to my father's signature. On the manifest was listed a Chrysler Imperial in shocking pink. "I was stunned," my mother recalled. "I still believed it was a mistake."

She decided to wait until her husband came home from the office to clear it up, but when he got in and saw the car, he was ecstatic. When my mother complained, "But it's pink," he growled, "No it's not. Why the hell would you say it's pink? It's light purple."

That's when my mother discovered that her husband, Hollywood's emperor of taste and glamour, had become color blind. Although color blindness is not a symptom of dementia, at the time our family was convinced that it was, and the Pink Chrysler, as the family came to refer to it, seemed to be a concrete symbol of my father's deteriorating mental faculties.

And, of course, age and illness had made him no less of a menace behind the wheel. I dreaded the days when he picked me up from school, because driving with him was like taking a turn on Mr. Toad's Wild Ride at Disneyland. In that era before seat belts were standard equipment, at every turn I held on to my seat in terror. Whenever he lit a cigarette while driving, he let go of the steering wheel altogether and used both hands to light. Panicked, I would lunge across the seat and grab the wheel until the cigarette was successfully lit.

One afternoon after he had picked me up from school, he sideswiped a bus, and when I told him he had, he barked at me that he didn't know what I was talking about. Fifteen minutes later the same thing happened again. I reported this to my mother and that resulted in my being picked up less and less often by my father.

After several months of sideswiping buses and concrete pillars, the pink Chrysler Imperial resembled an entry in a demolition derby. Nothing made my father happier than being behind the wheel of a car, his elbow propped on the open window, a cigarette in his left hand and a poodle in his lap while listening to a ball game on the radio.

But as much as he tried to hold on to the simple pleasures of his routine, he knew that old age was catching up with him. In those years, my father would rise from the dinner table only to discover food droppings all over his expensive suit and tie. "One day while combing his hair in front of the mirror," Kennedy recalled, "the comb dropped out of his hand. He felt a terrific pain in his arm. He was having a stroke.

"He had to watch himself grow old," said Kennedy, "and he hated it."

He watched his friends grow old as well. In October 1961, my father paid a visit to the ailing Joe Schenck at his Beverly Hills residence, and when he came home he told my mother that before he left, the two men had embraced—a completely uncharacteristic move. My mother believed this one simple gesture encompassed decades of unacknowledged gratitude for their mutual support.

"Mr. Wilkerson loved Joe Schenck," said Kennedy, "and Schenck loved him. Besides Hughes, Schenck was really the only ally he had." Greg Bautzer said, "Without Joe's friendship and support, Billy would have had a tough time in Hollywood."

On October 22, 1961, my father learned that Schenck had died at the age of eighty-two. A few days later a courier delivered a small parcel to our home. When my father opened it, he discovered a gold fountain pen with Schenck's initials engraved on it. He instantly recognized it as the pen made famous by all the deals and correspondence it had signed—the same one the movie titan had used to pen notes to my father. Attached was a new note in Joe's hand that read, "Dear Billy, for you." A message from an attorney also accompanied the package, indicating that Schenck's will had instructed the pen be left to Billy Wilkerson. I watched as my father sat on the edge of his bed, his face buried in his hands, weeping uncontrollably with the open package by his side.

Six months later, in April 1962, my father's own health problems dramatically accelerated. One night at dinner, he leaned over to retrieve his napkin that had fallen on the carpet and cracked two ribs on his chair's wooden armrest. I watched him cry out in agony, but I didn't know what was wrong. With the help of our gardener, my mother slowly helped him upstairs and into bed.

After that an almost continual stream of doctors came and went from our home, and a myriad of specialists were in constant attendance. Horton & Converse Pharmacy made almost hourly deliveries; its delivery truck became a depressing reminder of my father's condition. Numerous procedures followed, leaving scars crisscrossing his torso. At one point a plastic tube with a metal clamp at the end protruded from his abdomen, draining bile; he emptied the black liquid into a drinking glass.

By that summer, my father was a wreck. Besides the cracked ribs, he was afflicted with burning piles, cancer of the anus, angina pectoris, corns, gas, gallbladder issues, seborrhea, sinusitis, and sciatica. With the onset of each of these conditions, he became even more intolerable, curtailing his socializing, rarely entertaining at home. Amazingly, despite all this, he rarely missed a deadline for his daily editorial.

On the night of August 28, my father's only remaining poodle, Pee-Pee, overturned his water bowl on the linoleum floor in the master bathroom before he was retired to his kennel for the night. When my father made a bathroom call in the middle of the night, he slipped on the wet floor. We were awakened by his agonizing screams. He was raced to the hospital, where doctors found he had suffered a broken vertebra. Still, my father refused to remain in the hospital, and when he came home, he informed my mother that he was going to die.

On Saturday night, September 1, I went to his bedside to kiss him goodnight. I remember the light of his solitary table lamp, the only illumination in that dark bedroom. In that dim light, I could see the railway of scars spanning the length of his torso. His once-handsome face looked leathery and weather-beaten. When I leaned over and kissed his forehead, I smelled the reek of medicine. He opened his eyes and said in his sandpapery whisper, "I've got something to say." He struggled for breath. "Listen to me carefully," he wheezed. "You're a Wilkerson. Remember that. Wilkersons aren't afraid to risk, aren't afraid of failure. Do you understand me?" I nodded, even though I was confused.

My father died at 4:00 AM on Sunday, September 2, 1962. His death certificate certified the cause of death as a coronary, but Kennedy was adamant on the real cause of death. "Mr. Wilkerson died of a broken heart. He never got over the death of his mother."

No priest came to administer last rites. I entered my father's bedroom that afternoon after the mortuary had removed his body, wearing my dress uniform from St. John's Military Academy, the school I attended. I stood there for a long while as the last rays of the late-afternoon sun flowed across the room. The bedroom was quiet as a library, stilled by the departure of the spirit that had inhabited it since 1935, but all the signs of his life were still present. The bed was neatly made, as if he had just left for work. At his bedside, resting at the bottom of a half-filled glass of water, were his dentures. Rows of medicine bottles lined every available inch of his nightstand, standing like toy soldiers at attention. His reading glasses were neatly folded next to a worn deck of playing cards. Two tins of his favorite chocolates and licorice sat side by side.

For a man so deeply committed to Catholicism, our home was strangely devoid of religious symbols. We had not a single Bible. The only testament to his devotion was a color depiction of the Virgin Mary propped against the lamp, on the same night table that held his cocked Army .45. In that moment, feeling both his presence and his absence, I stood at attention at the foot of the bed and saluted.

To see the original breakup letter that Edith Gwynn wrote to Billy Wilkerson and some of Wilkerson's actual Tradeviews columns that called out alleged Communists in Hollywood, visit https://issuu.com/hollywoodgodfather.

ACKNOWLEDGMENTS

THERE WERE THOSE WHO would not discuss Billy Wilkerson with me. Their silence only increases my gratitude to the many who did. In some cases, I was given certain information with the promise that I would not publish until after my source's passing. I have kept my promise. To all those who gave so graciously of their time and energy, I offer my sincere thanks.

Thank you to: Bob Christianson, Jim Heimann, Las Vegas historian Alan Hess, Susan Jarvis at UNLV Special Collections, Patrick Jenning and Marshall Croddy, Donn Knepp, David Millman of the Nevada State Museum, Charles Rappleye, Colin Russell, Kate Stadelman, Armen Tavitian, Mike Trent, Ross Velderrain, Dick Weaver, and Rob Wilhite.

PEOPLE PAST: David Alexander, Greg Bautzer, Marcia Borie, Grace Bouliance, Cubby Broccoli, Estelle Jackson "Brownie" Brown Franson, Bill Diehl, Harry Drucker, Vivian DuBois Wilhite, Jack and Vic Enyart, Bill Feeder, Murray Fields, Don Carle Gillette, Edith Gwynn, Radie Harris, Howard Hawks, Cliff A. Jones, Walter Kane, Howard W. Koch, Norman Krasna, Carl "Junior" Laemmle, Mervyn LeRoy, Perry Lieber, Herb McDonald, Kurt Niklas, Mr. and Mrs. Donald O'Connor, Alex Paal, Joe Pasternak, LeRoy Prinz, Rev. Mother Regina, Joe Rivkin, Beatrice Sedway, Howard Strickling, Lana Turner, Peter Viertel, Raoul Walsh, Louis Wiener, Tichi Wilkerson, and Frank Wright.

THE MEDIA: Art Durbano, Denny Arar of the *Daily News*, Lowell Bergman of CBS's *60 Minutes*, Kenneth Turan and Sharon Bernstein of the *Los Angeles Times*, and Bob Shemeligian of the *Las Vegas Sun*.

SPECIAL THANKS TO: George H. Kennedy Jr., Billy Wilkerson's faithful secretary and general manager for thirty years, who worked beside the man who created Hollywood history; Thomas F. Seward, Billy Wilkerson's business partner for close to a decade; and Hollywood historian Val Holley for his excellent research in helping me acquire practically the entire oeuvre of Billy Wilkerson editorials.

A heartfelt thanks to British biographer and historian Robert Lacey. It was Robert who, in his biography of Meyer Lansky, published the first accurate account of the building of the Flamingo Hotel, citing Wilkerson as the project's originator. Throughout the long writing process, he has been a wonderful mentor, teacher, and friend, who painstakingly edited the manuscript for my previous book *The Man Who Invented Las Vegas* twice for historical inaccuracies.

To my cousin Ron Wilkerson and our showrunner Robert Cooper, my coproducers on *Dreamland*, the TV series based on my father's life. Both of them believed in his story from the very beginning.

To my son, Will, my biggest cheerleader, and to my sister, Cindy, who provided memories when they were not too painful.

I have been truly blessed to work with some wonderful editors. Yuval Taylor, senior editor at Chicago Review Press, had the guts to publish *Hollywood Godfather* when others did not. I'm deeply grateful for his unfaltering guidance with this project.

To Greg Bautzer biographer James Gladstone, who not only brought me to the attention of Chicago Review Press but also provided a superb historical review of the material that greatly aided the narrative.

To Devon Freeny, my developmental editor at CRP, who spent countless hours smoothing out this very difficult and complicated tale. His patience cannot go without mention. He contributed an alchemy to this project I will forever be indebted to him for.

And last, to Amy Friedman, my Max Perkins, who took the building blocks of my father's story and helped me construct a beautiful home for it. Part shrink, part editor, Amy helped weave the fabric of his story into a seamless tapestry, guiding both his biography and me to safety. She always, without exception, caught me when I fell, and for that I cannot express my gratitude enough.

APPENDIX
BILLY WILKERSON'S
BUSINESSES

Years in parentheses indicate dates of operation under Wilkerson's ownership.

Publications

Hollywood Reporter (1930–1962)
1606 North Highland Avenue, Hollywood (1930)
5746 Sunset Boulevard, Hollywood (1930)
6715 Sunset Boulevard, Hollywood (1931–1962)

London Reporter (1936)
154 Wardour Street, London

Restaurants, Nightclubs & Cafés

Speakeasies (1926–1927)
*Dodge Townhouse (Fifth Avenue near St. Patrick's Cathedral), New York City
(1926–1927)*
Fifty-Second Street and Park Avenue, New York City (1927)
Various locations (Mayor Jimmy Walker's speakeasies), New York City (1927)
Maximum occupancy: Unknown

Vendôme Wine & Spirits Co. (1933–1936)
6666 Sunset Boulevard, Hollywood
Maximum occupancy: 400

Café Trocadero (1934–1938)
8610 Sunset Boulevard, Hollywood
Maximum occupancy: Louis XVI Room, 50; French-Blue Room, 250; Main
    Dining Salon, 400

Ciro's (1940–1942)
8433 Sunset Boulevard, Hollywood
Maximum occupancy: 300

Restaurant LaRue (1944–1954)
8631 Sunset Boulevard, Hollywood
Maximum occupancy: 280

L'Aiglon (1947–1948)
Beverly Drive and Wilshire Boulevard, Beverly Hills, CA
Maximum occupancy: 150

Club LaRue (1950)
Highway 1 (future site of the Sands Hotel), Las Vegas
Maximum occupancy: 100

Hotels

Arrowhead Springs Hotel (1939–1940)
Lake Arrowhead, CA
Maximum occupancy: 100–200 (hotel and casino combined)

Flamingo Hotel (1946–1947)
Highway 1, Las Vegas
Maximum occupancy: 200 (hotel and casino combined)

Other

Sunset House Haberdashers/Hairdressers (1936)

6715 Sunset Boulevard, Hollywood

Maximum occupancy: 20 (haberdashery and barber shop combined)

NOTES

MOST QUOTES IN THIS BOOK are drawn from my original interviews and correspondence with the people who knew my father. See "Original Interviews & Author Correspondence" in the bibliography, p. 325, for a full list of these primary sources. Additional sources and explanatory notes for each chapter are laid out below; a full name listed alone indicates a primary source not attributed in the text.

1. The Corpse

Notes of condolence: All are from the author's collection, dated to September 1962 (a few of the notes are dated more specifically: Thomas M. Pryor, September 4, 1962; Harry Brand, September 3, 1962; and Joan Crawford, September 4, 1962). Wilkerson's eulogy: Author recollection.

2. Rosebud

Big Dick's gambling and the Wilkersons' tobacco farm: George Kennedy. Wilkerson's quotes about his childhood on the farm: Author recollection, circa 1957. Wilkerson's sexual solicitation by a priest: Tichi Wilkerson. *His heart was never in medicine*: "'Billy' Wilkerson," *Hollywood Close-Up*. Big Dick's death: Clipping, *Birmingham News*, February 1916, author's collection. *"The only thing I knew"*: Author recollection, circa 1957. *When a friend once asked*: Bill Feeder.

3. Lubinville

Fires in the silent era: "In the Beginning," *Hollywood*, episode 2, directed by David Gill and Kevin Brownlow (Thames Television, 1979). *"What the hell"*: "Nightlife of the Tin Gods," *Los Angeles Mirror*. History of nickelodeons: Joe Pasternak; Jacobs, *Rise of the American Film*, 56; Bowser, *Transformation of Cinema*, 4–6; Grieveson and Krämer,

eds., *Silent Cinema Reader*, 80–81, 120, 126; Allen, *Film History*, 202. Records center
fire: "The 1973 Fire, National Personnel Records Center," National Archives official
website, accessed March 20, 2018, www.archives.gov/st-louis/military-personnel/fire
-1973.html. *In later years, he'd talk*: Tichi Wilkerson. The influenza pandemic: Molly
Billings, "The Influenza Pandemic of 1918," Stanford University official website,
February 2005, http://virus.stanford.edu/uda; American Experience, "Timeline:
Influenza Across America in 1918," PBS official website, accessed March 10, 2017,
www.pbs.org/wgbh/amex/influenza/timeline/index.html (site discontinued). *The very
next day she learned*: George Kennedy. *"Snakes love warmth"*: Author recollection. *His
visit to St. Petersburg*: George Kennedy. *Wilkerson acknowledged to friends* and *"In our
hour of need"*: George Kennedy. *"We were like a Roman slave ship"*: Author recollection, circa 1957. Joe Pasternak's L.A. story: Pasternak, *Easy the Hard Way*, 74–75.
Twenty-two thousand speakeasies: Birmingham, *The Rest of Us*, 152. *"The townhouse
was the first"*: Murphy, *Say . . . Didn't You Used to Be George Murphy?*, 52. *Opened in
February 1927*: "Hollywood Institution," *Time*. *"A boozer is a loser"*: George Kennedy.

4. The Crash

Speakeasy raid: "Hollywood Institution," *Time*. *In fact, some historians believe*:
Adler, *Hollywood and the Mob*, 6. Manhattan trade paper and Wilkerson's Black
Tuesday: "Hollywood Institution," *Time*.

5. Life in the West

Daily Screen World letter: Louis Jacobino to Billy Wilkerson, July 31, 1930, author's
collection. *The paper's premise*: Early *Hollywood Reporter* advertising rate card,
author's collection. *They woke to the same breakfast*: Tichi Wilkerson. *"Wisps of
smoke rising"*: Wilkerson and Borie, *Hollywood Reporter: The Golden Years*, 3. *"To
Raoul Walsh"*: George Kennedy. *Schenck was an unapologetic carouser*: Tom Seward.
"A large man of imperious bearing": Rappleye and Becker, *All American Mafioso*, 61.
According to Paul Ivano: "Swanson and Valentino," *Hollywood*, episode 6, directed
by David Gill and Kevin Brownlow (Thames Television, 1979).

6. The Bet

"Mirthful, infectious smile": Rappleye and Becker, *All American Mafioso*, 7.
Wilkerson would make many social loans: "A Tale of Two Willie's," *Daily Variety*.
Story of the bet: Tom Seward. *Five thousand press clippings*: "'Billy' Wilkerson,"
Hollywood Close-Up. *Mayer grew pale*: Howard Strickling.

7. Vendôme

Fortnum & Mason deal: George Kennedy.

8. The Cut

Louis Mayer call, Max Albert Schlesinger, and sample Wilkerson memo: "'Billy' Wilkerson," *Hollywood Close-Up*.

9. Café Trocadero

Île de France encounter: "'Billy' Wilkerson," *Hollywood Close-Up*. Actresses' nightlife complaints: Tom Seward. Myron Selznick: "Nightlife of the Tin Gods," *Los Angeles Mirror*. Troc's opening night: "'Billy' Wilkerson," *Hollywood Close-Up*. Jack Benny quote: Marcia Borie. "Siberia" seating: Tom Seward.

10. The Shakedown

Wilkerson was playing a private card game: Tom Seward. Bioff and Browne background: Olsen, "The Mob and the Movies." Balaban & Katz shakedown: Tuohy, "Gone Hollywood," www.americanmafia.com/Feature_Articles_208.html; Olsen, "The Mob and the Movies." *The time for that takeover had come* and *Rosselli was adamant*: Tom Seward.

11. The Breakup

"I want to be free": Edith Gwynn to Billy Wilkerson, circa mid-1935, author's collection. *She returned every advance check*: Edith Gwynn. *When she did greet visitors*: Author recollection.

12. Sunday Night at the Troc

"The price of my train ticket": Joe Rivkin. *"You're in a dying business"*: Tom Seward. *Wilkerson took credit*: "'Billy' Wilkerson," *Hollywood Close-Up*. *"Get the hook"*: Broccoli, *When the Snow Melts*, 52. Joe E. Lewis background: Cohn, *The Joker Is Wild*, 16–25, 117–136. *He guided Lewis back*: Tom Seward. *Fifty-seven consecutive weeks*: Cohn, *The Joker Is Wild*, 142.

13. The Gambler

He traded cars with Kennedy: George Kennedy. Joe Schenck and Lázaro Cárdenas: Raoul Walsh. *The minimum buy-in was $10,000*: Tom Seward. *He even pursued his* *quarry*: George Kennedy. The Gambling Syndicate and Wilkerson's stake in their clubs: Eyman, *Lion of Hollywood*, 184.

14. Hollywood's Bible

Thalberg obituary: "Hollywood in Gloom," *Hollywood Reporter*, September 15, 1936. *"A heavy, slickpaper yearbook"*: "Hollywood Institution," *Time*. *"The paper had become"*: "'Billy' Wilkerson," *Hollywood Close-Up*. *"The toilet bible"*: Tom Seward.

15. The *London Reporter* to Sunset House

"We believe that in a period": Frank Pope, Tradeviews, *London Reporter*, March 18, 1936. Wilkerson and J. Arthur Rank: George Kennedy.

16. Daily Life at the *Reporter*

"A Central Casting Corporation gambler": "Hollywood Institution," *Time*. *"Mad Margaret"*: George Kennedy. *"And don't forget my friends!"*: Tichi Wilkerson.

17. Friends and Allies

Shearing off the car doors: Author recollection. Death of Ted Healy and Strickling's role in the cover-up: Fleming, *The Fixers*, 175–178. Pat Di Cicco's wives: Adler, *Hollywood and the Mob*, 85. *"Gave us the valuable commitment"*: Broccoli, *When the Snow Melts*, 102. *"What does it have?"*: Tichi Wilkerson. *"Influence in the industry"*: Broccoli, *When the Snow Melts*, 102. *An infusion of up to $25,000* and *Interrupted by a phone call*: David Alexander. Procuring women for Hughes: George Kennedy; Tom Seward. Walter Kane's 1947 suicide attempt: Gladstone, *Man Who Seduced Hollywood*, 170–171. *Proved himself so useful* and *"Billy, looks like"*: George Kennedy. Sheilah Graham vendetta and quoted articles: Graham and Frank, *Beloved Infidel*, 134–135, 231–233. *Graham had returned to Hollywood* and *"I want you to be my second"*: Westbrook, *Intimate Lies*, 47–48. *"Presumably for his regular stool"*: Rasmussen, "Man Behind the Sunset Strip."

18. The Starmaker and Lana Turner

"The Professional Againster": George Kennedy. *Down on his hands and knees*: David Alexander; George Kennedy. *"Jailbait"*: George Kennedy. Lana Turner's discovery: Lana Turner; W. R. Wilkerson III, "Writing the End of a True-to-Life Cinderella Story," *Los Angeles Times*, December 10, 1994. *"This young lady has"*: Gladstone, *Man Who Seduced Hollywood*, 29. Lana Turner and Greg Bautzer: Ibid., 29–35.

19. "He'll Bring Us All Down"

We can't get along: Louella O. Parsons, "Former Actress, Married One Year, to Seek Divorce," *Pittsburgh Post-Gazette*, May 3, 1937. *$50,000 a year*: Olsen, "The Mob and the Movies." *A cartoon caricature of a gangster*: George Kennedy. Bioff and Jules Brulatour: Adler, *Hollywood and the Mob*, 65. *He summoned film company executives*: Adler, *Hollywood and the Mob*, 67; Tom Seward. IATSE backlash and state assembly hearings: Olsen, "The Mob and the Movies." Wilkerson/Bioff meeting and aftermath: "A Tale of Two Willie's," *Daily Variety*. *"For whatever mistake"*: Ibid. Bioff targets Joe Schenck: Tom Seward. *"Taking care of the problem"* and *"He wouldn't do that"*: George Kennedy. *"Looking just like the inside"*: "Hollywood Institution," *Time. Complete set of Reporter printing plates*: Author recollection. Trocadero sale: Tom Seward. *Not only the most successful*: Jim Heimann.

20. Women and Marriage

The publisher would remain in hiding: Tom Seward. *"Y'know, Billy's real mistress"*: "Hollywood Institution," *Time*.

21. Joe Schenck and the Arrowhead Springs Hotel

He presented Bioff with a Fox company check: Adler, *Hollywood and the Mob*, 70; Tom Seward; Greg Bautzer. *Schenck immediately contacted*: Higham, *Merchant of Dreams*, 340. *A meeting of the Hollywood Syndicate*: Tom Seward. Otis D. Babcock's grand jury probe: Olsen, "The Mob and the Movies." *In retrospect, the legal retainer* and *Schenck and Wilkerson met again*: Tom Seward. *Wilkerson felt an obligation*: George Kennedy. *He wanted to lease the hotel*: Estelle Jackson Brown; Tom Seward. *Wilkerson leased the building*: *Los Angeles Examiner*, October 8, 1941, in Los Angeles Examiner morgue, University of Southern California Regional History Center. Schenck grand jury appearance and indictment: Olsen, "The Mob and the Movies." Arrowhead backroom games: George Kennedy.

22. Ciro's

"I want to tell you": Ciro's advertisement, *Hollywood Reporter*, February 16, 1940. Ciro's menus: Sunday dinner menu, April 13, 1940, and Monday dinner menu, April 15, 1940, both from author's collection. *The club played host* and *Bugsy Siegel was also*: Tom Seward.

23. Trials

Joe Schenck's plea bargain: Olsen, "The Mob and the Movies." Willie Bioff's plea bargain: Tuohy, "Gone Hollywood," www.americanmafia.com/Feature _Articles_208.html. *He also squealed about*: Relayed by FBI agent Frank Angell to Billy Wilkerson (date unknown), per Tom Seward. *He paid gangster Tony Cornero*: "Hollywood Institution," *Time. They probably first met*: George Kennedy. *A cordial if formal relationship*: Vic Enyart. *Wilkerson's guest in his private box*: Tom Seward. *Sent Greg Bautzer to seduce her*: Gladstone, *Man Who Seduced Hollywood*, 59. Wilkerson/Seward partnership: "$150,000 Suit Hits Wilkerson on Partnership," *Los Angeles Times*, December 4, 1952. *Wilkerson gave his testimony*: "A Tale of Two Willie's," *Daily Variety*. "*Wilkerson's life has been*": "Hollywood Institution," *Time. His goal on the stand*: David Alexander. *A verdict was reached*: Olsen, "The Mob and the Movies."

24. Restaurant LaRue

Four-star chef Orlando Figini and "*The fashionable place*" and *The restaurant's weekly take*: "Hollywood Institution," *Time. Discreet card games* and *He would make good later on*: Tom Seward. "*When I feel the table*": Tichi Wilkerson. *He also turned to his mother*: George Kennedy; Tichi Wilkerson.

25. The Flamingo

Wilkerson's gambling losses: George Kennedy. *Bartered away Reporter advertising* and *Too dire for even Wilkerson* and "*If you are going to gamble*": George Kennedy. *Frequently horses were doped*: Jennings, *We Only Kill Each Other*, 135. "*Gambling halls*": George Kennedy. *Taking over the El Rancho Vegas*: Tom Seward. *Bautzer learned even more*: Greg Bautzer. *Folsom sold Bautzer the property*: Tom Seward. Recording the deeds: Clark County, NV, Book of Deeds, 40:381–382 (title first recorded under Moe Sedway, then under Greg Bautzer acting for Billy Wilkerson; both deeds recorded the same day, November 21, 1945). *Wilkerson was pleased*: George Kennedy. *All his passions under one roof*: Greg Bautzer. Instructions to Russell and Douglas and naming the Flamingo: George Kennedy. *Sedway was a loyal associate*: Beatrice Sedway. *Running Vegas's El Cortez Hotel*: Lacey, *Little Man*, 152. Wilkerson and "the Boys": Tom Seward. Russell and Douglas's designs: George Kennedy. Wilkerson's fundraising attempts and budget cuts: Tom Seward. "*I have become convinced*": Billy Wilkerson to Moe Sedway, undated, mailed to the El Cortez Hotel, Las Vegas, NV, courtesy of Beatrice Sedway. *He had gambled away $60,000* and *Owed Moe Sedway $5,000*: Tom Seward. *Deeded the land to Sedway*:

Clark County, NV, Book of Deeds, 40:381–382 (title and deed of transfer indicate
that the land was formally transferred from Margaret Folsom to Moe Sedway, but
a check from Wilkerson to Folsom dated March 5, 1945, for $9,500 indicates that
funds were transferred between them eight months before Sedway quitclaimed the
property to Wilkerson's attorney, Greg Bautzer; Tom Seward confirmed that this
was, in fact, an initial down payment to Folsom for the land's purchase). *Joe Schenck
still had faith*: Greg Bautzer. *Repurchased the Flamingo land*: Clark County, NV,
Book of Deeds, 40:381–382 (title and deed of land transfer executed and recorded
on November 11, 1945). W. R. Wilkerson Enterprises: Greg Bautzer. Early construction: Tom Seward. *Wilkerson had already sunk $300,000*: George Kennedy. *Bargain-
basement advertising rates*: Jennings, *We Only Kill Each Other*, 152. *The publisher
even went so far*: Tom Seward. Wilkerson abandons the project and Sedway brings it
to Lansky's attention: George Kennedy. Harry and Sam Rothberg background: Lowell Bergman; Messick, *Secret File*, 206. Harry Rothberg's offer: Greg Bautzer. *Rothberg and Wilkerson signed*: "Release of All Demands," Nevada Project Corporation,
March 19, 1947, author's collection. *Rothberg had organized them*: Greg Bautzer.

26. Bugsy Siegel

Siegel's temper and his charm: George Kennedy. *Established himself as a playboy*:
Patrick Jenning and Marshall Croddy. *Financed his own glossies*: George Kennedy.
Hollywood regarded him as a failure: Patrick Jenning and Marshall Croddy. *She
would say as much*: George Kennedy. *His violent temper tantrums*: Beatrice Sedway.
Harry Greenberg trial: Giesler, *Jerry Giesler Story*, 237–239. *Well acquainted with
Siegel's brother* and *He deferred to my father*: George Kennedy. *"Because of people
like me"*: Greg Bautzer. *Wilkerson shipped Siegel off* and *Late-night meeting in Vegas*
and *Dissolve into jealousy*: George Kennedy. *Siegel began to feel intimidated*: Greg
Bautzer. *"This is my fucking hotel!"* and *The mere mention of Wilkerson's name*:
George Kennedy. *He began to see himself* and *Wilkerson agreed to a compromise*:
Greg Bautzer. Siegel's restaffing decisions: Ibid.

27. The Crusade

Wilkerson at confession: George Kennedy. *"If you could make a buck"*: Goldstein,
"Hollywood's Blackest Hour." Trumbo's response: Trumbo, *Additional Dialogue*,
59–60. *"Germany had Goebbels"*: Anonymous source. *Arthur Miller grew to loathe*:
George Kennedy.

28. Exile

Hughes's drug addiction: George Kennedy; Tom Seward. *Wilkerson had a small table installed*: George Kennedy. *The site began to swarm*: Greg Bautzer. *Carpenters, plasterers, and other workmen*: Jennings, *We Only Kill Each Other*, 152. *Siegel decreed that each bathroom*: Louis Wiener. *More toilets were ordered* and *The steel ceiling beam*: Greg Bautzer. *The heavy curtains Hill had ordered*: George Kennedy. *Building, destruction, and rebuilding*: Jennings, *We Only Kill Each Other*, 152. *By day, trucks regularly delivered*: Greg Bautzer. *Stamped* INSUFFICIENT FUNDS: Jennings, *We Only Kill Each Other*, 176 (Nevada Project Corporation check no. 1384). *Siegel abjectly apologized*: IRE, *Arizona Project*, 15. *Webb ordered trucks full of materials*: Tichi Wilkerson. *Siegel summoned architect Richard Stadelman*: Kate Stadelman. *Siegel was in a hurry* and *He called Siegel directly*: George Kennedy. *He hired press agent Paul Price*: Jennings, *We Only Kill Each Other*, 173. *Also accompanying Siegel*: IRE, *Arizona Project*, 15. Siegel's threats and Wilkerson's escape to Paris: Greg Bautzer (author was unable to locate copies of the affidavits Bautzer described). Wilkerson's plan and routine in exile: George Kennedy. *Welcomed by a cacophony of construction noise*: Tom Seward. *Thousands of Flamingo matchbooks* and *Siegel had decided to rely*: George Kennedy. *The locals in particular were put off*: David Alexander. *"Found their rhythm"*: Lacey, *Little Man*, 152. Flamingo buyout deal: Greg Bautzer. *Bylined from the French capital*: Tradeviews, *Hollywood Reporter*, June 3, 1947. Siegel's murder: Lacey, *Little Man*, 157–158. Wilkersons' return from Europe: SS *Queen Elizabeth* passenger list, Southampton to New York, June 25, 1947, via Ancestry.com, www.ancestry.com/interactive/7488/NYT715_7405-0808. *Investigation into Siegel's finances*: Beatrice Sedway. FBI inquiry: George Kennedy. *She was a key witness*: Investigation of Organized Crime in Interstate Commerce: Hearings Before the Special Committee to Investigate Organized Crime in Interstate Commerce, 82nd Cong., vol. 7 (testimony of Virginia Hill Hauser, March 15, 1951), 1144, 1168, 1170. *An egalitarian establishment*: Greg Bautzer.

29. The Blacklist

My father later received confirmation: Greg Bautzer. Studios' antitrust battles: Aberdeen, "Hollywood Antitrust Case," www.cobbles.com/simpp_archive/1film_antitrust.htm. Waldorf meeting: Greg Bautzer (Joe Schenck shared the details of the meeting with Bautzer as well as Wilkerson, since the two had also become close friends through my father); "'Billy' Wilkerson," *Hollywood Close-Up* ("He once borrowed five grand" interjection).

30. L'Aiglon

Hercules test flight and airline crash near miss: Tom Seward. United Airlines flight 624: "Crash of DC-6 Kills All 43 on Board in Pennsylvania Emergency Landing," *New York Times*, June 18, 1948.

31. *United States v. Paramount Pictures*

Supreme Court arguments: "Byrnes Defending Movies in Supreme Court Antitrust Suit," *Corpus Christi Times*, February 10, 1948; "Film Industry Fighting for Life—Byrnes," *Los Angeles Times*, February 12, 1948 (*"the freedom of American life"*). *"I think the ruling means"*: Aberdeen, "Hollywood Antitrust Case," www.cobbles.com /simpp_archive/paramountcase_6supreme1948.htm. *Regular payoffs to his contacts*: Tom Seward. Rosselli is paroled: Olsen, "The Mob and the Movies." Rosselli's return to Hollywood: Tereba, *Mickey Cohen*, Kindle ed., ch. 8. *Their lobbying relied more on lip service*: Tom Seward. RKO and Paramount relinquish their theater holdings: Aberdeen, "Hollywood Antitrust Case," www.cobbles.com/simpp_archive /paramountcase_6supreme1948.htm. *Joe Schenck suspected*: Tom Seward.

32. "That Was Who He Was"

Hughes did indeed have a paid informant: Wilkerson and Borie, *Hollywood Reporter: The Golden Years*, 6. Divorce from Vivian: "Wife Involves 'New Look' in Divorce Action," *Los Angeles Times*, December 4, 1947; "Fifth Spouse Divorces Publisher and Cafe Man," *Los Angeles Times*, March 8, 1949.

33. Club LaRue

Restaurant LaRue buyout deal: *Los Angeles Daily News*, July 22, 1954.

34. The Next Chapter

"You are": Tichi Wilkerson.

35. The Partnership

Ronald Reagan visits: George Kennedy. Meredith Harless's confirmation: Adler, *Hollywood and the Mob*, 126. *"Grabbed sole control"*: *Hollywood Citizen-News*, August 11, 1951. *"Questioned the propriety"*: *Hollywood Citizen-News*, December 4, 1952. *Proceedings were delayed*: *Daily Variety*, July 16, 1952. Willie Bioff's murder: Olsen, "The Mob and the Movies."

36. The Shadow

Peter Viertel's military inquiry: *Dangerous Friends*, Viertel, 53–54, 273–274. Blacklist-era corruption: "None Without Sin," *American Masters*, season 18, episode 1, directed by Michael Epstein (PBS, 2003). *"There was a pall of fear"*: Goldstein, "Hollywood's Blackest Hour." Darryl Zanuck phones Wilkerson: George Kennedy. Elia Kazan Oscar protest: Patrick Goldstein, "Oscar-Night Cliffhanger," *Los Angeles Times*, March 15, 1999. Garson Kanin lawsuit: "Kanin Sues Magazine for $2,025,000 Libel," *New York Times*, April 9, 1952. *"Legally," he told the court*: Greg Bautzer. *Mailed to Reporter headquarters*: Ross Velderrain.

37. The Old Days

"He was, of course, Louie B. Mayer": "'Billy' Wilkerson," *Hollywood Close-Up*. Howard Hughes's later years: Gladstone, *Man Who Seduced Hollywood*, 182–195. *"It won't be long"*: Grace Kelly biography, Turner Classic Movies official website, accessed March 20, 2018, www.tcm.com/tcmdb/person/100310%7C63086 /Grace-Kelly/biography.html. *By the time the police arrived*: Tereba, *Mickey Cohen*, Kindle ed., ch. 21.

38. Curtain Call

"Of course this is Billy Wilkerson": Author recollection. *Find her on the roof*: George Kennedy. *TV host Ed Sullivan*: Greg Bautzer. *"Brash, colorful and controversial"*: Arelo Sederberg, obituary for Bart Lytton, *Los Angeles Times*, June 30, 1969.

SELECTED
BIBLIOGRAPHY

Original Interviews & Author Correspondence

Alexander, David. Interviews, August 1972 and June 15, 1973.

Bautzer, Greg. Interviews, March 5 and May 5, 1972.

Bergman, Lowell. Interview, July 23, 1992.

Borie, Marcia. Interview, September 1987.

Bouliance, Grace. Interview, 1992.

Broccoli, Albert "Cubby." Phone interview, 1992.

Brown Franson, Estelle Jackson "Brownie." Interview, May 6, 1993.

Diehl, Bill. Correspondence, March 29, 1993.

Drucker, Harry. Interviews, June 4, 1973, and July 18, 1983.

DuBois Wilhite, Vivian. Interview, October 1972.

Enyart, Vic. Interviews, February 25, 1973, and December 1980.

Feeder, Bill. Interview, August 16, 1993.

Gillette, Don Carle. Interview, February 28, 1973.

Gwynn, Edith. Interviews, May 17, 1972, and February 10, 1973.

Harris, Radie. Interview, February 17, 1973.

Hawks, Howard. Interview, August 1972.

Heimann, Jim. Interview, September 2002.

Jenning, Patrick, and Marshall Croddy. Interview, September 2, 1993.

Kennedy, George H., Jr. Correspondence, May 25, 1970, and July 8, 1971, and interviews, February 5 & 12 and August 1972, January 13 & 20 and June 9, 16 & 23, 1973, January 18 and March 16 & 23, 1974, and December 24, 1987.

Koch, Howard W. Interview, February 9, 1993.

Lacey, Robert. Interview, 1992.

LeRoy, Mervyn. Interview, January 1974.

McDonald, Herb. Interview, February 10, 1993.

Niklas, Kurt. Interview, February 16, 1993.

Paal, Alex. Interview, May 10, 1972.

Pasternak, Joe. Interview, September 12, 1972.

Prinz, LeRoy. Interview, April 17, 1978.

Regina, Rev. Mother. Interview, January 15, 1973.

Rivkin, Joe. Interviews, May 20, 1972, May 20, 1973, and February 13, 1974.

Russell, Colin. Interview, September 1, 1992.

Sedway, Beatrice. Interview, May 23, 1992.

Seward, Tom. Interviews, September 9, 1972, April 7, 1973, January 11 and February 13, 1974, and December 15, 1992.

Stadelman, Kate. Interview, July 23, 1992.

Strickling, Howard. Interview, February 24, 1973.

Turner, Lana. Interview, January 1974.

Velderrain, Ross. Interview, November 28, 2003.

Viertel, Peter. Correspondence, April 28, 1993, and interview, 1993.

Walsh, Raoul. Interview, September 1972.

Wiener, Louis. Interview, April 22, 1993.

Wilkerson Kassel, Beatrice Ruby "Tichi." Interviews, August 21, 1991, August 21, 1992, and March 7, 1993.

Books

Adler, Tim. *Hollywood and the Mob*. London: Bloomsbury, 2007.

Allen, Robert C. *Film History: Theory and Practice*. New York: McGraw Hill, 1985.

Birmingham, Stephen. *The Rest of Us: The Rise of America's Eastern European Jews*. New York: Berkley Books, 1984.

Bowser, Eileen. *The Transformation of Cinema, 1907–1915*. Berkeley: University of California Press, 1990.

Broccoli, Albert R., with Donald Zec. *When the Snow Melts: The Autobiography of Cubby Broccoli*. London: Boxtree, 1998.

Cohn, Art. *The Joker Is Wild: The Story of Joe E. Lewis*. New York: Random House, 1955.

Eyman, Scott. *Lion of Hollywood: The Life and Legend of Louis B. Mayer*. New York: Simon & Schuster, 2005.

Fleming, E. J. *The Fixers: Eddie Mannix, Howard Strickling and the MGM Publicity Machine*. Jefferson, NC: MacFarland, 2005.

Giesler, Jerry, as told to Pete Martin. *The Jerry Giesler Story*. New York: Simon & Schuster, 1960.

Gladstone, B. James. *The Man Who Seduced Hollywood: The Life and Loves of Greg Bautzer, Tinseltown's Most Powerful Lawyer*. Chicago Review Press, 2013.

Graham, Sheilah, and Gerold Frank. *Beloved Infidel*. New York: Henry Holt, 1958.

Grieveson, Lee, and Peter Krämer, eds. *The Silent Cinema Reader*. New York: Routledge, 2004.

Higham, Charles. *Merchant of Dreams: Louis B. Mayer, MGM and the Secret Hollywood*. New York: Dutton Adult, 1993.

Investigative Reporters and Editors Inc. (IRE). *The Arizona Project*. Columbia: University of Missouri, 1977.

Jacobs, Lewis. *The Rise of the American Film*. New York: Harcourt Brace, 1939.

Jennings, Dean. *We Only Kill Each Other: The Life and Bad Times of Bugsy Siegel*. New York: Pocket Books, 1992.

Lacey, Robert. *Little Man: Meyer Lansky and the Gangster Life*. Boston: Little, Brown, 1991.

Messick, Hank. *Secret File*. New York: G. P. Putnam's Sons, 1969.

Murphy, George, with Victor Lasky. *Say . . . Didn't You Used to Be George Murphy?* New York: Bartholomew House, 1970.

Pasternak, Joe. *Easy the Hard Way*. London: W. H. Allen, 1956.

Rappleye, Charles, and Ed Becker. *All American Mafioso: The Johnny Rosselli Story*. New York: Doubleday, 1991.

Tereba, Tere. *Mickey Cohen: The Life and Crimes of L.A.'s Notorious Mobster*. Toronto: ECW Press, 2012. Kindle edition.

Trumbo, Dalton. *Additional Dialogue: Letters of Dalton Trumbo, 1942–1962*. New York: M. Evans, 1970.

Viertel, Peter. *Dangerous Friends: At Large with Hemingway and Huston in the Fifties*. New York: Doubleday, 1992.

Westbrook, Robert. *Intimate Lies*. New York: HarperCollins, 1995.

Wilkerson, Tichi, and Marcia Borie. *The Hollywood Reporter: The Golden Years*. New York: Coward-McCann, 1984.

Articles

Aberdeen, J. A. "The Hollywood Antitrust Case." Hollywood Renegades Archive, 2005. www.cobbles.com/simpp_archive/1film_antitrust.htm.

Daily Variety. "A Tale of Two Willie's." November 26, 1943.

Goldstein, Patrick. "Hollywood's Blackest Hour." *Los Angeles Times*, October 19, 1997.

Hollywood Close-Up. "'Billy' Wilkerson Called Legendary Giant of Hollywood History in First Biographical Interview on Eve of 70th Birthday, Reporter's 30th." September 15, 1960. Reprinted September 13, 1962.

Hollywood Reporter. September 3, 1930–September 2, 1962.

Los Angeles Mirror. "Nightlife of the Tin Gods." May 25, 1953.

Olsen, Richard L. "The Mob and the Movies." *Los Angeles Times*, July 5, 1987.

Rasmussen, Cecilia. "The Man Behind the Sunset Strip." *Los Angeles Times*, December 7, 1997.

Time. "Hollywood Institution." Restaurants, July 3, 1944.

Tuohy, John William. "Gone Hollywood." AmericanMafia.com, May 2002. www .americanmafia.com/Feature_Articles_208.html.

FBI documents obtained via the Freedom of Information Act.

Modern-day currency equivalents via the CPI Inflation Calculator, Bureau of Labor Statistics, accessed March 20, 2018, www.bls.gov/data/inflation_calculator.htm.

INDEX